Furs by Astor

Books by JOHN UPTON TERRELL

Furs by Astor · Journey into Darkness · Plume Rouge · Sunday Is the Day You Rest · The Little Man · Adam Cargo · Jean Blue · *For Young Readers:* The Key to Washington

Furs by Astor

JOHN UPTON TERRELL

William Morrow & Company
New York 1963

To Donna,
whom I sometimes address as Mrs. Astor.
In fun, of course.

Contents

Prologue

The American Fur Company, born of a plunderer's dream and a legal mirage, was swaddled in fiscal luxury behind the screens of a Liberty Street countinghouse. A birth certificate was issued by the New York State Legislature on April 6, 1808. DeWitt Clinton, politically influential in both Albany and Washington, was named godfather. Thomas Jefferson, the President of the United States, sent his congratulations.

As he considered his newest progeny with understandable pride, John Jacob Astor could rub his rugged hands in anticipation of enormously profitable new conquests. Almost since the day he had bought his first muskrat skin, more than twenty years before, he had dreamed of monopolizing the American fur trade. Experience, endless study and the trend of political events had brought the conviction that this could be accomplished only in one way: by obtaining a deceptive charter that would suggest official sanction of company policies and actions, and would open the way for both legal and illegal operations in the great fur-producing areas west of the Allegheny Mountains.

His inherent shrewdness, his knowledge and understanding, told him that each step had to be taken cautiously, that there could be no leaps toward the ultimate goal. Each area of combat had to be fully secured, and all adversaries destroyed beyond possible recovery, before the next advance was undertaken. Neither sharp practices nor sound business methods could be relied upon, alone or in combination, to bring victory. If they were generally adequate weapons in the fur markets of New York, London and Montreal, they would be woefully vulnerable and ineffective before the forces of international diplomacy, frontier lawlessness and political corruption. These were forces which must be countered in kind, with violence, bribery and unrelenting destruction.

The enormity and boldness of the plan illustrated the measure of the man who had conceived it. He was setting out to do what nations, with all their civil, military, political and financial strength, feared to attempt.

More than simply a dream of empire, and far more than the hallucination of an incurable egotist, it was the coldly calculated scheme of an unqualified realist. If the plan as Astor had formulated it was diabolical in its aspects, so was it admirable. If it was piratical, so was it commendable, so was it contributory to the national interest. If it was selfish, so was it more vital, more dynamic, more momentous, than any plan ever originated and carried forward by one man in the history of America. This one man was casting himself in the role of supreme ruler of an earthly domain into which all the countries of Europe could have been dropped and lost from sight. He was appropriating for himself the prerogatives of an economic royalist and the rights and privileges of an indisputable sovereign.

If Jefferson had been able to see behind John Jacob Astor's dark brow, he undoubtedly would have withheld his approval of the corporate enterprise. The President relied on the advice of trusted friends, and they were no more clairvoyant than he. Among these confidants were George Clinton, the Vice President; Henry Dearborn, the Secretary of War; and Albert Gallatin, the Secretary of the Treasury.

The approbation of these high officers might have been enough to convince any Chief Executive that Astor's proposal was worthy of official cognizance. But Jefferson also was influenced in his attitude by his own great dream of opening the immense western wilderness for the exclusive use and benefit of

Americans. Orderly expansion over plains, deserts and mountains to the Pacific was a vision he had long held. It had prompted his decision to send Lewis and Clark on their epic journey, and they had given to it the first touch of reality.

If Thomas Jefferson was deceived, it was not his fault. No one ... not even Astor's close friend DeWitt Clinton ... knew all of the machinations fermenting in the perspicacious brain of the former German butcher boy.

Part One

Overture with Seven
Flutes

1

When John Jacob Astor went up the Hudson River in April, 1785, at the age of twenty-one, on his first venture into the wilderness, the North American fur trade was nearly three hundred years old. Yet its greatest days were to come in his time.

Since the beginning of the sixteenth century . . . possibly shortly before that . . . Europeans had been trading with the forest Indians for the valuable pelts of wild animals.

The fishermen had come first. Portuguese, Basques, Bretons, Englishmen, nameless in history, miraculously navigating their staunch little boats in circular courses westward from the fishing grounds off Iceland, saw the mountains and forested shores of Labrador and Newfoundland. Soon they had looked into the Strait of Belle Isle. They had touched at Bonavista, and they had beaten around Cape Race into the great Gulf of St. Lawrence. A few of them had struck on southward, quartering the headlands of Nova Scotia, standing off the rocky coast of Maine and clearing the sand spits of a queer hook of land that was to be called Cape Cod.

In 1500 the age of metal had not yet come to the aborigines who lived in the limitless forests of northern America. Their tools and utensils were made of wood and stone, hide and bone. Then suddenly strange men with pale skins had come out of the sea in search of fish. The things these invaders valued the least had been nothing less than marvels to the Indians. The utility of a commonplace European article . . . an ax, a cooking pot, a knife, a tempered nail . . . surpassed anything they had imagined, even in dreams. One unbreakable, unburnable iron kettle did away with all the labor and care required of a whole series of bark or pottery vessels.

The fur trade began.

2

Astor could not justifiably have been accused of living in the past, but it could have been said with accuracy that he constantly studied it, and that he was shrewd enough to see it as an important prologue. Nor did he live in the future; yet he often gazed into it, and his practicality did not preclude him from harboring great dreams. He lived in the moment at hand, facing the problems and affairs of life as they were presented to him, but he forgot neither history nor the years that were ahead.

Religious, political and territorial conflicts notwithstanding, the fur trade had expanded commensurately with the advance of civilization. North America, except for the eastern seaboard, was still largely wilderness. If the trade followed its historical pattern . . . and Astor held an unshakable belief that it would . . . only the pace would be different in the future; it would be faster.

Astor understood, as he strode for the first time onto the Canadian stage, that his own era had much in common with the century in which Samuel de Champlain, the greatest of all early fur traders and explorers, had lived. In the light of this conviction, he set out to take advantage of the situation.

The time of Champlain had been one of commercial confusion, impending political crises and menacing religious controversies. The fur trade was on the verge of attaining an invulnerable healthiness, perhaps susceptible to prolonged sickness, but not to destruction. Not many years before Champlain and his young men gazed into the wilderness, only the nobility and the rich could afford furs . . . they had demanded the princely marten, sable and mink . . . but other classes had begun to prosper, to acquire social rights and privileges, and new markets for less valuable pelts had been created. Hides of animals such as elk and deer were wanted for leather. Wolf, bear, buffalo, fox, lynx, raccoon and muskrat were sought for moderately priced coats, linings, collars and gloves. It had been found that for hats nothing could surpass the American beaver, the downy hairs of which were incomparable in their natural cohesion into a durable felt.[1]

As for the kings and the wealthy, a swiftly developing economic system known as capitalism was causing them to give serious attention to mercantilism. The capitalistic theory was not especially complicated, and it appeared to proffer a badly needed practical program for increasing national wealth.

Also, an apparently insatiable demand for European merchandise had been created among the Indians. How great it might become could only be guessed, for no one knew how many Indians there were nor how extensive was the land in which they lived. The wildest speculations might well turn out to be conservative.

A new age, a new way of life, had begun for the Indian, and the stage had been set for the bloodiest dramas of all North American history. As the traders fought each other to secure the Indians' furs, so the Indians began to fight one another to control distribution of the traders' marvelous merchandise. The St. Law-

[1] So durable was it that in the latter part of the seventeenth century beaver hats worn by Frenchmen were remade and sold in Spain, and after being worn there were returned to New Rochelle and again remade for sale in Brazil, whence they were brought back again after being worn, remade once more, and sold to the Portugese, to be used in trade in Africa.

rence River tribes sought to set themselves up as middlemen, and they gouged their brothers of the interior and fought to keep them from coming eastward to trade. They became as dishonest and as vicious as their white counterparts. The goods the Indians sent inland were often damaged, the esteemed cooking pots often burned black and worn thin from long usage.

By the time European goods reached people as far away as the Sioux, in the valleys of the upper Mississippi and the Red River of the North, over Indian trading routes, they were of little use or value. Yet so eager for them were the have-nots that they gave generously of their furs for worthless articles, treasuring them as curiosities and manifestations of the white man's genius.

South of the St. Lawrence, in a beautiful land of fine forests, lakes, streams and lush valleys, incredibly rich in furs, was the heartland of the remarkable confederacy of the Iroquois. Their empire reached from the Hudson to the Ohio and the Great Lakes. Intermittent trade, often at exorbitant prices, for the magical goods possessed by the St. Lawrence River tribes was not long endurable. At last the Iroquois legions . . . the incomparable warriors who "approach like foxes, fight like lions, and fly away like birds" . . . swept into the valley of the St. Lawrence.

Champlain, seeking to hold the friendship and trade of the river tribes, the Hurons, Algonquins and Montagnais, invaded Iroquois territory and attacked them. It wasn't much of a battle, but it marked the beginning of a hundred years of brutal, vicious warfare between the French and the Five Nations, and it made the Iroquois friends of both the Dutch and the English.

It was the young men Champlain sent out who broke the trails into the unknown West, to the inland seas of Ontario, Erie, Huron, Michigan, Superior—men like Étienne Brulé, Grenolle, Lavalée, Nicolet, Radisson, Groseilliers. They knew the headwaters of the Mississippi, and a lake called Winnipeg, and they saw rivers flowing to the north, emptying into a great bay an Englishman named Hudson had found.

The great region that was to be known as the Middle West,

the richest fur country on earth, had been opened, and simultaneously a new breed of men, men of a kind the world had never known, had been created. They were *les seigneurs des lacs et forêts*, the *coureurs de bois*, the *voyageurs*, and their humble brothers, the *mangeurs de lard*.

They were the incomparable canoe men; the human beavers; the lustful, superstitious, gay adventurers; the "white Indians" with red squaws; the peerless hunters and trappers and traders. Their log shelters and their camps rose in strategic locations along the routes of wilderness travel. They opened the way, and their furs poured into the rendezvous, were carried on in canoes and bateaux down the Ottawa to Montreal, through the Great Lakes to Niagara and down the St. Lawrence, overland to Albany and down the Hudson to the sea, and the prolificacy of the rich cargoes gave new fuel to the turmoil of the Western world.

The traders of the Netherlands had swarmed into the Hudson Valley behind its discoverers, and were prospering from their commerce with the Indians. The British, already holding an iron grip on Virginia and New England, had begun to encroach on this lucrative traffic in furs. The Swedes stuck their noses in briefly, withdrew them and selected other locations. The French had become alarmed, for the Hudson-Mohawk valleys and New Amsterdam, on Manhattan Island, comprised the key to domination of the Iroquois country. The commander of Fort Frontenac, one René Robert Cavelier, Sieur de La Salle, struggled to halt an immense stream of furs flowing from the west and southwest to the Iroquois traders, who carried them on to the English at Albany.

Two events, occurring at widely separated places, had marked the beginning of the actual war between England and France for control of the forest empires of America and the fabulous fortunes in furs produced in them. These were the seizure by the British of New York and the Hudson Valley, and the granting of a charter to a powerful group called the Governor and Company of Adventurers of England Trading into Hudson's Bay. The charter, by which the British capitalized on their discoveries in the far North, created the strongest and most enduring fur-trading monopoly of all time—the Hudson's Bay Company.

These two actions created a great pincer movement against the French, but another hundred years were to pass before the jaws could be completely closed. The final victorious pressure was applied on Lake George, at Ticonderoga, and Crown Point, on the Plains of Abraham and in the shadow of Mount Royal. On September 8, 1760, Canada passed into the hands of the British, and they controlled all of America from Florida to Hudson Bay, from the Atlantic far westward to the vague and undefined headwaters of a river with a name difficult to pronounce —Mississippi.

The French fur traders stayed on, but they were no longer the supreme masters. The names of men from Northumberland, Glasgow and Edinburgh, from Devonshire and Cornwall and Liverpool, were on the packs of furs . . . McDonald, Henry, Stuart, McKenzie, McGillivray, Frobisher, McKay . . . even though the names of the remote wilderness posts which *les seigneurs des lacs et forêts* had built were unchanged . . . Nipissing, Sault Ste. Marie, Nipigon, Niagara, Vincennes, De Chartres, La Baye, Chequamegon and Michilimackinac.

When the treaty bringing independence to the United States, and giving to it all the rich fur lands westward to the Mississippi River, was signed at Paris in 1783, John Jacob Astor was setting out on the course that would lead him to supremacy in that vast wilderness region and make him the greatest fur trader of all time.

3

It was on a wintry November day in 1783 that a young German, speaking English with a heavy accent, accosted the mate of an American vessel lying in the harbor of Bristol and inquired about passage to New York. The mate, whose name was John Whetten, noticed that the young man had with him, in addition to a baggage roll, what appeared to be a "pacotillo of musical instruments."

Whetten might have dismissed John Jacob Astor with a few morsels of gruffly delivered information, but he was impressed by Astor's neat appearance and quiet, polite manner, and he took the trouble to inquire into Astor's personal situation. At the conclusion of a friendly, if difficult, conversation Whetten went out of his way to be helpful. He told Astor that another vessel, the *North Carolina*, then lying in a nearby anchorage, could provide a more comfortable voyage for less money than his own ship, and he advised Astor to take passage on it.

If Whetten and Astor could have looked into the future at the moment of their chance meeting on the Bristol wharf, they might have accepted without question the belief that every man's course was preordained when he was born. Whetten was one day, not many years away, to become master and part-owner of an Astor ship, to be related to Astor by marriage, and to be named sponsor of one of Astor's sons.

Astor took his new friend's advice. He paid five guineas for his ticket. This entitled him to a wooden bunk in the steerage of the *North Carolina*, and to salt beef and biscuit for the duration of the voyage. The word "duration" was soon to acquire a special significance.

The *North Carolina*, Captain Angus in command, cleared

England for Chesapeake Bay.[2] The five guineas Astor paid for his passage represented a third of the money he had been able to save during four years of backbreaking labor in London. He had invested another five guineas in flutes . . . assertedly seven of them . . . made by the musical instrument company of which his elder brother George was the head. He hoped to sell them in New York, but not only for the profit he might make. One of his several ambitions was to become a musical instrument dealer, and to represent George Astor and other British firms in the United States. When he went aboard the *North Carolina,* he carried the flutes as personal baggage, wrapped in his one good suit and his extra shirts and underwear, to avoid paying duty or freight charges on them. It is quite possible he also carried a packet of music and some other small instruments in the "pacotillo" described by Whetten.

The winter of 1783–84, during which the little *North Carolina* pitched and rolled her way across the raging North Atlantic, was distinguished for its severity. As the dreary, interminable weeks passed into sunless oblivion, the twenty-year-old Astor had more than enough hours in which to ponder the wisdom of the drastic step he had taken in putting Europe and everything he knew and loved so far behind him, more than enough cold black nights in the steerage hole when retching with sickness, he might wonder if life as a butcher boy back in Walldorf was, after all, as dull and difficult and unpromising as it had seemed.

---

[2] The files of Lloyd's record the vessel's name as *Carolina,* and show that she sailed from the Thames on November 18. Astor always insisted the name of the ship was *North Carolina.* He must have boarded her in the Bristol Channel late in the month, possibly early in December.

4

Walldorf was a village lying between Heidelberg and the Rhine in the Duchy of Baden. There was nothing to distinguish it from a thousand other German villages, except that nature selected it as the birthplace of John Jacob Astor. This event, which occurred on July 17, 1763, preserved Walldorf's name in reflections which still may be seen in various parts of the world, an honor quite disproportionate to its deserved place in history. If John Jacob Astor had not happened to begin life there, in all probability the place would never have been heard of at all.

The child was given the name of his father, Jacob, a convivial butcher who seemingly preferred quaffing the lager dispensed in the local tavern to delivering ham hocks and rump roasts to *Hausfraus*. Some confusion, other than that caused by the paternal waywardness, developed from having two males named Jacob in the house, and it was decided to address the son as Johann, although the other troublesome given name was not discarded.

The lineage of the Astors failed to inspire the rapt attention of early genealogists, but the male line reputedly descended from a Huguenot family which fled to Lutheran Germany after the failure of the Edict of Nantes made life in France intolerable for the Protestant peasantry. How many there were in the family was not recorded, but one member of it, a Jean Jacques d'Astorg, appeared in Walldorf in the 1680's. He acquired a small farm, and in 1692 married a Walldorf girl named Anna Margaretha Eberhard. Thereafter he proceeded with commendable industriousness to labor in his little fields and sire offspring, and when he passed from the Walldorf scene the nucleus of the Astor clan had been established on the earth.[3]

---

[3] More than one descendant of John Jacob Astor possessed a craving for at least the outward trappings of gentility, but the most fantastic attempt to smother the

John Jacob Astor's paternal grandfather, Felix, was born in Nussloch, in 1693. It was during Felix's earthly journey that the name of D'Astorg was changed, not by legal decree, but by the guttural tongue of South Germans, to Ashdor, Ashdour and Ashtor. This transformation, however, apparently did not influence Felix's way of life. If Jean Jacques had established the Astors, Felix made them indestructible.

In 1713 (or 1719) he married Eva Dorothea Freund, and she gave birth to four children, the youngest of whom, Jacob, was to become the father of a male prodigy. When Eva died in 1725, Felix promptly took another wife, who bore him at least sixteen children before she, too, found escape in the Lutheran graveyard.

When Felix himself passed on in 1765, not only had the name

---

family's rustic background under an aristocratic cloak was made by William Waldorf Astor in 1899. Worth in the neighborhood of a hundred million dollars, William Waldorf Astor abandoned his American citizenship, went to England, and became a British subject. He bought the Cliveden estate, at Taplow, Bucks, the old seat of the Duke of Buckingham. He also bought a newspaper, a magazine and a title. Possession of the latter was his greatest ambition, and King George V made him happy by fulfillling it. He became Lord Astor.

Before he ascended to the nobility, however, William Waldorf Astor took pen in hand and created a genealogy of his family which, as far as he was concerned, left little to be desired.

It went something like this:

Jean Jacques d'Astorg, the fleeing French Huguenot who settled in Walldorf, was the great grandson of Joseph d'Astorg, Marquis de Roquepin, whose grandfather had been Antoine d'Astorg, Baron de Monbartier in Haute-Garonne, twelfth in line from Pierre d'Astorg, Seigneur de Noallac in Limousin, who could trace his lineage to Pedro d'Astorga, a knight of Castile, who fell at the taking of Jerusalem, in 1100. The name of Pedro d'Astorga came from a grant of arms conferred upon him by the Queen of Spain. It depicted a falcon, silvery white and shining, on a gloved hand.

Inasmuch as Lord Astor owned a magazine, he had no difficulty getting his family history published. Disinterested genealogists, however, took a somewhat jaundiced view of it, and respectfully pointed out some discrepancies. Not the least of these was recording the date of the marriage of John Jacob Astor's mother as July 6, 1766, which was three years after his birth. At least five other children had been born to her before that date. Another slight error made by Lord Astor was placing the marriage of John Jacob Astor's grandmother fifteen years later than the birth of his father.

The portions of Lord Astor's contrived history that dealt with the family's noble Spanish origins were bluntly shown to be false by the unkind genealogists.

It was suggested by one that a more appropriate coat of arms than the silver falcon would contain a butcher's apron, with perhaps a few spatters of Spanish goat blood on it.

of D'Astorg vanished from Walldorf and its environs, not only had the Astors found a permanent niche in world history, but their French blood had become diluted to the vanishing point by frequent and prolific consummations among the Baden peasantry.

John Jacob Astor's mother was Marie Magdalen Vorfelder. She had married Jacob Astor in 1750, at the age of seventeen. Five sons and a daughter were born of the union. The first child, a son, had succumbed in infancy. The others were George Peter, born in 1752; John Henry, 1754; Catherine, 1757 or 1758; and Johann Melchior, 1759.

Marie Astor died in 1766, three years after John Jacob was born, and all memory of her, of course, soon left him. Her place was taken by Christina Barbara, by whom his father had six more children, two of whom died at an early age.

In some contemporary accounts . . . but not from John Jacob's own lips . . . the commonplace situation of a drunken father and a cruel stepmother was described in varying degrees of horror. That the household was not altogether a happy one was suggested by the swiftness with which both sons and daughters forsook it as soon as they had the means. On the other hand, there were indications that matters were not so severe and unpleasant as some of the strait-laced and jealous neighbors enjoyed painting them.[4]

Unquestionably the family lived in restricted circumstances. Jacob Astor was stupid, pigheaded, lusty, optimistic, gay, a stout trencherman and a heavy drinker of beer, but he was not a complete wastrel, nor was the toll of his dissipation disastrous. For

[4] If it was true, as some said, that John Jacob had no respect for his father and detested his stepmother, then he successfully removed these weights from his memory. After he had grown wealthy in New York, he commissioned an artist to paint portraits of them as he pictured them in his recollections. The portraits showed his father selling fish and game and his stepmother selling flowers in the Walldorf market place. It was an expensive and touching gesture, hardly one a bitter man would have performed, but it was not without a psychological aspect. He did have both Jacob and Christina portrayed in commonplace commercial occupations, indicating that he took a certain pride in the fact that he came from a long line of peddlers.

some forty years he operated the leading Walldorf butcher shop, and after that he enjoyed life in relatively good health for another three decades. If, however, he never suffered in his old age for the need of a pfennig, he was often quite confused. He could understand that his youngest son was very rich, but how that happy state had been achieved by John Jacob was beyond his comprehension. Nature had not endowed him with the capacity to grasp the true meaning of Astoria or the international significance of the fur trade. If he held any vision of America at all, it contained no sweep like the sweep of the plains beyond the Missouri, it was not of the Shining Mountains in their grandeur, it did not echo the deep-throated rumble of a money-mad metropolis beside a harbor large enough to hold all the big ships of the world.

Jacob Astor died in 1816, at the age of ninety-two, regretting to the last that his youngest boy, who had been able to cut out such a neat and clean roast without waste, and who had a fine head for figures, had not carried on in his place as Walldorf's best butcher.

Whatever trying circumstances John Jacob may have known as a youth, they interfered little with his schooling. He received an education that was exceptional for the time and the place. This was due to a talented and highly intelligent teacher named Valentine Jeune, also a descendant of Huguenot refugees. Jeune worked in close association with the village pastor, John Philip Steiner, but he was in no way inhibited by Biblical teachings. He strove to drive into the heads of his pupils not only reading and writing and ciphering, but worldly knowledge. He believed that boys especially should know something of true history, of philosophy, of geography, and that they should keep their eyes lifted to far horizons.

Both men recognized in young John Jacob a distinct and compelling personality and an exceptionally able mind, and they made special efforts to guide and assist its development. World affairs appeared to have a special fascination for him. He eagerly sought information about foreign countries, and he spent hours lost in the few books and newspapers available.

The revolution raging in America absorbed his attention, and he thoroughly enjoyed hearing Jeune and Reverend Steiner discuss it. On this issue the two men did not see eye to eye. The pastor contended that freedom could be a dangerous thing for the common man with no experience in handling it. Besides, the Bible made it plain that kings had their heavenly purpose.

Jeune thought otherwise. He believed that kings should be tolerated only so long as they were just and gave all freedom and privilege possible to their subjects. When oppression was inflicted, people should rise in revolt and throw off the royal yoke. There was no reason to believe that a government of the people could not function with success. Kings had no monopoly on brains. The principles of democracy advanced by the American revolutionary leaders were doctrines of which self-respecting men could be proud. This fellow Washington seemed to be as brilliant as he was forceful. His demands for primary rights for the little man composed a great step toward the justice to which all people on earth were entitled.

John Jacob was not certain in his own mind that either his teacher or his religious mentor was altogether correct. He suggested that the delegation of too much authority and privilege to the masses might lead to the disorderly conduct of vital affairs and in the end destroy the benefits it had been intended to bestow. Perhaps democracy had its advantages, but control of both government and property should be retained by vested interests. An attempt to achieve an equitable distribution of wealth and political franchise could result in putting too much power in the hands of irresponsible people.

It was a view which gave pause to Schoolmaster Jeune and Reverend Steiner, and it increased their awe of their acute pupil, but it impressed John Jacob's father not at all. It was nothing less than idiocy, in Jacob's opinion, to think that a band of ragged rebels could overthrow the might of England. Everyone seemed to be forgetting that not only the great forces of the English king were opposing the colonial uprising. Thousands of good Germans, Hesse-Hanau men, Hesse-Kassel men and Brunswickers had also been sent to quell the upstarts. People should think of that before they spouted about such newfangled things as freedom for the peasants and the rights of man.

Young John Jacob was not to be blinded by patriotic fervor. His mind was too calculating, too practical, for that. Besides, there were fragments of concrete evidence to indicate that the power of the English king and his Hessian mercenaries was not insuperable. These were to be found in tales recited by travelers passing through Baden, in the newspapers and in the soiled, travel-marked letters, not only from the Hessians themselves who had been leased to England, but from John Jacob's two older brothers, George in London, and Henry in the Colony of New York.

5

On Palm Sunday of 1777, John Jacob Astor was confirmed in the Lutheran Church. Customarily for a German peasant boy the ceremony marked the end of school days. He was expected at age fourteen to become apprenticed to a tradesman or to take employment as a servant or laborer.

John Jacob's course was to be an exception to the normal pattern. His father refused to obligate himself for an apprenticeship fee. He wanted his youngest son, as he had wanted all his sons, to follow in his footsteps.

John Jacob, being penniless, had no alternative but to comply with the edict. His head, however, remained filled with bold plans.

The next two years were the unhappiest of his life. He toiled in his father's shop, delivered meat to village doors, and endured a dreary home life. Walldorf became an empty, stagnant place, incapable of providing the stimulation and challenge his swiftly developing intellect craved.

He was more than capable of handling the responsibilities placed on him. At fifteen he was an expert meat-cutter and a competent businessman. He was physically strong, his muscles were well developed, his body was thick and heavy. If he despised every phase of his life, however, discouragement failed to bring frustration, and he never ceased scheming to escape.

He appealed to both of his brothers, George and Henry, for advice and assistance, and at last it came.

Henry, who was two years younger than George, had settled in New York. His career since he had put Walldorf behind him had been both dangerous and dramatic. Butchering was a trade for which he had a genuine liking, but he had refused to follow it under the aegis of his father.

As George had done, Henry went to England, but he had not long remained there. Henry's heart had been set on getting to America, which, he was convinced, would become a land of un-limited opportunity. Under the circumstances of war, ordinary migration had been impossible, but Henry had found a way to accomplish it. He had no stomach for the life of a soldier, but he had no objection to traveling with soldiers as a civilian. He became a sutler, and when the British troops and the Hessians paraded along Broadway, after their victory in the Battle of Long Island, Henry was on the seat of a supply cart in their wake.

At the first opportunity he deserted, and it was not long before he had begun to prosper as a meat-seller in the Fly Market. The letters he wrote home to his family and friends indirectly in-fluenced the course of American history, for they were in a large measure responsible for bringing John Jacob Astor across the Atlantic.

Crude, ungrammatical letters, they glowed with enthusiasm. They delineated in awkward terms the reality of an unbounded opportunity. In their thoughts they reflected the spirit of an un-paralleled freedom. They filled the chafing, straining, dissatisfied mind of John Jacob with a determination to reach the United States.

That was a feat difficult to accomplish. A poor youth who spoke little English simply didn't pack a bag and depart. John Jacob took Henry's letters to Reverend Steiner and Jeune. The stumbling missives contained assertions that were difficult to believe. Soldiers of the ragged rebel army were freezing and starving to death, yet somehow they continued to fight, they refused to be beaten. Henry was convinced they would win.

There was much about his activities, as well as his private thoughts, that Henry did not disclose. He did not reveal that at the same time he was professing sympathies for the rebels he was acting as a kind of middleman for meats "confiscated" from colonial farmers by British and Hessian raiders.

It was Henry's custom to slip out of New York on horseback and meet a raiding party somewhere in the rural reaches of Westchester. He would buy the stolen livestock, and under cover of night drive the animals into town, butcher them, and sell the meat to any customers who desired to purchase it. His prices were generally lower than those of the butchers who secured their supplies through more legitimate channels.

Charges hurled by angry competitors failed to detract Henry from his nefarious ways. He was not one to permit his emotions to interfere with business. Patriotism was a fine thing, and he believed everyone should have it, but he saw no relationship between it and operating a meat stall. He cared no more who ate the swine and cattle and sheep than the poor animals themselves. As for the work, it was just as hard to quarter rebel beef as a Tory bull.

By all means, Henry told John Jacob, find a way to get to America. In New York even a dumb butcher boy could earn three times as much as he could in Walldorf. A smart young man could soon be his own master. Restrictions were not imposed on a man's brains, even though he had barnyard straw in his hair. But, cautioned Henry, it would be best to learn English before making the leap. Americans were stupid about foreign languages.

George Astor had been in London several years. He wrote that the British merchants were extremely uneasy over the way the fighting was going in America. The Ministry was being severely criticized for its obstinacy in dealing with the demands of the rebels. Yankee privateers were punishing English shipping. The sensible thing was to secure peace through a just compromise.

George Astor, too, was a good businessman. On his arrival in London he had gone to work for the firm of Shudi & Broadwood, makers of pianofortes. Within a short time he had formed his own company and was manufacturing musical instruments. He had prospered and achieved a standard of living virtually inconceivable to the farmers and small tradesmen of Baden.

It was George's thought that Melchior should be the next member of the family to emigrate, and he invited him to England, but Melchior had become a tenant farmer on the estate of the Prince of Neuwied, and did not want to leave. George then urged John Jacob to come to London, promising to see that he got work.

In his inherently thoughtful and methodical manner John Jacob discussed the matter with the pastor and the teacher, his only true friends. They concluded that it would be wisest for him to go to England first, and there learn to speak English well while working for George, and they offered to talk to his father about it for him.

Jacob Astor was adamant in his refusal to permit his valuable remaining son to leave. Months passed before the two men were able to persuade the intemperate butcher to give John Jacob the same opportunity that his other sons had taken for themselves.

On a spring day in 1779, John Jacob, a small bundle of clothes slung over a shoulder, a few small coins in his pocket, stood at the edge of Walldorf and gazed back at the only home he had ever known.

Several people had walked with him to the end of the cobbled street, where it joined the old Roman road that drove through the green countryside to the Rhine. His half sisters wept. His father looked sullen, feeling self-pity. Some of John Jacob's boyhood friends stared enviously at him.

In all the little knot of people only Valentine Jeune was cheerful and spoke encouraging words. The teacher, who was beginning to show his age, admonished the others not to fear for John Jacob. John Jacob had a good head, and the world would hear of him.

Plans had been carefully worked out. John Jacob would walk to the Rhine. It would not be difficult for him to get a job on one of the timber rafts that regularly descended the river. The raft would carry him to the Netherlands, and by working on it he would earn enough to pay his passage to London on a North Sea packet.

He said good-by and turned away. There were tears in his eyes, and he did not look back.

Valentine Jeune had extracted a pledge from him. It was to be honest, to be industrious and never to gamble. Thinking of it as he plodded on, he took a qualified oath. He swore that two of the resolutions would compose the foundation of his credo. He was a little dubious about the third—honesty. It was, after all, largely a state of mind.

6

If the weather of the North Atlantic was cruel, the hand of good fortune rested on John Jacob Astor's shoulder in the bleak, cold and cramped steerage of the storm-battered *North Carolina*.

Several of the first-class passengers were officers of the Governor and Company of Adventurers of England Trading into Hudson's Bay, already famous throughout the world in 1783 as the largest and most powerful organization in the international fur trade.

The executives, being privileged to move about as they desired, stretched their legs and held conversations in various sections of the ship. They were unaware that an alert and inquisitive young German was attentive to every word they spoke within his hearing, and that he was thoughtfully filing away in his sharp mind their remarks for possible future use.

The fateful pattern was carried out further by one of Astor's fellow passengers in the steerage. He was a German who had immigrated to America before the Revolution, and was then returning from a business trip to Europe. His name was soon forgotten, but his business was furs, and the more he told of his experiences in buying and selling them, the more an astonished and intrigued Astor questioned him. Perhaps he found in Astor's seemingly insatiable demands for details a means of alleviating the tedium of the voyage. Perhaps he had a sincere desire to help a young countryman, or perhaps he enjoyed the opportunity to build himself up in the eyes of his inquisitive young listener.

Whatever the case, he imparted knowledge without stint, and his talk was often technical in nature: how to buy, pack, transport and preserve skins, and how to judge the quality of them. Grade was especially important in beaver skins, for there was a wide variation in value in the markets of Europe. The most highly prized by the hatters were *castor gras d'hiver*, which were taken in the winter from prime beaver. The raw side was scraped, a process which weakened the roots of the long hairs, allowing them to drop out. A number of pelts were sewed into a robe, and it was worn for several months by an Indian with the fur next to his skin. The robe became soft and greasy, the fur downy, a condition which made it suitable for fine hats. Pelts worn only a short time were called *demi-gras*. Beaver taken in the summer were known as *castor gras d'été*, and they had thick skin and little fur and were of small value in hatmaking. *Castor sec* were skins which had not been worn at all, and their value depended upon the season in which the beaver had been killed.

Of the greatest interest to Astor at the moment were the economics of the trade as they were recited by his loquacious counsel. The German trader had gone to London to dispose of the furs he had acquired during the past year. These had been sufficient in both quantity and quality to pay for his trip, enable him to purchase a stock of British manufactured articles for use in future trading, and still leave him a good profit for his year's work. He had with him several packs of such things as tin and tinsel trinkets, glass beads, ribbons, shiny wire, imitation gold and silver buttons, cheap buckles, brass watch cases and fake medals.

Hardly any capital was required to start in the fur trade. With nothing more than a basket of toys, or even a tray of cakes, a young man could begin in the streets and on the wharves of New York. Farm boys, Indians and Hudson River boatmen brought pelts into the city, and they were glad to exchange them for souvenirs or a bite to eat. The pelts could be sold to New York furriers, or even better, they could be sent to Europe.

The profits were enormous. If a man could establish a connection with a reliable London fur house, the profits were even greater. In fact, they were fabulous. Beaver skins, for instance, were worth from six to ten times in London what they were in New York.

John Jacob Astor trembled inwardly with excitement as he gazed out on the cold and tempestuous North Atlantic toward the promised land. Six hundred to a thousand per cent profit! It was unbelievable!

The *North Carolina* stood into Hampton Roads sometime in the middle of January, and pointed her stubby prow into Chesapeake Bay, which was filled with floating ice. Slowly she twisted her way through the floes under winds that froze sails. She was in constant danger of being wrecked.

On one occasion, when large bergs threatened to stove in the little ship's hull, Astor appeared on deck wearing his best clothes.

He had reasoned that if the *North Carolina* went down and he were saved, his good British suit would be on him. If the ship were wrecked and he lost his life, it would make no difference what clothes he wore.

The *North Carolina* did not founder, and at the end of another week the passengers were excitedly preparing to land. In a day or two the mansard roofs and red brick chimneys of Baltimore would come into view.

Winter had another plan. Bitter cold suddenly descended. The bay was solidly frozen from shore to shore. There was no wind. The *North Carolina* lay helpless in the frigid grip of a relentless vise.

Days, weeks, months, crept away in maddening monotony. Some of the passengers made their way ashore over the ice, but Astor chose to remain aboard. He had been guaranteed his food, poor as it was, for the *duration* of the voyage, and the voyage would not be completed until Baltimore Harbor had been entered. The delay cost him nothing, except his own time, and he was not certain that that had any value at all.

By the third week of March, however, he found himself unable to endure the situation any longer. Rations were short, and there was no prospect that the implacable cold would end long enough to allow the ice to weaken. Taking his bundles, he struggled through the white silence to the Maryland shore. He reached Baltimore by stage on the twenty-fourth or twenty-fifth of March, 1784. The trip from England had taken approximately four months.

7

Astor was no longer a Walldorf greenhorn. He had spent four years in the largest and most important city in the world, and the bucolic plainness of the Baden villager had surrendered to a certain sheen of urbanity. He had less than five guineas in his pants pocket when he reached Baltimore, but his impecuniosity was not a shadow on either his native intelligence or his burgeoning sophistication.

He was never to forget the detailed events of his first day in America. Half a century later he was to write to his good friend Washington Irving: "I took a walk to see the town. getting up Market St. while standing and looking about, a little fat man came out of his shop. This was Nicholas Tuschdy he addressed me saying—young man I believe you are a stranger, to which I replied yes.—Where did you come from.—from London—but you are not an Englishman no a German. Then he says we are near country men I am a Swiss—we are glad to see people coming to this conitry from Europe. On this he asked me into his house and offered me a glass of wine and introduced me to his wife as a countryman. He offered his services and advice while in Baltimore and requested me to call again to see him."

Astor had called again. He was desperately in need of money, and he mentioned to Tuschdy that he had brought with him some musical instruments which he would like to sell. The kindly Swiss promptly offered to display them in his shop window.

Astor remained in Baltimore about three weeks, astonished by the friendliness and hospitality of the people he met and thoroughly enjoying his first taste of the American way of life. A flute or two was sold, enabling him to pay his living expenses and take a coach for New York. When he stepped ashore from the Jersey ferry at the Battery, only a few shillings jingled in his pocket.

It was imperative that he find his brother Henry at once. He had not forgotten how some wiseacre in Walldorf had predicted he would go hungry in a country where bears invaded churches and Indians wilder than bears roamed the streets, scalping people. He did not propose to let the prediction come true.

His meager possessions slung over a shoulder, he swung up Broadway, fascinated by the sight of West Indian Negroes in bright headbands and earrings, by the cries of hawkers selling drinking water, Jersey straw for bedticks, candied pears on sticks, by the rumble of strange-looking drays and carts on the cobbles, by the tulip trees that shaded the walks from the bright spring sunlight.

Strikingly blond, muscular, he had a somewhat heavy, strongly-chiseled face, and his eyes, set under thick brows, were lighted in brown depths. Stopping now and then to inquire in a guttural accent the way to Heindrich Ashdour's house, he marched on with a self-assured, determined manner.

He was only a few steps and fewer months from the conquests which would make him the richest man in America.

Part Two

Trinkets in Stardust

1

Henry Astor was prospering. Only a month before the arrival of his younger brother in New York, he had married Dorothea Pessenger. She was the stepdaughter of John Pessenger, a meat-seller who occupied Stall Number One, the most advantageous location in the Fly Market. The union did not injure Henry's prestige as a butcher, but he was truly devoted to his pretty wife, whom he described fondly to his Fly Market colleagues as "de pink of de Powery."

Henry and Dorothea had set up housekeeping in small but comfortable quarters at First and Fisher Streets. "Brudder Yakob" was given a warm welcome, but they were less than enthusiastic about taking in a boarder so soon after their wedding. Henry suggested that he help John Jacob to find lodgings near the Fly Market, and offered to put him to work delivering meat and making himself generally useful in the Astor-Pessenger shops.

Despite his poverty, John Jacob rejected the offer. He wanted no more of butchering. He wanted complete freedom, and he was determined to make his own way, no matter how difficult it might be.

Henry was not a little disappointed and irritated, but his brotherly affection was not irreparably injured. He took John Jacob to the home of George Dieterich, a German baker, at 150 Queen Street, and arranged to have him lodged there.[1]

---

[1] Queen Street later became Pearl Street.

As good fortune would have it, Dieterich needed an assistant. He had plans for enlarging his business, and he wanted to engage a capable youth to peddle cakes, cookies, doughnuts and rolls about the streets, and to delivery bakery goods to regular customers. He offered his lodger a job.

John Jacob had no more wish to become a baker boy than he did to work in a butcher shop, but he reasoned that by peddling for Dieterich he would quickly learn the city, meet people and have an opportunity to dispose of his remaining musical instruments, while at the same time looking about for more profitable employment. He took the job, and the next day set out to add his strong voice to the hawkers' cries that made the New York streets of the day a bedlam of discord.

2

The New York that Astor came to know in 1784 was filthy, poverty-stricken, crime-ridden and permeated by political corruption. It had a population of slightly more than twenty thousand, and it extended in a disorderly pattern from the Battery only to Warren Street. There the open country began, meadowland and groves rolling gently between the rivers to the rockier heights of Harlem.

The noise of the Revolution's guns still echoed in the ears of the residents. Returned soldiers, penniless and emotionally disturbed, wandered in the ugliness, finding it difficult to comply with the rules of civilian life in the new nation they had helped to create.

The general economy was just commencing to show signs of recovering from the losses inflicted by the conflict and from commercial and financial setbacks caused by the flight of the Tory families . . . most of them employers and landowners . . . on the heels of the British troops.

Acquisition of fifteen guineas, more than enough to pay his passage, had not alone influenced Astor to strike out for America. The deciding factor had been the signing of the treaty of peace. With astuteness uncommon in a young man of twenty, he had seen the advantages to be gained with the development of a new and unrestricted trade between the old and the young nations.

The Declaration of Independence had, of course, thrown a great new light over the land, giving rise to strong, fresh hopes in a weary and impoverished people. The common man could mouth its exalted sentiments with savor, even if he found them a bit unbelievable, while he watched for a favorable turning of the road.

That years would pass before the noble doctrines would be interpreted and carried out in ways that resulted in general benefits, that the infant government would have trouble surviving from week to week and have neither time nor funds for launching truly significant experiments in practical democracy, that the peace would turn out to be tenuous and the most important provisions of the treaty would not be carried out until another war had been fought, some thirty years later, were events of the future no man could have predicted.

Astor could do no more than deal with the conditions before him at the time.

He soon came to understand that the ordinary former colonial, fighting for enough bread to sustain his family and himself, was still at the mercy of laws and customs which had come down through generations of European jurisprudence. They favored the propertied man, and gave no rights to the struggling worker who owned nothing of real value.

Not only commerce and industry were controlled by the landowners and wealthy merchants, but all political bodies as well. Their British forebears had taught them the value of class government, and they had no intention of sacrificing this advantage to social reforms. Independence from the Crown of England did not mean that the basic structure from which British statutes stemmed was to be abandoned. Such a procedure would have been unthinkable. Because laborers, farm boys, clerks and factory workers had shouldered guns and fought for their freedom from oppression was not reason enough to let them have it.

The proprietary forces, the landed gentry, had made certain that the new state constitutions left as little power in the hands of the people as possible. Provisions were most rigid and discriminatory in treating with property rights. In most states no man could hold high political office unless he was the owner of substantial acreage, possessed a heavy purse, and was free of all debt. Under the New York Constitution of 1777 a man was prohibited from voting for state officers unless he had assets worth one hundred pounds and no financial encumbrances. The citizen who had no property of such value was disenfranchised until he acquired it.

Astor thoughtfully noted that the landholders, the rulers of the overall economy, were staunch supporters of the churches. At the same time they kept their political guns loaded and maintained a sharp lookout for breaks in the legal dikes they had erected, on which they depended for protection.

It was a shrewd observation for a young peasant in a strange land, but even more to his credit was the fact that he understood its significance. There was an advantage in being seen each Sunday morning and evening in the same pew while some sincere but deluded minister preached of equality and the Ten Commandments. A man could enjoy especially the admonitions to the humble to be content with what the Lord saw fit to provide, to respect high office and authority, and to look only to heaven for a reward for faithful service.

If the conditions Astor found in America in some ways were not as salubrious as he had thought they would be, in other ways they proffered even more promise than he had dreamed of finding. The general laws were hardly different than they had been in Europe, and the social and economic burdens on one of his class and financial standing varied only in a few respects from those he had found in London.

But there was a difference, a very great difference, and when he recognized it his spirits soared and his blood raced. Fundamentally the difference, as he saw it, was that in America no important door was closed to him. The circumstances of a man's birth could no more bar his financial progress than the color of his eyes. Only ignorance and indolence could do that.

Freedom wasn't yet all that the men of Lexington and Valley Forge and Yorktown had thought it would be, but there was no doubt about the future. All a man had to do was to gaze westward to understand that. And looking that way, Astor was deeply stirred.

It was this inherent perspicacity, this great gift of farsightedness and keen vision, that set John Jacob Astor apart from all the other laborers and poor workers about him. Other butcher boys and peddlers and dock workers and ditch diggers, looking in the same direction as he, at the same things, did not in reality see what he saw. Nor did they comprehend as he comprehended. Even if some understanding and recognition came to them, they had no means of utilizing such weapons. They were not possessed of the qualities, the force and the ability with which, by some mysterious quirk of nature, a Walldorf peasant had been endowed.

But, in all the world, few have been so endowed.

3

Astor had not long remained in Dieterich's employ, but during that period, short as it was, he found time to look into the business of buying and selling furs, as he had promised himself he would do at the first opportunity.[2]

---

[2] Brief as was his employment by the baker, Astor wished to conceal it from public knowledge in later years. He became irritated if it was mentioned by members of

He soon received from George a shipment of flutes. It was the custom of the time for a person who had articles to sell, but did not own a shop, to place them with an established merchant to be disposed of on commission. Astor made such an arrangement with Samuel Loudon, a job printer and publisher of the *New York Packet.*

On September 20, 1784, an advertisement in the *Packet* announced: "GERMAN FLUTES of A Superior Quality to be Sold at this Printing-Office."[3]

Astor's faith in musical instruments as a means of aiding him to achieve the independence he craved, did not abate, but he was unwilling to depend entirely on them. It was his conviction that security required numerous and varied sources of income.

Some time in the summer of 1784, he traded for his first fur pelt on the New York waterfront, giving in exchange for a beaver skin some sugar buns or some toy or trinket, and thereupon not only proving to himself that what his German shipmate had told him was true, but casting the die which was to shape the course of his life for the next half century.

Although he was inspired and excited with the prospect which his first small venture in the fur trade created, he was unwilling to learn the business only through his own experiences on the

---

his family. After his sister Catherine reached New York—the wife of a distiller, George Ehninger—she and John Jacob frequently differed sharply over business and personal questions. When Ehninger died she continued to operate the cordial distillery he had founded. For some reason it was a business Astor intensely disliked, and he expressed the view it was beneath the dignity of the family. This superciliousness brought a sharp rejoinder from Catherine. She criticized him for being overly conscious of his wealth, and reminded him that he at one time "vas noting put a paker poy, und solt pred und kak." She apparently understood that she could make him retreat from his contemptuous pose by reminding him of his own lowly beginning in New York.

[3] Inasmuch as this story is primarily about Astor and the fur trade, details of his career as a dealer in musical instruments are omitted. Similarly, descriptions and accounts of the hundreds of real estate transactions which won him the title of "landlord of New York" and made him millions of dollars are excluded. Astor also was one of the largest shipowners of his time, but only his maritime operations connected with the international trade in furs are included. It should be kept in mind that the fur trade was the foundation of Astor's success, and from it came the money that permitted him to launch his careers in various other fields.

streets and wharves; to secure more knowledge of it he obtained employment in the shop of an elderly Quaker, a fur dealer named Robert Bowne. He was hired as a beater, that is, he was to beat furs to keep out the moths. He received his room and board in Bowne's home and a wage of two dollars a week.

Within a matter of days Bowne knew he had made a good bargain. Astor's sound business instincts and his inherent ability as a trader soon revealed themselves. Bowne was shrewd and seldom missed an opportunity to make a profit, but he was eminently fair in his dealings with all persons, and no more than a few weeks had passed before he had increased Astor's wages and given him more responsible duties. His attitude and his act rewarded him. Whatever assignment was given to him, Astor carried out with dispatch and efficiency.

Although he worked hard and gave Bowne a full measure of service, Astor did not, however, let his duties and obligations interfere with his private ambitions and plans more than was necessary. His meager income was supplemented by money from the occasional sale of a flute or piccolo or mouth organ, and he promptly invested it in goods to be traded for skins. In his spare time, with a basket of cheap jewelry, pottery birds, pins, needles, ribbons and beads, he went aboard sloops and barges lying in the New York docks. Sundays and evenings he sought out rivermen, degraded Indians and wandering farm laborers who might have a pelt or two to trade. He lugged his acquisitions home, beat them, cleaned and packed them, and scurried out to find more.

But he did not sell them.

Steadily he built up a stock of furs, and by the time the first frigid blasts of winter struck the Hudson River he was ready to make the move he had contemplated privately for months.

If the story appeared incredible, it was no less than that. A young German immigrant arrived virtually penniless in New York in the spring, and by the late fall he had not only gained a remarkable knowledge of the fur trade, but he had acquired

enough pelts to make it worth his while to sail across the Atlantic to dispose of them.

On both the outward and return voyages Astor was favored by
comparatively good weather. It was as well a highly successful
trip. He not only sold his furs at a good profit, but he established
a connection with a dependable London trading house. He also
obtained agreements under which he would represent both his
brother and the musical instrument firm of Shudi & Broadwood
in New York. He invested part of his returns from the furs in
British goods suitable for the Indian trade, an indication that
greater plans were taking shape in his thoughts.

Astor also brought back from London a large assortment of
musical instruments, again arranged to sell them through the
Packet office, and then returned to work for Bowne. The furrier
was delighted to have his gifted protégé back, and soon decided
to send him on a fur-buying journey into the wilderness of northern New York State . . . the Iroquois country.

It was a dangerous assignment, and one that might easily result in a loss of money, if not injury or death, for a young man
unfamiliar with life on the frontier.

Astor was eager to go. The truth was that he had for some time
been considering making such a journey in his own interests,
but he did not yet feel himself prepared for the arduous undertaking. It was risky business, and he did not have much to risk.
His unobligated capital at the time approximated $500. It would
be decidedly more judicious, he reasoned, if he could make his
first trip as Bowne's agent, secure the experience he needed, yet
endanger nothing more than his own hide. Bowne would be footing the bills, paying him a commission, and making all the investment.

When word came down the Hudson in the spring of 1785 that
the ice was breaking up in the north and the Indians were beginning to move, Astor boarded a sloop bound for Albany. He
wore the durable rough clothes of the woodland trader: a fur
cap, a heavy mackinaw, stout boots into which his thick woolen
trousers were tucked, woolen shirt and underwear. At his belt

was a skinning knife. He puffed nonchalantly on a clay pipe. In his pocket was a purse heavy with copper and silver pieces, mostly British coins. The Indians of the Five Nations understood something of the value of British money. They would have nothing to do with paper, which was unsuitable for personal adornment and did not glitter. In a heavy pack Astor carried his articles of trade, the trinkets and notions and utensils which so delighted the red people of the forests and for which they willingly exchanged their valuable beaver, muskrat, lynx, fox, wolf, marten and mink skins.

Approximately twelve months had passed since Astor had first seen the dirty streets of New York. In that time he had made enough money to travel to London and back, to acquire a substantial stock of musical instruments, and to leave several hundred dollars in Robert Bowne's strongbox.

He had established a connection with a London fur house which would benefit him greatly when the time came for him to strike out for himself. He was the American representative for two reputable British piano makers. He had earned the respect and won the trust of a leading New York fur dealer. He had been furnished with money and goods and sent alone on a perilous trading expedition, an assignment that only a man with a level head, courage and acute business sense would receive.

He had . . . although he had told no one . . . met the girl he intended to marry as soon as he could see his way clear to support her.

He was not yet twenty-two years old.

4

Somewhere in that dark, beautiful, cold land along the Mohawk west of Albany, Astor met the Iroquois. The people of the Long House, descendants of the once supreme Five Nations, still preserved a shadow of their sovereignty. Doggedly they clung to a proud heritage: the elders through living memories, and the young in feverish dreams that would never come true. The sun of their day was falling low, but it had not set.

If Astor had anything in common with the intrepid *voyageurs* and *coureurs du bois* it was that both he and they were engaged in the fur trade. In contrast to their buoyancy, love of life and improvident ways, he was stolid, deadly serious, and excruciatingly thrifty. He had no desire for licentious personal adventures. He had no real love for the forests, little appreciation of natural beauty, and he held an intense dislike for the discomforts and hardships one was obliged to endure on a trading expedition. He had no thought of entering into life in the wilderness on the native level, as his illustrious French predecessors had done in the posts and camps. Indian women repelled him.

Yet, in certain ways he was intrepid, and he possessed an abundance of both physical stamina and courage. Only poor business, never the presence of danger, could have turned him back as he trudged westward on the woodland trails.

All the years that had passed since the pathfinders had first gone that way had brought only small changes to the wilderness. A few forts had been built, but it was still Indian country. Some settlers were there, but they barred their cabin doors and windows at night. The tomahawk, if antiquated, had not lost its might nor is usefulness, and bloody scalps still adorned the thighs of vengeful warriors.

He had journeyed to the Iroquois country for one purpose . . .

to secure pelts at the lowest possible cost. Yet, furs were not all that he thought about. As he traded his trinkets and notions for skins, he contemplated the political situation of the northland, it and all the regions to the west, and he never ceased to increase his knowledge and understanding.

In both London and New York, even in Walldorf, he had done the same thing. Always had he sought answers to an unending flood of questions in his mind. He had wearied himself in struggles by candlelight to read newspapers and books in German, French and English . . . especially books about exploration and discovery . . . believing that only through an understanding of history could a man evaluate sensibly the events of his own times and look with even partial clarity into the future.

One question to which he attributed great significance involved the Northwest Territory, that vast region bounded roughly by the Great Lakes, the Mississippi River and the Ohio. It belonged to America, but the British still controlled it, simply because they dominated its economy by occupying the trading posts. Astor had reached the conclusion that not much time would pass before the British would be driven from the field, and American fur traders would supplant them. The conviction was not based only on right, not only on the premise that it was American territory and Americans had every legal right to exploit it. Those factors influenced his thinking, but he was also influenced by geographic and economic considerations. He held the belief that the next few years would witness a natural westward expansion of American trade and commerce, and its force would be irresistible.

This reasoning was contrary to a belief popular at the moment. Many Americans thought that their weak government would tolerate the British domination rather than chance another war, and would, in the end, despite the provisions of the peace treaty, seek some kind of a compromise that would permit both British and American traders to operate in the area.

Rumors, invariably without foundation, were never lacking in the Hudson River settlements and the lonely outposts which Astor visited. Congress would create an American royal family.

An Indian nation would be established in the Northwest Territory, and only troops and government agents would be permitted to enter it. The new American Crown would retain a monopoly of the fur trade and maintain posts. Americans would be the losers, for the British were smarter traders, who had the benefit of long experience in dealing with Indians.

Astor made many such trips over a period of several years. He walked, rode and drove a wagon hundreds of miles on spring, summer and fall expeditions. However, he went on only two trading trips as the agent of Robert Bowne. Never after his twenty-fourth year did he serve any master except himself.

How successful he was in Bowne's behalf, and how much the old Quaker appreciated his good service, might never have been known had it not been for an incident which occurred nearly a hundred years later at Michilimackinac. There in an excavation a silver watch of the so-called English bulldog type was found. Still legible on it was an inscription which read: "Presented to John Jacob Astor by R. Bowne, 1785."

Astor not only trudged the trails of the country north of the Mohawk. He traveled the rutted traces of the Catskills, of the forested hills of northern New Jersey, of the woodlands and swamps of Long Island, of the farthest reaches of the Adirondacks. He knew the Finger Lakes country, the valley of the Allegheny, and the mountains of Pennsylvania.

Wherever they took him, they were all difficult and dangerous journeys. He suffered frequently from exhaustion, hunger and cold. But rewards came in several ways. He made money and established his own name. He learned things that eluded less perceptive men. In a real sense, he discovered America for himself. He gained an intimate and revealing perspective of the new and growing nation that he could have gained in no other way. He acquired knowledge of geography, trade, people, resources that the most intelligent and well-informed businessman of New York, Philadelphia and Boston could not hope to match.

On he went until he came to the big water, the falls of Niagara, the shores of Lake Ontario and Lake Erie. He knew the little frontier clearings of Syracuse, Rochester, Utica, Buffalo, and he told hunters, trappers, traders and Indians: *someday cities will stand in these places.*

He was seen in the taprooms of the frontier taverns, and he was well remembered for his inquisitiveness, his constant quest for information, news and opinion. He was remembered even more for the things he said.

A generation before the Erie Canal became a reality, he expounded on the subject of building it. To his astonished listeners, who had never dreamed of such a thing, he explained the commercial advantages to be gained by having a means of good transportation between the Great Lakes and the Hudson River, thus to the sea and all the world.

Indians, traders, wilderness storekeepers, farmers, hunters, long recalled seeing him tramping along with a heavy pack on his back, a rifle in the crook of his arm, bullet pouch, powder horn and knapsack slung from his powerful shoulders, skinning knife at his belt.

His burned face was hard and swollen from the bites of insects. His clothing often was torn and dirty and strong with the smells of sweat, campfire smoke and raw pelts. He drove himself unsparingly. He gave little or no time to self-indulgence, although sometimes at night before a cabin hearth or an open fire, if there was no bargaining to be done, he might tootle a bit of Mozart on a battered German flute, and permit himself the shock of a mug of fiery homebrew.

No deal was too small for him, none was too large. He would dicker as patiently for a single skin as he would for a hundred-pound pack, always holding firmly to his offer until his adversary gave in. Then he would quickly hand out the agreed price, and vanish into the trees.

Seldom was he fortunate enough to make his bed on the dirt floor of a settler's cabin, or scratch fleas with Indians in a bark lodge. He knew many a lonely campfire, a pallet of fir boughs or a lean-to hastily thrown up to break a bitter night wind.

One contemporary wrote that before the settlement of Canandaigua was founded in 1789, "John Jacob Astor, with a pack of Indian goods upon his back, wandered from the Indian trail, got lost in the low grounds at the foot of Seneca Lake in an inclement night, wandered amid the howl and rustling of wild beasts, until almost morning, when he was attracted by the light of an Indian cabin . . . and following it, obtained shelter and warmth."

James Wadsworth, Squire of Geneseo, told how he once came upon his friend Astor in "a sad plight." Astor's wagon had broken down in a swamp, and in the struggle to free it, the pack in which he had his money rolled off the tail-piece and vanished into the ooze. Next the frantic horses stampeded into quicksand, and they and the wagon slowly disappeared. Astor emerged from the ordeal with an ax over his shoulder, "the sole relic of his property." Squire Wadsworth was greatly impressed by his imperturbability. Astor had shrugged, as if to dismiss the disaster from his thoughts, and had set out to acquire a new outfit.

If Astor had known the word *psychology*, it would have meant *tricks of the trade* to him. According to a story, he discovered that quite a few Indians liked music, and when the occasion was opportune he would brighten the sour visage of some Seneca or Mohawk with a few trills and runs from German folk dances on his old flute.

Perhaps . . . but if that story belonged in an Astor apocrypha, there was no lack of evidence to show that he influenced numerous persons, and that he made a number of important and lasting friendships.

Peter Smith was one, both friend and close associate. Smith was three years younger than Astor, but he was fully as precocious and intelligent. When they met, Smith was employed as a clerk by Abraham Herring, a New York importer. He was as determined as Astor to be independent, and he quit his job to open a bookshop. To supplement the infrequent sales of literature, he stocked lace, beeswax, walking sticks and snuffboxes. Prosperity avoided the hopeful establishment, however, and at the end of a year, Smith looked about for a more profitable occupation.

In 1788, Smith and Astor entered into a partnership. Their

original plan called for Smith to remain in New York and handle the furs Astor sent down the Hudson from his trading expeditions, but this arrangement soon proved to be unsatisfactory, if not unnecessary. Smith was attracted by the idea of settling upstate, and he preferred action rather than the sedentary life of a New York fur dealer.

He and Astor made a number of trading trips together, going to Albany by boat and then on foot to the interior. Old Fort Schuyler stood where the city of Utica was to rise. Smith was attracted to the place, and at last decided to set himself up there as the proprietor of a general store. He opened his business in 1789, but he and Astor continued as associates in the fur trade until 1792. Smith's store for some time served as an upstate headquarters for Astor. Furs that he collected were stored there. Astor saw to the marketing in New York himself. When Smith married Elizabeth Livingston, a young lady of well-to-do and socially prominent parents, she induced him to give up the fur trade and shopkeeping for a more aristocratic life as a country gentleman and landowner.

In 1787, a "gentleman of Schenectady" stated: "Many times I have seen John Jacob Astor with his coat off, unpacking in a vacant yard near my residence a lot of furs he had bought dog-cheap off the Indians and beating them out, cleaning them and repacking them in more elegant and salable form to be transported to England and Germany, where they would yield him 1,000 per cent on the original cost."

Another man who became a close friend of Astor and had an influence on his spiritual life was, strangely enough, a former resident of Walldorf. He was the Reverend John Gabriel Gebhard, and when Astor came to know him he was the pastor of the Dutch Reformed Church at Claverack on the Hudson.

Astor built up his trade in the Catskills to the point where hunters and trappers brought their furs to him. He maintained a headquarters in this area in Cornelius Persen's store at Katsbaan. Each spring, Astor, coming up the river on the earliest sloop, would stop there. Some years his trade was so heavy that

Persen's store would be filled with packs of furs he had purchased, and the overflow carried into the Persen kitchen, "against the indignant protests of the mistress of the house."

Another field station was set up by Astor in the home of Peter Sailly at Plattsburg. Sailly was appointed collector of customs at Plattsburg, supervising traffic crossing the Canadian border. He and Astor became involved in some international transactions of a highly dubious nature.

Albany was, in Astor's time, and had been since shortly after Henry Hudson turned around there in 1609, the eastern fur trade headquarters for the Iroquois country, and even for regions beyond its borders. The Walloons had made it a permanent settlement in 1623, calling it Fort Orange. The British drove them out, and for another century or more the French had bled and died in their attempts to dislodge the British. Once they succeeded in destroying nearby Schenectady, but Albany's strong garrison discouraged them, and they retreated to Canada.

All through the years, from the woods of western New England, from the lakes and rivers bordering Canada and from the big waters of Niagara, the Indians, the independent French and English trappers, and the American colonials brought pelts into the posts of Albany. Men whose names were to live forever in the annals of the fur trade, men who performed incredible feats of exploration, who made fortunes and lost them, had padded in their moccasins along Albany's rough streets, bartered over the scarred boards of crude trading counters, and sent their valuable packs on to New York or Montreal.

Many of these notorious and distinguished men were there when Astor first jumped ashore from a Hudson River sloop. He heard them talk, he studied their methods, and he boldly sought their friendship and their advice.

One of them whom he came to know . . . one of the most distinguished and successful . . . was the Canadian, Alexander Henry.

Henry was much older than Astor. He had been a soldier under General Amherst. After the fall of Montreal in 1760, he elected to enter the fur trade. The French merchants of Montreal, however, striving to control the remnants of their once great empire, refused to sell him any trade goods. He had gone to Albany, where he had secured a licence and the merchandise he wanted.

In the next few years, Alexander Henry had become known as an enterprising and shrewd trader throughout all the vast wilderness territory from the St. Lawrence to the Saskatchewan, from the Great Lakes to the Hudson. He had eventually established his own house in Montreal.

That such a veteran of the trade, whose fame and fortune had not yet reached their greatest heights, should become more than a speaking acquaintance of a young German immigrant was an extraordinary development. It was also one of the most important events in Astor's life.

Astor first met Henry in Albany in the spring of 1785. Certainly he was honored and impressed to be in the company of such a famous and experienced man. But Henry, as certainly, saw something in Astor that he did not see in other youthful traders. Perhaps he sensed an extraordinary ability, a keenness and astuteness, that made him regard Astor with more than ordinary interest.

The evidence to support such an assumption was revealed in the fact that a chance acquaintanceship within two years developed into both an enduring friendship and a business association.

5

When Astor returned to New York in 1785 from his first trip into the wilderness, his head was full of important plans bearing upon his own immediate future, and not all of them had to do with the fur trade.

At 81 Queen Street was the home of Sarah Cox Todd. She had been for fifteen years the widow of Adam Todd, and although she was connected with the prominent Brevoort family by marriage, she was obliged to take in boarders to make ends meet.

Sarah Cox Todd had a daughter, also named Sarah, who was a year older than Astor. He had first become aware of the younger Sarah's charms when he was peddling cakes for George Dieterich, but he had postponed his approach on a social level until he could achieve a more suitable station. This self-imposed requirement, he felt, had been fulfilled when he became an agent with regular employment for Bowne.

Astor launched his courtship of Sarah Todd with the same forthrightness, intensity and thoroughness that he would have displayed in a new business venture. He met with no objection from Sarah Cox Todd. She had liked him from the beginning, and was appreciative of his good manners and his serious attitude toward life. The American young men Sarah (the daughter) knew were inclined to wildness. Many of them had been in the army, and they exhibited a restlessness which Sarah (the mother) thought boded them no good. Also, young Astor had a taste for fine music, worked harder than the proverbial beaver, in which he was very much interested, and regularly attended church.

Oddly enough, Astor was also known and liked by one of the male members of the family. Adam Todd also had been the father of a daughter, Margaret, by a previous marriage. She was some twenty years older than her half sister Sarah who held Astor's eye, and she was the wife of a Capt. William Whetten. It had been John, the son of Margaret and William Whetten, who had met Astor on the wharf at Bristol.

Also, a daughter of Margaret and William Whetten was the wife of Henry Brevoort, and it was through this alliance that the Todds had come into the circle of the prominent Brevoort clan.

The resistance of Sarah to Astor's attentions was hardly less than that of her mother. She quickly became betrothed. The marriage ceremony was performed on September 19, 1785, in the German Reformed Church of New York.

Sarah Todd brought to her husband a most welcome dowry of $300. It was money her mother had saved over a period of years while cooking and caring for boarders. Astor promptly stowed it in his strong box. He had plans for putting it to good use. The young couple took no honeymoon. They moved immediately into living quarters, consisting of two rooms which had been arranged for them in the Todd house.

Astor had gained a lovely wife and a good home.

Sarah Cox Todd had gained another boarder.

It could not have been denied that Astor's romantic instincts were colored by certain degrees of practicality, but it was equally true that he possessed a deep and abiding love for Sarah, and that he was a kind, considerate and devoted husband.

The morning after his marriage Astor was back at work in Robert Bowne's fur house. In that September of 1785 he had been in America seventeen months. Great schemes had formed in his head, but they were not the products of youthful dreams. They were schemes based on the most factual foundations he could devise for them through careful thought and cold analysis.

They were as well schemes touched, by no doing of his own, with sprinkles of stardust.

6

Beaver skins sold in London in 1785 for twenty shillings a pound. A two-pound prime pelt could be obtained in an Iroquois lodge for knickknacks worth no more than three or four shillings, and sometimes for less if the trader happened to have a jug of rotgut rum with him. Four shillings against forty, or a gain of 900 per cent. Transportation cut this overall margin, but not a great deal. The profits on other pelts were comparable, oftentimes larger.[4]

Astor plunged into the trade, feeling the weight of his new domestic responsibilities, and the two rooms he and Sarah occupied were at times so crowded with packs of furs that there was little space remaining in which they might engage in the customary pursuits of a newly wedded couple. The furs overflowed into the woodshed and the Todd stable, and the general odor was hardly that of a florist's shop.

Although he labored from dawn until dark and often far into the night, trading, beating, packing, grading, shipping, Astor was disturbed by a conflicting ambition which would not be stilled. It was to have a musical instrument store of his own.

This represented a peculiar twist in his nature. He understood that his greatest opportunity was as a dealer in furs. Yet, he was determined to enter a business in which the profits were not a tenth of those to be made in the fur trade.

It was as if, in this rare instance, emotion had influenced him to such an extent that his love for an industry . . . if not for the instruments themselves and the music they produced . . . was irrepressible. At last he surrendered to the pressure. Securing merchandise on long-term credit from his brother in London, he opened a small shop on the ground floor of the Todd house.

That done, he seemed to be no longer concerned with this venture. The story went that he was not even present to receive the first customer, but was on his way at the time to the Niagara frontier for furs. Sarah, breaking away from her own domestic duties, from beating furs, and from helping her mother cook for the Todd boarders, was alone behind the counter. But Sarah was fully capable of launching the enterprise by herself.

[4] The price of mink on the London market in 1784 was twenty-eight shillings per pound, and otter sold at thirty to fifty shillings per pound.

7

The American Revolution had ended officially with the signing of the treaty in 1783, but it was not over as far as the Canadian fur traders and the Montreal dealers were concerned.

It was not permitted to export furs from Canada directly into the United States. If a New York dealer wished to obtain Canadian pelts, he was obliged to buy them on the London market. Even if he bought them in Montreal, he had to ship them first to London, then reship them across the Atlantic to New York.

The Northwest Territory had gone to the United States over the conference table . . . a loss the Canadians disliked to think about . . . yet the posts in it still remained in British hands, both military and civilian, while the diplomats continued to wrangle. Americans were kept out.

Furthermore, American commerce on the Great Lakes was prevented by the continued enforcement of a wartime prohibition against the use of the lakes by private vessels. Only royal ships were permitted to carry goods. This restriction had been modified by the British a year after Astor reached America to permit Canadians to move their own furs by water between Niagara and Montreal. Subsequently another amendment had been made which permitted British subjects to transport merchandise in their own craft on all the lakes. But the door was still kept tightly bolted against American trade.

Astor's wilderness trips and his conversations with men, such as Alexander Henry, who had ranged halfway across the continent, had given him a sound understanding of the real value of the territory surrounding the Great Lakes. It was apparent why the Canadians became depressed by the thought that it would be opened to their American counterparts. This could mean that they would be completely forced out of the immensely rich fur trade at such places as Detroit and Michilimackinac.

During the winter of 1786–87, Astor gave his close attention to the subject. The case was simple: Americans had been victorious in the war, yet they were barred from trading in the country they had won . . . which was one of the most productive fur regions on the continent, indeed in the world.

Astor's thinking on the problem was not influenced by loyalty to his adopted country. Not at all. He was not as sympathetic with the plight of the Americans as he was desirous of finding a way to circumvent the British regulations. The man who did that on a large scale, he told himself, could make money.

He was motivated in his assault on the matter, as well, by the knowledge that the American demand for furs of high quality was steadily increasing. The cheaper skins, such as muskrat, raccoon, deer, wolf and bear, had always been used for clothing, but before the Revolution American prodigality had not encompassed a desire for the finer furs . . . beaver, marten, ermine, mink, otter . . . with which the nobility and the wealthy of Europe adorned themselves. Ostentation had not found a place in the plain American character, and least of all did the recently liberated colonials wish to be accused of imitating their foppish European cousins.

But emotions engendered before the war, and augmented during it, were diminishing, swallowed in the flood of social and political conflicts confronting the people of the new states. If a man wanted a tall beaver hat, he damn well bought it, and he thought not so much about its popularity in England as he wondered how it favored his own appearance.

Americans were changing, becoming less conscious of their former status as poor relations of the British Crown, and more aware of the fact that they were, in truth, proprietors of an enormously rich empire, and, in constitutional theory at least, masters of their own destiny.

Nevertheless, without a strong or even a dependable government behind them, Americans were obliged as individuals to stand on their own feet. A man could look to no one but himself, and if he needed protection and support in some enterprise, it came not from Philadelphia but from friends and sympathizers, if it came at all. Generally it did not come. And as the nation was born, so was born a new kind of man, a man free in his heart and hardened by disappointments and bitter experiences, a man independent, stubborn and determined, a man who would not be stopped by the weakness of his own government any more than he would be intimidated by the machinations of selfish and bigoted diplomats.

There was no one in all the world to be compared with the American individual created by the surrender at Yorktown. If he wanted land, he went out and took it. The same thing was true of furs, a valuable commodity. If he could obtain them in no other way, he smuggled them, ironically enough in the case of the Northwest Territory, from his own country into his own country.

He slipped off into the wilderness, which he owned, but which he could not occupy, and he brought furs out. He brought them up the Ohio River, through Pittsburgh. He could not transport them on the Great Lakes, so he carried them along the shore. Under the very muskets of the British garrisons, he moved quietly across the Appalachians, through the hardwood forests, into Pennsylvania and New York and Virginia. He paddled his canoe silently down Lake Champlain and Lake George, pushed a packhorse down into the valley of the Hudson, with pelts bought or trapped on Canadian territory.

Altogether it was really a small business, it did not amount to much in dollars and cents, but like all significant events it cast a shadow before it.

Some men who saw the shadow understood its meaning. One of them was Astor.

Early in 1788, he went up the ice-filled Hudson. He left Sarah with their first child, a girl born only a few weeks before, whom they had named Magdalen after his mother. This year he did not follow the trail into the valley of the Mohawk.

From Albany, Astor rode a horse up the Hudson Valley until it turned westward; from there he went northwestward through

Whitehall to Lake Champlain. A sloop carried him to Plattsburg, where he stayed overnight with his friend, Peter Sailly,
"sleeping in the front of Sailley's big open fire in the kitchen."

A lake boat took him on to Rouses Point. In a smaller craft
he descended the Richelieu River to St. Jean. He traveled in
a wagon from that settlement to the vicinity of La Prairie on
the St. Lawrence, and was ferried across the great river to Montreal.

The trip from New York took two weeks. He had advanced
with the spring, and the St. Lawrence was not free of ice. It would
soon be gone, however, and the Ottawa River as well would be
open. There was excitement and bustle in the city. The brigades
were preparing for the long spring journey into the wilderness.
Soon the fleets of immense canoes, loaded so heavily with men
and trade goods that their gunwales were only a few inches above
water, would push up the Ottawa against the rushing spring
current.

Astor went to the home of his friend Alexander Henry. The
old trader welcomed him and invited him to be a house guest.
A few days later Astor was a passenger in a cargo canoe, ascending the Ottawa with one of the first spring brigades to leave.

8

Astor could not have gone on such a journey had not Alexander
Henry arranged it for him. American traders were not permitted
to visit the interior of Canada without a legitimate reason and
assurances that they did not propose to engage in any business
while there. An excuse that he wanted to go simply as an adven-

turous traveler would not have been sufficient. Space in every canoe and bateau was at a premium, and taking a passenger meant that his weight in goods had to be left behind.

Astor had sworn allegiance to his adopted country, but he was too commercial-minded to permit patriotism in any degree to interfere with either his own advancement or the carrying out of his personal plans. His first loyalty, with the exception of his family, was to the dollar. Citizenship, like honesty, was a relative thing. He had become an American because he had believed he could make more money and have a greater future by being one than he could by becoming a naturalized British subject.

Astor went on the Canadian expedition that spring as a spy. He went, not simply to gain experience but to gain firsthand knowledge of the operations of the British companies in the region of the Great Lakes, the Northwest Territory. He wanted to see for himself their methods, to learn the size of their profits, to secure information on the type and quality of the goods they used in trading with the Indians, to see their strength in the fur country with his own eyes. And he wanted to know all these things because he was already planning to enter the trade in competition with them.

He did not deceive Henry. Henry was wily and shrewd, and he had been in the trade for many years. He understood what Astor was up to, but he saw no danger in letting the likeable, enterprising young German go along with the *voyageurs*.

Henry was wealthy, lived in a fine house, belonged to the Beaver Club, and was socially prominent. He was amused by the suggestion that Astor, a struggling New York trader, could be a threat to such strong and experienced organizations as the North West Company. It would have been the case of a mouse becoming overly ambitious and failing to realize its own limitations, or a foolhardy rabbit hopping in the pad marks of a lion.

Henry was soon to learn how fallacious was his judgment.

From the time he had entered into it, the manner in which the fur trade was conducted . . . barter and exchange . . . had been a magnet to Astor. The system proffered an unlimited range for his superb merchandising instincts. Under such a method of doing business the amount of profit to be made was governed almost entirely by the ability of the trader, and Astor enjoyed the challenge.

The best method of obtaining furs, and the most profitable, was in direct trade with the Indians. This eliminated the middleman. Besides, securing a prime beaver pelt worth from six to ten dollars in London for a few cents' worth of baubles or a cheap cooking pot brought an incomparable sensation of delight and no end of satisfaction.

It was not strange that the Indian knew the same sensations. He was unable to comprehend the eagerness of the traders to obtain furs, for he had never lived in the world of the white man. He was constantly astonished that they would travel hundreds of miles and suffer great hardships to get pelts. The Indian could only conclude that a man who would part with a bright tin mirror for a buffalo robe was not in his right mind.

At least to this extent the industry was a mutual pleasure, each party holding profound contempt for the stupidity of the other. Worldliness and ignorance worked amicably together.

But there were serious drawbacks. Indians, for instance, could not always be depended upon to take skins with regularity. The Indian lived with the freedom of the wind. Regular employment and scheduled production were customs he had to be taught, induced to adopt, and he was a poor pupil. He dwelt in the earth, not simply on it, living out his years in the natural way of life about him, superior to the animals which gave him sustenance only in that he possessed mental powers which created spiritual images and transcended instincts with forces of reason.

The fur companies supplemented the Indian hunters with trappers of their own. These men served in two ways. They trapped, and as company representatives they also traded. They worked generally on fixed wages, but, like the Indians, they received little actual cash for their services. Amounts they earned were credited to their names on the books of their employers, and usually this credit was quickly consumed by the purchase of new equipment, puffed away in the costly smoke of cheap Virginia tobacco, and puked out in the course of battles with expensive rotgut whisky. The end of summer normally found most of them broke and sick, returning to far rivers and valleys, a thousand miles beyond the reach of such civilized refinements as whorehouses and saloons, to the wilderness silence where a plate of buffalo hump and beaver tail had nothing in common with a silver dollar.

Another source from which the Canadian houses obtained furs was the free-trapper. He worked only for himself. He could not have been more Indian if his skin had been red. He wandered alone . . . or perhaps with one or two other free-trappers . . . into fastnesses never before penetrated by white men. Like a deepwater sailor, he had his squaws in remote camps. When he had taken a few packs of peltries, he struck out to travel hundreds of miles across mountains, plains and forests on horseback, or he came down the rivers in a bark canoe, to a trading post or a summer rendezvous. He cared not so much for hard money as for the things it would give him . . . new blankets, powder, traps, tobacco and whisky. He, too, generally penniless and disillusioned by his brothers, vanished each season into the silence he loved and preferred, and which was his home.

There were these three chief systems of supply for the companies . . . direct trade with the Indians, company hunters, free-trappers . . . but there was a fourth. It was through the purchase by one company of furs owned by another in such northwest trading centers as Detroit and Michilimackinac. It was the least desirable system, for it frequently required an outlay of cash. Payment for furs and services with trade goods brought two profits . . . one on the goods and one on the furs . . . and it established an advantageous spread between initial investment and final return that provided a greater opportunity to absorb losses which might occur through disaster or theft.

When Astor made his journey out from Montreal, the North West Company had only shortly before completed the sound foundation that was to endure through future decades. Previously there had been only one monopoly in Canada, that of the Hudson's Bay Company, and it operated in the great basin that drained into the Arctic body of water from which it took its name. South of this region, all the way from the Saskatchewan to the Ohio River, competition between companies and individual traders raged unabated and uncontrolled. Men fought to the death for a pack of beaver skins, for the trade of a tribe, or to hold their rights in a certain area. They pirated, pillaged and destroyed. Hatred curdled their thoughts and filled their hearts.

When the American Revolution ended, the Canadians realized that if Montreal was to remain the leading fur trade center of the Western world . . . indeed, if they were to survive . . . they had to work together.

It was an understanding easier to think about than to carry out. Getting the bitter enemies to co-operate with each other, to lay aside their guns and knives, to quell their hate and their burning desires for revenge, to share the trade and the profits, appeared an insurmountable task. Men with less courage and determination than wilderness traders, who had faced danger and seemingly insuperable problems all their lives, would not have made the attempt.

But there were giants in the Montreal trade, big men, fearless men, men who could imprison emotions in themselves and who understood the wisdom in fighting for financial security rather than a chance to stab an adversary in the back.

Actually the guns of the Revolution were still barking when they had begun to preach the doctrine of co-operation. For a time their efforts brought little success. In 1779, however, a significant step forward had been made with an agreement at Michilimackinac that united nine groups into a weak partnership for one year. Most of the nine came to like the taste of the unprecedented arrangement, and when it expired they signed a new agreement which was to continue for another three years. It lasted only two. The old order of cutthroat competition and bloodshed returned.

It was 1784 before the hostilities could be halted once more. By that time the fate of the Northwest Territory had been sealed, and many of the Canadian traders, but not all by any means, were ready to listen to reason.

A five-year agreement was formulated, and the organization took the name of the North West Company, a name destined to be imperishably carved into fur trade history.

The company was divided into sixteen shares, one for each group or house participating. Famous names were on the roster, among them Benjamin and Joseph Frobisher, Simon McTavish, Todd and McGill, Alexander Henry, Angus Shaw, Alexander Mc-Leod, William McGillivray, Cuthbert Grant, William Thor-burn, Alexander McKenzie, Forsyth & Richardson, John Gregory, Roderick McKenzie.

Studying the structure of the company, Astor could understand that for the first time knowledge, political influence and wealth had been welded together into a formidable force. The North West Company's announced intention was to operate in the Great Lakes region, the Northwest Territory "and beyond." How far beyond was an interesting question. The company not only had petitioned the Crown for exclusive control in the enormous central territory, but it had let it be known that it intended to explore "western regions," and it requested that it be awarded charters for exclusive rights to the fur trade in any areas it "discovered and opened."

Dissension, jealousy and the old brand of hatred soon troubled the company, but it had not collapsed. A group of disgruntled Montreal merchants formed a rival organization, which they called the General Company of Lake Superior and the South . . . popularly termed the General Store . . . but it soon succumbed to mismanagement. Six dealers in Detroit formed the Miami Company, but it also faded from the scene. The North West Company steadily grew stronger.

On his wilderness journey, Astor also obtained firsthand information about events taking place in a town called St. Louis. Spanish and French traders there were clashing with hunters from Michilimackinac in the Illinois country, and along the Wabash and the lower Ohio.

These Frenchmen and Spaniards were taking advantage of the difficulties which harassed the Americans. Back in 1763, Spain had opened the Mississippi to navigation by British subjects. In the peace treaty of 1783, Great Britain had confirmed the same right of navigation to citizens of the United States. But Spain had rejected this agreement, declaring that since Americans were no longer British subjects, the 1763 grant of navigation could not apply to them. Thus, American exports by way of the Mississippi were halted, even though the river bordered American territory. Spanish traders at New Orleans, Mobile and Pensacola reaped large profits on furs taken out of the United States and shipped down the Mississippi by the foreign traders of St. Louis.

Astor's education in the fur trade was significantly augmented even as the brigade with which he was to travel from Montreal prepared to depart. He quickly came to understand that the famed French-Canadian *voyageur* was "as full of latent tricks and vice as a horse," had the instincts of a pirate, and was occupied by all manner of ghosts.

Most of them drank themselves into insensibility, caroused with hopelessly degraded Indian sluts, and then scurried to the ancient chapel of Ste. Anne, the patroness of the wilderness hunters, to make confession. Having purged themselves and made their vows, they hurried back to wallow in the gutters until they were dragged off to start the hazardous voyage.

The big canoe to which Astor was assigned was forty feet in length, constructed of birch bark, and caulked with pine resin. The cargo, weighing some four thousand pounds, was wrapped and tied in hundred-pound packs, which could be easily carried over portages. Despite its great size, the craft could be transported on the shoulders of ten or twelve men. When waterborne, it could be propelled swiftly and efficiently by ten paddlers, who were called middlemen. At the bow rode a foreman to watch for sandbars, snags and other obstructions. A steersman in the stern gave all commands to the paddlers. Both foreman and steersman were veterans, selected because of their experience and ability to counter the whims and solve the mysteries of the northern rivers, and they received double wages. On big water, under a favorable breeze, a sail sometimes was used.

The brigade put off under the doubtful benefit of drunken songs and chants. Some of the *voyageurs* were sound of body, but green. Some were experienced, but lazy. Some were both expert and willing, but exhausted from their debauches, and of little use.

After the passing of a few days, however, the evil effects of their carousing and the bad whisky had begun to wear off. Senses were regained, strength seeped back into their hard bodies, and they were once more the masters of the life and the environment they loved and understood so well.

The *coureurs de bois* and the *voyageurs* had been from the beginning of interior exploration the masters of the fur trade. They had not been as happy working for the British as they had been when France ruled the American wilderness. The British were too staid, they dampered the free French-Canadian spirit, they frowned on their licentiousness, inflicted punishment for minor infractions a French trader would have overlooked, they ridiculed their childlike ways and their superstitions, and the British did not know how to dance, to sing and to be gay. But one thing the British did understand. It was that they could not succeed without the *voyageurs* and *coureurs de bois;* they could not carry on a profitable trade with the Indians without them, nor without them could they have built and maintained their posts in the wilderness.

The route of the brigade with which Astor traveled lay up the Ottawa River from the St. Lawrence to a point near the present little town of Mattawa. There the bateaux were unloaded and the short portage made to French River. Swiftly the French carried them down to Georgian Bay, and they were on the big water. Through the maze of a thousand islands, big and little, they paddled on into the North Channel that opened on the northern end of Lake Huron.

Some of the big canoes turned southward between Drummond

Island and the shore of the mainland that was to become the upper peninsula of Michigan, and reached the end of their outward voyage at Michilimackinac. There the packs of furs gathered the previous winter and spring in regions as far south and west as the Illinois, the Wisconsin and other streams of the Mississippi basin would be awaiting them.

Other canoes continued on westward to the North Channel, passed St. Joseph's Island and pushed up the St. Marys River. The falls of the St. Marys necessitated another portage, and then the *voyageurs* gazed across the cold, steely waters of Lake Superior.

Driving onward, they held to the northern shore of the immense lake until at last they came to Grand Portage and Fort William on the western shore. This was the gateway to the water routes that reached through the limitless western wilderness to the Lake of the Woods, Lake Winnipeg and the Saskatchewan.

The principal partners of the North West Company resided in Montreal, and they composed a kind of commercial aristocracy, living in lordly and lavish style. Two or three of them journeyed in the trade canoes each year out to Fort William to meet with the company's traders and to plan affairs for the coming season. They traveled in state, like Highland chieftains, wrapped in rich furs. In their retinues were cooks and bakers, and in the cargoes, for their private use, were European delicacies and choice wines.

Of far more interest to the sober, practical Astor than high living and merriment were the dimensions of the North West Company profits, the size of its trade, and the methods by which the traders operated, and these things he did note carefully, if not on paper, in the files of his scheming mind.

At Michilimackinac . . . where he apparently lost his watch . . . he saw the most important fur-trading center in all the Northwest Territory. All traffic from north, west and south passed through it, and not only the large companies but small ones and independent traders had posts or agents there.

For the first time Astor had an opportunity to observe the use of liquor in the Indian trade. As an individual tramping the Iroquois trails with all his worldly goods on his back, he had not been able to carry much rum with him. Packing a few jugs along in a wagon, or even on a horse, had been more feasible. But a man traveling alone placed himself in great danger by trading rum for pelts.

This danger was largely eliminated when a strong company traversed the wilderness, as the trading occurred at established posts which could be defended. At Michilimackinac, Astor not only saw for the first time the extent to which the Montrealers used liquor in the trade, but also came to understand its truly enormous power as a medium of exchange.

Canadian traders were forbidden by law to supply the Indians with alcohol in any form. Yet, a large part of the canoe cargoes was cheap and impure New England rum made from West Indies molasses. If the traders from Montreal were inclined to abide by the prohibitory statute at Canadian posts . . . within reasonable limits, that is . . . they had no need to regard it at Michilimackinac. The island at the head of Lake Michigan was in United States territory, and so was all the vast fur country south and west of it. At the posts in Michilimackinac liquor was dispensed freely over the counters. And in such a place, where the companies and independents were in close and direct competition, each agent sought to outdo his rivals by providing numerous and sizable drinks to break down the resistance of the Indians who came there with furs. The result was that during the trading season the place was bloody bedlam.

In the late summer the brigades, their bateaux as heavily loaded with fur packs as they had been in the spring with merchandise, would set out for home. As the forests turned red and gold, they swept down the Ottawa River to the St. Lawrence and Montreal. Fortunes in pelts were carried into the warehouses of the British and Canadian companies. There would be mad, wild, bloody, brutal scenes as the *voyageurs* celebrated their safe return. Candles would be lighted and prayers said for those who had not survived the perilous journeys through the Indian country. Each year these rites were performed, and the participants saw in their thoughts the graves and wooden crosses left behind them in the forest silence.

Astor was back in Montreal . . . once again enjoying the linen sheets in Alexander Henry's fine home . . . in September, 1788. A document in the Palais de Justice, among the "Notarial Records of John Gerbrand Beek," discloses that on September 30, Astor, described as a New York furrier, and one Roseter Hoyle, a Canadian merchant, signed a contract for shipping furs from Montreal to New York and Rotterdam by way of London.

This was the first legal agreement Astor was known to have made in the fur trade.

Under its provisions, he was to ship "Two thousand dollars in Furrs and Peltries more or less" to the order of Hoyle in London. Hoyle was to reship them to him in New York. From New York, Astor was to ship "one thousand Dollars more or less in [different type American] Furrs and Peltries" to London, which Hoyle was to send on to Rotterdam. Later invoices showed that six bales of furs were shipped to Astor in compliance with the agreement, and that their value was £783 0s. 3½d. currency or £704 14s. 3d. sterling.

It was a significant indication of his progress that Astor, a beginner in the fur trade, on his first trip to Montreal could muster sufficient credit to enable him to contract for furs valued at $3,000. Seemingly his friendship with Alexander Henry had begun to pay dividends.

Equally significant was the appearance of an advertisement in the *New York Packet* on October 28, 1788, under the signature of "J. Jacob Astor," which said: "He gives cash for all kinds of Furs; and has for sale a quantity of Canada Furs, such as beaver, beaver coating; raccoon skins, raccoon blankets, and spring muskrat skins; which he sells by large or small quantities—a considerable allowance will be made to every person who buys a quantity."

The advertisement ran in the *Packet* until the seventh of November, and it appeared in the *Daily Advertiser* for December 29.

The wording was revealing. Astor had Canadian furs for sale in New York. He offered them in "large" quantities. Among the pelts offered were "spring muskrat skins," which meant skins taken early in the year 1788. None of the furs advertised, however, could have been those Hoyle had shipped to him only a month previously from Montreal by way of London.

Astor had left Montreal early in October for New York. He traveled alone, but he had made arrangements to meet smugglers somewhere on the border of United States territory. In view of events which were subsequently to occur, the rendezvous undoubtedly took place at or near Peter Sailly's house in Plattsburg. Transporting the furs onward from that point on Lake Champlain would have presented no problem. Horses would have carried them from the south end of the lake until the Dutch gabled rooftops of Albany came into view. A sloop would have taken them down the Hudson to Old Slip or the Battery. No questions would have been asked.

9

Astor's first trip to Montreal had convinced him that further expeditions by himself, or even with Peter Smith of Utica, into the Iroquois country would be inadvisable. The profits to be gained from these personal expeditions were small. Besides, Astor found himself dissatisfied with the prospect of continuing in the trade with the small volume which had passed through his hands in the past. The journey to the Northwest Territory not only had stirred his ambition to new heights but had awakened in him a new determination stronger than any he had dared to harbor.

A chapter in Astor's life ended in the winter of 1788–89. Never again was he to be seen bent under a heavy pack on a wilderness trail.

His musical instrument store, under Sarah's efficient management, was bringing him satisfactory returns. He corresponded with hunters, merchants and traders, and soon furs began to arrive on consignment to him. From London came furs which he ordered from his friends in Montreal. To Europe he shipped American furs desired in that market.

The extent of his prosperity was indicated by an important event which took place in the summer of 1789. He made his first purchase of real estate, launching the career that would make him the largest and richest property owner in New York. On May 18, he bought from his brother Henry, two lots and four half-lots in the "out ward of the city on the Bowery Road and Elizabeth Street." For them he paid in cash "the Sum of forty seven pounds current money of the State of New York."

Astor's relationship with Alexander Henry continued to develop. In August, 1789, he was back in Montreal, once again a guest in the Henry home, and for the first time the two became partners in a business transaction. In the fur trade the word *partner* did not necessarily mean that a man was a member of a firm. One trader could be a partner of another on a single trading expedition or in a single transaction.

On August 29, 1789, Astor made an agreement with William Hands, a Detroit trader, under which Hands was to deliver to him at Montreal by August 20, 1790, some 15,000 "Good and Merchantable Musquash Skins." The price was to be "four pence half penny per skin," payable upon delivery. Hands and Astor bound themselves, as was the custom, to carry out the contract "in the Penal Sum of One hundred and fifty pounds Sterling." It was later revealed that Alexander Henry was a silent partner in the agreement.

In September, Astor negotiated a similar deal with Ephraim Santford, a Montreal hat-maker.

Here, in these two instances, he was for the first time dealing in "futures." It was an indication of his belief that the market for muskrat skins would rise in the coming year.

Both of these contracts brought him trouble, and he was obliged to take legal steps in an attempt to enforce them.

Astor was in Montreal in August, 1790, to take delivery of the 30,000 skins, but found that neither of the agreements would be carried out on schedule. On August 23 . . . three days after the delivery date agreed upon . . . he sought the services of the notary, J. G. Beek, whom he had previously engaged.

Beek was instructed to file legal protests against Hands and Santford, and to notify them that Astor would demand payment of the full penalty, and in addition would bring suits for damages against them.

Beek carried out his instructions. He went to Santford's house in the suburb of St. Lawrence. Finding that Santford was absent, he made a demand for immediate delivery of the skins before the hatter's wife, and departed.

Santford was an established businessman and property owner. The muskrat-skin market had risen, as Astor had believed it would, and Santford would have liked to escape from his commitment. In the face of a legal, written and notarized contract, however, he had no alternative but to comply with its provisions, even though he suffered a loss. Santford delivered the skins.

Hands was in Detroit, and was not expected back in Montreal until late in the fall. Beek filed a protest against him, but Astor had no intention of waiting for a settlement which might not be possible before winter had set in and travel to New York would be difficult and hazardous.

Evidence that Alexander Henry was a silent partner in the deal with Hands was disclosed by Astor's assignment to him of his own interest in the matter. The notarial records in the Palais de Justice for August 26 contain a notice of transfer from Astor to Henry of the entire agreement with Hands.

The document stated: ". . . That for and in Consideration of the said agreement being one half of the account and risque of Alexander Henry of Montreal Merchant and for the Consideration of Fifty pounds of lawful money to him the said John Jacob Astor now in hand paid by the same Alexander Henry . . ." Astor made over to Henry all his interest in the skins and in the penalty demanded.

If Astor got no muskrat pelts from Hands, he did get fifty pounds in cash, and he left Henry with the task of collecting from Hands.

Another troublesome deal beset Astor in Montreal during the fall of 1790, but the circumstances clothing it suggest that it was colored by ulterior motives.

On September 21, the same notary, J. G. Beek, called on Astor at the home of Alexander Henry in Notre Dame Street, and charged him with failing to carry out an agreement he had made to sell "twenty thousand musquash skins" to one Richard Dobie.

The agreement assertedly had been a verbal one, which Astor had made when he met Dobie in Sullivan's Coffee House. Beek announced that Dobie was prepared to pay Astor "at the rate of . . . seven pence currency" per skin.

The price should be noted. Astor was to have paid Hands 4½d. and Santford 5½d. per skin.

Beek was dismissed with Astor's categorical denial that he had ever made such an agreement with Dobie. Inasmuch as there was no written contract, and not even a witness to the verbal agreement, the issue was a stalemate . . . Astor's word against Dobie's. Beek departed with the admission that Dobie had no means of collecting.

The truth was that Dobie had no intention of attempting to collect. The whole matter was a scheme contrived by Astor, Beek and Dobie. With it Astor could show through the medium of notarial documents the price of muskrats at the time, and therefore how much profit he would have made had Hands kept his bargain. It also would serve to bolster evidence which would be presented, if needed, by Alexander Henry in a damage suit against Hands.

Back in New York in October, 1790, Astor consummated an association with Thomas Backhouse & Company of London that was to give him greater prestige in the fur trade and to be exceptionally profitable.

Astor's son was Wm Backhouse Ast

For some time in New York he had enjoyed a friendship with William Backhouse, an important merchant, who was a brother of Thomas, the head of the London house. It was through the influence of William that the connection was established.

The first transaction between Astor and the Backhouse firm occurred on November 6, 1790, when two cases of merchandise were shipped from London on the brigantine *Two Brothers*, of Newburyport, Massachusetts, which was commanded by Captain Peter Ceely. In the months following, casks of skins bearing Astor's mark ⊣⊦A , which was becoming familiar in the international fur trade, were shipped from New York to Thomas Backhouse in London.

Early in 1790 Sarah had given birth to her second child, who had died shortly after being christened Sally. Long before her grief had subsided, Sarah was carrying her third child. She was determined, however, that she would not bring another into the world under the distressing and disorderly conditions in which they lived.

For four years she had struggled vainly to maintain clean and respectable living quarters among crates of flutes, pianofortes, violins and packs of ill-smelling animal skins. She did not propose to endure this hardship any longer.

Her rebellion, however, was not marked by fiery proclamations or harsh threats. She was too clever and too much of a lady to conduct herself in that manner. Besides, she understood fully that soft words and womanly wiles were most effective in dealing with her thrifty, hardworking husband.

Quietly she pointed out to him that both the musical-instrument business and his fur trade had increased to such proportions that they could no longer be carried on efficiently in the crowded, unattractive rooms at 81 Queen Street. As a result of this situation, business was being adversely affected. Profits would be greater in larger and more presentable quarters, such as an attractive store and a showroom in which furs and other merchandise could be adequately displayed.

This was something Astor could understand, and he realized the wisdom of Sarah's suggestion.

On May 18, he bought a store with living quarters above it at 40 Little Dock Street, including the land on which it stood, from the estate of James Wells "and others." The price was £850. The move apparently impressed the editors of the *New York City Directory*, for they printed his name for the first time.

He had been in America approximately seven years.

He was the proprietor of a thriving musical instrument company, and a rapidly expanding fur business.

He had an aggressive, devoted and talented wife, and a fat, bouncing baby daughter.

In Montreal he had an association with the great Alexander Henry and connections with other merchants. His agents operated through the Iroquois country, buying pelts from the Indians, the settlers and from smugglers who brought them in from the Northwest Territory.

He was represented in London, the largest fur market of all, by Thomas Backhouse & Company, one of the most prominent, influential and wealthy houses in the international fur trade.

He owned a business building, five full lots and five half-lots on the lower end of Manhattan Island, and their value was steadily increasing.

He was worth in all probability between $30,000 and $40,000 in cash, merchandise, furs and real property.

He was twenty-seven years old.

Part Three

The Golden Ladder

1

During the last decade of the eighteenth century, Astor completed the foundation on which he would build his fur empire. As he laid each stone he gave long and careful thought to permanence and impregnability. Up to this time the world had seen nothing like it, and nothing like it was to be seen again. The economic and social changes which were to come soon after Astor's era were to put an end to empire-building by an individual. Only in America's first hundred years was such a thing possible.

Astor was no more religious than he was gregarious by nature, and he boldly displayed a liking for musichalls and the theater that more circumspect people . . . if they had such a vice . . . took pains to conceal. Still it was an exception rather than a custom for him and Sarah to go out in the evening. If she wished to be entertained, he preferred that she invite friends to their home. She seemed to be satisfied. Actually, her home was her world.

Astor's few social activities were predicated on his belief . . . which he was later to abandon as illogical . . . that he could advance his own business career by engaging in them. For instance, it gave him standing to be seen at church on Sunday mornings among respected bankers, merchants and lawyers, and talking with such men in the churchyard after services often gave him knowledge of financial and political affairs he might not otherwise have acquired. For the same practical reason that he became more active in his church, where he swiftly elevated himself to a trusteeship, he decided to become a Mason. He was accepted by Holland Lodge No. 8, which had been established in 1787 with a charter which allowed the members to perform "their Labours in the Low Dutch Language."

Astor took Freemasonry seriously, but his enthusiasm for it was bolstered not a little by the prominence of some of his fraternal colleagues. Among them was DeWitt Clinton, who was to become Governor of New York; Cadwallader D. Colden, with whom Astor was to be associated in a notorious land deal; and Henry W. Livingston, a member of a leading mercantile family. If the homes of their distinguished parents and relatives were not open to Astor, he had the satisfaction of sharing with them the secrets of the Masonic Order, and this circumstance alone made him their brother. It was a position of which he took good advantage. Clinton rose unusually fast in the degrees, but the German immigrant who talked at times as if he had marbles in his mouth was not far behind him. Astor eventually caught up to Clinton, and it was not until he bore the title "Sir J. J. Astor" and was registered as treasurer of the Knights Templar that his interest diminished. By that time, the year 1801, he felt that neither his social nor his financial position needed to be strengthened by artificial aids.

Astor continued to watch closely as the stage was set for a showdown between the United States and Great Britain over the Northwest Territory.

His conviction that the Canadians, and no doubt the French and Spanish trespassers, would be forced to withdraw from the Northwest Territory remained unchanged. Just how the weak American Government would bring this about, he was not willing to predict. Another war with England had to be avoided at all costs.

Certain factors, however, pricked his interest. New western names were being heard in the trading and counting houses of Montreal and New York: Auguste and Pierre Chouteau, Charles Gratiot, Gabriel Cerre, Jacques d'Eglise, James Baptiste Trudeau, John Evans and James McKay. The latter two were reputed to be of Spanish descent.

New states were being created west of the Alleghenies. Americans generally did not seem to believe that the west could remain in the possession of the Indians, nor would it be set aside as wilderness only to support the fur trade. Settlers were moving into the country where British military power was not strong enough to keep them out. Land companies were being formed. Congress had debated problems of civil government in the new areas, and there had been proposals to sell lands to provide pensions for war veterans and to help defray the national debt.

Taking office as Secretary of State, Thomas Jefferson promptly sought to put pressure on Great Britain for the surrender of the Northwest Territory, and on Spain to open the Mississippi. He advocated commercial retaliation, and he bluntly rejected a British suggestion that a buffer Indian state be established, with the reply that any cession of American territory was out of the question.

In 1791 the greatest tragedy of Astor's life occurred. Sarah gave birth to their first son, who was promptly and proudly named John Jacob Astor, Junior. By the time the boy was baptized, on August 11, with John Whetten acting as sponsor, it was known that he was mentally deficient.

The child's disorder was variously diagnosed as insanity, imbecility, lack of muscular control, and softening of the brain. There were indications that some kind of an accident, perhaps during the delivery, was responsible, but the medical knowledge of the time did not permit the truth to be established.[1]

Astor's love for his wife and children reflected a side of his character that was diametrically opposed to his cold attitude toward

---

[1] Through a long life of seventy-six years, John Jacob Astor, Junior, was never to recover, and as long as they lived, his father and mother were never to cease praying that he would. A friend of the Astors wrote that he "had periods of restored mentality, when he wrote verses of some merit." If that were true, it was the closest he ever came to recovery. He lived always in luxury, for years in a mansion built for him by his father on Fourteenth Street. He received the finest nursing care, companionship and medical treatment obtainable. At one period a doctor gave his attention exclusively to him, and was highly paid for his services.

those with whom he did business. Both qualities in him were un-adulterated. His affection and consideration for his family . . . even for those related to him only through the marriages of his brothers and sisters, nephews and nieces . . . were as unqualified as his hardness in commercial transactions and his unwavering de-votion to the almighty dollar. Between these two ways of his life there was nothing. He took no half-steps, gave no half-measures.

Whoever were his vague ancestors, how high may have been their positions, Astor himself was born in the atmosphere of the slaughterhouse. Yet, his thinking, his convictions, his practices, were those of a Federalist aristocrat. If there was one thing Astor could not understand, it was Jeffersonian Democracy. In his mind, liberty was one thing, equality was another, and the two had nothing in common. An unbridgeable gulf existed between the man of wealth and the man who had no property, and in his estimation, rightly so. Freedom was fine and noble, for it gave a man of humble birth a chance to advance himself, but freedom that permitted a poor man to vote with a rich man, that gave the common worker as much voice in political affairs as the wealthy merchant, was wrong and dangerous.

The Federalist, with his aristocratic tradition, was for freedom within certain limits and under certain conditions. He repudiated the rabble and its guillotine. And he favored Britain against the mob of the Place de la Revolution.

So did Astor. It was not the American counterparts of Robes-pierre, Marat and the upstart Corsican Napoleon who were then . . . in the 1790's . . . saving the United States from disaster. It had not been the propertyless common laborers who had en-abled the American Confederation to survive the crises which had faced it before and after the treaty with England had been signed. Nor had they steered it through the storms which came close to wrecking it . . . the fight over the Articles of Confedera-tion, the economic depression, Shay's Rebellion, the fight to build a sound government through a constitution of a kind never before known. It was the landowners and the employers, the traditional ruling class, the wealthy merchants and traders, who had accomplished all that.

Astor was not born to this tradition, but he was of it. Perhaps its precepts had been indelibly stamped on his brain by his German background and training. Or perhaps his belief in it was entirely the work of nature. Whatever the case, it was religion to him, and he used it to give emphasis to his authority and prestige as he acquired them.

Astor possessed no democratic instincts; it never seemed to occur to him that only a democracy of the American type could have given him his opportunity, the freedom to have and to hold without limit. He thought not at all about the guarantees of the American Constitution as benefits to mankind, but as guarantees that opened doors to unlimited exploitation.

Astor was a bigot. He possessed a great egotism. His self-assurance and vanity were displayed in a bland, childish fashion. He was opinionated and narrow-minded. All of these unadmirable traits became more pronounced as his financial status improved and his confidence in himself increased. He never thought of working for the community or for the country that was doing so much for him. He worked only for John Jacob Astor.

Yet, for all his unshakable and profound belief in the aristocratic tradition, he knew only one side of it. He never knew the obligations of gentility, and if they had been pointed out to him, he wouldn't have understood them. An appraisal of money as a vehicle to a certain end would have been inconceivable to him. Money was the end.

The assertion that he worked only for himself demands qualification. Astor really had two goals. The first was to make himself rich and independent. The second was to do for each of his children as much as he did for himself. He established an individual program for each of them as they came into the world.

In 1792 he bought a share in the Tontine Coffee House in Wall Street for his little daughter Magdalen. The Merchants' Exchange ... precursor of the New York Stock Exchange ... met in the coffee house. Astor went there frequently to pick up market news, to discuss political issues with other merchants over a bit of raw codfish and a glass of wine.

Another place habitually frequented by Astor was Mrs.

Keese's boarding house, which stood at the northeast corner of Broadway and Wall Street, across from Trinity Yard. Mrs. Keese's was both the residence and the meeting place of many of the prominent politicians and lawyers . . . some of them Astor's age . . . of the time.

It was on Mrs. Keese's veranda, or in her parlor . . . and possibly he took a meal there now and then . . . that Astor met several men who were to play active and important roles in his life. Among them were William P. Van Neess, a young lawyer who was to become a prominent Democrat and judge of the Southern District Court of the State of New York; Thomas J. Oakley, also an attorney, who was to represent Astor in land litigation; John Armstrong, whose daughter was to marry one of Astor's sons, and who was to be President Madison's Secretary of War; Brockholst Livingston, the attorney who was to be retained by Astor and who was to become an influential politician.

Other men of importance whom Astor came to know through friends at Mrs. Keese's were Gen. Stephen Van Rensselaer, the patroon, of Albany, and a fiery, dapper United States Senator named Aaron Burr. Burr and Astor were to become close friends and to be involved in several land deals of historical significance and doubtful propriety.

By 1792 Astor's fur business had grown to the extent that he felt it would be expedient for him to take in a partner who was qualified to relieve him of some of his burdensome responsibilities. He selected Cornelius Heeney, who had held an executive position in the mercantile firm of William Backhouse & Company.

Backhouse, whom Astor greatly respected and admired, recommended Heeney for the post. The partnership was in reality nothing more than a glorified clerkship. Astor hated above all else to share profits, and did so only when forced to in order to complete a transaction. Also, he was by nature secretive and disliked to have anyone know his private affairs. It must have been because of Backhouse's advice that he placed his trust in Heeney.

William Backhouse died suddenly on August 25, 1792, only a

short time after Heeney had left him to join Astor. Heeney and William Laight, a partner in the Backhouse company who also was to become associated with Astor in various business activities, were named executors of the Backhouse Estate.

A month later, on September 19, 1792, Astor's fourth child and second son was born. The boy was baptized November 17, and given the name William Backhouse Astor. Anna Backhouse, Backhouse's widow, acted as sponsor.

2

The soundness with which Astor built and conducted his various enterprises was first demonstrated in 1792, a year in which the Duer Panic caused widespread financial setbacks. In June he wrote a letter to his friend Peter Smith in which he commented on the number of bankruptcies in New York. They had, he declared, "affaceted my property but not So as to affacet my business." Property values declined, but not his fur trade. Indeed, in the face of adverse economic conditions it had continued to develop.

Astor's annual trips to Montreal were not undertaken only for the purpose of buying furs. He wanted to observe at firsthand conditions there, and to strengthen his association with individual traders and fur houses. He would leave each year some time between late June and early August, and return to New York in late October or early November. Enroute he conferred with his agents at various points.[2]

[2] Astor made large investments in wilderness lands in Lower Canada and upper New York State, but these activities had no connection with the fur trade.

As a corollary of the fur trade, he served as agent for numerous back-country merchants, purchasing supplies and importing merchandise they required on a commission basis. Two letters . . . one written by Heeney . . . to Peter Smith at Utica reveal this phase of Astor's business, and provide a comparison of fur prices for the years 1792 and 1793.

Heeney's letter quoted the following prices:

Bear	40/	Mink	4/6
Otter	42/	Fisher	7/6
Marten	4/8	Raccoon	6/
		Muskrat	2/7

On May 14, 1793, Astor wrote Smith:

Sir

You^r fav^r. of Ult^o I duly rec^d. I have now to inform you that I have bad acco^{ts}. from Europe concerning the Sales of Furs, and unless you can buy Furs at or under the annex'd prices. I wish you not to buy any on A/cco^t. of

Your Hble Servt

John Jacob Astor

Good	Bear	40/ to 42
"	Otter	32 to 36
"	Martin	5 to 5/6
"	Mink	3/6
"	Fisher	6/
"	Raccoon	6/
"	Musrat	6/

Astor's only full sister, Catherine, and her husband, George Ehninger, arrived in New York in 1792, and continued the distillery business Ehninger had established in Europe. Catherine gave birth to a son, also named George, soon afterward. When

Ehninger was killed accidentally "while burning spirits," Catherine determined to carry on his business, much to Astor's displeasure. She soon married a Michael Miller, "taught him the secrets of the business," and continued in it despite Astor's antagonism.[3]

In 1794, with his business continuing its rapid increase . . . and commensurately his income . . . Astor once more deemed it necessary to secure a larger establishment. A building at 149 Broadway proffered sufficient commercial space, and also offered more room for his growing family. He bought it. The ground floor contained enough space for a display area for furs, counters for musical instruments and musician's supplies, a stock room and a bookkeeping office.

On the second floor were residential quarters more spacious than any the family had previously enjoyed. Sarah would have liked to live apart from the store, but Astor opposed the idea. He was averse to revealing his prosperity. A separate home, he believed, would indicate affluence he did not care to display. It was just as well, he maintained, to let those with whom he traded believe he was obliged to live in modest circumstances. The truth probably was that he did not wish to incur the additional expenses of a separate establishment.

If by nothing else, the extent of Astor's wealth in 1794 was indicated by the fact that he could afford to sit for two portraits by the renowned painter Gilbert Stuart. Astor had not reached his thirty-first birthday when the first portrait was completed. He did not like it, and Stuart accepted a commission from him to paint another.

[3] Elizabeth, one of Astor's half sisters, followed Catherine to the United States in 1793. At the time she was about twenty, a typical buxom, yellow-blonde peasant with a pleasant personality. John Gotlieb Wendell, a porter in Astor's employ, was attracted to her. Being penniless and homeless, she was not in a position to refuse any proposal that was sincere and would provide a measure of security. Obviously desirous of relieving himself of supporting her, Astor sanctioned their marriage. However, he did not abandon her to life as the wife of a porter. He loaned Wendell enough money to start as a fur dealer in Gold Street in a modest way, and gave him free advice about the business. Wendell was smarter than Astor had realized. He emulated his benefactor, began to buy lots, and in a few years became a wealthy man.

Both portraits showed Astor as spare, with a rather scholarly face: deeply set, intent eyes, an arched nose, straight mouth with thin lips, and a strong chin. At the time, not many years had passed since he had been a wilderness trader, trudging the trails with a heavy pack on his back, and his body was still lean and hard. He continued to ride a horse, both for business and pleasure, and this exercise helped to keep him in good physical shape.

But it was in this same year that for the first time his health became a matter of concern to both Sarah and himself. It seemed that the hard physical labor of previous years, the ordeals through which he had passed in the wilds, had at last begun to take a toll of his body. Added to this burden was the mental anxiety caused by constant pressure from business, constant demands for money, constant struggles in the fur market. Astor began to experience periods of exhaustion, excessive tiredness from which he was slow to recover, and a loss of appetite.

The course of political and economic events was of great concern to him. Throughout 1793 and 1794, the Canadians, still hoping to hold the Northwest Territory for its valuable fur trade, continued to incite the Indians against the Americans. Guns, money, ammunition, liquor and wild promises were dispensed from the British posts. In addition, British trade restrictions and the illegal seizure of American ships on the high seas were inflicting severe damage on the international trade which the new nation so badly needed.

Congress blazed with anger. War fever rose to a high pitch. Preparations for military and commercial retaliations were advocated. The Federal leaders were alarmed, and with the hope of averting a conflict they urged President Washington to send a special envoy to London. Hamilton recommended John Jay, long a partisan of Great Britain, but an able diplomat, a jurist, and a believer in a strong central government. Washington was agreeable to the choice. Jay accepted the appointment and left for London with instructions to make forceful efforts to solve the burning issues, especially those relating to commerce and the Northwest Territory.

This move influenced Congress to withhold hostile legislation, but it did not cool the anger against the Indians whose depredations, inspired by the British, had made the entire Northwest Territory a savage and bloody ground.

In August, 1794, Gen. Anthony Wayne threw his troops against the Indians at Fallen Timbers and struck a blow that shattered their powers of organized resistance. The victory stunned the British Foreign Office, and it rebuked the Canadian officials who had been inciting the natives to attack Americans.

Jay was courteously received in London, and the Foreign Office displayed a conciliatory attitude. The document known as Jay's Treaty was signed. It provided, in addition to commercial and navigation concessions favorable to the United States, that Great Britain would withdraw its "Troops and Garrisons from all Posts and Places within the boundary of the United States by June 1, 1796." Settlers and traders in the Northwest Territory might either remain or leave with all their property as they desired. Both British subjects and Americans were given the right to cross the boundary between Canada and the United States at will and to trade with whom they pleased.

When Astor read the terms of the agreement in the American newspapers, he uttered a brief, cogent statement:

"Now I will make my fortune in the fur trade."

Forthwith he packed his bags and on November 17, 1794, he sailed for London.[4]

---

[4] Some years ago a biographer of Astor said he traveled to Europe in the steerage. There is no evidence to support such an assertion. Astor was parsimonious, and frequently deprived himself of comforts he could well afford. However, he was not a miser, and at this time he had achieved a position of prominence in the business world. Taking steerage passage to Europe would have injured him in the eyes of associates, and meant a loss of prestige. He was not stupid enough to let that occur.

3

A few days previous to his departure Astor had sent a letter to Peter Smith which provided a revealing view of a major facet of his character. If he was capable of real friendship with any man, that man was Smith. Probably he trusted Smith more than any other person, with the exception of his beloved Sarah, and undoubtedly he felt more kindly disposed toward him than any other associate. But Astor's kindness, affection and trust were imprisoned by barriers placed about them by nature, and beyond which they could not go, regardless of the amount of emotional pressure driving them.

Astor had advanced Smith considerable money in an enormous land deal in which they were associated with William Laight, the Backhouse partner, and he was concerned about it as he wrote: "Being about to depart for Europe & not knowing when I Shall return I find Occasion to write you this long letter with respect as to our lands you will no Doubt doo what you think for Our mutual Interest . . . Dear Peter how will it be with the payment on your part . . . you Know that I would as Soon Injure myself as to do it to You . . . you Know that I have put every Confidence in you that One man can in another & which I have found you have always Kept Sacred altho' its probable that I may want money very much next Summer yet I would not ask you for any more than what you can pay without Injuring yourself . . . I don't know what may be your Situation tho I hope its good nor am I affraid of being paid every Shilling by you in time which I will give you provided Laight does the Same but what if he should sue you have you property to pay him & Secure me at Same time I hope you have but if not I hope youlnot pay him without Seeing me at Same time Secured . . . & at any rate I think I ought to be the last who ought to lose by You . . . at any rate

I shall expect it from you that youll at least pay me as soon as M^r. Laight . . . I hope you'le excuse me for writing you this plain manner . . . I have and wish to Show you as much real Friendship as can be expected from any person who at same time wishes to do his duty to his family I wish you well god Bless you & keep you in health . . . My Best Respets to Mrs Smith and Remaen Deare frind . . . Yours . . . a Line Dericted for me to Care of Thos Backhause at Landan thill 1 of March will cum to hand . . ."

Astor took a large quantity of prime pelts to London with him, and gave his personal attention to their disposal. Although his connection with Backhouse was satisfactory, he was forever searching for new and more profitable associations. During the several months he was in London, he was in daily touch with dealers, and he secured orders from several of them.

Not the least of his accomplishments in this respect was the relationship he established with agents of the North West Company. He developed personal friendships among them and when he left London he had in his pocket a contract under which he could purchase furs from the company in Canada. The new treaty . . . when it became effective in 1796 . . . would permit furs to be shipped directly from Canada to the United States, eliminating the cost and the delay of sending them by way of London. With this understanding, Astor cemented his relations with the North West Company . . . he already had good friends in it in Montreal . . . on both sides of the Atlantic.

In London, Astor also bought a large amount of merchandise suitable for the Indian trade. The quantity indicated the size and scope of his plans. He intended to take advantage of the forthcoming peace in the Northwest Territory to a greater extent than merely buying furs through agents. It seemed certain that he had in mind establishing his own posts, and sending his own expeditions, fully supplied with trade goods, into the territory.

Also, Astor was fully aware that goods made in Britain, which were far superior to those manufactured in the United States, would be in increasing demand as American traders advanced into the west. Through his extensive purchases in London he would be in a position to supply them at a large profit to himself.

Sarah had been pregnant for seven months at the time Astor left for Europe. In the spring of 1795, he received a letter from her informing him that she had given birth to a daughter on January 11.

Sarah had emerged from the ordeal in good health and spirits. She had carried out his wish that the child be named after either his brother Henry, or Henry's wife. In February the girl had been christened Dorothea, with Henry and Dorothea in attendance as sponsors.[5]

Astor visited his birthplace in 1795, and also while on the Continent, established connections with new agents in Rotterdam, Paris and Leipzig. His French representative was John N. l'Herbette, whose son Astor was to assist when the young man fled France to escape military service.

Astor returned to New York in August, happy to find his second daughter and other members of his family . . . with the exception of the little boy who lived in a room and a world of his own . . . in good health.

Business conditions, however, were a disappointment. His investments and commitments in Europe had placed a heavy strain on his funds, and it would be some time before he realized a return on them. In New York he was discouraged to find out that Heeney had not possessed the acumen and ability attributed to him.

Astor wrote Peter Smith: ". . . while I was gon to Europe my Business has got mush Deranged at hame . . ."

Shortly afterward Astor announced that his partnership with Heeney had been terminated.

He made no plans to take in another partner, but he did conceive the idea of developing an assistant by training a young man from the ground up in the fur trade. His choice was William Whetten Todd, Sarah's nephew. When he went to Montreal in

---

[5] Ann Eve, another of Astor's half sisters, migrated from Walldorf to the United States in 1795. Most likely she came at the instigation of her sisters, Catherine and Elizabeth, rather than by invitation from Astor. She was twenty-four when she arrived in New York. Soon afterward she married Dr. Richard Corner. He died in 1799. The next year she married Peter Cook, a cartman.

September, he left Todd, then fourteen, working as a clerk and a bookkeeper in his store under the aegis of Aunt Sarah.

En route to Montreal, Astor wrote to Smith from "Fort Miller," expressing his regret at "not having Rec^d a line from you."

Astor informed Smith that he expected to return from Canada in a month, and requested Smith to write him at Albany. He said: "I Can not Describe to you an Black & white how much I am in want of Cash theare for If you Can Sent me any it will oblige me mush be the Sum ever so Smale . . . I am mush Pressd for Maney . . . I am told your making a grate fourtune & very fast which gives me mush Pleasure . . . believe me to be your well wisher."

In Montreal, Astor encountered the situation he had antici-pated. The market was unsteady, and the traders deeply con-cerned about their future. The provisions of Jay's Treaty would become fully effective the next year. How much enterprise and force the Americans would show in developing their own inter-ests in the region of the Great Lakes was a matter yet to be de-termined, but if Astor's attitude and activities were an indication of things to come, the days ahead could well be dark for them. He represented a formidable threat.

Alexander Henry perhaps understood better than any other Ca-nadian the extent of Astor's ambition. He knew him better than the other traders . . . Astor continued to be a guest in Henry's home . . . and he realized Astor's capabilities. He saw wisdom in maintaining a close relationship with the energetic, sharp New Yorker, while at the same time he warned his colleagues that Astor's operations could become extremely dangerous to the Ca-nadian fur trade. Henry correctly judged that Astor's private plans eclipsed those of the swiftly growing North West Com-pany.

When Astor returned to New York from Montreal in 1795, he was pleased to find out that young William Whetten Todd had applied himself diligently to learning the rudiments of the fur trade and had shown not a little business talent. Astor, there-upon, sent the youth off to Montreal to study French in a boarding school. Within a few months, William had had all he wanted of the Canadian climate and the fur trade. He came home and resigned. Astor was angry and disappointed, but his efforts to induce William to reconsider the decision were futile.

Astor was happy to see that the troubles of the North West Company continued to increase. Dissension over policies and personal jealousies injured the morale and shattered discipline in the organization. Another group of traders calling themselves the New North West Company, but better known simply as the XY, had formed an alliance. Most of the best traders remained with the old company, but one of the ablest of all, Alexander Mc-Kenzie, broke away.

McKenzie, famous as an explorer, had made a trip to the Pacific in 1793. Although he became head of the XY, he saw wisdom in a union of the two companies. Under one strong organization, he maintained, the peaceful expansion of the Canadian fur trade to the Pacific coast could be accomplished with good profits for all. This achievement would open the door for direct exchanges of Canadian furs for the commodities of China, a highly lucrative commerce.

Finally, McKenzie advocated the amalgamation of all Canadian companies into a gigantic combine. The governors of the Hudson's Bay Company in England were men of great influence in British trade policy. The heads of the old North West Company held positions of high standing in British politics. Together these two powerful groups, and the growing XY Company, might be strong enough to break the monopoly of the East India Company in Asia.

Montreal traders, fearing a loss of both profits and prestige, refused to go along with him. McKenzie became embittered. He sent XY men to the Saskatchewan, the Athabasca, the Assiniboine, the Red River, the Souris, the Qu'Appelle, all in the far west. He invaded the North West Company's territory adjacent to Lake Superior.

A period of unprecedented violence and lawlessness followed.

Large quantities of liquor were used in the trade. Hunters were murdered. The fighting extended all the way from the waters draining into Hudson Bay to the upper Missouri River. The size of the operation involved was illustrated by the fact that the old North West Company had 117 trading posts, and the XY about a third as many.

It was, of course, the continued loss of profits that finally brought a halt to the vicious conflict. As some of the older leaders died, younger and cooler heads were able to effect a reconciliation. Another new organization . . . still called the North West Company, however . . . was formed and divided into a hundred shares. Twenty-five went to partners of the XY, and seventy-five to members of the old North West Company. It was an organization with impressive resources.

As the eighteenth century drew to a close, Astor's name as a fur trader was established on an impregnable foundation and was well known to every man in the business, from Montreal to Norfolk, from New York to the western frontier beyond the territory of the United States. Now, however, the traders, dealers and even the trappers in the wilderness began to hear of him in a new way. Agents, armed with letters of credit from him, appeared in the trading centers of Michilimackinac and Detroit, and in the lonely posts along the Ohio River and the Great Lakes.

4

Of all the fine furs to be taken in North America, in its forests or in the waters washing its shores, nothing could compare in beauty and texture with the sea otter of the North Pacific.[6] Jet-

[6] They were almost completely exterminated by hunters, and the few remaining today are rigorously protected.

black, smooth, shorthaired loveliness gleaming underneath with silver, the sea otter was the prize of the international fur trade. Little known in the western world at the beginning of the nineteenth century, sea otters had been from remote times highly valued by the Chinese, who secured them in small numbers from northern Asiatic seas.

Only a handful of Russian, Spanish and British mariners had seen the Northwest Coast of America before Captain James Cook saw it in February, 1778. Along it, from Spanish California to Alaska, lived enormous herds of sea otters.

Cook anchored his ships off the southwest shore of Vancouver Island, where he found Indians anxious to trade. They offered the skins of "bears, wolves, foxes, deer, raccoons, polecats, martens; and in particular, of the sea otter." In return they wanted "knives, chisels, nails, mirrors, buttons, iron and other metal." Cook believed that these Indians had traded previously with white men.

Cook's ships had been at sea two years, and the clothing of his crews was worn out. Chiefly in an effort to cover themselves adequately against the cold North Pacific winds, the sailors struck up a trade with the natives. For a dozen large green glass beads six of the finest sea otter pelts could be obtained.

When the ships reached Canton, the crewmen found out the true value of the otter skins. They sold them for the fabulous sum of $120 each, and they came close to mutiny in their demands that they be permitted to return to America and make their fortunes. The officers forced the disappointed sailors to return to England, and before releasing them, issued an order commanding them to keep secret the discovery of the wealth in sea otters on the American West Coast. Needless to say, the order was violated.

England was not then in a position to take advantage of Cook's discoveries. The American Revolution, and the ensuing conflicts on the Continent, absorbed her time and money. Another complication was the clash between British monopolies. The monopoly of the South Sea Company included the Northwest Coast of America. The monopoly of the East India Company kept all other British traders out of China. Trade between the two places was, therefore, illegal, but that did not mean it was impossible. Whenever good profits were to be obtained in a trading venture, British mariners usually found a way to circumnavigate political and legal red tape.

American ships were barred from trading with the British Dominions by England's navigation laws, kept out of the trade with France by prohibitive French tariffs, and kept out of Spain by restrictive Spanish trade policies. There was little demand in the other countries of Europe for American goods.

But there was nothing to keep American merchants out of the trade with China . . . unless it was the extortionate practices and the piracy of the Chinese . . . and America had one product for which the Chinese were willing to pay high prices. That was ginseng. In turn, the teas, silks, and the coarse cotton cloth known as nankeen of China brought good returns in the United States.

The merchants of Salem and Boston were the first to carry the American flag into the ports of China. The first American ship to return from Canton carried a cargo that brought her owners a $30,000 profit.

However, the Americans needed more than ginseng to support such a trade. John Ledyard, a native of Hartford, Connecticut, solved the problem. He had been with Captain Cook, and he published a book about his adventures. In it he told of the great amount of money to be made in the sea otter trade.

Thereupon, on their way to China, American ships went first to the Northwest Coast, and traded with the Indians for furs. As Washington Irving wrote: "It was as if a new gold coast had been discovered."

Sarah Astor, always informed on current affairs, reproved her husband for not taking advantage of the opportunity to sell furs in China. Astor protested that he had no ship and could not afford to buy one. He also felt that the trade was too dangerous

for a person who did not possess a large reserve of capital to fall
back on in the event of disaster.

"Charter a ship," Sarah is alleged to have told him. "Let someone else carry the insurance and bear the losses."

Whether this wifely advice inspired Astor to take the steps he
did take, or whether he made up his mind before he received it,
was not known, but the circumstances gave birth to one of the
most famous of the many fabulous stories about Astor's career
. . . the Case of "Permit No. 68." Those who first disseminated
the tale offered no documentary evidence to support it, and official records suggested it did not happen in the way it was recounted.

However, the old adage about smoke and fire was applicable
. . . a series of incidents of some kind unquestionably occurred.
It was not Astor's way to boast of his victories or to explain his
defeats. Sarah was his only true confidante. Yet, he was known
on occasion to invent romantic tales for the edification of people
who annoyed him with questions about his success as a trader
and businessman. Men who knew him best were, therefore,
neither ready to discredit completely all legends about his exploits nor to repeat them as gospel. The truth, they wisely suspected, lay somewhere between the two extremes.

There was no question that if "Permit No. 68" did exist it
was fraudulent. Purportedly it came into Astor's hands before
he left London late in the winter of 1795–96 in the following
way: He happened to learn that one of the highest officers of
the powerful East India Company had the same name as a young
man, somewhat older than himself, who had once lived in Walldorf. Curiosity prompted him to investigate, and he found to his
pleasure that the prominent executive and his boyhood acquaintance . . . whose name was known only as Wilhelm of Walldorf
. . . were, indeed, one and the same.

Wilhelm, reportedly, was delighted to see Astor, took him to
dinner, and inquired as to how he might be of service. Astor had
no request to make of him, and Wilhelm thereupon insisted that
Astor accept a permit to send a trading ship to China, where the

East India Company held an ironclad trade monopoly. The "permit" gave to the "bearer" . . . an important word in the tale . . . the privilege of trading "at any of the ports monopolized by the East India Company."

Astor, it may be supposed, smiled to himself. He was fully aware that since the American Revolution, American vessels needed no permit from anyone to engage in trade with China. As a matter of record, they had been doing it since February, 1784 . . . twelve years before he found Wilhelm . . . when the Yankee vessel, *Empress of China,* sailed from New York for Canton. Not wishing to be impolite, however, he stuffed the paper Wilhelm proffered into his wallet, and went on to France, Belgium and Germany. It was not until three years later, after the admonishment from Sarah about his reticence in entering the China trade, that he pulled "Permit No. 68" from a desk drawer in his New York office.

Next, according to the legend, Astor called on a shipper named James Livermore who was in hard straits because the trade with the West Indies, in which he had been engaged, had been stopped by British restrictions and French privateers. Astor offered to furnish "Permit No. 68," which gave the "bearer" permission to trade at Chinese ports monopolized by the East India Company, if Livermore would supply a ship and a cargo. The profits were to be equally divided.

Livermore protested that Astor would not be investing a cent in the enterprise. Astor replied that without the permit there could be no enterprise.

Whatever his objections and misgivings, Livermore signed an agreement with Astor, who thereupon handed over "Permit No. 68." Livermore loaded his largest vessel with ginseng, lead and scrap iron, stowed $30,000 in Spanish silver in her strongbox, and dispatched her on the long trip. Perhaps she stopped on the Northwest Coast for some sea otter skins. Perhaps she paused in the Hawaiian Islands to take on sandalwood, which brought a high price in China. No one knew any details of her voyage.

One morning some eighteen months later, a dray stopped at

Astor's door. Several heavy kegs were rolled into his counting-house. They contained 55,000 Spanish silver dollars, his half of the profits from Livermore's China trip.

Several questions quite naturally arose: Was Livermore stupid, or was it that he simply did not keep abreast of the news? Was "Permit No. 68" an invention of Astor? Did he get the idea for it in London? Did he counterfeit it?

The answers were never found. The name of James Livermore was obviously a pseudonym, for it was not to be found on the roster of American shipowners of the time. The ships' registers of the Port of New York did not reveal that Astor had an interest in any vessel during the final years of the eighteenth century.

But these mysteries were not difficult to explain by men who knew Astor. He had simply concealed Livermore's real name. That was in keeping with his usual deviousness and his reticence in disclosing the true circumstances of any of his slippery enterprises.

5

William Backhouse, Astor's second son, was healthy and alert, and he helped to compensate his parents for the burden of sadness placed on them by the subnormal condition of John Jacob Astor, Junior. The boy to whom Sarah gave birth on December 26, 1797, however, brought a new weight of profound concern to them. He was handsome, appeared to possess normal senses and faculties, but his body was frail and did not respond to their efforts to give him strength. He was christened Henry, after Astor's brother, but at the age of twenty-three months he died.

The same year in which Henry was born brought Astor into the spotlight of notoriety in a new and curious guise. He was suspected of organizing a filibustering expedition . . . or at least of giving financial aid to one . . . against Canada. However, Astor's full intentions and the complete structure of the plot . . . if there was one . . . were never revealed, due mainly to two circumstances: his inherent habit of keeping his mouth shut about himself, and the later destruction of most of his personal papers.[7]

On August 31, 1797, Robert Prescott, Governor-in-Chief of Canada, wrote to Robert Liston, British envoy to the United States, regarding the strange activities of a fur dealer and importer named "Oster."

Prescott's letter contained extracts from a communication he had received, signed only "R.P.", which said that "a German person Jacob Oster . . . has imported in the last ship from London 6,000 stand of arms and 100 casks of gunpowder . . . he frequently visits Canada . . . deals largely in furs, and is at present ('tis said) in that country."

The British envoy sent Prescott's letter to Timothy Pickering, the United States Secretary of State, in Philadelphia. On October 6, Pickering sent it on to Joshua Sands, Collector of the Port of New York, with a request for an investigation.

Governor Prescott was deeply concerned about a threatening French-Canadian revolution in Canada. (A leader of the plot against the Canadian Government was David McLane, who had the support of Pierre Auguste Adet, French Minister to the United States.[8]) Prescott feared that Astor planned to use the arms to supply a filibuster against Canada from the United States.

Collector Sands responded quickly to Secretary Pickering's request, and a few days later in October, Pickering wrote the

[7] Between 1873 and 1875, fifteen large packing cases containing business papers and records of John Jacob Astor were destroyed on orders from his son, William Backhouse Astor. A few years later, "to save a few dollars' truck hire," when the office of the Astor Estate was moved, the remaining business books and personal papers of John Jacob Astor were similarly destroyed.
[8] McLane later was executed for an attempt at insurrection in the Province of Lower Canada.

British envoy: ". . . it appears that M^r. Oster has imported no arms, and only a small quantity of gunpowder, in the usual course of his trade, and that the powder chiefly remains on hand."

Pickering, of course, was relying on what he had been told by Collector Sands. Sands, it appeared, was being deliberately deceptive and evasive in an effort to protect himself and a prominent New York merchant, from whom he regularly received payments under the table.

The inadequacy of Pickering's reply to the British was enhanced by the fact that in the summer of 1797 Astor was advertising for sale in the *New York Gazette & General Advertiser* some 14,000 pounds of English gunpowder.

If Astor was apprised of the insinuations made against him, he was not dissuaded by them from continuing to deal in weapons of war. He had discovered a new and lucrative phase of general merchandising to supplement his fur trade and musical instrument business. Thus, in his store he was surrounded by a curious combination of goods: flutes, furs and firearms.

At various times he offered for sale: "Ten Ton of the best english FF gun powder . . . at the Rate of Fifty Cents p lb wight" delivered, "800 wt. refined salt setre," "a few casks of water colours, for paper," "some elegant looking glass plates, 7 feet high," "1100 red sheep skins . . . beaver, raccoons, musrats, dressed and row cooney skins, Camels and Germ hare wool."

In an advertisement in the *Gazette* on November 15, 1798, under the heading "ARMS and AMMUNITION," Astor offered a formidable array of military supplies. Among them were "24 CANNONS, 4 pounders, 1240 4 pound round shot, 20 barrels of Cannon Powder, 600 quarter casks of fine Musket do. of superior quality, 300 half casks do, 90 whole casks do., 12 Muskets with Bayonets, 14 Swords."

It was in this advertisement that Astor first informed the public that he was interested in trade with Canton. Besides the weapons, he offered "10 chests Hyson Tea, first quality, 10 do. Souchong do., With a small assortment of Indian Sattins, Lutestrings and

Taffities."[9] Whether these goods were brought back by the mysterious Livermore vessel, or were purchased from other New York merchants engaged in the China trade, was not stated. Astor had not yet become a shipowner.

His trade in military supplies continued to increase rapidly, and his store and warehouse became a veritable depot for large and small arms. He advertised: "18 very neat 4 pound cannon, 100 musquets with bayonets, well suited for ships use, 100 do very neat and light, fit for Military, 26 pair pistols, 1 carbine, complete, with bayonet, I Riflegun, and some very elegant London made fowling pieces, 10 tons musquet and cannon powder . . . 2 ton London Patent Shot . . . 500 Musquets with Bayonets, 200 Pistols, for ships use, 5 pair double fortified 6-pounders with Carriages, shot, Spunges, &c—complete . . . Beaver, Raccoon and Muskrat Skins . . . 6000 lb. Spanish Lambs Wool . . . 3 boxes Indian Silks, 1 do. Silver Watches . . . a quantity of very excellent Hyson and Souchong Tea, imported in ships Grace and Jenny . . ."

In considering the suspicions cast against Astor by Governor Prescott, persons close to him deemed it illogical to presume that he would risk his high position in the Montreal fur market, and chance being barred from the Canadian trade in which he was making so much money, for a comparatively negligible profit from the sale of arms to a band of Vermont raiders and French-Canadian rebels. Moreover, a man intent upon supporting a filibuster normally did not advertise weapons for sale.

Astor possessed a German's inherent dislike for the French. More than once in his life he publicly disclosed his conviction that they were not to be trusted. He made it clear in act and statement that he favored the British, both in business and politics. It seemed reasonable to his friends to conclude that the "R. P." who warned Governor Prescott of Astor's activities was either a bored British spy or a rival merchant hoping to get Astor into trouble with the authorities.

[9] Lutestrings, mentioned in the advertisements, had nothing to do with lutes. They were pieces of a certain kind of silk, sometimes spelled "lustrings" or "lustrines."

Firearms . . . even small cannon . . . and gunpowder were staples in the Indian trade, and Astor furnished them to traders on the frontier. Also, weapons of all sizes and types were necessary equipment on all ships. Pirates operated in the Atlantic, the Caribbean and in Asiatic waters at the time. French privateers were a scourge in international sea commerce. Astor imported his weapons from England, and he sold them to shipowners to arm their vessels and their crews . . . a traffic that brought no protest at the time from the British.

However, not all traders and merchants were naïve enough to think that Astor was above furnishing raiders, or supplying arms and ammunition to rebels of any nationality, and some knew the inaccuracy of such a suggestion. He may have been unjustly accused in the Canadian case, but he did sell "all the swords required" for at least one Latin-American insurrection, that of Gen. Francisco de Miranda in Caracas. His go-between, or shield, in this deal was Samuel Gouverneur Ogden, also a prominent New York merchant.

On New Year's Day, 1800, Astor had been in the United States slightly less than sixteen years. He was not yet thirty-seven years old, but he was the possessor of a truly enormous fortune for the time, between $250,000 and $300,000.

Part Four

The Wide Horizon

1

Astor was an advocate of a strong central government, but he was violently opposed to governmental infringement upon private enterprise. In his view, it was the government's duty to keep the peace, collect taxes, defend the country against foreign invaders, make laws and enforce them, deliver the mail, and protect the rights and property of American citizens, especially those of landowners and businessmen. Beyond the limits of these areas, he maintained, the government should have no prerogatives, least of all in the indefinite field of social reform. He often reiterated his maxim that no one ever made any money giving it away to the poor.

As far as the fur trade was concerned, this conviction placed him in opposition to the humanitarian efforts of Washington and Jefferson, and into open conflict with the policies of later administrations.

President Washington had sent troops to halt the Indian depredations west of the Alleghenies, but he told Congress that a final peace with them could be secured only by giving them justice. "Next to a rigorous justice on the violators of peace," said Mr. Washington, "the establishment of commerce with the Indian nations on behalf of the United States is most likely to conciliate their attachment. But it ought to be conducted without fraud, without extortion, with constant and plentiful supplies, with a ready market for the commodities of the Indians, and a stated price for what they give in payment, and receive in exchange. Individuals will not pursue such a traffic, unless they be allured by the hope of profit, but it will be enough for the United States to be reimbursed only."

Anyone who proposed a ceiling on profits was, in the estimation of Astor, beyond comprehension. His attitude was bolstered by the fact that Congress itself displayed no immediate interest in Mr. Washington's recommendations. The President repeated them, and in 1794 added the proposal that Congress should establish Government trading houses to operate on the principles he had previously outlined.

Astor had not yet begun to organize the fur trade lobby he was to head in the future, but he understood the necessity of immediately opposing such a program. Before he could take any effective steps, however, Jay's Treaty had been signed, the way had been opened for American traders in the Northwest Territory, and President Washington had succeeded in wringing from Congress an appropriation of $50,000 for the purchase of goods to be sold to the Indians at cost.

An appropriation of such magnitude required an agency to handle it. Congress took the next obvious step: it approved Mr. Washington's recommendation for the establishment of Government trading houses.

The move struck Astor with dismay, and it was with great relief that he learned, upon investigation, that Congress had no intention of awarding a monopoly to the Government posts. Private traders were to be given licenses to operate. The door was, therefore, only partially closed.

Astor at once spotted several weaknesses in the Government's plan. The Federal posts would be prohibited from giving credit to the Indians, and the wages of the government agents were to come out of other funds, and would not be charged against the Indian trade. Prices charged the Indians were to be set at such a level "that the capital stock furnished by the United States may not be diminished." A markup of only 33 1/3 per cent was to be permitted on trade goods, which must be paid for either in cash or skins. No liquor was to be dispensed.

Only the Government could afford to conduct a business on such premises. Astor regarded the situation with abhorrence. The Government houses could continue to operate even if they lost money.

Angry and incredulous, Astor moved fast. He was aware that no private trader like himself could succeed unless he employed methods which Government agents were prohibited from using. He saw ahead of him three courses of action he must follow: (a) large-scale buying, (b) the giving of strategic credit, (c) the use of liquor. Of the three, he considered the last as the most important and advantageous.

While Astor moved swiftly to entrench himself, the Government moved slowly. Before 1800, only two houses were opened, and both of them were in the South. There they met with opposition from private traders that was encouraging to Astor, and strengthened his confidence in his own plans. Independent southern traders . . . whose business was small in comparison with that of the North . . . were doing exactly what Astor planned to do in the Northwest Territory. For one thing, they were carrying their trade goods directly to the Indian camps and arranging tempting displays, while the Government agents were obliged to remain within the confines of the posts. Also, the private traders of the South were holding the loyalty of the Indians by gifts of strong drink and various trifles. The news that the Government houses were getting only 10 per cent of the business was, indeed, happily received by Astor.

Congress, however, was prevailed upon to enlarge the program. Federal factories were established at Chickasaw Bluffs, on the Mississippi; on the Tombigbee River, at Detroit and Fort Wayne. The only one ever located west of the Mississippi stood on the Missouri, about forty miles south of the mouth of the Kansas River.

The administration of John Adams gave little attention to frontier problems, but Thomas Jefferson, upon assuming the

Presidency, at once showed that he was vitally interested in them. He believed that he could control the Indians by just and favorable trade policies, and he inaugurated them in the Government's posts at Fort Wayne and Detroit, although he took no steps to restrict the operations of the private traders. On the contrary, Mr. Jefferson, no Anglophile, saw decided advantages in a program under which both private and Government interests were served. The stronger the American operations were, the more the Canadian traders would be checked. In furtherance of this determination, he vigorously enforced the regulation requiring all traders in the Northwest Territory to hold American licenses.

President Jefferson long had dreamed of American expansion to the west. After he took office in 1801, the time was not far distant when he would know even greater fulfillment of that dream than he had dared to hope for.

Astor, who considered Mr. Jefferson naïve, thoroughly approved, however, of his desire to strengthen the position of American traders. He held a similar desire, the difference being that Astor thought in terms of the singular rather than the plural.

His agents, duly licensed and voicing the Jeffersonian doctrine of supremacy for Americans, set up shop in Michilimackinac, Detroit, Fort Wayne, Chicago, Green Bay, Chillicothe, St. Joseph, and at various other places between the mouth of the Cuyahoga River on Lake Erie, the Wisconsin and the Ohio.

From all of these places . . . from Montreal, from Albany and Fort Schuyler, from the valleys of the Hudson and the Mohawk, where he once had traded with a pack on his back . . . the bales of furs poured into his big warehouse in New York City. There they were processed and packed for shipment to American hatters and furriers and to the houses of Europe in which the name of Astor was rapidly becoming synonymous with the American fur trade.

Attesting to Astor's power and his influence was a letter Alexander Henry wrote to a friend, John Askin. In it he commented on the tendency of the Canadian market to decline. Because he and Astor had joined forces to bid for muskrats against the North

West Company, the price of this fur had been maintained. "As-
tore and me bought the whole . . ." Henry told Askin. They had
bought all the muskrat skins offered at Montreal that season,
cornering the year's supply.

When young Edward Ellice, whose father had founded the
noted British fur house of Inglis, Ellice & Company, was sent to
Montreal to learn the trade, he traveled first to New York so he
could meet John Jacob Astor. At the time, Astor was about to
leave for Montreal, and he and young Ellice traveled together.
At Albany they were entertained by Gen. Stephen Van Rensselaer and by the wealthy merchant John Bayard.

As usual, Alexander Henry's fine house was open to Astor.
Dinners were given for him in the homes of the rich and influential traders, Joseph Frobisher and William McGillivray. On
several occasions he was a guest at the Beaver Club, the exclusive
social organization sponsored by the North West Company and
to which most of the prominent men of the city belonged.

At the very time Astor was being shown the hospitality of the
partners of the North West Company and other leading Montreal traders, he was scheming to destroy them. At this time, as
well, he was applying himself to finding ways and means of dis-
crediting and wrecking the Government factory program once
and for all.

2

One day shortly after the century began, Astor entered a New
York bank to negotiate for some mercantile paper. A pompous
clerk questioned whether his signature was sufficient without

collateral in the transaction. Astor calmly inquired how much the clerk thought he was worth. The bank employee suggested a sum ludicrously small. Still unruffled outwardly, Astor mentioned the names of several well-known merchants and asked the clerk's opinion as to their worth.

The clerk admittedly based his judgment on the manner in which the merchants were known to live, and mentioned sums excessively high. Astor smiled, and quietly remarked that he was worth far more than any of the men named.

The bank clerk registered his disgust, and muttered that if Astor was as wealthy as he stated, he was a fool to work as hard as he did and live in such modest circumstances.

Astor told the story himself, and sought to give the impression that he considered it a good joke. This attitude was fallacious. In reality, he was embarrassed and angered by the incident. On several other occasions he had been similarly criticized in the same way by friends and business associates. The experience in the bank may have been the stroke that brought to an end his refusal to assume a style of living more in keeping with his financial position.

In 1801, shortly after his fourth daughter, Eliza, was born, Astor moved his business headquarters and store to 71 Liberty Street. It was the first time it had been separated from his home.

He continued, however, to keep his family at 149 Broadway, and it was not until the following year that their home was moved to 214 Broadway. This was a temporary domicile he took while looking about for a more desirable permanent residence. In it his last child, a son, was born in November, 1802. The boy died in infancy, before he was christened.

Of the eight children born to Sarah and Jacob Astor, three daughters . . . Magdalen, Dorothea and Eliza . . . and two sons . . . John Jacob, Junior, mentally unbalanced, and William Backhouse . . . were living.

Either late in 1802 or early in 1803, Astor found the house which he thought provided an environment suitable to a man of his wealth and business prominence. It was at 223 Broadway, above Vesey Street. The owner was United States Senator Rufus King, who had built it as his own residence. Astor bought it from King for $27,500.

The price suggests that it was closer to being a mansion than an ordinary large dwelling. It was described by Astor's contemporaries as being very handsome and commodious, with open porches fronted by massive pillars. The neighborhood was one of the best in the city. The neighbors were no less desirable, and among them were several families whose social position was far above the highest level obtainable by a man of Astor's butcher shop heritage. Not even Sarah's somewhat tenuous affiliations with such substantial and prominent families as the Brevoorts and the Whettens could open all doors, and money had not the influence upon everyone that breeding, good taste and manners commanded.

Sarah was delighted that her family might dwell in close proximity to members of the gentility, the cultured, but most of all she was grateful that at last they possessed a home in which they might take pride, and which presented the atmosphere of respectability and refinement in which she wanted her children to grow and develop. No longer must they all endure the animal odor of raw furs, and have customers, draymen and unbathed trappers from the wilderness crowding into their front hallway or even invading their parlor.

There was more than one parlor in the spacious structure at 223 Broadway. There was room for a fine piano or, perhaps in good time, an organ. There was room for books and pictures. There was a gracious paneled dining room, an adequate kitchen, servants' quarters, a stable above which a coachman might live, a big woodbin, and fireplaces in which large logs could be burned. There was a room for each of the children, and, most important of all, a room for the little boy whose eyes were vacant and whom visitors were not permitted to see. Now he could have the facilities and the privacy his condition demanded.

Astor liked to boast that he was a millionaire before anyone knew it. He seemed to derive satisfaction from the knowledge that he had deceived people into believing he was a man of modest means, when actually he was the second richest man in America. Only the resources of the Philadelphia banker and shipper Stephen Girard, were greater, and Girard was a true miser, a wretched, ragged individual without kith or kin, who dwelt in a shabby house. Astor could boast that he had provided his wife and children with a fine home. Girard would not have loaned God a two-penny whistle without usurious interest.

It may have been that Astor was driven by criticism to improve his standard of living . . . and there was no doubt that he found the change pleasant and invigorating . . . but no force could make him adhere to the admonition that he should adopt a more leisurely way of life. On the contrary, he drove himself harder than ever. He was in his counting house or in conferences from early morning until exhaustion forced him to bed late at night. His dreams and his schemes became greater than ever before.

He fully understood the danger of having the United States flanked by European powers, and especially by France. Any plans for expansion, such as those President Jefferson harbored . . . as well as the personal plans taking shape in Astor's mind . . . could be set back for years by the disruption of diplomatic relations with the swaggering Napoleon.

Astor kept in close touch with informed friends and neighbors, such as DeWitt Clinton and Gouverneur Morris. He gave his support to President Jefferson's attempt to purchase West Florida and New Orleans from France, although he considered the plan inadequate. It was a step in the right direction, but it would not bring the results which the United States must win if both its territory and its commerce were to be secured.

When it became apparent that Napoleon considered Louisiana of diminishing importance, Astor advanced an almost inconceivably bold plan. He proposed to Clinton and Morris that they form a syndicate to buy the entire territory of Louisiana and sell it to the United States at a commission of 2½ per cent.

If Clinton and Morris considered Astor's scheme feasible, they were too slow in reaching a decision. Once Napoleon had permitted his ministers to open negotiations for the sale of all of Louisiana, Robert R. Livingston and James Monroe, given the authority by President Jefferson, wasted little time in completing the purchase.

Almost overnight the size of the United States was doubled, and its territory reached from the Atlantic to the Pacific.

Some time later an overly inquisitive acquaintance asked Astor to name the largest amount of money he had made at any one time. Astor replied that he would rather talk about the largest amount he had ever lost, and he told of the failure of his plan to buy Louisiana. If it had succeeded, he estimated that he and his associates would have made a profit of $30,000,000.

3

The inducements to enter the China trade were numerous, but Astor moved toward the decision to import goods in his own ships with customary cautiousness.

He had the advantage of reliable information supplied by relatives. Sarah's niece, Margaret Whetten, had married Stewart Dean, master of the second vessel from the United States to trade at Canton. Also, both Sarah's nephew, John Whetten, and her brother, Adam, were sea captains.

The inducements which finally influenced Astor to finance his own participation in the trade were two in number . . . he saw them as equally attractive. The fact that large profits were to be made on merchandise from the Orient was not one of them, for it went without saying that if large profits were not to be made he would not have considered the matter at all.

Canton would provide him with another major outlet for the flood of furs descending upon him in New York. He needed it if he were to maintain his supremacy in the fur trade.

The leniency of the Federal Government with regard to the payment of import duties provided an incomparable opportunity to operate with money that did not belong to him.

A round-trip voyage between New York and China took fifteen to twenty months, yet profits were enormous. Capital was easily built up. There was a good reason for this. The Federal Government had adopted a very lenient policy with big shipowners. It allowed them as long as eighteen months to pay the duties on merchandise imported from China. As a result, a ship operator could sell a cargo from China in New York . . . normally at a profit of a 100 to 150 per cent . . . and need not remit the customs duties due the Government. This money could be used to pay for loading and sending another vessel to China. The shipowner operated with Government money as he grew rich.

Joseph A. Scoville, a contemporary of Astor, had this to say in his entertaining work on the early merchants of New York:[1]

"John Jacob Astor at one period in his life had several vessels operating this way. They would go to the Pacific and from thence carry furs to Canton. These would be sold at large profits. Then the cargoes of tea would pay enormous duties which Astor did not have to pay to the United States for a year and a half. His tea cargoes would be sold for good four and sixmonths paper, or perhaps cash; so that for eighteen or twenty years John Jacob Astor had what was actually a free-of-interest loan from the Government of over five millions of dollars."

Of the shipping firm of John H. Smith & Sons, Scoville wrote:

"This house went enormously into the Canton trade, and, although possessing originally only a few thousand dollars, Smith imported to such an extent that when he failed he owed the United States three millions and not a cent has ever been paid."

If Astor privately looked upon this policy as the essence of

[1] Scoville wrote under the pseudonym of Walter Barrett. He was a great admirer of Astor.

poor business, he was very willing to take advantage of it. He could agree openly with the arguments with which Congress defended it, while laughing to himself at the naïveté and ignorance of the political boobs in Washington.

The policy ostensibly had been inaugurated to assist American shippers in their struggle with foreign competition. The country was woefully short of hard money, and the structures of the few banks in existence were afflicted with fiscal termites. The owners of British, French, Dutch, Spanish and Scandinavian bottoms were accorded infinitely greater facilities for obtaining loans and credit than were the operators of American vessels.

A period of eighteen months' grace, during which an American shipowner engaged in trade with China might retain the duties on a cargo before paying them to the Treasury, permitted considerable leeway in competing with foreign flag carriers financed by such powerful institutions as the Bank of England, the Baring Brothers and the Rothschilds. However, the temptations inherent in such a system were too great to be resisted. Honest shippers balanced their accounts with the Treasury to the best of their ability. Dishonest shippers, of which Astor was one, found means of evading their obligations.

The Government, of course, required that shippers give bonds for the amounts they owed. This was a laughable procedure, and no safeguard at all. A man's bond, as Astor and the other abusers very well understood, was only as good as his ability to pay. And prominent merchants and landowners were not put in jail for nonpayment of debts. That was a privilege reserved for the poor.

The fact that in less than a quarter of a century the Government lost more than $250,000,000 in import duties because of the attempt to bolster international sea commerce was of no concern to shippers of Astor's persuasions. They considered it a windfall of which they would be fools not to take full advantage.

Even though he saw before him an open gate to a fabulously lush field, Astor still did not plunge through it. His first venture in the China trade was not made as an individual but in association with several other men. One of them was William Laight, his partner in Mohawk Valley land deals. The combine bought the *Severn*, an eight-year-old ship of 280 tons. Astor was influential in placing Stewart Dean, the husband of Sarah's niece, in command.

The *Severn* sailed from New York on April 29, 1800. In her hold were "3,573 seal skins, 1,023 beaver skins, 351 fox skins, 103 otter skins, 4,769 covids of camlets, 132 piculs of ginseng and 27 piculs of conchineal." On the return voyage, the *Severn* left Canton late in December, and passed Sandy Hook on May 11, 1801, after a trip of 130 days. She brought "black and coloured sattins . . . silks and silk handkerchiefs and shawls, yellow and white nankeens, Hyson skin and Souchong teas, black Indian lutestrings and taffities, colored sinchews, Canton and Nankin fans, nutmegs, cloves, chinaware and sugar."

Now Astor moved faster in the trade. He shipped large quantities of Canton products imported by others to his agents in Europe. The *Severn* also was dispatched to Europe with teas, nankeens, and other Asiatic commodities. She brought back dry goods and sixteen passengers. Then off she went again on the long voyage to Canton, with ginseng, skins and $43,000 in bullion.

When she made her third China voyage in 1803, she carried her most valuable outgoing cargo. It consisted of 6,133 beaver skins, 3,000 seal skins, 1,270 fox skins, 697 otter skins, 169 piculs of ginseng, and $62,000 in bullion.

It was not always easy for Astor to obtain the amount of specie he wanted for a China voyage. However, he hit upon one arrangement that was of considerable help in this regard. It involved his taking up in New York notes of the Bank of Albany. A friend of his, Gerrit W. Van Schaick, was cashier of the bank. The notes were transmitted to Albany, and Astor received payment in dollars. Some of these exchanges amounted to more than $50,000. Bright silver delighted the customs gangsters and greedy Cantonese merchants as much as furs.

But one ship would not satisfy Astor's growing appetite for more profits from the China trade. While he squeezed his partners out of their shares in the *Severn* . . . he became its sole owner in May, 1804 . . . he built a vessel especially suited for the long and hazardous voyage around the Horn to the other side of the world.

The new ship, built in the yard of Eckford & Beebee, in New York, he appropriately named the *Beaver*. She was a fine craft of 427 tons, her frame made of imperishable live oak, and she had capacity for 1,100 tons of cargo. Astor placed Whetten in command on her maiden voyage. Her strongbox contained more than $60,000.

The *Beaver* was fast and lovely to behold. She had two decks and three masts. Her length was 111' and her breadth 29.6' and she drew 14' 9". She had a square stern, a square tuck, quarter galleries, and a woman head.

Driving fast under tall white sails through blue water, she completed her first round-trip voyage in nine months, about half the time many ships took. She ran from Canton to the Bermudas in the remarkable time of seventy-five days.

Still Astor was not satisfied, and he built a consort for the *Beaver* which was christened *Magdalen*, after his eldest daughter, who was then a striking young lady of eighteen. The *Magdalen* sailed on her first voyage on May 5, 1806.

The captain of the *Magdalen* was John Cowman, a master mariner and a veteran of innumerable voyages to far places. Astor spoke of him as the "king of captains," but this admiration did not preclude Astor from engaging in a bitter and costly argument with Cowman over the purchase of a chronometer.

On a later voyage, when the *Magdalen* was ready to sail, Cowman informed Astor that the insurance company had demanded he have a chronometer on the ship. Astor told Cowman to buy one. The captain protested that he did not have $500 to spare for such a purpose, and he maintained that a chronometer properly should be supplied by a ship's owner.

Astor refused to make the purchase, insisting that it was a captain's responsibility to obtain the navigating equipment needed. When Cowman remained adamant, Astor, not wishing to delay the departure of the *Magdalen*, capitulated. He instructed the captain to buy the instrument and charge it to the ship's account.

Cowman carried out the order, and in keeping with custom submitted an accounting of disbursements for the crew, supplies and his own expenses before he weighed anchor. Astor, scrutinizing the list with his usual care, noted the item of $500 for the chronometer, and refused to pay it. Cowman thereupon resigned in disgust and walked off the ship. It took Astor several days to obtain the service of another captain and get the *Magdalen* off to China.

Cowman took command of another trader's vessel, but he left for China almost two months after the *Magdalen* had sailed. Harboring a bitter grudge against Astor, he made every effort to overhaul the *Magdalen*. His great skill as a navigator and his experience in the trade showed their value. He arrived back in New York with an immense cargo of tea only seven days after the *Magdalen* had docked.

Astor had not expected another ship in port for some time, and he was holding the *Magdalen's* cargo for a rising market. The goods from Cowman's ship were offered at auction immediately and sold at attractive prices. The result was that Astor was unable to dispose of his tea because of a temporary oversupply. By the time he was able to sell, several other ships had arrived from China, and the market became even more glutted. He suffered a loss of $70,000.

Captain Cowman himself told friends that some days later Astor stopped him on the street, and said: "You vass right, Cowman. I had better pay for dot chronometer."

Then, said Cowman, Astor rehired him.

Astor, with unusual fickleness, also applied the title "king of captains" to another able master he employed, F. A. De Peyster. De Peyster's long experience in the China trade and his knowledge of the piratical practices of Chinese officials enabled him to render a great favor to Astor.

Nicholas G. Ogden, a brother of the prominent New York merchant, Samuel Gouverneur Ogden, was Astor's agent in Canton. He died suddenly shortly before an Astor ship commanded by a Captain Rossiter arrived there. At the time, merchandise belonging to Astor, valued at nearly three quarters of a million dollars, was in Wampoa warehouses. Because of Ogden's sudden death, the incredible Chinese red tape and the machinations of thieving Chinese officials had combined to entwine the goods in a so-called legal snarl.

Captain Rossiter was young and inexperienced, and he was unable to extricate any of Astor's property. The situation was somewhat desperate, with Astor standing to lose the goods by confiscation through the connivance of grafting customs men and Chinese merchants acting under a dishonest court order.

De Peyster, an old China hand, was not to be brow beaten or swindled in such a manner. He forthwith ended the difficulty with a strong show of force and the greasing of influential palms. Ogden's affairs as well as Astor's were straightened out, and the two ships sailed low in the water with valuable cargoes.

When Astor was apprised of the matter, he thanked De Peyster profusely, clapped him on the shoulder, and said: "I would have taken a big loss if it had not been for you."

That was all. That was De Peyster's reward.

It was not only the Chinese who were making things difficult for American shippers at Wampoa. The British Navy used the slightest pretext to delay a Yankee ship. On at least two occasions Astor's vessels were tied up by legal actions . . . one of them not so legal . . . inspired by Commander John Wood, of H.B.M.S. *Phaeton*, stationed in the Bay of Chuenpi.

Astor was working on plans to expand his trade still more, both by buying additional ships and taking shares in others, but in the fall of 1806 the menacing attitude of the British China squadron aroused forebodings in him. He believed that an open armed conflict between Yankee merchantmen at Canton and the English naval vessels there would occur. American cargo vessels were well armed, and the overbearing attitude of British officers served to revive the intense feelings engendered by the late Revolution. If the British did not start violence, angry American sailors might well do it.

Astor did not propose to withdraw entirely from the trade until the situation calmed down, but he did determine to decrease the chances of loss by selling shares in his own ships to other merchants. In May, 1807, Elias Kane & Company, and the firm of Corp, Ellis & Shaw became part-owners of the *Magdalen*. The next month, Elias and Oliver Kane joined Astor and John Whetten as operators of the *Beaver*.

In accordance with his conviction that serious clashes in the Far East were inevitable, Astor wrote Secretary of State James Madison to inquire whether "under present circumstances it will be adviseable to let . . . a Ship called the *Beaver* being Coppered and 430 Tons burthen, carrying 12 guns, ready for Sea, say to sail for Canton in China, her funds on board will consist of about 250M in value . . . go to Sea on so long a Voyage?"

This letter was accompanied by another from George Clinton, Vice President of the United States, an indication that Astor had reached a place where he could hold the interest of high officials of the Government in his troubles. Astor also told Madison he had heard that the British would attempt to halt American shipments of tea to Canada, and suggested that the American minister in London be notified.

The replies Astor received were discouraging, and the *Beaver* was held in port. Instead of going to Canton, the *Magdalen* was sent to Calcutta.

Astor's fear of an open clash with the British was well founded, but the end result was not what he had anticipated. Instead of the British tying up American trade, President Jefferson himself did it by invoking an embargo on all foreign shipping. Only coastwise trade was permitted, and ships in this commerce were required to give bond that they would land their cargoes at American ports.

One idle vessel in harbor was all Astor cared to support, and he sold his interest in the *Magdalen*. Then with characteristic determination he began a search for loopholes in the embargo proclamation, so that he might put the *Beaver* into operation.

He thought he had found one in the provision which allowed

the President to grant American citizens permits to send vessels in ballast to foreign ports for the sole purpose of bringing back cargoes purchased before the embargo became effective. Astor wondered if he might use specie as ballast. He reasoned that once he had got the *Beaver* to Canton, he could easily arrange with crooked Chinese merchants to load it. Papers could be prepared to show that he had contracted for the cargo the previous year, and that therefore it was not subject to the embargo.

He applied to Washington for permission to bring back property alleged to belong to him in Canton. Secretary of the Treasury Albert Gallatin, who knew Astor well, rejected the request "on general grounds," not because it "appeared unfair." Gallatin's true convictions were not divulged.

Astor's ingenuity was never better illustrated than it was immediately following the refusal of the Government to clear the *Beaver* for China. It so happened that at the time President Jefferson thought very highly of Astor, and had spoken of him as "a most excellent man." Astor was also *persona grata* with other high officials . . . Secretary Gallatin, despite his action, among them.

In mid-July, 1808, President Jefferson received a letter from Senator Samuel Latham Mitchell of New York. Mitchell was also a professor of natural history in the College of Physicians and Surgeons in New York City. He was described by the Whig politician, auctioneer and loquacious diarist, Philip Hone . . . a friend of both Astor's and Mitchell's . . . as "distinguished for scientific and literary acquirements," but "strangely deficient in that useful commodity called common sense." Jefferson, however, considered Mitchell's word quite acceptable.

Senator Mitchell's letter to the President said in part: "Punqua Wingchong, a Chinese merchant, will be the bearer of this note of introduction. He came to New York about nine months ago, on business . . . he is desirous of returning to Canton, where the affairs of his family and particularly the funeral obsequies of his grandfather, require his solemn attention.

"The chief object of his visit to Washington is to sollicit the

means of departure . . . to China . . . he will be accompanied by
M^r. Palmer . . . who will aid him [Palmer spoke Chinese] in
stating his request . . ."

President Jefferson was in Monticello when Wingchong arrived in the capital and did not have the pleasure of meeting
him. Wingchong quickly wrote the President "praying permission to depart for his own country with his property in a vessel
to be engaged by himself."

By some mysterious means, word had got about Washington
that Wingchong was a distinguished, wealthy and powerful Mandarin. Secretary of State Madison was apprised of the matter, and
he also wrote the President in favor of Wingchong's request.

Jefferson approved it, and advised Secretary of the Treasury
Gallatin: "I consider it a case of national comity . . . the departure of this individual with good dispositions may be the
means of making our nation known advantageously at the source
of power in China to which it is otherwise difficult to convey
information."

Jefferson saw the "national good" as outweighing the effect of
making an exception to the rigorous embargo, and he told Gallatin: "I think therefore he should be permitted to engage a
vessel . . . and for this purpose send you a blank passport for the
vessel &c . . ."

When Gallatin learned that the ship Wingchong intended to
engage was the *Beaver*, he smelled another kind of animal. Gallatin was much better acquainted with Astor's character than
the guileless Jefferson. However, he complied with the President's
request, and wrote to David Gelston, Collector of the Port of
New York, to permit the *Beaver* to sail under the following
provisions:

"The vessel to be allowed such . . . Arms for resisting Malay
pirates . . . sea-stores as is usual and proper . . . and also such as
may be wanted for the accommodation of Punqua Wingchong
and attendants . . .

"The property of Punqua Wingchong and attendants consisting, besides their baggage and personal affects, of about forty five

thousand dollars . . . either in specie or in furs, Cochineal, Ginsang, or any other species of merchandise at his choice."

The ship was to be allowed to bring as a return cargo, only the proceeds of property owned "bona fide" by a citizen prior to the embargo.

Gallatin had carried out the President's orders, but he felt it necessary to advise him: "I have complied with your directions respecting the Chinese & he has engaged Astor's vessel to whom we had on general grounds refused permission. Had I had any discretion as to the application itself I would have hesitated."

A small notice in the New York *Commercial Advertiser* brought a roar of indignation from American shippers. The notice said simply: "Yesterday the ship *Beaver*, Captain Galloway, sailed for China."

Angry letters, some of them anonymous, were received by Jefferson and Gallatin. One, signed by ten merchants, all of whom had been in China and some of whom had lived there for a number of years, flatly charged that far from being a Mandarin, Wingchong was nothing more than a petty Chinese merchant, utterly incapable of giving credit. Furthermore, in addition to being altogether undistinguished, Wingchong was unknown to any of them, which they maintained could not be the case "were his character and standing in any degree respectable."

The merchants accused Jefferson and Gallatin of letting "avarice and turpitude" frustrate the intentions of the Government. They charged Astor with surreptitiously obtaining permission for the voyage.

Between the time he received the letter from the ten merchants and the day the *Beaver* sailed, Gallatin had plenty of opportunity to investigate their charges. He elected to do nothing, and he refused to admit that the administration had made a mistake. In fact, Gallatin did not reply to the letter from the ten merchants until the *Beaver* had cleared New York Harbor. He defended the right of the President to allow a vessel to sail for China, and declared that if the *Beaver* violated regulations, the bond furnished by its owners would be forfeited.

The uproar, however, was not quieted by Gallatin's diplomatic statements. The Federalists jeered. The press called Astor's Mandarin a "fraud," "a Chinaman picked up in the park," "a common Chinese dock loafer," an Indian "dressed up in Astor's silks and coached to play his part."

Jefferson began to believe he had been hoodwinked, and he got off a note to Gallatin declaring that he "had no means of judging" the truth of the charges and suggesting that if the vessel had not already gone "she should be detained till the facts . . . are inquired into." He added, however, rather hopefully: "I presume her gone."

The *Beaver* was gone. She was rolling under full sail down the Atlantic, with Punqua Wingchong, garbed in a Mandarin's robes, and with hard silver dollars jingling in his big pockets, loafing on deck.

The ship's strongbox contained $45,000, but her cargo was light, consisting of only 3,000 beaver skins and five piculs of cochineal. Presumably that was all the "property" Wingchong "owned." At least, it was all the property Astor was able to get on board under Wingchong's name.

The *Beaver* brought back from Canton 3,274 piculs of green tea, 1,070 piculs of black tea (more than 500,000 pounds of tea), and large quantities of nankeens, silk piece goods, chinaware and cassia. Because of the embargo these types of merchandise were in heavy demand. Astor's profits on the voyage were estimated to be about $200,000.

Neither the origin nor the end of Punqua Wingchong was ever revealed. At Canton he went ashore and vanished.

4

Astor's capacity for work, and his ability to cope with the details of several major operations at one time, were nothing short of phenomenal. All the time he was developing his Canton trade and struggling with the problems it presented, he was buying more wilderness lands and New York City property . . . including a theater, engaging in a heavy general merchandising business as a retailer, wholesaler and shipper, and increasing his fur trade to immense proportions.

In two purchases of Manhattan Island property made by Astor, the profit motive was of secondary importance. One was his residence at 223 Broadway. The other was his country estate of thirteen acres at Hell Gate, in the vicinity of Sixtieth Street and the East River. The property was known as Hurlgate. On it was what Washington Irving called a "spacious" and "well-built house" of colonial type, surrounded by trees, "with a lawn in front of it, and a garden in the rear." The greensward swept down to the water's edge, and in front of the house was "the little straight of Hellgate," which formed "a constantly moving picture."

Astor loved Hurlgate, and there he was to spend the only really pleasant and peaceful years he ever knew.

The most vital and most significant of all his activities was, of course, the fur trade. It provided the income which permitted him to engage in other enterprises, and to make immense investments in real estate. The plan he was slowly developing for his future conduct in the trade was to bring him the greatest power of any individual of his time.[2]

[2] Profits from his domestic and international fur trade allowed Astor to invest more than $700,000 in Manhattan property during the first two decades of the nineteenth century. He made a profit of more than $500,000 on one single large transaction in Putnam County. In the last two decades of his life purchases of

As trying and time-consuming as the journey was, Astor continued to make an annual trip to Montreal. In the fall of 1806, he took Magdalen with him for the first time. They were lavishly entertained by social and business leaders. Rumor had it that Astor would give his eldest daughter a dowry of £25,000, and the young bucks of the best families hovered about her at gay parties.

Samuel Bridge, a young merchant from Manchester, England, wrote in his diary of one brilliant affair in the home of Alexander Henry: ". . . we consisted of abt 40. Lady Johnston amused herself at Whist while the sprightly dance was kept up till past twelve—chiefly country dancing but some few Reels & one Cotillion in compliment to Miss Astor, as they scarcely dance anything else in New York."

None of the eligible young blades of Montreal was to be successful in wooing Magdalen. On September 14, 1807, she married Adrian Benjamin Bentzon, who earlier in the same year had been ousted by the British from his post as Governor of Santa Cruz Island in the West Indies. But Bentzon didn't need a job as a qualification for marrying Magdalen, and he was soon to play an important role in the fur trade affairs of his father-in-law.

While his handsome daughter was being courted and married, Astor was giving thought to matters far removed from any drawing room or church.

Two events had taken place which graphically demonstrated to him the need for decisive action if he was to carry out any part of the complicated and hazardous plan he was contemplating.

One was the purchase of the Louisiana Territory by the United

---

New York City property amounted to $1,250,000. In addition he held innumerable long-term leases on property that soared in value. In one period of eight years his income from rents alone amounted to $1,265,000. In 1803 he concluded that selling pianos and violins was not worth the time he was obliged to give to that business. He had made money selling musical instruments, and he was one of the leading, if not the largest, dealer in New York. That was a satisfaction to him in itself, but not reason enough to continue. Sentiment in him was always blended, if not dominated, by practicality. He sold out to his rivals, Michael and John Paff, and relinquished his rights as the agent of European manufacturers. But he still tootled on his old flute now and then, for sentimental reasons.

States. The other was the successful journey of Lewis and Clark.

Having performed one of the most comprehensive and successful feats of exploration in all of history, Lewis and Clark had provided Americans with some knowledge of the magnitude of the
enormous wilderness area their Government had acquired for
them.

Probably no more significant event ever took place in the West
than the meeting of Lewis and Clark, when they were almost
home from their epic journey, with several parties of American
fur hunters who were ascending the Missouri. The course of empire had been charted, and no one understood that better than
the observant, thoughtful Astor in New York.

The Government fur houses in Detroit and Fort Wayne were
showing encouraging results, encouraging, that is, to a skeptical
Congress. They were serving as supply bases for American traders
competing with the Canadians, and they were attracting the Indians with honest practices and reasonable prices. Jefferson was
delighted, and asked Congress for additional funds to build more
Government houses farther west. He got them, and new Federal
posts were established at Chicago, Sandusky and Michilimackinac, much to the discouragement of the Canadians and the aggravation of the ambitious Astor.

In an effort to counter the growing power of the Americans
who were asserting their rights with such vigor and determination, the Canadians formed a new organization. It was to operate entirely in the Old Northwest and the country beyond the
Mississippi. They called it the Michilimackinac Company. Ostensibly owned by the merchants of Michilimackinac and the
Canadian traders who made their headquarters there, it was in
truth nothing more than a strong subsidiary of the North West
Company.

In 1806, this offspring, with thoughtful camouflage, entered
into an agreement with its parent by which the fur trade of all
Canada, outside of the territory controlled by the Hudson's Bay
Company, was to be divided. The Michilimackinac Company
would have the trade of the upper Great Lakes and the upper

Mississippi, and it soon took over the posts, supplies and equipment of the older organization in that area. The rest of the immense land, including the upper Missouri and the Far West, would remain the domain of the North West Company.

The Michilimackinac Company had one purpose, and that was to exploit as fast as possible the furs of the United States. No one understood that better than Astor, and the thought bristled the hairs on his thick neck.

While Astor chafed and studied the situation, the American Government was taking some steps to make clear its intention. Zebulon M. Pike ascended the Mississippi and warned traders not to display any British insignia on United States territory. Jefferson extended his trade policies west of the great river. Government houses were built on the Arkansas, on the Natchitoches, at Bellefontaine and Fort Madison.

In New York during the winter of 1807–08, Astor spent long hours alone behind the screens of his countinghouse. Frequently he worked far into the night, a shawl about his shoulders against the cold drafts which a small coal fire failed to defeat. Meticulously he put down figures and scratched in a cramped hand words and sentences that were to lose none of their potency and their impact on the American economy because of atrocious spelling and bad construction.

He was ready to make his great move.

Part Five

The Genesis of Empire

1

It was late in January, 1808, when Astor disclosed to Governor DeWitt Clinton the plans which had been germinating in his mind for some time. They were predicated on simple facts that would infuriate any loyal American who wanted to carry out the noble program to develop the West which Jefferson had advocated. Two main Canadian companies were operating in the area. They were the North West Company with a capital of $1,200,000, and the Michilimackinac Company, its offspring, with a capital of $800,000. By far the greater proportion of the furs secured by these companies came from United States territory. Both of them recently had begun to trade west of the Mississippi River.

Three-quarters of the furs consumed in the United States, Astor told Clinton, passed through the hands of this powerful foreign combine. At least $400,000 worth of furs were taken by the Canadians each season on the upper Mississippi and Missouri rivers. In order to obtain the furs he needed, Astor was forced to buy American furs in Montreal. Therefore, he not only was obliged to pay a premium on the American furs he bought, but the United States Government was being deprived of revenues to which it was justly entitled, and American consumers were forced to pay higher prices than would be the case if western furs came directly to New York.

Moreover, Astor declared, both the North West Company and

the Hudson's Bay Company had well-formulated plans for expanding their operations to the Pacific, and establishing themselves on waters draining into the Columbia River. If they were successful in securing domination of the land trade in this vast area, they would be in a good position to control the valuable trade in sea otters and other furs on the entire Northwest Coast. Thereby, they also could monopolize the China trade from that vantage point.

Astor spread before Clinton the papers he had prepared with great care during the previous months. They disclosed a plan for building a series of trading posts along the route taken by Lewis and Clark, from St. Louis to the headwaters of the Missouri River, thence across the Rocky Mountains and down the various streams flowing into the Columbia, and so to the western ocean. At the mouth of the Columbia, a headquarters post would be established through which furs taken in the interior west of the Continental Divide could be funneled for shipment to China and New York. Furs taken east of the mountains would be brought down the Missouri to St. Louis, then transported overland to New York or sent down the Mississippi to New Orleans for shipment.

Astor expressed the conviction that this immense operation not only would be profitable, but would be highly beneficial to the entire country. For one thing, the security of the United States would be enhanced, and laws could be enforced with greater facility. For another thing, enormous quantities of merchandise would be required for the trade that would develop, hundreds of persons would be employed, there would be immense expenditures for wages, transportation and provisions . . . all of which would benefit the general economy.

Another important point to be considered was that the creation of such an organization as he proposed would relieve the Government of the expensive and controversial trading factory program.[1]

[1] Trading posts were called factories, especially by the British. The agents in charge of the posts were spoken of as "factors." In the posts furs were sorted as to grade and quality, treated, pressed into bales and otherwise prepared for shipment. Literally, a factory was a trading station where factors resided and transacted business.

This burden would be shouldered by the private company. The hope of the Government to secure the loyalty of the Indians through fair trade practices could be fulfilled without any cost to the people as a whole. Being a permanent organization, and having the field to itself, the private company would find it advantageous to deal honestly and liberally with the Indians. Irresponsible traders interested in making a quick killing in the trade and then getting out, with no regard for either the Indians or the future, and who would employ dishonest methods, would be eliminated.

The investment in such a gigantic program would, of course, be greater than any one man could afford. Heavy initial expenses probably would prevent a profitable return for at least two or three years. It was Astor's opinion that if he could induce ten or twelve responsible men to associate themselves with him, the enterprise could be carried forward with a good chance of being successful. He stood ready to venture as much as $100,000 of his own money in it.

The presentation Astor made to Clinton was unmitigatedly dishonest.

Astor had only one goal: a monopoly of the fur trade of the whole western United States. He had no intention of permitting any other capitalist to join him. His avowed purpose was to concentrate the western fur trade, and thereby the economy of the West, in the hands of only those American traders who had been born in Walldorf, Germany, in 1763, and had arrived in the United States in the year 1784.

Astor understood that his scheme could not be carried out without certain favors from the Federal Government. He needed official sanction, and it was most unlikely that one man alone . . . especially a German whose operations already had been the subject of official wrath and widespread condemnation on several occasions . . . could obtain it. Americans were inherently opposed to monopolies of any type. If he appeared as spokesman for a group of wealthy, reputable and influential men, his chances of obtaining an official blessing would be greatly increased.

Astor had gone first to Clinton for a good reason. He wanted to

know if the Governor would recommend to the New York Legislature that it grant him a charter. This had to be sought, however,
in the strictest secrecy, for if word of the plan reached Canadian
ears, international difficulties might ensue. "You know," he wrote
Clinton, "that I do considerable business with the people in
Montreal. They would take it unkind of me to prepare an opposition to them and on the other hand if they knew the extent of
the plan they would take measures to oppose with more effect."

If Clinton would quietly ask the Legislature for a charter, Astor
declared, he would go to Washington and seek governmental
sanction of the plan. He maintained that he had no intention of
proceeding without it. This assertion, too, was deceptive. Astor
had every intention of proceeding without governmental sanction. In fact, he didn't need it to enter the trans-Mississippi fur
trade. What he wanted was official approval of his efforts to be on
record. This would give him prestige not enjoyed by other companies.

To Clinton, Astor expressed the belief that if he held an exclusive charter from New York State to trade in "the Lusuanas &
Missourie" the Federal Government might "grant additional advantages—the benefits resulting to the country from the trade
. . . the Enthusiasm of Intercourse & good will with the Natives
would itself be a great object to the country and without it the
company could not succeed for it would be the best & True Policy
to trade honourably with them & to treat them well, with Independent traders its not so, they go one year to trade with the Indians perhaps never to see them again, why then they care little
how much they Cheat them." He believed the Government
"would give very considerable aid to Insure its success, they have
no [now] some trading houses which would be withdrawn."

Astor did not disclose to Governor Clinton that he had first
planned to try to secure a Federal charter . . . in other words a
government monopoly . . . rather than merely a charter from New
York, but that he had come to the conclusion such a thing was
not possible. Such high officers as Gallatin and Vice President
Clinton might have been receptive to the idea, but it was antipa-

thetical to democratic principles as Jefferson conceived them. With this barrier facing him, Astor had turned to the next most powerful government, that of New York State.

Clinton knew Astor intimately, knew his true character, and knew the nature of the business code to which Astor adhered. He understood that in the cunning, perspicacious brain of the former butcher boy was a plot fantastic in scope and of frightening proportions. He knew that Astor's proposed American Fur Company was not being created merely as another promising business venture, but as the cornerstone of a cartel to dominate national and international markets. Whoever controlled the fur trade between the Alleghenies and the Pacific not only could control the economy of that vast and little-known territory, but the life of virtually every man, woman and child in it. Clinton knew, too, that Astor's contention that the establishment of licensed American Fur Company posts in the West could greatly augment the prosperity of the country and create good will among the native tribes was completely false.

DeWitt Clinton said nothing of these things to his good friends in Washington. As for the members of the New York State Legislature, they cared not so much what Astor did, or what schemes he had in mind, as how much he paid for their favors. Money could get a man pretty much what he wanted in the New York capital, anything from a French *fille de joie* to a pardon for tax evasion.

If Clinton had any misgivings, if his knowledge of the truth of things burdened his conscience, he understood the futility . . . and perhaps the political indiscretion . . . of refusing Astor. Moreover, he was obliged to concur with Astor's argument that Washington obviously was unable to take steps which the situation in the West demanded. The United States owned the territory, but all the way from Niagara to the upper Missouri the Canadians continued to ladle off the cream of the Indian trade. If private enterprise could accomplish what the government, with its cumbersome methods and confused theories, could not, Clinton felt himself obligated to support it. He not only agreed to place

To counter govt ineptness

Astor's proposal before the Legislature, but pledged himself to urge its passage.

As Astor viewed the situation in 1808, the chief difference between his past operations and those to come would be in size. His trade in the East had been affected at times by both stubborn competition and dwindling production. Opportunities to reap immense returns in the incredibly vast and almost untouched far western regions would continue for years. This thought alone created a mental picture of a chain of posts, rather American Fur Company forts, running from St. Louis up the Missouri to the Shining Mountains, and down the western slope of the continent through the valleys of the Snake and Columbia Rivers to the sea. But not even the Pacific shore would mark the limit of his empire, for there his ships would meet the hunters and carry his furs on to the rich markets of the Orient. He had studied carefully the reports of Lewis and Clark.

With Clinton's support won, Astor's next step was to advise President Jefferson of the project. He requested Jefferson's approbation, and informed the President that he did not propose to go forward unless it was received, for he felt strongly that without such sanction he could not succeed.

This appeal to Jefferson was made before Astor had contrived the shenanigans involving the Chinese Mandarin. Astor suggested that Jefferson inquire of Vice President George Clinton as to his character and ability. George Clinton, the uncle of DeWitt, had been the first Governor of New York under the new state constitution, and he had been associated with Astor in political and commercial considerations. There was, Astor informed the Chief Executive, some need for urgency, as the New York Legislature, which he intended to ask for a charter, would adjourn in a few weeks, and he did not wish to make any final move until he had been advised of the President's sentiments.

Jefferson's sentiments were favorable. He saw in the scheme strong support for his own plans for opening the West, which were at the time enmeshed in a web of political intrigue and red tape. A sound and fair trade with the Indians was a vital necessity, and would become more vital as time passed, for Jefferson was struggling to advance his program of moving the tribes to new homes west of the Mississippi River.

Jefferson asked the Secretary of War, Gen. Henry Dearborn, to look into Astor's reputation, and General Dearborn wrote De-Witt Clinton about the matter. Within a few days, having received a reply from Clinton, Dearborn advised the President: "Govr. Clinton speaks well of Astor, as a man of large property and fair character, and well acquainted with the fur and peltry business."

While Astor very much wanted governmental sanction, he did not permit his progress to be interrupted while waiting for a decision from Washington. He and Clinton went ahead with their negotiations with the Legislature. On April 6, 1808, "An Act to Incorporate the American Fur Company" was passed.

This was a week before Jefferson replied to Astor. Assured of Astor's ability and respectability, on April 13, Jefferson gave his benediction to the plan as he understood it. This understanding, however, did not include the knowledge that Astor intended to carry it out alone. Jefferson had the impression that a number of American citizens would join together to engage in the western fur trade. This conclusion obviously was derived from Astor's statement that a number of prominent men would be invited to partake in the enterprise.

Only Astor . . . and possibly Governor Clinton . . . understood that Jefferson's approval was qualified and based on false information. That was good enough for Astor. Armed with the written approval from the Chief Executive, he had an incomparable advantage over every other fur trader in America.

The articles of incorporation of the American Fur Company were, indeed, born of a countinghouse dream and a legal mirage. They had no more basis in truth or reality than the words and gestures of a puppet show.

Stating that John Jacob Astor was desirous of forming a trading company for the purpose of dealing extensively with the Indians, the act explained that "an undertaking of such magnitude would require a greater capital than any individual or unincorporated association could well furnish, and who would be less able to support a fair competition with foreigners who are at present almost in the exclusive possession of the fur trade."

Astor, said the act, prayed that he and other persons may be incorporated, "the better to enable them to carry into effect this design . . . and such an establishment may be of great public utility, by serving to conciliate and secure the good will and affections of the Indian tribes toward the government and people of the United States, and may conduce to the peace and safety of our citizens inhabiting the territories belonging to the native Indian tribes."

Astor had submitted the names of four friends as commissioners of the corporation . . . James Fairlee, William Edgar, William Denning and Edward Laight . . . and they were duly approved by the Legislature. The stock was to be offered for public subscription, and stockholders were to elect a board of nine directors. The price of the stock would be $500 a share.

The company was incorporated for twenty-five years, and the capital stock for the first two years would amount to one million dollars, after which it might be increased to two million. The nine directors would manage the company, and would elect a president. One-third of the shares might be retained by the company for the purpose of rewarding its employees. An annual dividend was to be paid at the discretion of the directors.

All this was unadulterated hogwash. Viscount Astor was to write, with greater integrity than was shown in his fraudulent genealogy of the Astor family, that Astor's corporation was simply "a fiction intended to broaden and facilitate his operations." As the official historian of Astor's fur-trading enterprises, Washington Irving was to state that Astor furnished the capital for the American Fur Company "by himself—he, in fact, constituted the company; for, though he had a board of directors, they were really nominal; the whole business was conducted on his plans, and with his resources, but he preferred to do so under the imposing and formidable aspect of a corporation, rather than in his individual name, and his policy was sagacious and effective."

The magnitude of the undertaking, while almost inconceivable in the light of the time and the state of the American economy, was not beyond the means of either an individual or an unincorporated association. Astor could put up all the money needed with little strain on his total resources.

The four commissioners were paid for the use of their names, either with cash or a share or two of stock. They had no more authority, no more voice in the affairs of the company, than did the Indians it intended to rob.

The stock was never to be offered to the public. Ninety-nine and nine-tenths of it was to be held in one name . . . John Jacob Astor. The board of directors was a sham, and it had no powers at all. Astor elected himself president, and his term in office was subject only to his own desires. Only he could remove himself.

No employee would be rewarded with stock whose name was not Astor. A dividend would be paid whenever Astor chose to take the money from the till, and if any other man received one, it was only because Astor felt that he should be paid something for the use of his name and for keeping his mouth shut. Although Astor would have liked to eliminate all names except his own, not even the liberal New York State legislators could be induced to approve a one-man corporation. There simply wasn't any such thing.

Astor saw to it that his well-meaning but naïve mentor, Thomas Jefferson, was kept informed of his thoughts and activities. He told Jefferson, both directly and through Gallatin, that the embargo was preventing him from carrying on the Michilimackinac trade, and that he was considering making a trip to St. Louis to survey the situation from that vantage point.

Meriwether Lewis had become Governor of Louisiana Territory, and Jefferson wrote him recommending Astor. The President informed Lewis that a powerful company was being organized to carry on the Indian trade in the West on a large scale, with the intention of securing for the United States "exclusive possession" of that commerce, and would employ a capital of $300,000 the first year and later increase it to $1,000,000.

Astor had implanted in Jefferson's mind the idea that once the

American Fur Company became active, the Michilimackinac Company would fold its tents and fade away. Jefferson passed this news on to Lewis, adding that the new American company would be "under the direction of a most excellent man, a mr Astor merch', of New York, long engaged in the business & perfectly master of it." Lewis, in turn, gave the news to St. Louis traders, most of whom received it with something less than enthusiasm. Charles Gratiot, however, eagerly wrote Astor to offer his services. But Astor did not accept Gratiot's offer. Neither did he go to St. Louis.

He went instead to Montreal.

Astor's complaint that Jefferson's embargo was preventing him from carrying on the Michilimackinac trade was based on the contention that a large part of the pelts from that area had to be sold in London. He had told Gallatin, "We cannot consume a large proportion of those furs."

This statement was in direct contrast with the assertion he had made previously that "we are obligd to Drow ¾ of aur furrs for ham Consumption from canada."

The truth was that Astor was trying to work out some scheme, comparable to that involving the fake Mandarin, by which he could get governmental permission to ship furs from Michilimackinac to Montreal and Europe through the barrier of the embargo. Gallatin was inclined to agree that the Michilimackinac situation was unjustly punitive, and he wrote to Jefferson asking for instructions in replying to Astor. Should he give Astor any encouragement? Gallatin inquired.

By this time Jefferson was wiser, and he made no reply. The last time Astor had secured his permission to send a ship through the embargo . . . to carry a homesick Chinese named Punqua Wingchong to Canton . . . was an experience Jefferson would have liked to forget. He did not intend to be burned twice in the same way.

Astor made no mention, either in Canada or the United States, that it was his plan to build a fort at the mouth of the Columbia River, and control the fur trade of that area with a strong garrison and a battery of cannon. This was the most private of his secrets having to do with the American Fur Company, but he had not originated it. Strangely enough, he had got it from his old friend Alexander Henry.

As early as the spring of 1786, the astute Henry had written the New York merchant William Edgar, advocating the building of forts on the rivers of the Northwest Coast for the purpose of trading with the Indians. Henry had called the idea "my favorite plan." Later, in the course of his long association with Astor, Henry had made some mention of the plan, which he had never been able to carry out himself, to his friend.

It was not without good reason that Edgar was selected by Astor to be one of the commissioners of the American Fur Company. Astor was not always an original thinker nor a pioneer in business. His genius was never better illustrated than when he was carrying out the ideas of other men. He profited most from the successes and failures of others, as well as from his own. As Kenneth Wiggins Porter was to remark in his study of Astor's business methods, this was "a feat more difficult than it sounds."

In Montreal in the fall of 1808, Astor let it be thought that he was amenable to enlarging his associations with the Canadian companies beyond the confines of a buyer-and-seller relationship. The Canadians listened attentively. They seemed to be especially interested in Astor's suggestion that it might be possible to "create spheres of influence" which would contribute to their mutual benefit.

While they gave thought to the matter, they entertained him in lavish style. He dined with Joseph Frobisher and other leaders of the trade in the home of William McGillivray, president of the North West Company. On September 13, he was the guest of honor at a dinner in Frobisher's home "with a large number of gentlemen," among whom were executives of both the North West and the Michilimackinac Companies. On the 17th, he was entertained at a dinner in the Beaver Club.

Although their courtesy and hospitality knew no bounds, the Canadian traders took Astor's suggestions under advisement, and made no commitments. He returned to New York empty-handed, which was exactly what he had wanted to do.

If he had several purposes in making the journey north that year, they were all predicated on a single desire. That was to determine what his next major move would be. With this in mind he had made an effort to deceive the Canadians into believing it might be possible to soften his competition in the Northwest Territory. He reasoned that if they saw the possibility of an alliance with him, they might hold in abeyance the plans he knew they harbored for westward expansion. This would aid him in getting a bigger jump on them.

His suggestions to the Canadians were advanced as well for another reason. Through observation of their reactions he could acquire knowledge of their true beliefs, how great their fear of him was, and the extent of the discouragement or optimism that influenced their thinking. The last thing he wanted was a crippling alliance, for he was convinced that if given the time and the opportunity, he could drive them out of Michilimackinac, and take over the bulk of the trade for himself.

As still another attempt to deceive and confuse them, he had sought to leave the impression that he was not fully certain of his own strength and his own ability, and in this he believed he had been successful.

2

Astor's master plan had the characteristics of a carefully programmed dynasty. Not only would marriages be arranged, they would be rigidly supervised. The American Fur Company was the founder of the line, and in its offspring, even though they might have no outward resemblance to their progenitor, the nature and qualities of the original blood would be predominant.

The first principality of the planned empire would be established on the Northwest Pacific Coast. Long before he took fundamental steps toward that achievement, Astor had a name for it ... Pacific Fur Company.

South of the mouth of the Columbia River reached the timbered ranges and palisades marking the coast of Spanish California. Off the foggy capes the sea otters swarmed in great herds, but taking them under the guns of Spanish men-of-war was a perilous and often unrewarding adventure.

North of the Columbia, higher mountains, innumerable islands, inlets and bays, steeper precipices and thicker fogs characterized the coast of Russian America. There, too, the sea otters thrived, seals blackened the rocky beaches, and the land produced an inexhaustible bounty of fine furs. The Russians attempted to guard their treasures, but they were bunglers, their government was diseased, and their colonies were badly managed and frequently hungry. Because their own supply ships arrived in New Archangel only spasmodically, and seldom when most needed, the garrison was forced to depend for succor on itinerant traders.

Despite these handicaps, the Russians managed to keep most foreign fur traders from making successful forays into Alaskan waters, but necessity obliged them to enter into transactions with some of the invaders. For one thing, Chinese ports were closed to Russian vessels, and this cut them off from the most lucrative fur market of all. They conducted some smuggling into Canton, but it was expensive and hazardous.

American ships, however, were not barred from China. There was nothing to prevent Americans from carrying precious cargoes of Russian furs from New Archangel to Canton as their own property. Such traffic would be illegal, but that was more of an annoying detail than reason for restraint. Agreements were contrived in secret, and both Russians and Yankees made money.

Corollary temptations were too great to be ignored by the

Americans, however, and the Russians soon complained that their clandestine partners were engaging in illicit trading with the natives, and moreover were furnishing them with arms. The Russians found it necessary to stop the agreeable traffic and forbid all foreign ships to enter their territorial waters.

If the maps of the Northwest Coast were incomplete and inaccurate, Astor's understanding of the situation in that area was not. The American embargo prevented him from sending a vessel to the North Pacific, but he quickly devised a scheme to circumnavigate that restriction, and it was a legal scheme.

When Andrew Daschkoff became Russian Consul-General to the United States in June, 1809, Astor was no less ready to receive him than the Department of State.

Daschkoff arrived with instructions to remonstrate against the practices of American traders on the Alaskan coast. He made a formal demand that they be prohibited from giving firearms to the Indians for peltries.

Astor sympathized with Daschkoff, and suggested that since the arm of the American Government was neither strong enough nor long enough to carry out this demand, he do it himself. This could be accomplished through an agreement between the American Fur Company and the Russian-American Company, which held a monopoly in the North Pacific colony. Astor would supply the Russian settlements with all the supplies they required for the exclusive right to trade in the Russian territory and its waters.

Furthermore, Astor would build a strong post at the mouth of the Columbia, but he would not trade directly with the natives near the Russian settlements. In return, the Russian-American Company would agree not to deal with any other trader nor with Indians adjacent to the Columbia.

Daschkoff jumped at the proposal. So enthusiastic was he that he suggested he be given credit for inventing it. With him as its originator and sponsor it would have more of a chance of receiving the full approval of his government.

Daschkoff urged Astor to dispatch a supply ship to Governor Alexander Baranoff at New Archangel, and arrange to fill the colony's needs at regular intervals. The captain of the ship should be given full power to sign a contract with Baranoff. Daschkoff wrote Baranoff a letter which the captain was to deliver. In it he expressed the hope that the trade in furs with Canton would be exclusively controlled by Baranoff and Astor, and that other adventurers on the Northwest Coast would be driven out.

Daschkoff's proposals dovetailed very nicely with Astor's overall plans. He had privately determined to make his first strike for control of the western fur trade at the mouth of the Columbia River, instead of at St. Louis. This, he was convinced, would not only be confusing to his competitors but would give him a distinct advantage over them.

The embargo inflicted by Jefferson had been repealed by President Madison in March. It had not brought England and France to terms, as Jefferson had hoped. On the contrary, it had served to worsen the international situation, and it had inflicted severe punishment on American shippers. The feelings of the voters toward it were reflected in the Federalist gains in the election of 1808.

During the embargo an immense fortune in furs had piled up in Astor warehouses. Many of them he had acquired at extremely advantageous prices because of the glutted market. With the gates opened again, he wasted no time in getting them on their way to China. He bought the brig *Sylph* and quickly sent her to Canton under the command of Edward Daniel. She carried an unusually valuable cargo: $92,000 in specie, thousands of otter, fox and beaver skins, cotton, ginseng and cochineal.

His brig *Fox*, with the celebrated Captain Cowman on the quarter-deck, sailed for Calcutta.[2] His ship *Huntress*, 225 tons, cleared for an unspecified destination in the "S Seas," and vanished.[3] The *Beaver*, of Mandarin fame, Richard Marner in com-

[2] The *Fox* made the round trip in seven months and fifteen days, the shortest time recorded up to that year for an American vessel.
[3] One day, several years later, the *Huntress* was to come limping into port, having at last escaped her unidentified captors.

mand, left for Canton, low in the water with an immense cargo of cotton, furs and hard dollars.

Within a few months Astor had five vessels of his own en route to the Orient. He also had obtained shares in several others engaged in the China trade.

In September, 1809, Astor bought the ship *Enterprise* for a specific purpose. She was to inaugurate his scheme to get control of the Northwest fur trade and carry out his agreement with Daschkoff. The *Enterprise* was of 291 tons burthen, and she had been built in Philadelphia in 1807.

Astor selected a captain for the important mission with great care. He was John Ebbets, not only a skilled navigator but a veteran of both the China and the Northwest Coast trade.

Another reason for the selection of Ebbets was that he, while on the coast of Alaska in 1802, had won the gratitude of the Russian American Company by rescuing a number of its employees during a bloody Indian uprising in Sitka. Ebbets, Astor stated, "enjoyed both the esteem and confidence of the Indians" and had "long been known to Mr. Baranoff, who had seen proof of his trustworthiness in many a business transaction."

As ships came into New York from Europe and the West Indies during the fall of 1809 with dry goods, hardware, gin, molasses, rum, tobacco, powder, brandy and other merchandise suitable for the Northwest trade, Astor loaded the *Enterprise*. On November 15, she cleared from New York on her celebrated voyage.

Astor's passion for detail was never better illustrated than it was in the instructions he gave to Captain Ebbets. There were, in fact, two sets of them, and they were drastically different . . . the result of thoughtful premeditation.

The first set of orders was written for the benefit of Daschkoff. If he followed them, Ebbets would proceed directly to New Archangel and deliver his cargo to Governor Baranoff. He would exercise the utmost caution in dealing with the Indians, and he would consult with the supercargo, Daniel Greene, regarding any problems that might arise in which the Indians were involved. Greene, a native of New Haven, had been captain of a sealing ship engaged in the Northwest–Canton trade. He was "resolute and hawkeyed," not inclined to frivolity, yet "humane" to the natives, and "indulgent" to his saliors without giving them any encouragement to presume upon his good nature. After delivering the cargo, and receiving furs in payment for it, Ebbets would return directly to New York.

Daschkoff was pleased that Astor apparently was placing the welfare of the Russian-American Company before other considerations, but Daschkoff had a lot to learn about Astor.

In a secret set of orders, Ebbets was instructed to touch at ports in California and determine whether it were possible to develop a profitable trade with the Spanish. Next Ebbets was to stop in the Columbia and "prepare the Indians for a friendly reception to some white men who would come to stay with them." He was to leave a letter containing the information he had gathered under a marked tree on the Columbia. The letter would be picked up by an Astor ship which would follow him.

Instead of concerning himself with the welfare of the Russian settlements, Ebbets was to trade for furs wherever he had an opportunity while en route to New Archangel. Astor obviously expected this trade to be successful, for he told Ebbets that in the event New Archangel was reached without supplies, Ebbets was to say that supplies had not been brought because the settlement was thought to have everything it needed.

Ebbets carried out the secret orders. He touched at several West Coast ports, and finally arrived at the Indian village of Newetee on June 11, 1810. This was the place where he was to leave a letter for the next Astor ship. His efforts to obtain furs had brought only moderate success, and he still had the major part of his cargo. The *Enterprise* reached New Archangel, which was on Norfolk Sound, at the end of June.

The dispatch furnished by Daschkoff brought Ebbets a cordial reception, but then difficulties arose. A letter and a contract from Astor were written in both French and English, but for some unknown reason Astor had failed to provide copies of them in Russian. Ebbets knew no Russian, and none of the Russians could read either French or English. It was a stalemate until a few days later when the Russian sloop-of-war *Diana* arrived. She was commanded by Capt. V. M. Golovnin, an able linguist, and he began to translate the papers into Russian.

Negotiations proceeded smoothly until Ebbets made an unfortunate mistake. In his efforts to convince the Russians of the great expense and trouble to which Astor had gone to aid the settlement, Ebbets gave Golovnin an account of the cost of fitting out the *Enterprise*. Inadvertently he also gave him a copy of his secret orders from Astor.

When Golovnin had translated these documents, the atmosphere at New Archangel became somewhat strained, and an unpleasant shadow fell over the course of American–Russian relations. The secret instructions clearly placed Ebbets in the role of a spy, for they told him to ascertain in the most minute detail the circumstances of the colony, to note the extent of its trade, its strength, its defences, to learn the dimensions of Govenor Baranoff's power, "and any other significant facts which might be available."

Captain Golovnin interpreted the instructions as indicating that the United States was considering the feasibility of seizing Russian America. He advised Governor Baranoff to submit the entire matter of an agreement with Astor to the board of directors of the Russian-American Fur Company.

Captain Ebbets had no alternative but to curse his own bumbling, and stand his ground. It would have done him no good to run, for the Russian warship was anchored in the harbor. He settled down to await developments, hoping for the best.

Baranoff indicated that he would follow Golovnin's advice, but he did not do it. He had recently applied for permission to retire, and he did not wish to become involved in a situation which might influence the government to postpone his request pending a clarification of the intentions of the Americans. Besides, Baranoff was weary of his job, tired of life in a remote and unimportant outpost. In all probability he didn't really give a damn what happened to Russian America, and it would have been all right with him if it were given back to the Indians. All he wanted was to be relieved, and return to the comforts and civilization of St. Petersburg.

Despite the unpleasant state of affairs, Baranoff entered into negotiations with Ebbets, but these bore no fruit. He found it impossible to conclude an agreement along the lines proposed by Astor and Daschkoff for several reasons. One was that Astor had failed to list prices for which goods would be sold, and therefore Baranoff had no way of knowing whether it would be more advantageous to trade with Astor or continue to depend upon transient traders.

Another barrier to a conclusive deal with Astor was that Baranoff had not heard a word from the Russian-American Fur Company's board of directors for three years, and he feared the company might have made an agreement with some other American trader. Also, Baranoff thought hopefully, Russia might have been able to straighten out its everlasting wrangles with France, Sweden and England. In that case, supplies would be coming with more regularity from St. Petersburg.

The best Baranoff could do under the circumstances was to purchase part of Ebbets' cargo for $27,000, payable in furs of various kinds. He also arranged with Ebbets to have the *Enterprise* carry 66,000 seal skins, 3,000 sea otter skins, and other Russian furs to Canton and sell them for specified Chinese goods. Ebbets . . . really Astor . . . was to receive a 5 per cent commission on the sale, and an additional $18,000 for freight. One-third of the freight charges were to be paid in cash at Canton, and two-thirds in furs when Ebbets returned to New Archangel. This was an indication of the tremendous profits to be made from furs in Canton.

Baranoff also gave Ebbets a list of prices at which he was willing to take goods. If the prices were suitable to Astor, he could send another ship or two to New Archangel. Payment would be made in furs. Therefore, despite the setbacks, Astor still remained in a position to obtain furs from the Russians.

Ebbets left New Archangel in August. As he still had cargo,

he stopped to trade at various places along the coast. At Newetee
he placed a letter under a tree. Early in October he started across
the Pacific for Canton.

In January, 1811, while Ebbets was selling his furs at Canton,
the *Beaver* came in, but, to the captain's great disappointment,
it brought no word for him from Astor. He wrote a letter telling
Astor that, even though there was no agreement, a ship sent to
New Archangel from New York would find a ready market for
various types of goods, "above all brandy." A "small invoice" of
the same commodity also should be sent for use in trade with
the natives. He cautioned Astor to say nothing to Daschkoff
about the liquor, but remarked that a whole cargo of rum would,
indeed, be a good investment . . . unless the Russians found out
about it.

In Canton, Ebbets made a profit of $20,000 on the compara-
tively small quantity of Astor's furs, and received more than
$74,000 for Baranoff's pelts. He deducted his commission of 5
per cent and $6,000 for freight, and invested this money with his
profits in Chinese merchandise. This merchandise he sent to
New York on the *Beaver*.

Ebbets set the *Enterprise* on a course for the Northwest Coast
in April, and on June 7, came in sight of New Archangel. Baranoff was delighted with the efficient and profitable manner in
which Ebbets had sold the Russian company's skins, had exchanged the money for Chinese goods, and returned with such
things as sugar, millet-meal, nankeens, teas, silks and chinaware.
He paid Ebbets the remaining freight charges, amounting to
$12,000, and also bought some European goods which Ebbets
had obtained from the *Beaver* for $35,348.15. These charges were
also paid in furs. Thus, on arriving back in New Archangel, Ebbets received nearly $48,000 worth of sea otter and seal skins. It
was a good start in the trading he was planning to do along the
coast during the summer.

By August, Ebbets had obtained a valuable cargo of furs from
the Indians, and again sailed for the Far East. He conducted

another successful trade at Canton, and departed for New York
on January 11, 1812, with a heavy cargo of Chinese goods.

3

Establishing land trade and constructing posts in the Far Northwest demanded able and experienced men, and Astor knew of
no better place to obtain such lieutenants than Canada. The
prospect of securing the services of veteran Canadian traders was,
as well, doubly satisfying. He not only would have the benefit
of their knowledge and training, but he would be taking them
away from the North West and the Michilimackinac Companies.

In Montreal, Astor wasted not a day. He approached the men
he wanted, agreed to give them time to consider his proposition
and went back to New York, leaving Montreal in a state of agitation. Rumors of Astor's negotiations with the Russians, despite
his attempts to keep them secret, had preceded him northward
via diplomatic channels and the medium of trade gossip. After
his visit there, the Canadian companies fully understood that
Astor's plans were alarmingly menacing to their own futures.

The success of Astor's personnel raid on Montreal was demonstrated before the spring of 1810 had arrived. On March 10,
he entered into a preliminary agreement with three veteran
Nor'Westers. They were Alexander McKay, Donald McKenzie
and Duncan McDougal. A final contract was to be drawn in the
near future.

The trend of the Canadians' thinking was shown by the fact
that in the preliminary agreement the possibility of Astor's buying out the Michilimackinac Company was mentioned, and it

was further provided, leaving the gate completely open, that the Michilimackinac and American Fur Companies might merge, if that appeared more advisable.

Meanwhile, Astor had been talking with several other men whose services he thought would be valuable to him. One of them was Wilson Price Hunt, of New Jersey, who for several years had had business interests in St. Louis. He had also negotiated with Ramsay Crooks, Robert McClelan and Joseph Miller, who were partners in fur-trading ventures on the Missouri River. Two other Canadians, as well, were attracted by Astor's proposals. They were David Stuart and his nephew Robert Stuart.

These men represented a formidable array of both talent and experience, and their identities demonstrated Astor's thoroughness, in addition to delineating the structure of his plan. He had selected men who had been trained in the trade on both sides of the North American continent.

In June, 1809, they gathered in New York. After lengthy discussions they affixed their signatures to a document which created an organization to be known as the Pacific Fur Company. The incontestable strength of Astor was revealed throughout the thirty articles which comprised the agreement. He was to manage all the business of the company. He was to advance all necessary funds, not to exceed $400,000. He was to bear all losses for the first five years. Profits were to be divided according to the number of shares held by each man.

A hundred shares were to be issued. Astor would get fifty of them, while fifteen would be reserved for the use of the company. Holding half of the shares, Astor undoubtedly felt that his control was assured, but it would have taken only one additional share . . . which might be issued to a dependable friend or a member of his family . . . to make his domination a certainty.

Astor retained the privilege of making his shares over to the American Fur Company under certain conditions, none of which appeared insuperable. The company's lifespan was set at twenty years, but after five years all losses as well as profits would be apportioned on the basis of the number of shares held by each partner.

Of the thirty-five remaining shares, McKay, McKenzie, Mc-Dougal, David Stuart, Hunt and Crooks received five each, and McClelan and Miller each got two and one-half shares.[4]

Measures to put Astor's great plan into full operation were immediately taken. It called for the dispatch of two major expeditions to the Northwest Coast. One was to go overland from St. Louis, following the route of Lewis and Clark. On the way, it was to select points at which trading posts might be advantageously established.

The other expedition was to go by sea from New York around Cape Horn in a vessel fully equipped and supplied for trade with Indians and for establishing a strong post, or fort, near the mouth of the Columbia River. Its name was to be Astoria.

The boldness of the plan was no greater than its significance. Its vitality could not then, and could not afterward, be overemphasized. One man was setting out to do what the American Government was not strong enough to do, and that was to conquer . . . not for his country, but for himself . . . an immense land few white men had ever seen, the boundaries of which had not been officially established, simply because its extent was not fully known.

One man was appointing himself arbiter of any international disputes which might arise. He alone was to be the antagonist of any foreign power with ambitions to acquire legally or through piratical actions a portion of the potential riches of the vast and untouched empire.

[4] Robert Stuart was to acquire a part of his uncle's interest at a later date.

4

When word of Astor's dynamic movements got out, the Canadians reacted with swift decisiveness.

For three years Astor's agents had been cutting deeply into the trade at Michilimackinac, and the Montrealers had tolerated it only because they saw no means of halting it. In the interim, cautious feelers extended by both sides had brought no results. Astor's pressure had continued to grow, and at the same time regulations promulgated by the United States authorities, largely at his instigation, had been strengthened. The difficulties of the Canadians were becoming insupportably manifold. The formation of the Pacific Fur Company was a blow that presaged disaster.

Even before the Astoria papers were completed, William Mc-Gillivray, president of the North West Company, and John Richardson, head of Forsyth, Richardson & Company, were in New York for the purpose of inducing Astor to purchase a share in the Michilimackinac Company. Astor delayed his decision. The disadvantages of such an arrangement were patently clear to him. It would have served to weaken his position in the Great Lakes region, but, more importantly, it would aid the Canadians in getting around the restrictions of the United States Government. Astor finally countered the proposal with an offer to buy the interests of the Michilimackinac Company which were on United States territory, but his terms were so astringent that Mc-Gillivray and Richardson scurried home to save what little blood remained in their business.

The Michilimackinac Company traders who resided on the island were despondent. In the summer of 1810, they abandoned hope, and sold out to two firms prominently associated with the

North West Company. These were McTavish, McGillivray & Company, and Forsyth, Richardson.

While the executives of these two concerns sought new ways of solving the problem, Astor took another step to force the Canadians to accept his terms. He let it be known that he had ordered an immense quantity of goods from England to be used specifically in the Great Lakes trade, and that he was increasing his force of agents in that area.

In the summer of 1810, Astor, of course, had heard nothing regarding the progress of the *Enterprise*, and he proceeded on the theory that all was well with the ship. A new Russian Minister, Count Frederic Petrovich Pahlen, had taken office in Washington, and Astor sent his son-in-law, Adrian Benjamin Bentzon, to the capital to win Pahlen's support for the plan formed in collaboration with Daschkoff. Bentzon was chosen for the mission because of his experience as a Danish diplomat and Governor of the island of Santa Cruz before the British took it over and ousted him.

Count Pahlen had no hesitancy in informing Bentzon that he was very much displeased with the way the Federal Government had failed to take stern measures against American adventurers in the North Pacific. Bentzon had a soothing explanation. A popular government . . . by that he meant a government controlled by the people . . . could never give Russia the satisfaction it demanded. However, a plan such as Astor was advocating had a good chance of succeeding in solving such a problem. Private enterprise often was stronger under the American system than the authorities, and it unquestionably was more efficient.

Count Pahlen seemed to be placated. He advised Bentzon that a final decision, of course, would have to be made in St. Petersburg by the head of the Russian American Fur Company and the Minister of Foreign Affairs, Count Nikolai Petrovitch Rumiantzoff. He suggested that Astor send an authorized agent to St. Petersburg with the full plan, to which he would attach his own recommendations. Count Rumiantzoff, Pahlen hinted, had no love for the British and would be favorably impressed by a program which would diminish British influence in the North Pacific.

Bentzon prepared for the trip. As a move toward that end, Astor wrote Secretary of the Treasury Gallatin for assistance. He asked Gallatin to persuade President Madison to write a letter to John Quincy Adams, the American Minister at St. Petersburg, requesting him to help the American Fur Company obtain an agreement with Russia, and he furnished Gallatin with an outline of the proposal.

Madison's refusal to place the government in Astor's camp was predicated on Astor's attempt to exclude all other American traders from doing business on the Northwest Coast, and to obtain an exclusive right to export American furs into Russian territory. The President did not propose to open himself to charges of granting a monopoly in any branch of American business. He was not averse, however, to instructing Adams to "promote the opening of the Russian market generally to articles which are now excluded, and which may be imported from the United States."

It was qualified encouragement, but Astor had no alternative but to be content with it. He applied to Gallatin for a passport for Bentzon and permission for his son-in-law and daughter Magdalen to sail on the official frigate, *John Adams*. The *John Adams* was being sent to Denmark for the express purpose of carrying George W. Erving, a special minister charged with pressing certain claims of the United States. Astor reinforced his request by casually mentioning that he and his wealthy friends might be of assistance to the Government in its difficulties over the charter of the Bank of the United States.

The Secretary of the Treasury took up the matter with the President, and Astor's request was honored.

When Bentzon boarded the *John Adams*, he gave the unmistakable impression that he was going to Russia on business vital to the American Government. It was a small ship. One stateroom was highly preferable for the accommodation of a man and wife. That stateroom had been assigned to the special minister, Erving, for whom the voyage had been scheduled in the first place.

Bentzon was so unyielding and unreasonable in his demands that Erving was ousted from his quarters. He never forgave Bentzon. So enduring was his wrath that later he was to write President Monroe warning him against any schemes that Astor or his arrogant son-in-law and impossible daughter might propose.

Bentzon was courteously received in St. Petersburg. The terms of the agreement were acceptable, with one exception. That was Astor's demand for the exclusive right to import American furs into Russia. In objecting, Count Rumiantzoff declared that giving Astor such a right would violate the monopoly held by the Russian-American Fur Company.

Bentzon capitulated, and an agreement was signed with the sanction of the Russian Government. It said in part that "the two companies bound themselves not to interfere with each other's trading and hunting grounds, nor to furnish arms and ammunition to the Indians. They were to act in concert, also, against all interlopers, and to succor each other in case of danger. The American company was to have the exclusive right of supplying the Russian posts with goods and necessaries, receiving peltries in payment at stated prices. They were also, if requested by the Russian governor, to convey the furs of the Russian company to Canton, sell them on commission, and bring back the proceeds, at such freight charges as might be agreed upon at the time. This agreement was to continue in operation four years, and to be renewable for a similar term, unless some unforeseen contingency should render a modification necessary."

It was a major victory for Astor. The provision referring to "interlopers" was especially gratifying to him. *Interlopers*, under his definition, meant nothing else but the Hudson's Bay and the North West Companies, whose covetous eyes, he well knew, were focused on the northwestern United States and western Canada. The failure to secure an exclusive right to import American furs into Russia had been a small concession to make in the light of the other benefits.

5

In the fall of 1810, Astor had somehow found time to make his annual trip to Montreal. It availed him nothing concrete. As worried and discouraged as they were, the Canadians were cordial and hospitable. Astor was a guest of the Beaver Club at a dinner given in Dillon's Hotel on October 6. At no time during his stay did the traders permit their irritation and fear of Astor's known plans to get the better of their prudence.

The new year of 1811 had hardly begun, however, when the situation was drastically changed. Both sides had adopted new attitudes, but for different reasons. Peculiarly enough, the result was to be that while the North West Company and the American Fur Company were to be bitter rivals in the Far West, they were to be allies in the region of the Great Lakes.

The two firms which had purchased the Michilimackinac Company, appending Montreal to its name, had come to the conclusion that Astor's enormous capital, which came from both the fur trade and his commerce with China; his advantage as an American citizen; and his incomparable shrewdness, comprised a force too formidable to combat in open competition. They sent William McGillivray to New York with instructions to conclude an agreement with Astor virtually on his own terms.

McGillivray not only represented the two companies, but also the North West Company. Thus, the forces and the resources of almost all of the Canadian fur trade, excluding the Hudson's Bay Company, were embodied in the man who sat in the new Astor headquarters at 69 Pine Street.

Astor concealed the fact that he himself was anxious to come to an understanding, and would have made important concessions to achieve it at once. He also kept hidden the reason for this reversal of attitude. The reason was that he was deeply concerned by the state of relations between the United States and Great Britain. In the past months they had steadily worsened to a point where they were cause for serious alarm. While he fervently hoped that an open conflict would by some means be prevented, he was realistic enough to understand that the outlook gave little promise that such a tragedy would not come in due time.

He and McGillivray sparred adroitly, but never allowed a stalemate to be reached. On January 28, they found themselves in accord.

The agreement they signed gave birth to a Canadian-American organization to be known as the South West Fur Company. Their reasons for establishing it were clearly stated. Some of the goods needed for the Indian trade could be most readily secured through New York, others through Montreal. If there were two companies in opposition to each other in the Great Lakes area, both would suffer handicaps that could be eliminated by a single organization.

The South West Fur Company was to operate for a minimum of five years, unless dissolved by mutual consent. Astor and the Canadian partners would each bear half the expenses and receive half the profits. A provision stated that in the event the trading houses established by the United States Government should be abolished, Astor was to bear two-thirds of the expenses and receive two-thirds of the profits. The basis for this provision was that with the discontinuance of the government factories, a larger share of the trade on American territory would automatically go to independent American traders.

The most important provision of all, as far as Astor was concerned, involved the position of the North West Company. Under the terms agreed upon, for the year 1811 the South West Fur Company would take the place of the Montreal Michilimackinac Company in its relations with its parent, the North West Company. After 1811, the North West Company was to abandon every post and surrender every interest it held in territory belonging to the United States. In return for this concession, the South

West Fur Company agreed not to trade in the part of the Lake Huron area which was not within the limits of North West Company posts. These territorial limitations did not extend "to any Countries beyond the ridge of the Rockey Mountains nor the river Missouri nor to the North West Coast or in the Pacific Ocean."

One other provision was significant. It permitted the North West Company to acquire an interest in the South West Fur Company in the maximum amount of one-third of the 50 per cent owned by the two Montreal firms. Only a few weeks had passed before the North West Company exercised this right.

In a strict analysis it was a pact highly favorable to Astor. Once more he had accomplished alone what the United States Government had not been able to do. He had brought peace to the fur trade of the Old Northwest Territory . . . indeed for him a very desirable and lucrative peace.

6

Three events occurring in 1810 gave Astor cause to celebrate. John Jacob Bentzon, his first grandchild, was born. The overland expedition to the Columbia River got under way. The *Tonquin*, inaugurating his conquest of the fur trade in the Far Northwest by sea, sailed from New York.

Astor's choice of commanders for the two expeditions was inexplicable, and reflected on his ability as a judge of men. His experience in the fur trade was great, his competence and shrewdness as a businessman were beyond question. Yet, his orders pertaining to field operations revealed an astonishing lack of understanding of the problems to be faced. The result was to be disaster on all fronts.

The Pacific Fur Company partner Donald McKenzie was a veteran Indian trader. For more than ten years he had been in the service of the North West Company. He was fully seasoned to the hardships of the wilderness. His training and ability as a fur hunter, his knowledge of Indians were outstanding. He was rough, uncouth and not above being unscrupulous in his dealings with both white and red men. He was a man of many moods, and these moods influenced both his personal loyalties and his enmities. Hatred and vengeance were as quick to rise in him as admiration and kindness, but in such practical matters as survival and warfare he was without a peer.

The value of Wilson Price Hunt as a partner rested in two categories. He was scrupulously upright, amiable and he had the manners of a gentleman. He was a competent merchant and businessman. For some time he had been connected with St. Louis firms which supplied traders, but he had never ventured very far into the wilderness. Therefore, his knowledge of the Indian trade and of the countries in which the various tribes lived had come to him at second hand.

Perhaps because Astor thought the favorable qualities of one would counterbalance the deficiencies of the other, he decided the two men should share in the command of the overland expedition. It was an error in judgment that no experienced and competent field general would have made.

Early in 1810, Hunt joined McKenzie in Montreal to prepare for the journey. They failed to acquire all the men and supplies they wanted largely because North West Company agents induced some merchants not to sell the Astor corporation any goods and discouraged Canadian *voyageurs* from joining it. Liberal terms, however, at last secured enough men and supplies for a start, and the company set out from La Chine on July 5.

Hunt was both disappointed and appalled by the situation. He had seen for the first time the resentment of Astor . . . really in some cases genuine hatred . . . in the Canadians. Also it was the first time he had encountered the *voyageurs* on their home ground, the few he had known in St. Louis having been working far afield and displaying the obedience and diligence they customarily displayed in the wilderness.

Progress was slow and difficult. The men seemed to sense Hunt's inexperience, and took advantage of it. They sought every few miles to land, build a fire, brew a pot of tea, smoke, chat and sing. The first leg of the trip, to Mackinac Island, required seventeen days.

On the island they gave themselves over to frolicking, drinking, whoring and dancing, interspersed with confession. McKenzie wore a sour countenance and said nothing, allowing Hunt to face alone the problem and the task of employing additional *voyageurs*. There were a number of unengaged men on hand, but for several days Hunt's efforts to enlist them were futile. Those with whom he spoke merely shook their heads and wandered away along the beach before the crude log buildings of the famous post. A few of them frankly admitted they did not want to go into a country that was unexplored.

By a generous offer, Hunt at last managed to engage an influential *voyageur*, and he, like a Judas goat, helped to decoy others into the fold. But this was not easily accomplished, even with the payment of substantial advances on their wages. The advances were squandered overnight, and the men who had received them appeared with pitiful tales of how they were being prevented from going by obligations of various kinds. Some of them had forgotten that they had made previous commitments to other companies, and these could be discharged only by "reasonable considerations." Hunt paid the "considerations," but none of them were reasonable. For one man he paid a court fine. Another he relieved of a judgment. Others owed bills for goods and liquor which had to be settled before they were free to depart.

Ramsay Crooks, another partner, appeared to join the expedition, and it was he who came to Hunt's rescue with a trick that solved the recruiting problem.

Crooks was experienced and intelligent. Born in Scotland, he had immigrated to Canada at the age of sixteen. He had been sent to Mackinac Island as a clerk, and after a year's service there had gone to St. Louis. In 1807, as an associate of Robert Mc-Clelan, he engaged in the trade with Missouri River tribes.

Shortly after Crooks reached Michilimackinac, Hunt succeeded in hiring the desired number of men. This was accomplished by the simple means of offering bright feathers, brassy ornaments, and other doodads, as inducements to enlist. A voyageur could no more resist such gaudy decorations than could an Indian. Mc-Kenzie could have told Hunt that, but he had not done it.

On August 17, thirty voyageurs and the three partners began working their way through the dangerous waters of northern Lake Michigan toward Green Bay. From Green Bay their route took them up the Fox River, down the Wisconsin to Prairie du Chien, and down the Mississippi to St. Louis.

St. Louis presented a different scene, but no fewer problems. Hunt wanted to increase the company to sixty voyageurs. The majority of the Canadians loitering about the streets, the Vide Pouche and the Rue Principale, had already pledged their services for the next year to Manuel Lisa and the Missouri Fur Company.

St. Louis was on the verge of the boom that was in a short time to make it the fur-trading capital of the West. It was filled with a conglomerate population, Canadian voyageurs, Mississippi boatmen of several nationalities, Kentucky and Virginia hunters, soldiers, and Indians of various tribes. Enterprising American shopkeepers were beginning to establish emporiums of numerous kinds, and new brick and stone buildings were rising among the dignified old French houses with their open casements and spacious gardens. Billiard parlors, saloons and brothels were doing a good business day and night, and for the first time in its history the old frontier settlement knew a serious crime rate.

The entrance of Astor, with all his money and prestige, into the trans-Mississippi fur trade brought instant and strong resentment from St. Louis traders. They made an effort, as had the houses in Montreal and Michilimackinac, to thwart Hunt's efforts to obtain supplies, guns, ammunition and *voyageurs*. Once again, it was another partner who stepped into the breach and relieved Hunt's difficulties.

He was Joseph Miller, a wilderness Indian trader of wide experience and great ability. Miller's popularity with the leading St. Louis traders made it possible for Hunt to acquire both the men and the supplies needed. Not the least important of these was a good keelboat and a large barge to carry the tons of cargo which the company required for such a long journey.

Fall was at hand, and within a few weeks the upper Missouri would be closed to travel by ice, but Hunt was determined to avoid the great expense and trouble of wintering the expedition in St. Louis. He announced that they would push up the river as far as possible before cold weather stopped them, after which they would set up winter quarters.

The departure was made on October 21. For nearly four weeks they paddled, poled and hauled their boats steadily up the Missouri, covering in that time about 450 miles. Even in the season of comparatively low water it was a strenuous and perilous trip. Great snags frequently obstructed the way, and floating trees were a constant danger.

Under the adverse circumstances the value of the Canadian *voyageurs* was amply demonstrated. They seemed never to be disheartened by hardship. They bent to their backbreaking oars hour after hour, cheering themselves with filthy stories of strumpets, red, white and black, they had known, or with bursts of song. They laughed in the cold water, joked about their own weaknesses and their wounds. They danced and sang about the campfires at night, and recounted terrible experiences with ghosts and their wild and narrow escapes from death at the hands of Indians.

On November 16, the company reached the mouth of a small stream called the Nadowa, a short distance above the site of the present city of St. Joseph, Missouri. There they began to build log and earth shelters for their winter quarters. The decision to stop had been made none too soon, for on the second day after their arrival at Nadowa Creek the river was choked with ice.

Idleness and the prospect of long and dreary months in isolation brought from some of the partners and the American hunters unpleasant remarks. The essence of their criticisms was that if McKenzie had been in complete charge of the company from the time it was organized in Montreal, it would then be on the headwaters of the Columbia instead of on the lower Missouri, scarcely beyond the frontier. McKenzie had been trained in the swift operations of the North West Company brigades, and he would have solved promptly the problems which had baffled Hunt.

Two men who were to play important roles with the company rode into the camp at Nadowa. One of them was the partner Robert McClelan, and the other was the Virginian John Day.

McClelan had served with distinction under Gen. Anthony Wayne in campaigns against the Indians. Moving westward, he had become an associate of Crooks in the Missouri River trade. He was a man of iron nerve and fiery spirit, and sometimes of ungovernable temper. As a result of nasty experiences he and Crooks had once suffered at the hands of the Sioux . . . for which he blamed Manuel Lisa . . . he held an abiding hatred for that tribe, and it was his hope that he would have an opportunity for revenge against both the Indians and the Spanish trader.

John Day joined the company as a meat hunter. He had for several years been employed in such a capacity, and as a trapper, by several St. Louis companies. Forty years of age, he stood well over six feet, walked, dressed and thought as an Indian.

McClelan had brought several letters for Hunt from Astor. One of them contained instructions which were to have a vital bearing on the conduct and success of the expedition.

Astor ordered Hunt to assume full command on the overland journey. McKenzie was divested of his authority. What brought about this reversal of his original plan, Astor did not reveal. It was, however, one of the most serious mistakes he ever made.

When he was shown the letter, McKenzie became furious. He

stated in blasphemous words that he considered the order not only a personal affront but a violation of his agreement with Astor.

If the harmony of the partners had been disturbed previously, it was now dangerously strained and near a breaking point. Hunt decided that it would be wise for him to return to St. Louis and send dispatches to Astor regarding the progress and condition of the company. He also wanted, if possible, to obtain the services of a Sioux interpreter. This appeared to be extremely sensible after he had learned of the attitudes of Crooks and McClelan toward those Indians.

Hunt, traveling by horseback, reached St. Louis on January 20. He was approached at once by two British scientists who asked permission to travel with the Astor brigade for some distance up the Missouri. They were John Bradbury, a naturalist sent out by the Linnean Society of Liverpool, and Thomas Nuttall, a botanist and writer, who had come out to make a collection of American wilderness plants. Hunt agreed to take them as far as the Mandan Villages, where in the late summer or early fall they probably would meet traders descending the river with whom they could return to St. Louis.[5]

The problem of securing the services of a competent Sioux interpreter was not easily solved. Hunt learned there was only one man in St. Louis at the time who could qualify for the post. He was a half-breed named Pierre Dorion, a son of the Dorion who had been an interpreter for Lewis and Clark.

The previous year, Pierre Dorion had worked for Manuel Lisa.

[5] Bradbury and Nuttall were intrepid, brave, and noted authorities in their respective fields. They were to write famous books about their travels in the West. For the ignorant *voyageurs* they were a constant source of amusement. A story is told of how Nuttall, when suddenly surrounded by 300 unfriendly Arikara Indians, turned to one of the white partners and said calmly: "Sir, don't you think these Indians much fatter, and more robust than those of yesterday?" Nuttall was called *"le fou"* (the fool) by the *voyageurs*. No sooner would his boat touch shore than he would leap out and go scrambling about in an examination of the vegetation. Both he and Bradbury would wander off in the face of dangers that would have given a mountain man pause. More than once they got lost. *"Où est le fou?"* the boatmen would ask with laughter. The answer would come: *"Il est après ramasser des racines."* (He is gathering roots.)

He had proved himself not only an able linguist but a notorious drunk. While he had been with Lisa among the Mandans, his great craving had manifested itself to an extent that was insupportable. The only whisky to be had was that which Lisa had brought upriver for the trade, and he did not propose to waste it in the gullet of an alcoholic half-breed. When Dorion's demands became unbearable, Lisa opened his stock. He charged Dorion at the rate of ten dollars a quart, and the interpreter soon succeeded in running up a big bill.

When Dorion returned to St. Louis, he refused to pay the extortionate price, and a furious argument ensued. It was still in progress when Hunt arrived from Nadowa.

Apprised that Hunt was trying to lure Dorion away from him, Lisa's wrath rose to great heights. His company had met with some severe reversals, and he was in no mood to have his problems complicated by an Astor agent. He demanded that Dorion sign an agreement to work for him during the coming season. Dorion ignored him, and accepted a liberal offer from Hunt.

Hunt also secured the services of several more hunters and *voyageurs*, and bought a boat in which to travel up to Nadowa as soon as the weather permitted. This condition did not occur until early in March. Hunt set the departure for March 12, but when on that date the boat was fully loaded and ready to leave, Bradbury and Nuttall announced their intention to wait for the next day's post from the East. They would take horses and catch up to the boat as it passed St. Charles, a village a short distance above the Missouri's mouth.

Moreover, Dorion arrived at the wharf with his squaw and two children, and refused to leave without them. Hunt at last gave in to both requests, and the boat put off.

During the evening, Bradbury and Nuttall learned that Lisa had secured a writ for Dorion, charging an attempt to escape payment of just debts. A deputy was to be sent to intercept the boat at St. Charles and arrest the interpreter.

At midnight, Bradbury and Nuttall, their loyalty to Hunt being greater than their need to wait for the next day's mail, took horses and set off across country. They reached the boat before it came into St. Charles, and Dorion was informed of Lisa's intentions.

Pierre wasted not a moment in landing and taking to the woods. His squaw, staggering under two small children and a great bundle containing the family's worldly possessions, quickly followed in his wake.

When the boat reached St. Charles the deputy boarded, but Dorion was not to be found, and no one seemed to know what had happened to him. The deputy returned to shore and suspiciously watched the boat pass out of sight around a bend of the river.

Dorion had already received half a year's wages, and Hunt sadly concluded that not only was the interpreter gone for good but the money as well. He was delighted and relieved when the lookout sighted Dorion waiting on a point of land a short distance ahead, with his little family gathered about him.

En route to Nadowa, the boat touched the French hamlet La Charette. Among the villagers who came to meet it was an old man named Daniel Boone. Still keeping in advance of civilization, the famous pathfinder, at seventy-seven, recently had returned from a trapping trip with sixty prime beaver pelts. He stood erect, sadness in his keen eyes as he watched the Astorians move away on their journey into an unknown country, obviously full of regret that he could not go with them.

On the next day, Bradbury had an opportunity to talk at length with another great explorer and mountain man, John Colter, who resided on a small wilderness farm. He was to give the world the story of Colter's incomparable western discoveries and adventures.

On April 8, Hunt's boat passed Fort Osage, a post standing about forty miles below the present site of Kansas City. Crooks and several men were awaiting it there, and the two parties went on together.

Full spring was in the air, and the river was rising. Heavy rains fell. The bodies of drowned buffalo floated past them in great numbers. Immense flocks of turkey buzzards fed on the carcasses rotting along the banks, while others constantly watched the boat, wheeling majestically high overhead on great wings that seemed not to move at all . . . birds with all the majesty of an eagle in flight, and on land disgusting, revolting in appearance and loathsome in their stench.

Bradbury was delighted to find the snakes emerging from their winter torpor, and collected a number. Enormous flocks of passenger pigeons filled the air. They appeared "absolutely in clouds." They moved "with astonishing velocity, their wings making a whistling sound . . . wheeling and shifting suddenly as if with one mind and one impulse . . . If suddenly startled while feeding . . . the noise they make in getting on the wing is like the roar of a cataract or the sound of distant thunder." Bradbury shot more than three hundred with a fowling piece one morning, and the company enjoyed a hearty meal from them.

The winter quarters at Nadowa were reached on April 17. Four days later the expedition pushed out into the current of the Missouri. The Columbia was still more than three thousand miles away.

Hunt did not know that Manuel Lisa already had left St. Louis in pursuit of him.

It was not for the purpose of recapturing the renegade Dorion that Lisa had set out. Lisa was going north to collect furs taken during the winter by his trappers, and especially to learn the fate of a group of his men, led by the redoubtable Andrew Henry, which had been driven from their trapping grounds at the Three Forks of the Missouri and had moved westward across the Continental Divide to escape the ravages of the implacable Blackfeet.

Lisa fully understood the dangers of passing through the Sioux, and he wanted to overtake Hunt so that the two companies, comprising a formidable force which any number of Indians would hesitate to attack, might make the most perilous part of the trip up the river together.

When Lisa left St. Charles, Hunt was nineteen days and 240

miles ahead of him. Lisa's drive to catch the Astorians was the most remarkable keelboat trip ever to take place on the Missouri.

7

On September 8, 1810, the sea wing of the great venture, counterpart of the overland expedition, was started.

The *Tonquin*, carrying partners who already were disloyal to Astor, and commanded by a fool, sailed from New York.

Astor's selection of Jonathan Thorn as captain of the ship, however, had been based on sound deductions. Relations between the United States and England were becoming more strained each day. The conservatives with pacific views were being driven from office by younger men, many from the Middle West, who had no patience with a peace policy. They were called the War Hawks, and they were especially aroused by the resistance of the Indians to the advance of white settlement. The people generally seemed to be convinced that this resistance was inspired and supported by Canada, and there were increasing cries for a war with England.

Thorn was a naval officer on leave. He was a veteran of the war with Tripoli, in which his courage and his ability to command a warship had been thoroughly established. Astor believed that Thorn's training and experience in battle would be invaluable in the event the *Tonquin* ran afoul of an armed privateer or a British man-of-war.

The *Tonquin* was a fine ship, of 300 tons, mounting twelve guns, and carrying a crew of twenty-one. Under Thorn's command, she undoubtedly would have given a good account of herself in an engagement.

Astor, however, saw no advantage in giving Thorn an opportunity to demonstrate his ability as a seafighter, and when he heard that an armed brig from Halifax was believed to be lurking off the New Jersey coast, he applied to the Navy for protection. The Halifax vessel, according to rumor, had been sent by the North West Company specifically to intercept the *Tonquin* and disrupt the progress of Astor's enterprise. Washington acted promptly, apprising the Navy commandant at New York that the Government held a deep interest in the expedition. The United States frigate *Constitution* was ordered to escort the *Tonquin* down the coast.

Astor had spared neither expense nor careful thought in loading the *Tonquin*. She carried a capacity cargo of merchandise, equipment, stores and ammunition for the establishment of a permanent fortified post on the Columbia. In addition to small craft for river travel, the frame of a schooner to be used in coastal waters had been stowed aboard. Quantities of seeds were sent so that the colony might in the first year enjoy fresh vegetables and grain.

The partners assigned to sail on the *Tonquin* were Alexander McKay, Duncan McDougal and David and Robert Stuart. With them went eleven clerks, thirteen Canadian *voyageurs* and five mechanics. As he had done when Captain Ebbets departed in the *Enterprise*, Astor gave Thorn and the partners long and detailed instructions. There was no reason or need for secret orders this time, and, indeed, the only duplicity that existed was in the minds of the men in whom Astor had placed an unqualified trust.

Before sailing, two of the partners, McKay and McDougal, called on Francis James Jackson, the British Minister. They gave Jackson the full plans of the Pacific Fur Company, the purpose of the *Tonquin's* voyage, the equipment shipped, and asked for instructions to be followed in case of war. Jackson informed them that in such a case they would be "respected as British subjects and traders." The minister expressed his "surprise and admiration . . . that a private individual should have conceived and set on foot at his own risk and expense, so great an enterprise." One man was setting out to gain control of a land several times the size of Europe.

While Astor did not learn of the secret conference between the British minister and his two partners until after the *Tonquin* had left, he may have suspected that something like it was afoot. This was indicated in his suggestion that inasmuch as the Canadians were to be connected with the Pacific Fur Company for some years, all of them should take an oath to become naturalized American citizens. Neither the Canadian partners nor the *voyageurs* voiced objections, and a few days later Astor was informed that they had complied with his suggestion. This, of course, had not been done, but neither was this deception disclosed to Astor until the *Tonquin* was well at sea.

Astor's parting letters to his associates enjoined them "in the most earnest manner, to cultivate harmony and unanimity, and recommended that all differences of opinions . . . should be discussed by the whole, and decided by a majority of votes." He especially cautioned them "as to their conduct on arriving at their destined port; exhorting them to be careful to make a favorable impression upon the wild people among whom their lot and the fortunes of the enterprise would be cast." He wrote: "If you find them kind, as I hope you will, be so to them. If otherwise, act with caution and forbearance, and convince them that you come as friends."

The injunction containing these democratic expressions and high principles went overboard at once.

In his orders to the captain, Astor admonished Thorn to give the "strictest attention to the health of himself and his crew, and to the promotion of good-humor and harmony on board his ship." Emphatically Astor told Thorn: "I must recommend you to be particularly careful on the coast, and not to rely too much on the friendly disposition of the natives. All accidents which have as yet happened there arose from too much confidence in the Indians."

The significance of these words was soon to be realized, but not by Jonathan Thorn. He forgot them as fast as he read them.

Numerous adjectives were used to describe Captain Thorn by his passengers, but if each was applicable, not one was complimentary. Aside from admitting that he was a skilled navigator, no one uttered a word in his favor. Even his blind loyalty to his employer, ordinarily considered a commendable quality, was seen as reflecting pathetic ignorance and a complete lack of understanding of the enormous scope and importance of the Astoria undertaking. Every view he held was limited by the confines of his ship; anything beyond that small world was out of his sphere, and therefore of no moment. Anything that interfered with his routine duties, even a passing thought or a casual word, infuriated him.

He stared down from the quarter-deck on his passengers with surly contempt, seeing them as unkempt braggarts, undisciplined backwoodsmen who would sit down to a stew of dog with filthy Indians, as disgusting landlubbers without property or pride who were living at the expense of a rich man.

Thorn lumped partners, clerks, *voyageurs* and mechanics together on a single low level, finding additional confirmation of their degradation in their jovial attitudes, their gaiety, their camaraderie. He completely abhorred the spectacle of the elder Stuart and a group of *voyageurs* sitting on the deck, as if around a campfire, laughing and gossiping while passing a pipe from mouth to mouth in the manner of Indians. He appeared to struggle with his temper whenever the company broke into songs of the wilderness, and he could only stare in utter amazement when some of them danced to the tune of a sour fiddle and the clapping of hands.

He refused to associate socially with the partners, but he disdained even to speak in a friendly or informal manner to the clerks. He chose to ignore the fact, if he were aware of it, that all eleven of them were young men of good families going out for a hundred dollars a year to serve a hard apprenticeship in the wilderness fur trade. Their high spirits and curiosity aggravated him. The desire to flog them was reflected in his eyes.

The antics, customs and appearances of the *voyageurs* stirred a terrible loathing in Thorn. He was not only unsympathetic but furious when any of them suffered the horrors of seasickness. He cursed them for remaining below in their berths in a squalid state, and he cursed them when they appeared "like spectres from the hatchways, in capotes and blankets, with dirty nightcaps . . . shivering about the deck, and ever and anon crawling to the sides of the vessel, and offering up their tributes to the windward . . ." But more than anything else, the French patois of the *voyageurs* and the Gaelic which the Scotsmen spoke when they did not wish him to overhear them threw him into an almost uncontrollable rage.

From the time the anchor was weighed, Thorn sought to impose upon the passengers the stern regulations and discipline of a naval vessel. His order that all lights were to be extinguished at 8 P.M. brought a scene indicative of the troubles to come. The partners considered the command an invasion of their personal rights. They reminded Thorn that he was working for them, and that they were on their own ship. The argument became furious, and Thorn thundered that unless he was obeyed, the partners would be clapped in irons. This was an insult McDougal could not bear. He was an "irritable, fuming, vainglorious little man," who held an inflated opinion of himself, and he promptly drew a pistol. Bloodshed was averted only by the quick actions of cooler heads.

Bitterness, hatred, resentment and hostility continued unabated, however, as the *Tonquin* moved into the tropics. These emotions were manifested in various ways, but did not reach a stage of violence until the Falkland Islands came into view. Captain Thorn announced that a stop would be made for repairs and to obtain a supply of fresh water. Joyously the landlubbers went ashore. They swam, hunted and explored. When a signal came from the ship for them to return, they were slow in obeying it. Infuriated, Thorn ordered sail raised, and the *Tonquin* stood out from the harbor.

The shore party consisted of McDougal, McKay, David Stuart, and five clerks. Seeing the ship moving off, they all leaped into their boat and set out in pursuit. Thorn swore that he would leave them behind, and it was "in vain that those on board made remonstrances and entreaties, and represented the horrors of abandoning men upon a sterile and uninhabited land . . ."

The eight men in the small boat bent to the oars, but they were unable to gain on the ship. After more than three hours had passed they obviously were becoming exhausted and were beginning to fall far behind.

It was more than Robert Stuart could endure any longer. Taking a gun, he charged up to the bridge. What happened at that moment was construed by several witnesses as Divine Providence. The wind suddenly died. The *Tonquin* began to wallow in the seas. Within a short time the small boat had come alongside, and the badly frightened men clambored aboard.

After this incident not even a pretense of good will could be maintained. The partners spoke exclusively in Gaelic, and the *voyageurs* employed French whenever they were within earshot of the captain. This led Thorn to conclude that a conspiracy to seize control of the vessel was in the making, and he kept a strong guard about himself night and day.

The *Tonquin* doubled Cape Horn on Christmas, and struck out across the Pacific. On the 11th of February, 1811, she dropped anchor in a small bay on the island of Hawaii.

The sailors began at once to desert. Most of them were brought back, flogged and thrown into the brig. For the good of the expedition, the Canadians submerged their feelings. They volunteered to stand guard to prevent more desertions and to serve as crewmen.

Green vegetables were obtained at Hawaii, but pork was unavailable due to a proclamation forbidding its sale to anyone except the king. The *Tonquin* was moved to Oahu, the residence of the royal family, anchoring in Honolulu Harbor on February

21. The company was hospitably received by the sovereign, and the meat they sought was sold to them.

On February 27, Thorn once more displayed his sadistic tendencies. Two sailors who overstayed their shore leave by fifteen minutes were brutally flogged and put in irons. A third who remained absent overnight was beaten unconscious, and thrown overboard to drown. Some natives rescued him, and he was left behind.

It was on March 1, that the *Tonquin* put out to sea for the Columbia River. The weather became severe. When the partners attempted to obtain warm clothing from the cargo for themselves and the crew, Captain Thorn drove them away with a pistol. Astor's cargo would not be touched, he declared, until it had been delivered to its destination and was taken out of his hands.

Cape Disappointment, a promontory on the north side of the Columbia River, was sighted on March 22. Here Thorn branded himself forever as a stupid and incompetent commander.

He was fully aware of the navigational dangers in the wild and tempestuous entrance to the great river of the West. When the *Tonquin* arrived, it was in vicious flood. No one but a madman would have attempted to sound for the channel in the raging waters. Thorn was that madman. In the face of pleas from his own officers, he ordered the first mate, Mr. Fox, to take a whaleboat and find a passage for the ship. John Martin, an old seaman who had previously visited the coast, was to accompany Fox. Thorn also ordered three *voyageurs* to go along as a crew. When Fox asked that experienced sailors be sent to handle the oars, Thorn replied that they could not be spared. Besides, he said with a sneer, the *voyageurs* were supposed to be experts on water. Let them demonstrate their vaunted skill.

According to Washington Irving, who had access to official Astor papers, Fox had a premonition of death, and he appealed for help from the partners, telling them with tears in his eyes: "I am sent off without seamen to man my boat, in boisterous weather, and on the most dangerous part of the north-west coast.

My uncle was lost a few years ago on this same bar, and I am now going to lay my bones alongside of his." Thorn's reply to an appeal from the Canadians was that Fox was a coward.

The five men moved away into the mists that hung over the rough and treacherous entrance. They were never seen again.

Captain Thorn appeared to be unconcerned by the loss. The next morning he ordered a second boat dispatched. McKay and David Stuart volunteered to go in it, but only because they hoped to find the lost *voyageurs*. Wind and tide conspired to prevent them from reaching shore, and they got back to the ship only after several close brushes with disaster.

Undaunted, Thorn sent out a third boat under the command of the second mate, Mr. Mumford. It accomplished nothing, and was almost capsized by breakers before making a safe return.

His disgust and aggravation mounting, Thorn ordered out a fourth boat. In it he sent Mr. Aiken, a navigator; John Coles, a sailmaker; Stephen Weeks, an armorer; and two Sandwich Islanders who had been signed on at Oahu. It, too, vanished.

A wild night of wind and raging ebb tide descended, and the *Tonquin* came close to drifting to destruction on rocky reefs. Toward daylight, the weather improved, and with a flood tide and a more favorable wind, she crossed the bar after scraping her keel several times.

Shore parties immediately began to search for the missing men. They came across Weeks and a badly injured Hawaiian. The other eight had perished.

The *Tonquin* was anchored in Baker's Bay, and as if he had completely forgotten the terrible toll of his criminal negligence, Thorn impatiently demanded that the site for the post be selected at once, as he was anxious to begin unloading. The Canadians, however, understood the importance of locating the fort in a strategic place, suitable for both trade and defense. They refused to be hurried, and began a systematic examination of the surrounding countryside.

At the end of three days, Thorn refused to wait longer. He ordered a shed erected on shore. As soon as it was ready, he began to move merchandise and equipment into it. The Canadians could continue their wasteful "sporting excursions" about the woods if they wished, but he would not be a party to such delinquency.

Thorn's arbitrary actions forced the partners to settle on a site they felt to be unsatisfactory in several respects. It was on the south side of the bay, and although it had some drawbacks, it did overlook a good harbor in which ships could anchor within fifty yards of the shore. Thorn moved the *Tonquin* there, and continued to unload. He retained aboard a large manifest of merchandise to be used in trading with the Indians northward along the coast.

With Astoria well on its way to completion . . . the foundations of the buildings were in place by May 18 . . . Thorn left to carry out his assigned mission of securing furs from the coastal tribes. McKay, wise in the ways of the red people and a veteran of the trade, sailed as supercargo. At Gray's Harbor an Indian named Lamazee was picked up from a fishing canoe. He proved to have ability as an interpreter, having learned some English from previous traders, and he was taken along in that capacity.

About a week later Thorn dropped anchor at Nootka Sound against the advice of Lamazee. The natives in the area, warned the interpreter, were treacherous and hated the white men. They had taken the lives of several traders. Thorn ignored the warning.

Daylight the following morning brought scores of Indians from shore in canoes loaded with the valuable sea otter skins. With the attitude of a small-town merchant in the safety of civilization, Thorn arranged tempting displays of blankets, cloths, knives, beads, fishhooks and other goods on the main deck. As the Indians swarmed on board, he stated the prices of the articles displayed. He was a little amazed to hear the Indians laugh and to speak with scorn of his offerings.

The Indians were willing to bargain, but Thorn abruptly refused. His utter contempt for them was made clear in his gestures and words.

McKay protested against permitting so many natives on the

ship at one time, but Thorn only waved him to silence. His face sullen, his hands thrust in his pockets, the captain paced the deck demanding that his offers be accepted. The bantering of an old chief seemed to be more than he could endure. Snatching up an otter skin, he struck the old man in the face with it, and had him thrown off the ship. He then kicked the furs to right and left as he stamped from sight. The trade ended, the Indians departing with their pelts.

Once again the interpreter advised Thorn to move the ship to safer waters. Once again McKay advised against permitting the Indians on board in large numbers. Once again Thorn ignored them. He considered as ridiculous the thought that naked savages would dare to attack in the face of the cannon and firearms on the *Tonquin*. Thorn went to bed, leaving only the usual watch on deck.

At daybreak the Indians were back with even greater numbers of skins. They carried no visible arms, but Lamazee called McKay's attention to the fact that many of them were wearing short "mantles of skins," and he expressed the belief weapons were concealed beneath them. McKay informed Thorn of the interpreter's suspicion. Thorn made light of it, but as the Indians continued to pour over the rail, concern began to show in his face. He ordered some men aloft to make sail, and told others to weigh the anchor. The Indians, observing Thorn's preparations to depart, quickly offered to accept his terms, and a brisk trade began. When the anchor was partially raised, and the sails were loose, Thorn, his apprehension increasing, ordered the deck cleared.

He had waited too long. As if at a silent signal, wild cries arose, knives and war clubs appeared like magic in the hands of the Indians, and they fell upon the white men.

Within a few minutes, Thorn, McKay, and sixteen members of the crew had been butchered. They all died bravely, leaving dead and wounded Indians scattered over the blood-smeared deck. Five crewmen, among them the badly hurt ship's clerk, a Mr. Lewis, had managed to barricade themselves in a cabin. They held out for the remainder of the day and through the night, sending a strong musket fire at any Indian who came within their sight.

At dawn Mr. Lewis cautiously emerged on deck to find the ship deserted. Its partially raised anchor had caught, and the *Tonquin* floated serenely on smooth water, its sails loosely flapping in a slight breeze. Several canoes containing Indians began to circle the ship, and Mr. Lewis signaled to them to come aboard, making the signs of welcome and peace. Then he disappeared.

Within a short time the deck once again was crowded with Indians, and they began to poke into the interior of their great prize. Lamazee, the interpreter, was among them.

Suddenly the *Tonquin* was lifted out of the water by a tremendous explosion.

Washington Irving, quoting from a Pacific Fur Company report, was to describe the scene this way: "Arms, legs and mutilated bodies were blown into the air, and dreadful havoc was made in the surrounding canoes. The interpreter was in the main chains at the time of the explosion, and was thrown unhurt into the water . . . According to his statement, the bay presented an awful spectacle after the catastrophe. The ship had disappeared . . . Upwards of a hundred savages were destroyed . . . many more shockingly mutilated, and for days afterwards the limbs and bodies of the slain were thrown upon the beach."

It was the interpeter who told also how four of the five men barricaded in the cabin had slipped away from the ship under cover of darkness in a small boat. Mr. Lewis, knowing he could not live, had declined to go with them. The four crewmen were captured by the Indians while they slept in a small cove into which the wind had driven them. They were tortured to death.

It was presumed that Mr. Lewis, his own life seeping from his body, fired the ship's magazine after enticing the Indians on board. If he derived any satisfaction in performing his heroic act, it was not to be known.

"Such," as Washington Irving said, "is the melancholy story of the *Tonquin.*"

8

The clouds of war were growing darker. Congress burned with fever, and impassioned speeches damning England rang to the rafters of the uncompleted Capitol. These sentiments were echoed and cheered in the new settlements west of the Appalachians, but they brought despondent looks and sad headshakes among the financiers and merchants of the Eastern seaboard.

The Nonintercourse Act of March 2, 1811, forbade the importation of goods from France and England. Astor quickly dispatched his agent and relative, Henry Brevoort, to Montreal to consult with his partners in the South West Fur Company on ways to meet the unfortunate situation. Brevoort went on from Montreal to St. Joseph Island, above Mackinac, to observe conditions there. It was the depot for the Michilimackinac trade on the Canadian side of the border. The Nonintercourse Act would prevent goods for the Indian trade from being imported through that station.

Brevoort found the situation discouraging, and he predicted heavy losses. Large quantities of merchandise brought from Montreal and Quebec by the South West Fur Company were piled up at St. Joseph. Stocks at Mackinac Island were insufficient to meet the demands of the trade for long. Not only Astor and other traders were disappointed. The chiefs of the various tribes which would have received the supplies for their furs were enraged. They expressed their fury in a series of bitter orations. Brevoort obtained copies of them, and sent them to his friend Washington Irving. "Shew old Astor the speeches if he wishes to see them," Brevoort wrote.

Astor didn't need to read the speeches to understand the seriousness of the situation. Brevoort's reports had convinced him of that. He applied directly to President Madison for permission to bring the Canadian goods into the United States. The Indians, he declared, were suffering for want of the usual supplies. There was no reason to penalize them. If the goods could be brought in, trade could be carried on, but if not, then all the goods so badly needed by American Indians would have to be sold at a loss to the Indian Department of Canada. If that happened, American Indians would cross the border to trade. American companies would lose their business, while their expenses, such as wages and maintenance, would continue.

Madison replied simply that "Congress left no power with the Executive to grant permission."

Late in 1811, Astor went to Canada. Learning that money was badly needed for the Canadian Army, he offered to arrange a plan of financial assistance. The Canadians accepted, but before the plan could be completed, hostilities began.

During his talks with Canadian officials, Astor obtained valuable information regarding the size and condition of British and colonial military forces. This information he transmitted to his good friend, Treasury Secretary Gallatin, who promptly passed it on to the President. Thus, Astor won the favor of the Canadian Government while at the same time placing himself in the light of a loyal American.

The alliance which the Canadians had made with Astor through the South West Fur Company did not prevent them from planning to counter his activities in the Far West. Astor's agents in London sent him word that the North West Company was fitting out a ship there which was to proceed to Quebec, take on traders, and then sail to the North Pacific Coast for the purpose of building a fort on the Columbia. Astor communicated the intelligence to Daschkoff with the suggestion that he might wish to inform the Russian Government of the British plan.

Then Astor busied himself with preparing another ship of his own to carry more men, arms and supplies to Astoria. He selected for the mission his favorite vessel, the *Beaver*, which had returned from Canton in July.

Into the *Beaver's* hold went not only supplies for the Indian trade and for the company which had gone out on the *Tonquin*, but merchandise and foodstuffs for New Archangel. Cornelius Sowle, who had been in the China trade, was named captain.

The *Beaver* cleared New York on October 13. Among the passengers were six clerks destined for service in Astor's posts in the Northwest, which Astor presumed were being built. One of the clerks was Ross Cox, who was to write a famous and controversial book about Astoria. Another clerk was George Ehninger, the son of Astor's sister Catherine. Also on board was John Clarke, an ex-North West Company trader, whom Astor had made a partner in the Pacific Fur Company. Clarke was said to be distantly related to Astor. His mother was a German whose maiden name had been Waldorf.

Meanwhile, far to the west of New York, and without Astor's knowledge, important events were taking place.

9

In the spring of 1811, Manuel Lisa with twenty picked men was driving his keelboat up the Missouri in an effort to overtake the Astorians so that the two brigades might travel through the Sioux country together. Almost constant bad weather made Lisa's forced trip more difficult. He pushed himself and his men to the limit. A colorful, dynamic, powerful wilderness conqueror, who might well have been a peer of Cortez had he lived three centuries earlier, he urged his company to supreme efforts with curses, whisky and promises, leading them in ribald songs as he manned the sweep of the heavy boat and fought the current of the raging river.

When Hunt reached the Omaha Villages on the 10th of May, Lisa was a hundred and fifty miles behind him. Nine days later, Lisa passed the Omahas, and realized that he could not catch Hunt before the Sioux country was reached. He dispatched a messenger overland asking Hunt to wait for him.

The messenger reached Hunt at the mouth of the Niobrara River. Hunt sent back a reply that he would wait, but as soon as the courier had departed, Hunt started on, redoubling his efforts to stay ahead of the Spaniard. It was an unconscionable trick, not at all justified by the keenness and bitterness of fur trade competition. Hunt, untrained in the ways of the wilderness and unfamiliar with its history, had been talked into going on by Crooks and McClelan, who despised Lisa. The two partners had convinced Hunt that Lisa had been responsible for their being detained by Indians on the river in 1809. All Lisa was trying to do was to get ahead, they declared, so that he could bribe the Indians to make trouble for the Astor company.

The charge had no merit. Lisa had only twenty men with him, not enough to guarantee his safety in the Sioux country. Hunt had more than three times that number. Moreover, Lisa knew that Hunt was going straight through to the Columbia, and did not intend to trade east of the Rocky Mountains.

Late in May, Hunt picked up Alexander Carson, Ben Jones, John Hoback, Edward Robinson and Jacob Rezner, all experienced mountain men. They were returning from the upper Missouri, but all agreed to turn about and go to the Pacific.

When Lisa reached the Niobrara he was only sixty miles behind Hunt. On he and his weary men drove, frequently rowing through a full day and night without stopping. Each day the ashes of Hunt's campfires told them they were gaining.

On May 30, Hunt was stopped by the Indians, but after threatening them with his guns he was allowed to pass. Lisa drove through the same gauntlet on June 1.

On the morning of June 2, when Hunt was again menaced by Indians, Lisa's boat came in sight. Lisa and his men had averaged eighteen miles a day for sixty days. During one period of twenty-four hours they covered seventy-five miles. It was a record that was never to be broken as long as keelboats were used. The combined forces reached the Arikara Villages on June 12.

Hunt originally had planned to follow the Missouri and Yellowstone rivers, but the mountain men who had joined him in May advised him not to expose the company to the Blackfeet. They urged him to turn westward from the Arikara Villages, and make the rest of the journey by land.

Hunt accepted the advice, and began to trade for horses. Three weeks were taken up in this occupation.

On July 17, the Astorians set out across the limitless plains. In the long file winding its way out of the valley of the Missouri were sixty-one men, one squaw and two small children. It was a serious hour. No one knew what lay ahead. They were in the truest sense pathfinders, for they were going into a land virtually unknown to white men. Only a few explorers and hunters had penetrated the western wilderness for any distance beyond the trail of Lewis and Clark, but the Astorians were crossing far south of that trail. Most of the country through which they would pass between the Missouri and the mountains had never been seen by anyone except the unknown Indians who inhabited it.

Eighty-two ponies had been obtained. The partners—Hunt, McKenzie, McKay, Crooks, Miller, McClelan—rode. Dorion, the interpreter, rode, and a pony had been assigned to his squaw and two children. The others walked. The remaining seventy-four animals were heavily loaded with supplies.

This was the summer of the plains. Constantly the earth

changed. Now it was flat and brown; as far as the eye could reach, there was no ripple to break the levelness. Now it was cut in myriad gashes, yellow coulees, umber washes, serrated ridges, marshy bottomlands from which rose arrays of ducks, geese, cranes, herons, sandpipers, blackbirds, snipe, curlews, killdeers; treacherous sands bordered springs and little creeks which ran away without apparent destination. Now it was aglow under a penetrating sun, rising and falling in a monotonous succession of powerful swells that seemed to carry the long horse train and the company on foot forward into the hollows, to hold them back as they crawled out. Now it was a heaving world of golden hills and green valleys, and the bright streamers, dancing from crest to crest, striking on broken ridge and bluff, made it a complicated network of contrasts.

This was the summer of the North, and it was a new world, for the world of the river was over the horizon at their back. This was the world of earth, not of water, earth beneath their feet, a wind with new smells in their faces, wind and buffalo grass and the blankets of cattails and lupine and roses and Indian tobacco and goldenrod and thistles, wind and sand and rock, a new way and a new life that changed thoughts and moods and words. And always the wind watched over the emptiness, over the hills and the horses and the people, as it had watched since the beginning, the greatest power on earth.

Big River in the country of the Cheyennes was left behind August 6. Thirty-six more horses had been obtained, and each person got a turn at riding them.

Hunt, feeling the pressure of the western emptiness and silence, gazed at the infinity of the sky's arch and searched for some comforting object on which to rest pained eyes. He found only a buzzard circling against the blue nothingness.

The buffalo moved like black smudges on the blankets of colored earth. The herds, grown greasy fat on the cured amber grass, brought concern to the scouts finding trail for the company. The buffalo crossed ahead of them, behind them, sometimes taking hours to pass, at times close enough so that the rumble of their hoofs on the dry summer sod was like thunder coming from a clear sky. Nothing could stop the stampedes, and the horses, like the men, seemed to understand the danger. Often a horse would stop abruptly, and with head high and ears erect, stare into distance. Often the scouts turned the train abruptly, or held it up while they rode ahead to examine the size of a herd and ascertain the direction in which it was moving.

The antelope always were frantic. At times their curiosity exceeded the bounds of their instincts, bringing them close to the train, and lead tore life from them. Ever since the company had left the Missouri, the antelope had run along its trail as if racing one another, then stopping and gazing in amazement and wonder. They pivoted suddenly and bounded away, only to whirl about and stare again. They stood on knolltops as if chatting with each other, then for no visible reason suddenly scattered in all directions as if a noiseless explosion had occurred in their midst.

The prairie dogs peered out from their doorways with blinking eyes, chattered wildly and piped warnings to one another.

The big jacks loped off and from vantage points watched in consternation, ears piercing the air like miniature steeples.

The coyote revealed no curiosity, no fright nor anxiety. It calculated distance with cold precision, moved in its thoughtful way in safety, slinking along the ridges, understanding the futility of attempting to bring down a horse, acting aware of the deadliness of the riders.

But not the gray wolf, not the lobo. Its howls drowned out the yapping of the coyote, and it came close to feast on carcass and scrap, to await a chance to sink fangs into ham cords. Sometimes the little horses would succeed in running one down and a rider's rope would drag it to death. At night the lobo crept in close to the grazing herd to make it nervous, to trouble the guards, but the hated smell of man kept it from coming too close.

The company skirted the Black Hills on the north and crossed the desolate wastes beyond. On August 17, the crests of the Big Horns could be seen in hazy distance.

Beyond the Big Horns was Wind River. They drank of its icy waters on September 9.

Union Pass opened a way for them, and they went down into the valley of the headwaters of Green River. They caught a glimpse of great mountains ahead. Hoback, Robinson and Rezner knew them. They had been beyond them, treading ground no white man had passed over before. The mountains were the Tetons.

A stream named for Hoback was followed until it poured into a fine gray-green river. The river was the Snake, a tributary of the Columbia. The day was September 26, 1811.

They had crossed the Continental Divide, and so they were in the region in which their orders told them to trade with the Indians and to begin the establishment of Pacific Fur Company posts. They had no idea how far they were from the mouth of the Columbia, or perhaps they would not have given so much thought to business.

The country was rich in furs, and two contingents were detached to trap. They were to remain behind through the winter, and bring in their catch to the Columbia the following summer.

In one detachment were Alexander Carson, Pierre Delauney, Pierre Detaye, and one St. Michael. In the other were John Hoback, Edward Robinson, Jacob Rezner and a hunter named Cass.

Suddenly the partner Joseph Miller announced that he, too, intended to stay behind. In a fit of wild rage he signed away his shares in the company. He was disgusted with the whole operation, and he wanted no part of it as an officer. He would become a plain trapper. Mystified by his violent act, the other partners regretfully agreed to leave him behind.

It was on the Snake that Hunt made the greatest mistake of the expedition. Seeing the big smooth river before them, the *voyageurs* clamored to abandon the horses and take to canoes. Indians who came into the camp and heard the proposal vigorously shook their heads. Travel by canoe, they said, was not possible, for the river was deceitful. The *voyageurs* laughed . . . the Indians did not know how well they could handle canoes. These were land Indians who had no knowledge of water travel. Hunt, the businessman from New Jersey, rejected the counsel of the Indians.

On October 19, the expedition started down the Snake in fifteen canoes which the *voyageurs* had constructed. They were ecstatic, and cried out their delight.

"We go, brother!"

"*Nous allons!*"

"*L'eau nous prend jusqu'à la fin maintenant!*"

"The river takes us to the end!"

"We come, Columbia!"

"Good-by, Horses!"

"*Au revoir, aux chevaux!*"

"We do not work with our behinds now!"

"This will be dreaming, cousin!"

They were dreaming. For nine days they sped on, borne on the strong green glass shoulders of the stream. Skillfully they guided their frail craft through torrents and rocky runs in the shadows of great hills. Suddenly the true character of the Snake, so appropriately named, was revealed to them in all its horror. Crooks's canoe was torn apart. Antoine Clappine was drowned. They had reached the terrible Cauldron Linn.[6]

For twelve days they searched on foot down the river and through the surrounding countryside, hoping to discover smooth water or a pass. They found only one way out, and that was by faint animal trails that wound away through the tortured country.

All the valuable supplies were stored in nine caches. On November 9, they started on, each man carrying a part of what little food remained and his weapons.

The journey of the overland Astorians from Cauldron Linn to

[6] *Lin* or *lyn* is a Scotch word. It means a pool of water in a perturbed state, for instance a whirlpool at the foot of a waterfall. The name *Cauldron Linn* (as Irving spelled it) undoubtedly was applied by one of the Scots in the company. Its exact location is not known, but probably was between American and Shoshone Falls in southern Idaho. Some members of the expedition called it the Devil's Scuttle Hole.

the mouth of the Columbia was one of desperation, hopelessness, sickness, injury, torturous hunger and death.

The company at times was divided into several bands. The *voyageur* Careière vanished and was never found. Dorion's wife gave birth to a child on December 30. It died a few days later Three men gave up, and went to live with the Indians. Another collapsed and had to be left in an Indian village. All were emaciated, and it was only through the help of the few natives encountered . . . and meals of dog, ground squirrels and beaver . . . that any survived.

On the last day of 1811 . . . long after the expedition should have been in Astoria . . . the parties were still struggling through the mountains and canyons of eastern Oregon.

10

During the spring and early summer of 1811, the men at Astoria worked diligently at erecting the post. Good relations were established with the Indians, and a profitable trade had begun. The future looked bright, and the company eagerly awaited the arrival of the overland expedition and the return of the *Tonquin* from the north.

On June 15, the first discouraging news was received. Two Indians, who turned out to be women dressed as men, came down the river with word that white men of the North West Company had built a post on the Spokane River, a tributary of the Columbia. It was clear that the competition which the Astorians had hoped to avoid had begun.

A lack of manpower had prevented an attempt to establish

trade with the Indians in the interior, although plans were made to launch this activity as soon as the overlanders arrived. It was decided, however, that the Canadians on the Spokane had to be opposed, and the assignment was given to David Stuart.

Before he could leave with a party, a large canoe manned by nine white men and flying the British flag, came down the Columbia. It was a group of North Westers led by the famed explorer, David Thompson.

The presence of Thompson at Astoria was resented by the Stuarts, but not by McDougal, who with McKay had visited the British Minister before sailing from New York. Thompson needed supplies and equipment for his return journey, and McDougal graciously furnished them. David Stuart made it clear that he did not approve of treating competing traders in such a hospitable and generous manner.

On July 23, Stuart set out to open trade on the upper river. He took four clerks, two *voyageurs* and two Sandwich Islanders with him. Thompson chose to leave at the same time. The two groups traveled together for some distance, but Stuart, disliking Thompson and distrustful of him, at last slipped away and went on alone.

At the mouth of the Snake River, near the present little town of Burbank, in the State of Washington, Stuart's band came upon a British flag flying from a pole. Attached to the pole was a slip of paper claiming the entire country for Great Britain. Stuart understood then that the North Westers were not in the country for trade alone. Only by a small margin of time had Thompson missed an opportunity to raise the flag of England at the mouth of the Columbia, where he had found the Stars and Stripes flying above Astoria.

Stuart went on to the Okanagan River, 540 miles above Astoria, and in September erected a trading house. It was a good location, considerably below the Spokane and the British post.

Back at Astoria, trouble of a different kind was brewing. Word reached the post that the Indians were planning an attack on it, and the work of building a strong stockade was accelerated.

War was averted only by the cleverness of McDougal. It was known that smallpox had ravaged the Columbia River Indians the previous year. McDougal summoned the chiefs of the various tribes into a powwow. He produced a bottle and told them it contained the germs of the dreaded disease. Unless they behaved, he declared, the bottle would be uncorked, and they would all be stricken. The terrified chiefs promised peace, and they kept their word.

In October, four men who had gone upriver with Stuart returned to report the building of the American post on the Okanagan. Their services were not needed there. With them came a free trapper, Regis Brugière, and an Iroquois hunter, Ignace Shonowane, who had performed the remarkable feat of traveling all the way from Michilimackinac over the route broken by Thompson.

Robert Stuart set out with a party to trap on the Williamette River. They were the first to open that great rich valley.

In October, also, Lamazee, the interpreter, arrived with the tragic story of the *Tonquin* disaster.

An atmosphere of gloom hovered over Astoria as the year 1811 ended.

Part Six

The War and
Mr. Astor

1

On May 12, 1812, the *New York Gazette and General Advertiser*
published intelligence brought by sea from the Northwest Coast
which told of the loss of the *Tonquin*. Astor refused to believe
the report, and eased his concern with the suspicion that his
enemies had circulated it to discourage him.

It appeared that groundless hopes were influencing his thinking more than usual. For instance, although he recognized the
sad condition of relations between the United States and England, he still held to the belief that war would be avoided. Just
how this was to be accomplished, he could not say. It was as if
he was showing a naïve faith in the superstition that calamity
could be averted by disbelief in its possibility. This state of mind
was indicated in a letter he wrote to Gratiot in St. Louis, in which
he said: "We are happey in the hope of Peace & have not the
Smalest Idia of a war with england."

Astor was not in New York on June 21 when the *Enterprise*
returned from Canton, but he was soon to hear from Captain
Ebbets about the *Tonquin* disaster. This tragic news was coun-
terbalanced to some extent, however, by the success of Ebbets'
long voyage. Despite Astor's own duplicity, and Ebbets' carelessness in presenting his papers at New Archangel, the first ship
in his great Northwest venture had made two lucrative trips to
Canton, and had returned with a small fortune in Chinese goods.
Besides that, Ebbets' skillful handling of matters had left the

door open for future voyages to the Russian colony. The scale was not yet tipped against him.

Having received no satisfaction from Secretary Gallatin and President Madison regarding the importation of trade merchandise from Canada, Astor appealed to ex-President Jefferson for advice. Jefferson replied that while strict adherence to the law was necessary, he felt assured that the Nonintercourse Act had not been intended to prevent the consumption of British goods by the Indians. He suggested that a proper and full presentation to the Government by Astor of the facts of the problem would receive favorable attention. That was all Jefferson felt he could do, for he believed the matter to be in abler hands than his own.

Astor was encouraged, but several weeks passed before he followed Jefferson's advice. When at last he did make a presentation to the Government, he did not rest it on the basis he had previously used. This time he informed President Madison that he had a large quantity of arms and ammunition on Canadian soil at St. Joseph, and if he was not allowed to bring this property into the United States, it would fall into the hands of the British and hostile Indians.

President Madison now saw the problem in a new light, as a war measure and not merely as a commercial matter. He ordered the Secretary of the Treasury "to instruct the [customs] collectors on the Lakes to receive and keep in their custody such of the above mentioned goods as thus might be brought in by Mr. Astor's agents . . ." Gallatin wrote to the collectors at both Detroit and Michilimackinac, transmitting the President's orders. A similar letter was written by Secretary of War William Eustis to Gen. William Hull, who was en route to Detroit with 2,000 soldiers in anticipation of a declaration of war.

For reasons known only to himself, Astor suddenly became convinced, early in June, that war was inevitable. He had much to do with a petition to the President . . . his name was at the head of a list of fifty-six prominent merchants . . . requesting that the embargo be continued as a substitute for war. He still felt that he had a very good chance of getting his Canadian furs and merchandise across the line. Some of the merchants who signed were openly suspicious of Astor's intentions, and sarcastically inquired if he was concocting some new "Chinese Mandarin" scheme.

If the suspicious merchants could have looked into Astor's head they would have seen that he had a far more diabolical and selfish scheme than that involving the fake Mandarin.

Becoming desperately concerned about his property, Astor set out for Washington to see if a personal appearance might serve him advantageously there. He traveled by horseback, and on June 18, he was between Baltimore and Washington when war was declared.

Astor rode into the capital on the evening of June 19. He worked fast, penning numerous letters in accordance with drastic plans he had swiftly formulated. He got off messages by private couriers to his agent at Michilimackinac, who at the time was L'Herbette, and to the representative of the South West Fur Company at St. Joseph, who was the French-Canadian Toussaint Pothier. He also wrote privately to the United States Collector at Michilimackinac, Samuel Abbott.

Next Astor left open letters with Secretary Gallatin, which were to be forwarded through Government channels, and thus bear official sanction, to L'Herbette and Pothier. Obviously this was done to impress the Government that he was operating in the open. Gallatin turned the letters over to the War Department, which was sending an express to General Hull at Detroit on June 24. Astor's private couriers had been four or five days on the way by that time.

How many other dispatches Astor got off by express riders on different routes to the north remained a matter for conjecture, but that at least one more, and probably two, couriers dashed out of Washington was to be shown by subsequent events.

On July 3, Reuben Atwater, the Collector at Detroit, attempted to send Astor's letters, which came to him through the War Department, on to Michilimackinac, but the messenger who started with them soon returned. He had learned British posts already had been informed that the war had started, and he feared capture. A week later Atwater made another attempt to forward "a copy of the Treasury letter" and "Astor's letters" to Michilimackinac by a messenger named Jacob Smith. Smith also failed to go through. He returned with news that the British already had captured Mackinac Island.

The undelivered letters came to the attention of General Hull, and he accused Secretary Gallatin of assisting in getting word to the British that war had been declared by sending a letter under Government frank.

The truth was that Astor's private messengers were the first to apprise the British posts of the war. It was also true that Gallatin knew of Astor's surreptitious action. He was to state: "I have it in my power to prove by whom and how the information was conveyed . . . But I do not wish, without an absolute necessity, to bring to public notice the name of the party concerned." Gallatin claimed the news had reached the British outposts on the Great Lakes by way of New York, Albany and Niagara, and added that to "Toussaint Pothier, agent at St. Joseph's in 1812, of the joint concern of Mr. Astor and the Montreal Company . . . was addressed the letter from New York which, in fact, gave the information there of the declaration of war. If that letter had my frank, it was forged, which I altogether disbelieve . . . it is probable that an account from New York via Niagara would reach St. Joseph's and Michilimackinac long before the news from Washington would arrive."

A letter from Matthew Irwin, Indian Agent at Green Bay, to Thomas L. McKenney, Superintendent of Indian Affairs, stated that Astor's agent "on his way to St. Joseph's communicated to the British . . . that war had been or would be declared. The British made corresponding arrangements and landed on the Island of Mackinac with regulars, Canadians and Indians before the [American] commanding officer there had notice that war would be declared."

A Canadian document revealed that word of the war was first received by the British on "the 27th of June, 1812," by a messenger sent by Astor "to Thomas Clark, Esq., of Niagara Falls.

An express was immediately sent to General Brock, who was at York [Toronto] the seat of the Government." Clark was a Canadian colonel, and a correspondent of Astor.

On July 3, the British commander, Gen. Isaac Block, wrote to Gen. Sir George Prevost that the "accounts" of a declaration of war were "received first through a mercantile channel."

The fact was that Pothier himself reached St. Joseph from Montreal on July 3, and he and Lewis Crawford, another Astor agent in Canada, were with the British forces when they took Mackinac Island on July 17.

Before he hurried back to New York from Washington late in June, Astor got Gallatin to write another important letter. It was addressed to Astor's old friend in the fur trade, Peter Sailly. Sailly was United States Collector at Plattsburg. The Secretary of the Treasury requested Sailly to allow Astor to bring his furs . . . which represented the catch for 1811 and the spring of 1812 by Astor hunters and agents throughout the vast region of the Mississippi headwaters, upper Michigan, Wisconsin and Illinois . . . into the United States from Canada. To escape a charge of favoritism, the same rule was applied to other Americans in the same predicament, of which there were very few.

Astor did not pause long in New York, but continued on to Plattsburg, where he received word that under the terms of the surrender at Mackinac, the British had agreed that all furs stored there should remain the property of their owners. Astor immediately dispatched couriers to all his agents in the Great Lakes region, instructing the agents to send all furs in their possession to Montreal. He wrote his Montreal representatives to forward them as fast as possible to the District of Champlain, in which Plattsburg was the port of entry.

Astor's furs at Michilimackinac, St. Joseph and other depots were worth several hundred thousand dollars. In the United States . . . that is, in New York . . . their value would be doubled or even tripled, due to the exigencies of war and the closing of ports. It was a pleasant matter to contemplate.

He reached Plattsburg on July 2, and sent to Montreal an

urgent request for a passport. While he waited for his friends there to secure it, he heard that the Canadian militia at Lachine had mutinied. He promptly sent this information to the American Government. His associates at Montreal worked swiftly, and a passport reached him on July 6.

He had been in Montreal only a short time before one of his agents arrived with twenty-six bales of furs, estimated to be worth $50,000. From Plattsburg they were taken by Benjamin Graves, one of Sailly's inspectors, to the public storehouse at New York City.

Convinced that his scheme would work, Astor sent more agents to assist in getting his property through Sailly's open door. It was not long before another consignment was on its way down the Hudson. However, the favoritism under which Astor was operating proffered temptations he was unable to resist. Soon some of his agents were applying themselves to moving traffic far beyond the scope of Gallatin's instructions to Sailly.

2

Good luck continued to favor Astor in his shipping during the first year of the war, as it did in the rescue of his furs . . . and his extracurricular smuggling . . . from Canada. Several of his vessels had got away to Europe shortly before the conflict began.

The *Enterprise* had reached New York three days after the opening of hostilities with an enormous cargo of teas and silks. Not long afterward the ship *Hannibal* came in from Canton with an extremely rich Oriental cargo. Strangely enough, Astor had not been the owner of the *Hannibal* when she left China. Her owner had grown panicky as international relations disintegrated, and feared his vessel would be captured by the British. He offered to sell out at an attractive price. Astor bought the *Hannibal* and her immense cargo of teas, and happily watched her sail unscathed into New York Harbor.

With little prospect of more tea arriving in the United States, the price began to rise. Astor put his cargoes from the *Enterprise* and the *Hannibal* in warehouses to await the inevitable shortage. He rubbed his hands in glee at the thought of the immense profits he would make.

In the fall of 1812, Astor's busy schedule and his frantic efforts to place himself in a position to gain from the war, were interrupted by a family problem which greatly disturbed him. His daughter Dorothea, who was nearly eighteen, had gone to Washington at the invitation of the Gallatins. While a guest in the Secretary of the Treasury's home she was introduced to Col. Walter Langdon of Portsmouth, New Hampshire. They had fallen quickly in love.

When Gallatin realized that the young couple were serious, he wrote Astor that Astor had "better send for his daughter to return home." Colonel Langdon, said Gallatin, "had every recommendation except wealth, being one of a large family."

Despite lack of wealth, the Langdons themselves did not approve of the romance. One of the colonel's relatives ungallantly described Dorothea as "this fat German, Dolly Astor."

However, before either the Langdons or the Astors could undertake remedial action, Dorothea and Walter eloped.

Astor was bitter. He swore that he would never forgive Dorothea, and he sought to drive her from his thoughts. His great love for all his children no doubt prevented this, but he made no effort to see her or her husband, and he closed the door of the Astor home to them. It remained closed, even after they had come to live in New York City.[1]

---

[1] The Langdons, Dorothea and Walter, had a large family. Some years later Astor happened to drop in at a children's party in the home of a friend. He was drawn to a beautiful little girl, and much to the distress of his hostess he asked her her name. "My name is Sarah Sherburne Langdon," she replied, and gave him a sweet smile. With emotion in his voice, Astor told her: "For your sake, I shall have to forgive your mother and father." Thereafter, Astor's affection for all the Langdons was unrestricted. He gave Dorothea a fine house, and made her wealthy with his gifts of money and property.

Astor's agents in both London and Montreal kept him well informed of the activities and plans of the North West Company. He was advised that not only had the company sent out an expedition to oppose the Pacific Fur Company on the Columbia, but it had petitioned the king for an exclusive charter to trade in that area.

The North Westers informed His Majesty that without a charter they would not be able to compete with Astor in the Far West, as had been demonstrated by the fate of the Machilimackinac Company. A share in Astor's Pacific Company had been offered to them, they said, but loyalty to their country had prevented them from accepting it. They recommended that a vessel be fitted out at their expense in London to be sent to the Columbia. "The progress already made by the American party," they declared, "renders this determination on our part absolutely necessary for the defence of our only remaining Beaver Country, and we know from dear bought experience the impossibility of contending from this side of the Mountains with people who get their goods from so short a distance as the Mouth of the Columbia is from the Mountains." Documents attesting to the situation were placed in the hands of Viscount Castlereagh, the British Foreign Secretary, and Lord Bathurst, president of the British Board of Trade, but no official action was forthcoming.

In a second and more desperate petition, the North West Company stated that it had taken steps of its own volition to establish a colony on the Northwest Coast, and pleaded for permission to export from England . . . not possible without special sanction because of the war. It also asked that a ship be sent under naval escort with the goods.

The British Foreign Office at last acceded to the request. A twenty-gun ship, the *Isaac Todd*, was fitted out by the company. It was to travel under convoy with a large fleet "of at least forty saile bound for all parts of the world."

Astor had planned to send out a vessel from New York in the fall of 1812, but he feared it would be captured. He asked Washington for protection, and also requested that a small garrison be sent to defend the fort at Astoria. Receiving no reply, he sent agents to London with orders to buy and supply a vessel there, and send it off to Astoria.

It was an extremely dangerous and bold plan. Under the very noses of the British he was proposing to send a ship from England with arms, ammunition and provisions with which to fight the North West Company.

Amazingly enough, the plan worked. His agents acquired the brig *Forester*, and outfitted her with the desired stores. Even more amazing was the fact that when the big convoy, of which the North West Company ship was a part, sailed from England, the Astor brig *Forester* was traveling right along with it, and the *Forester* was flying the British flag.

Astor had determined not to send another ship from New York to Astoria without positive assurance that she would not be intercepted. In an effort to secure this assurance he brought his agreement with the Russian-American Company into play. At his instigation, Andrew Daschkoff called upon the British Admiral, Sir John Borlase Warren. Daschkoff used the pretext that the sole purpose of sending an Astor vessel to New Archangel was to supply the Russian post with badly needed provisions. Not wishing to be the cause of the Russians in Alaska going hungry, Admiral Warren gave Daschkoff a license that would permit the ship to pass through without interference from British men-of-war.

Astor next wrote to Secretary of State James Monroe, requesting a letter from the President, or at least from the Secretary of the Navy, which would prevent his ship from being stopped and interned by American war vessels. He informed Monroe that his ship would have a passport from the Russian Minister, but he said nothing about the license obtained from the British admiral.

3

It was on January 18, 1812, that the first detachments of the overland expedition, led by McKenzie and McClelan, reached Astoria. The rejoicing was great, but it was burdened by the fact that the others were still lost somewhere in the upper reaches of the great river.

Nearly a month later, Hunt and his men staggered in, sick and emaciated from their long ordeal. This left only Crooks and the hunter John Day unaccounted for, and it was feared they had perished.

Hunt was dispirited by the situation at Astoria. A number of the men there had been sick. Indians were making trouble. The loss of the *Tonquin* had deprived the post of both manpower and trade goods, and no means were left by which furs taken during the year could be transported to Canton. While the arrival of most of the overlanders had brought the garrison up to sufficient strength to defeat Indian attacks, the matter of obtaining supplies was not solved.

Robert McClelan was more discouraged than Hunt. He saw nothing ahead, and he surrendered his shares and resigned as a partner, as Miller had done.

In March it was decided that the clerk John Reed should go to New York with dispatches for Astor. He was to be accompanied by McClelan, Ben Jones, a hunter, and two Canadian *voyageurs*. Another clerk, Russell Farnham, was to go after the supplies cached by the overland expedition. A third group under Robert Stuart was to set out for the post on the Okanagan.

The three contingents started together on the 22nd. At the Long Narrows they were set upon by Indians. Reed was badly clubbed, and the dispatches, which he had carried in a bright tin box strapped to his waist, were stolen. Robert Stuart and Mcclelan distinguished themselves in the fight. When the Indians had been driven off, the entire company continued on together to David Stuart's post on the Okanagan.

There they found that David Stuart and his men had been highly successful in trapping through the winter. More than 2,500 beaver skins and other pelts had been taken. These were loaded into canoes, and on April 24, the entire party started back to Astoria. On May 1, they came upon the missing overlanders, Crooks and Day, who had been robbed and stripped naked by the Indians and were nearly dead from hunger and exposure.

The company reached Astoria on May 11, to be greeted by the welcome sight of the *Beaver* lying in the harbor before the post. She had come in the previous day.

Leaving New York, October 13, 1811, the *Beaver* had reached Hawaii on March 26, 1812. Two sailors had been washed overboard and lost on Christmas Eve, and a hunter had died of scurvy, but otherwise the voyage had been without serious incident. She brought several Sandwich Islanders to augment the force at Astoria.

Even though it appeared that the Astorians might now begin to carry out their original plans, Crooks was too discouraged to continue. He, too, surrendered his shares and resigned, announcing that he would return east at the first opportunity.

The others went ahead with plans for the fall and winter operations. It was agreed that Hunt should go with the *Beaver* on its voyage to New Archangel. This decision was a serious mistake. Hunt, an American, was the one man who might have succeeded in opposing the advance of the British in the Columbia Valley. Perhaps McDougal had this thought in mind when he proposed that Hunt should go with the ship.

Robert Stuart was to lead a small party overland to St. Louis in another attempt to get reports to Astor. David Stuart was to return to the Okanagan, and build another post north of that point. McKenzie was to take a party to the Snake country, trap and trade through the winter, and recover the goods in the Snake caches. Clarke was to winter at Spokane.

It was June 29 when the combined groups set out for the interior. In the flotilla of canoes were three score men, and Squaw Dorion and her two children. All traveled together as far as the present site of Walla Walla, where they separated to continue on their respective missions.[2]

David Stuart arrived at the Okanagan on August 12, left Alexander Ross in charge of the post, and then went on to the Thompson River, where he spent the winter.

Clarke reached the Spokane River with clerks Pillet, McLennan, Farnham and Cox, and commenced the construction of a trading house. Farnham and Cox were sent to trade among the Flatheads, McLennan among the Coeur d'Alenes, and Pillet among the Kootenais.

McKenzie traveled up the Snake River to the mouth of the Clearwater, and after having begun to build a post, sent Reed to the caches at Cauldron Linn with the hope that he would rendezvous with the men who had been left behind to trap on the upper Snake. Reed soon came upon seven of them in a camp of Shoshone Indians. They were Carson, Delauney, St. Michael, Dubreuil, La Chapelle, Turcot and Landry.

The seven set out with Reed for the caches. It was found that Robert Stuart had beaten them there, but had left the three unopened caches intact, and had gone on. The goods were placed on horses obtained from the Indians, and taken by Reed and the other men back to McKenzie's post at the mouth of the Clearwater.

Robert Stuart, Crooks, McClelan, André Valler, Ben Jones and Francis Leclerc left Walla Walla by horseback on July 31. They reached the Snake on August 12, just above its entry into the Blue Mountains. Proceeding up the south bank of the river, on August 20, they met the hunters Miller, Hoback, Robinson and Rezner, who, with a fifth man named Cass, had been detached to hunt in the preceding October. Cass had vanished mysteriously in the immense wilderness through which they had been wandering.

---

[2] The noted hunter, John Day, became violently insane on the trip up the river, and had to be sent back.

Early in the previous winter the little band had been traveling southward when they came to a river which they believed ran into the Pacific Ocean. They caught sight of a great valley ahead of them. The river was the Bear, and they had discovered the valley of the Great Salt Lake.

Stuart's augmented party had reached the caches at Cauldron Linn on August 29. Hoback, Robinson and Rezner decided to stay in the mountains. Stuart outfitted them from the caches, and they vanished. Miller had had enough, and chose to go east.

The incredible journey of Robert Stuart and his little company to St. Louis opened important new gates in the unknown West. They suffered severe and prolonged hardships, and several times nearly died of exposure and hunger. The trip took 306 days.

The outward expedition led by Hunt and the eastward journey of Stuart opened the Oregon Trail, with the exception of a few parts of it, from the Missouri River, at the mouth of the Kansas, to the mouth of the Columbia.

4

The *Beaver*, with Hunt aboard, had sailed from Astoria on August 4, 1812, only a few days after the combined parties going to the interior had started up the Columbia. She was to exchange supplies at New Archangel for furs, trade along the coast, and return by the end of October. After disbursing excess provisions, she was to take aboard the furs gathered at Astoria and sail for Canton.

The *Beaver* reached New Archangel on August 19. It was found necessary to go to the island of St. Paul in the Bering Sea for the furs to be exchanged for the provisions. Early in November the vessel was blown off the coast and severely damaged by a storm. The month was half gone before the loading of the furs could be completed.

More than 75,000 seal skins were stowed in the *Beaver's* hold. They were valued at approximately one dollar each. In Canton they would bring twice that amount.

Astor's orders to Captain Sowle had given him no alternative. He was to return to Astoria before starting across the Pacific. Sowle informed Hunt that he did not wish to attempt the crossing of the dangerous Columbia bar with a damaged ship. Only in Hawaii could the necessary repairs be made.

Hunt wanted to return directly to Astoria, but he found it difficult to oppose a veteran captain in such a situation. Being a good businessman, Hunt also found merit in Sowle's argument that more delays would result in the *Beaver* reaching Canton in a season unfavorable for selling furs at a good price and obtaining a return cargo. Moreover, a ship from New York was expected to reach Astoria in the spring of 1813, and Hunt concluded that it would be better for the settlement to await these supplies than to risk the loss of a good market for the seal skins. The *Beaver* turned her prow down the Pacific for the islands.

At Hawaii, Hunt disembarked to wait for the Astor ship that was due in Astoria in the spring.

Of course, he did not know that the war had been under way nearly six months at that time. He bid Captain Sowle *bon voyage* at Oahu on the first day of 1813.

5

Meanwhile, significant events had been transpiring on the Columbia.

Affairs at Astoria, where Duncan McDougal was in command, were progressing under favorable circumstances, but this was not the case on the upper river.

On the Snake, where he had gone to open a post, Donald McKenzie found himself among Indians who preferred to hunt Buffalo rather than a trap beaver. Trade was sparse, and he had difficulty getting the natives to set out trap lines. Besides, McKenzie had never ceased to be disgruntled since he had been superseded by Hunt on the Missouri River. There in the loneliness of the Snake River outpost what little interest he had retained in the Pacific Fur Company speedily disintegrated. At last he decided to move, but before doing so he went to Clarke's post on the Spokane River for advice.

McKenzie was at Clarke's in December when John George McTavish of the North West Company, "with a strong reinforcement of men and goods," arrived from the east. McTavish brought word that England and America were at war, and that the armed British ship *Isaac Todd* would arrive with a naval escort in the mouth of the Columbia in the spring to capture the American fort there.

McKenzie gave no more thought to continuing his fur trading. Without even consulting Clarke, he dashed back to his post on the Snake, cached the goods there, and with his men set out for Astoria.

6

As the year 1813 began, the *Beaver* was en route from Hawaii to Canton; McKenzie was paddling down the Columbia with the first news of the war; the ship *Lark* was taking on supplies in New York for Astoria (six months after she had been originally scheduled to depart); the *Forester* was loading to sail in a British convoy from London; and Astor was in his countinghouse highly gratified with the way his furs were coming into the United States under the watchful eye of his friend Peter Sailly at Plattsburg.[3]

At Canton, Captain Sowle found a letter awaiting him from Astor advising him that the war had begun. Astor ordered him to return with all speed to Astoria with supplies and arms for the relief of the settlement. Unknown to most people, Sowle was inherently timid, and in the face of such circumstances he was almost a coward. He had no stomach for such a venture as attempting to run a British blockade, and he decided that the best thing for him to do was to stay right where he was. He wrote Astor that he intended to remain in China.

Day after day in Oahu, Hunt watched the horizon for the sail he most wanted to see. Having no way of knowing that a relief ship had not left New York because of the war danger, the fear grew in him that it had been sunk, and that another would not arrive for a year.

It was from the brig *Albatross*, which put into Oahu in June, that Hunt heard of the war. The *Albatross* had come from China! Hunt quickly chartered it, put aboard what supplies and equipment he could obtain, and set sail for the Columbia. Astoria was

[3] Astor's gratification was burdened by grief at the loss of Sarah Bentzon, the second child of his daughter Magdalen. The girl, named after her grandmother, survived only a short time after birth.

reached on August 20, a year and sixteen days after Hunt had left in the *Beaver*.

The situation which confronted him was more than disheartening. The settlement was doomed.

What had occurred since the first of the year was this:

McKenzie had reached Astoria with the first word of the war on January 13. He and McDougal quickly put their heads together to decide on a course. The two Scots not unhappily came to the conclusion that the British Navy would prevent Astor from sending any ships into the Columbia. With supplies as low as they were, Astoria would have to be abandoned by the beginning of summer, at the latest.

Their excuse for not taking others into their confidence was that it might lower the morale of the company. The truth was that they feared some of the clerks, and especially the Americans . . . even some of the French-Canadian *voyageurs* who had no great love for the British . . . might be foolish enough to want to defend Astoria.

Some announcement had to be made, however, for the men were restless and curious. McDougal ordered a halt in trade with the Indians, giving as his reasons that the supply of merchandise was running low, as were provisions, and in the event of trouble because of the war the volume of furs on hand would be greater than could be carried away overland.

Under the pretext of securing horses and notifying the winterers on the upper river of the seriousness of the situation, McKenzie departed with a company for Stuart's post.

He had gone only a short distance above The Dalles when he met the strong company of North Westers, led by McTavish. The two parties spent a jovial evening together, and in the morning continued on their respective ways.

During the next two months the winterers straggled into Astoria. Two clerks arrived from the Willamette in May with "seventeen packs of furs, and thirty-two bales of dried venison." Clarke, David Stuart and McKenzie and their men returned during June with 140 packs of furs, a valuable cargo.

Both Clarke and Stuart had enjoyed a profitable season, even though it had not been up to their expectations. But it had been good enough to make them angry at the thought of losing their catch to the North Westers. Ross Cox wrote: ". . . some idea of the profit may be formed, when I state that the wholesale price of a gun is about one pound seven shillings, while the average value of twenty beaver skins [demanded in trade for a gun] is about twenty-five pounds! Two yards of cloth, which originally cost twelve shillings, would generally bring six or eight beavers, value eight or ten pounds."

The value of twenty beaver skins in London or Canton, of course, would have been eighty to a hundred pounds, depending on size and quality.

The Astorians met in solemn conclave. No horses had been brought in, and McKenzie had never intended to secure any. His purpose had been to stop the Astorians in their trading on the upper river. No ship could be expected. McKenzie and McDougal frankly stated that they thought it wise to abandon Astoria and leave as best they could. Stuart and Clarke angrily opposed them.

The result of the stalemate was that a rather lopsided compromise gradually was worked out under which the Pacific Fur Company would retain Astoria until June 1, 1814, and during the interim trapping would be continued.

Clarke and Stuart suspected that McDougal and McKenzie had no intention of carrying out the agreement if a way could be found to circumvent it, but it was the best they could achieve under the circumstances. Reluctantly they affixed their signatures to it.

The document, dishonest in many of its assertions, stated:

The failure of the *Beaver* to return had left Astoria with insufficient supplies. Due to the war no relief ship could be expected to arrive. The interior trade had not come up to expectations. Astoria was not able to compete with the powerful North West Company. The Spokane post would be sold to the North Westers, and several of the Astor clerks would be given permis-

sion to enter the employ of the rival company, provided it agreed
to abandon all other posts in the Columbia region. Goods Mc-
Tavish and his men needed would be sold to them, payable in
horses the following spring. The North Westers would send an
express eastward across the mountains with dispatches informing
Astor of the agreement. McDougal would be given the power to
sell all furs and goods at Astoria to the North West Company
if he deemed conditions too dangerous to attempt to transport
them overland to the headwaters of the Missouri River.

In July the men went back to their interior posts. McTavish
moved his men upriver to await the developments he felt certain
would come.

Two men, Laroque and Cox, were assigned to carry the dispatches east. They did not get there. As they were starting out
of the Columbia Valley to cross the mountains, they met the
North West Brigade on its way to Astoria.

Two celebrated North Westers were in command, John Stuart
and Joseph McGillivray, and they were armed with full powers
to purchase the properties of the Pacific Fur Company. Laroque
and Cox forgot about dispatches for Astor, and turned back.

That was what had happened while Hunt was cooling his heels
in Oahu. Arriving at Astoria in the chartered *Albatross* in August, he was hurt, chagrined, astonished and angered. McDougal
and McKenzie would not have succeeded in their traitorous
scheme if he had been there to stand with Stuart and Clarke.

Hunt saw the futility of trying to change matters. The damage
had been done. He set about to devise some means of saving what
he could of Astor's investment. The only way that could be accomplished was to secure another ship. This meant returning to
Hawaii. The *Albatross* was not immediately available to him,
being already committed to sail to the Marquesas Islands, after
which it would return to Hawaii. Hunt had no alternative but
to travel on it.

The plan agreed upon was this: Hunt would go to Hawaii, secure a ship and provisions, and sail from the islands for the Columbia by January 1, 1814. He would leave with McDougal three

sets of bills of exchange for $20,000 drawn on Astor. These Mc-Dougal could use in the event Hunt failed to return and the company was forced to return overland. McKenzie would go up the river again and instruct Stuart and Clarke to send down their furs and all their men. McKenzie also would attempt to lure Mc-Tavish down to Astoria, but failing to achieve that, he would make a conditional agreement with McTavish . . . not to be binding if an Astor vessel did happen to arrive . . . to concur in the plan and under which some of the employees of the Pacific Fur Company would be engaged by the North West Company.

McDougal was to stay at Astoria, with powers to make arrangements for the departure, which would take place no later than May 1, 1814.

7

Early in 1813, Astor had heard again from his London agents that an assault against Astoria by the British was to be launched. In addition to an attack from the sea, an overland expedition, led by North Westers, would be sent to invade the region.[4] He wrote Secretary of State Monroe, pointing out the commercial and political importance of the post, and urging the Government to "throw forty or fifty men into the fort, which would be sufficient for its defence," until he could send reinforcements. Astor believed the expedition under Hunt had been in Astoria for several months, as it was supposed to be. Monroe seems to have have ignored his letter.

In March several events bearing upon the fate of Astoria occurred in widely separated parts of the world.

[4] The North Westers were already there, of course.

Supposedly the ship *Lark* was to carry provisions to New Archangel, and Astor had obtained, through the efforts of Daschkoff, permission from the British to send it there. He received similar permission from Washington.

The *Lark* got away from New York early in March under the command of Samuel H. Northrup. She was not destined for New Archangel, but for Astoria, and she carried equipment and supplies which would aid in the defense of the post.

The *Lark* got safely through the Atlantic, around the Horn, and had sighted the Hawaiian Islands when disaster struck. A storm drove her ashore on Maui, and she capsized, with a loss of five men and her entire cargo.

The Astor ship *Forester* left England under the protection of a British convoy. She flew the British flag, and her true colors apparently were not even suspected. By the time she had reached the Hawaiian Islands, the state of affairs at Astoria was well known. William J. Pigot, who had been supercargo, succeeded John Jennings as captain after an attempted mutiny. Pigot decided that it would be unwise to continue on to the Columbia. He slipped away for the Russian settlement of Bodega on the coast of California. He traded there and at other California ports for a time, then went south, wintering in the Gulf of California. The *Forester* never reached Astoria.[5]

Astor continued his efforts to get the Government to send a force for the protection of Astoria. A letter he wrote to the State Department from Philadelphia was well designed to hold the attention of Secretary Monroe. In it Astor explained with elaborate and studied carelessness that he was in Philadelphia to

[5] The *Forester* was sailed north to New Archangel in 1814. There Pigot learned that the true identity of his ship was known in the Hawaiian Islands, and the British were looking for him. Thus, he was prevented from going to China to sell his furs, as he had intended. He wintered again in California, hiding from the British, and in the spring of 1815 again sailed north to Russian territory, not knowing the war had ended. He conceived the idea of selling his furs to the Russians at Okhotsk, which he accomplished. Then he sent the *Forester* to Hawaii under command of the clerk Richard Ebbetts to be sold, while he went overland to St. Petersburg to collect his money. The *Forester* was sold to King Kamehameha, and paid for in sandalwood.

meet with Secretary of the Treasury Gallatin and several bankers in regard to loaning the Government money. He knew at this time details about the British ship *Isaac Todd*, and he made a sentimental appeal . . . a quality he seldom displayed . . . for an armed ship to be dispatched to Astoria.

The letter brought action. The American frigate *John Adams* was ordered to proceed to Astoria. She was commanded by Capt. William Montgomery Crane. Astor at once loaded the *Enterprise* to travel to the Columbia under the frigate's protection.

The two vessels were on the verge of sailing when the vicissitudes of war interfered. Commodore Isaac Chauncey, commanding American naval forces on Lake Ontario, made an urgent appeal for reinforcements. Captain Crane and the entire crew of the *John Adams* were sent to him, and the vessel was laid up.

Astor's fighting blood was stirred. He decided he would send the *Enterprise* without an escort. Daniel Greene, who had served as supercargo on the previous trip the *Enterprise* made to the West Coast, seemed to him a good choice for captain. Astor wrote to Greene, but he did not tell him the truth. In asking Greene to take command, he pretended that he did not own the *Enterprise*, but was acting for his friends, the Russians. This, of course, was part of a scheme to deceive the British. The cargo of the *Enterprise* would be valued at $20,000, and on the Northwest Coast would bring at least $40,000 in furs . . . which in Canton would be worth no less than $100,000.

Astor fitted out the *Enterprise* for both privateering and sealing. Greene proposed that he and the crew receive half the profits from prizes and sealing, and he wanted $5,000 himself if he succeeded in getting the ship to the West Coast. Astor agreed to the terms. But months passed, and he gave no order to sail. At last Greene grew tired of waiting, and resigned.

What had caused the delay was this: Astor had been trying to get the ship out of New York under Russian colors, and the Russians were doing what they could for him. They asked the British to "Suffer the Enterprise to pass." The British, doing well in

blockading the Atlantic Coast, had been politely obdurate in refusing. They saw Astor's fine hand in the scheme.

Astor's nerve failed him. He could not bring himself to chance
the loss of the ship and the cargo. The *Enterprise* was unloaded
and laid up.

Astor wrote despondently to Jefferson, hoping the former President could use his personal prestige to get protection for Astoria.
Jefferson's reply was polite, but its vagueness suggested that he
had not bothered to read the letter with care.

More agents were sent into Canada by Astor to bring out furs
and goods he purportedly had owned before the war. One of the
new agents was George Astor, Junior, the son of his brother in
London. The young man had arrived in the United States shortly
before the war had begun, and Astor, in keeping with his willingness to help his relatives, had agreed to teach him the fur trade.[6]

It was not long before the scandal of Astor's dishonest importing became public. Large amounts of goods he claimed to have
purchased in 1812, or before that, really had been bought only
a short time before they passed through Sailly at Plattsburg.
John Day (no relation to the noted hunter who went mad on the
Columbia), another Astor agent in Canada, was instructed to
buy Indian goods at Montreal if they could be brought into the
United States. Should Montreal be in danger of falling to the
Americans, Day was to buy especially large quantities of any
kind of manufactured articles and goods from the West Indies.

The fortune in furs and trade goods which reached New York
for Astor's account was channeled through government warehouses. Astor put up bonds for their value, and the goods were
released. This permitted him to dispose of them at enormous
profits, because of the shortages, or to hold them for even higher
prices, as he desired. Of course, after he had made arrangements

---

[6] Astor's brother George died in London in December, 1813. George had suffered
reverses in the musical instrument business, and Astor had sent him £3,000.
George's death occurred before he acknowledged receipt of the money. Astor advised George's widow, Elizabeth, not to try to carry on the business herself, but
she did not heed him. Astor gave Elizabeth "two hundred pounds sterling, yearly
for life."

with a New York court to intercede for him with the Federal Government, the bonds were remitted.

Astor was publicly charged with using Gallatin's instructions to collectors as a blind to cover extensive illicit operations. Another of his agents, John Bancker, who once brought in a consignment of dry goods, was accused of pursuing a "disrespectable and shameful business." Guy Catlin, another agent, was similarly branded for illegally importing trade goods. Astor stoutly declared, "I never in my life had any transaction direct or indirect" with Catlin. Yet Astor had written to Catlin telling him to consult with John Day, and guaranteeing to support any commitment they made.

Peter Sailly was openly accused by a shipping company operating on Lake Champlain of accepting bribes from Astor. Astor defended Sailly in a letter to Gallatin, saying the money he had paid to Sailly was "in Lew of any Claim" Sailly might have for a share of the imported furs, should they be condemned, "which I Did not exspct."

When Robert Stuart returned to New York from his great overland journey, Astor put him to work getting furs in Canada. Stuart bought pelts, and Day and Catlin, with the help of Sailly, got them across the line.

Although Crooks had resigned and had returned with Stuart, Astor did not leave him idle. He sent Crooks out to the Great Lakes region. A number of independent traders on both sides of the line owed Astory money, and Crooks was to collect the debts in furs. Crooks also was to buy Canadian furs whenever he could arrange with collectors to co-operate with him under a liberal interpretation of Gallatin's instructions.

Now, despite the war, Astor had furs pouring into New York from all directions. His organization might have been likened to a great wheel, the spokes of which were the channels over which the furs came to the hub. They came from Canada north of Plattsburg, from Canada north of the Great Lakes, from the Midwest, from St. Louis, from the forests and mountains of the South, passing through Baltimore and Philadelphia, where they often were diverted into the factories of the numerous hat and clothing makers who were Astor customers. Only on the Atlantic were the wheel's spokes broken.

But not all of Astor's sea trade was halted by the British blockade. A number of his ships had slipped through it. The schooner *Powhattan* reached New York from the Mediterranean early in 1813. His brig *Adolphus*, however, was captured. The *Rockingham*, not owned by him, but carrying a cargo in which he had an interest, successfully got through. The *Enterprise*, sent off to Europe with Oriental goods after returning from Canton, arrived the day after the *Rockingham*. The Astor ship *Hannibal*, which had returned from Canton in the fall of 1812 and had been sent on to Europe with nankeens and other Chinese products, also got back safely. Vessels carrying cargoes for him came in from the West Indies.

Astor's ingenuity was never better illustrated than in the *Hannibal* case.

Great quantities of valuable furs crowded his warehouses in New York, and it pained him that he was unable to send any to Europe to take advantage of the high market. He put his shrewd mind to work on the problem.

At the time the famous French general, Jean Victor Moreau, who had been exiled by Napoleon, was in the United States. Astor hated Napoleon as much as Moreau, but not for the same reasons. Considering Moreau in the light of his cold practicality, Astor saw the general as a distinct asset to him. Moreau was a supporter of the Loyalist cause, and therefore a supporter of Great Britain and Russia.

Moreau was living the life of a country gentleman on a New Jersey farm. One day he was visited by Paul Petrovich Svinin, a member of the Russian embassy staff, who inquired diplomatically whether the distinguished soldier would be interested in returning to Europe to assist in overthrowing Napoleon. Moreau, indeed, was interested, and he agreed to go.

It was not a coincidence that Astor happened to have a fine ship suitable for such a mission. Neither was the excuse a valid one that because of his great friendship with such Russian diplomats as Andrew Daschkoff he was willing to tender the *Hannibal* to Moreau.

Daschkoff managed to get in touch with the British, and they gladly agreed to let the *Hannibal* through the blockade to carry such an important ally to England.

Astor confided to Washington that he had managed to get permission to send a vessel to England for the Russians. President Madison asked that it carry secret dispatches to American Government agents abroad. Astor said nothing to Washington, however, about General Moreau.[7]

The *Hannibal* cleared for Europe on July 22, 1813. The dispatches President Madison sent from Washington were delayed, and missed the boat. In addition to General Moreau and his companion, Svinin, another passenger had hurried aboard just before the gangway was hauled in. He was Adrian B. Bentzon, Astor's son-in-law. Bentzon was in charge of a cargo of furs, listed as worth $60,000, but actually valued at three times that amount. In Europe they could be sold for at least $350,000, perhaps more. Also in the *Hannibal's* hold was freight which Astor was carrying for others, and for which he received $27,000 in freight charges, much more than enough to pay all the costs of the voyage.

The *Hannibal* went to Gottenburg instead of England. A month after he had stepped ashore, General Moreau was mortally wounded in battle.

Some months later the *New York Gazette* carried the news that the "Prussian ship *Hannibal*, Capt. Leisevitz . . . 50 days from Bremen . . . with assorted cargo . ." had arrived in the Hudson River. Among the passengers was William Backhouse

---

[7] Astor's friendship with President Madison was more than a purely formal one. He generally could obtain a private audience with the Chief Executive whenever he wished it. He trusted Madison and confided in him. Madison reciprocated. Astor's wealth and influence in the world of high finance made him valuable as a friend of the wartime administration. Most of the favors Astor received from the government, especially from Secretary Gallatin, could not have been granted without Madison's knowledge and blessing.

Astor, son of John Jacob Astor, who had been attending college in Europe.

In Germany, Bentzon allegedly had "sold" the *Hannibal* so that she might return under neutral colors. The sale was a fraud. A short time later the New York press reported that the "Hannibal, owned by J. J. Astor, cleared for Charleston" to load a cargo of cotton.

Astor had agreed to pay Daschkoff for his good work in helping to get the *Hannibal* through the British blockade, and some money was given to the Russian diplomat; but when a demand was made for the balance, Astor pleaded that the voyage had been unprofitable. He wrote Daschkoff: "I have at this moment great doubts whether I shall realize any thing more than the same agreed to be paid to you."

Astor welched on his agreement with the man who had made the voyage of the *Hannibal* possible.

Three days after he had turned Daschkoff down, Astor bragged: "Her cargo comes to a good Market . . . I have done very well in the voyage." His modesty was not becoming. The *Hannibal* had brought back, among other things, dry goods, steel, madder, wire, hare skins, Danish lambswool, Bohemian glass, wine glasses, Westphalian glass, milk glass lamps, toys, pocketbooks, lead pencils, gold paper, fiddle bows and drugs. Something of the value of the cargo was indicated in a letter Astor wrote to a Baltimore merchant, in which he said he had decided to sell most of the dry goods at auction, "otherwise I would have sent about $70,000 or $80,000 worth to you."[8]

Astor was prepared to make more attempts to get vessels off

[8] While the *Hannibal* was en route to Europe, Astor had again used Daschkoff's good offices to his advantage. He owned considerable cotton which was tied up at Charleston. Daschkoff got permission from the British to send a ship from Charleston with important dispatches for the Russian government. After considerable delay and numerous complications, the Astor ship *Caroline* sailed out of the South Carolina port. She was heavy with cotton and rice, and her destination also was Gottenburg. But the British had adopted a new view of the situation, and a few miles out of the Charleston harbor the *Caroline* was stopped by H.B.M. brig *Moselle*. Ship and cargo were "condemned to the captors." The pass obtained by the Russians from British admirals Warren and Cochran was ignored.

to Europe. He wrote to Secretary Monroe: "I have at present 2 fine ships in this port I would Licke to employ ane of tham as Cartel hawe I have no papers from the British Admiral if one could be employd without I wauld Licke it if government wish a fast Sailing vessel to go as a flag to Europe I can also furnish one."

The Government did want a ship to go to Europe with dispatches, and accepted the Astor offer. The *Fingal*, 380 tons, "coppered, and a very fine ship," was readied. She was to be allowed to carry passengers only. People fought for accommodations, paying $270 for passage, and seeming to have no fear of being captured and interned. There was a special rate of $250 for passengers who furnished their own liquor.

Astor made numerous other attempts to run the blockade. The *Flirt* left New Orleans for Bordeaux with cotton and furs, and apparently succeeded in getting through. The schooner *Boxer*, of 275 tons, made successful runs from New York to Havana, Havana to New Orleans and back, and from Havana to New York. Astor boasted that during these voyages the *Boxer* was "often chased & out sailed all she met with." There were other ships running their dangerous missions under the Astor flag, but their identities were not disclosed.

Astor seemed to enjoy the perilous game, not only for the profit it brought but for the excitement. Neither his profiteering nor his traitorous acts hurt his conscience.

Matthew Hale Smith, a contemporary, wrote that Astor ". . . fitted out several blockade runners for Gibraltar."

The Treaty of Ghent already had been signed when the *Boxer* stole out of New York Harbor, loaded with a cargo of furs and general freight, bound for Nantes. She was commanded by Captain Boyer, carried a crew of thirty-six, was armed with four twelve-pounders and two six-pounders, and "well provided with small arms." Outdistancing pursuing British warships, she reached her destination, only to learn that the war had ended before she had sailed.

The only vessel Astor equipped especially for running the

blockade to China was the brig *Macedonian*, 407 tons, and one of the fastest sailing vessels in the world. The war was nearly over when Astor purchased her for $27,000 cash. He spent another $40,000 coppering her and outfitting her for a dangerous career.

Astor heard that a group of naval vessels was to leave for the Pacific to attack British shipping in that theater of war. He arranged to have the *Macedonian* go along as a "store ship." He was obliged to put some naval stores aboard, but he also loaded her with furs and ginseng. Gleefully he predicted that if the *Macedonian* could make the round trip to Canton before the war ended, "she will clear $300,000." Even if peace came while she was at sea, she still would clear "150 to 200m." Not a disagreeable prospect at worst.

The *Macedonian*, under the command of Curtiss Blakeman, who had taken the *Hannibal* to Europe for Astor, put to sea in the company of the frigate *President* and several other naval vessels. In command of the *President* was the famed Stephen Decatur.

A British squadron soon came in sight, and after a bloody and desperate encounter the *President* was forced to surrender. With British ships straining to overtake her, the *Macedonian* vanished over the horizon.

On July 3, after a fast passage of 169 days, she sailed serenely into Canton. A British frigate which had chased her across the Pacific came in four days later.

Word that the war had ended reached China shortly afterward. The *Macedonian* was safe, and she sailed for New York with a cargo of merchandise. Because of the advent of peace, she brought no more than $200,000 profit to Astor.

8

Astor had been strongly opposed to the war, but when it came he wasted no time in proclaiming his disappointment. He set out immediately to turn it to his advantage, and in this effort he was highly successful.

Early in 1813, Congress, desperately in need of money to finance the conflict, authorized the sale of $16,000,000 in Government stock. Secretary Gallatin invited the four richest men in the United States to negotiate with him for underwriting at least $10,000,000 of the loan. The men were David Parish, Stephen Girard, Herman Le Roy and Astor.

Eventually Parish and Girard agreed to take $8,000,000 of the loan, and Astor took more than $2,000,000. The rate was $88 for a $100 certificate bearing interest at 6 per cent. Gallatin paid high tribute to Astor for bringing Parish and Girard into line.

Although they were rivals in the China trade and in other commercial activities, Astor and Girard were close friends. Astor was considerably younger than Girard, but the French-born capitalist both respected and feared Astor's shrewdness and ability as a businessman. It may well have been that the circumstances of their births . . . poverty and early struggles not to be excluded . . . and their European training and manner of thinking influenced them in assisting the Swiss Gallatin to some extent. However, the lives of Parish, Girard and Astor were dedicated to the making of money and the acquisition of power. Other considerations were invariably secondary.

Even though Astor was making handsome profits from speculations in Government stocks, he sincerely wanted the war to end. He was happier with the steadier, less spectacular and more certain returns from merchandising, legitimate sea commerce and the fur trade. He was never genuinely interested in stocks, bonds or banking. He was first of all a merchant and a trader. His greatest love was the fur trade, and throughout the conflict he looked forward to the day when war financing and the disruption of commerce would be matters of history.

This wish was not inspired by the realization of the tragedies and suffering war brought. Astor was not emotionally disturbed by the thought that instead of making money some men were being maimed and dying in the defense of their country. Such things he looked upon as the normal products of any war. If he displayed any emotion at all, it was based on anxiety for his property. The slaughter on a battlefield brought less anguish than the loss of a brig at sea. And even in the case of a ship disaster he was less concerned with the deaths of the men running the blockade for him than he was by the loss of the cargo. He was never known to utter a consoling word to the families of the seamen who died in his service, whether in peace or war, much less send them a few dollars to ease their financial difficulties.

Yet, Astor made an effort to clothe himself in the garb of a patriot. He denounced the policy of nonco-operation of the Boston Federalists, and he wrote a business friend: "I find the people to the eastward [New England] are determined to ruin the administration at the expense of the interest of the country & all that is & ought to be dear to man . . . we must endeavor to do without them . . ." In another letter, he said: ". . . nothing is so desirable for the good of us all as an union & states . . ."

This was pure hypocrisy. Astor's loans to the Government were made for the single reason that he could profit from them, and he would not have sacrificed a dollar to save America from being once again a British colony. While he denounced the Federalists, he was advocating a conciliatory policy toward Great Britain.

When peace finally came, he complained that it had not come at the right time for him. He wrote John Dorr, a Boston associate: "I am glad of Peace but 6 weeks earlier or 6 weeks later would have differ'd me 100 to 150m Dolls."

Astor made an enormous amount of money out of the war.

Yet, in a letter to a friend he said: "I am a great sufferer by the times as most all Men must be who have property."

The falsity of this statement was illustrated by the fact that before the treaty of peace had been signed, so great was his prosperity that he was able to state that he was more out of debt "than I have been for many years."

A month after the conflict ended, he told his old co-conspirator, Daschkoff, that he was glad of peace "because it puts every thing on safe ground & I can always make money if I will be prudent at all events I have enough, since it can make all my children independent, this I however mention only to you."

Whether Astor ever paid all the bribes he owed Daschkoff was not known.

9

It was evident from the first that John George McTavish had not led his brigade to the Columbia to take Astoria by force of arms. It was said that the partners of the North West Company were in the main upright men, not bandits, but the statement was irrelevant. They were not guided by gentlemanly instincts in their negotiations at Astoria, but by good business practices. They fully understood the power of Astor. Starting a shooting war with him would have gained them nothing that a few dollars could not gain. Violence on the Columbia might have brought serious repercussions on fur-trading fronts east of the mountains. As far as bringing the Northwest Coast under their flag was concerned, that was really not a conquest they needed to pursue. In the first place, they were businessmen, merchants and traders . . . not soldiers. In the second place, the British Navy was on the way, and territorial acquisition was properly its job.

Just to set the record straight, when negotiations were begun between McTavish and McDougal for the transfer of Astoria to the North West Company, McTavish produced a letter he had received from an uncle. The letter said word had come from London to the effect that a British frigate was en route "to destroy everything that is American on the N. W. Coast."

The disloyal McDougal had long before known what he was going to do, but the threatening letter provided a good explanation for his decision. He and McTavish had little difficulty reaching an agreement. In nine days the negotiations were completed.

Some of the Americans and Canadians viewed the proceedings "with shame and indignation," but they were in a small minority and in no position to do anything to halt it. According to Washington Irving, the feeling of some of them was that with the help of friendly Indians, the North Westers might have been "scattered." The furs could have been taken to caches up the river. A landing party from a British war vessel could either have been defeated or left to take possession of an empty fort, to which the Americans could have returned after the vessel had sailed away.

The Astorians did possess enough strength to drive off the North Westers, but none of them relished the idea of standing up to British marines supported by ship guns. And the experienced mountain men knew that the so-called friendly Indians, under a cannonading, would have decided quickly that the Astorians were doomed, and would have transferred their allegiance to the British. Moreover, it was difficult to believe that the British would be stupid enough to abandon a territory after they had gone to the trouble of capturing it. What seemed even more unreasonable was the assumption that any of the Canadians attached to Astoria would have been very enthusiastic in a battle against their countrymen.[9]

[9] It is, in fact, a matter of historical record that the strongest proposals for violently opposing the North Westers were made long after the British had taken possession of the Columbia, some of them as much as thirty years afterward.

McDougal, exceeding his authority, agreed to sell Astoria . . . the post, its contents, supplies, trade goods, equipment and furs . . . to the North West Company for $58,291.02. His explanation for his speed in completing the deal was that with a British warship due to arrive at any time he had to move quickly to prevent Astoria from being taken as a prize of war. It was difficult for others to argue with such a contention. However, McDougal had agreed previously with Hunt and the other partners to remove the furs, either overland or by sea, and he had let Hunt go off to Hawaii for a ship.

McDougal also defended himself with the statement that he had the consent of the other partners present, Clarke and Stuart, to act as he did under the pressure of the emergency. This was not true. Stuart was not there. Clarke's post on the Spokane had already been taken away from him by the North Westers, and his trade had been usurped. Neither Stuart nor Clarke consented. They did not sign the agreement. It was signed only by McDougal and McTavish.

Shortly afterward McDougal was made a partner of the North West Company.

The clerk Alexander Ross wrote that after the agreement had been completed, McTavish delayed in submitting bills of exchange for the property with the hope that he might secure better terms after the arrival of the British warship. McDougal and McKenzie, according to Ross, thereupon trained the fort's guns on the North Westers, and threatened to fire if the bills were not submitted at once. McTavish supplied them.

This story was fiction. Ross was not even present at the time, being upriver. Moreover, the bills were not actually delivered for several months, as it was impossible to make them out until a complete inventory had been taken.

Gabriel Franchere, who was at Astoria at the time, and who also wrote about affairs on the Columbia, did not even mention such an incident.[10]

---

[10] It is interesting to note, as well, that in the first edition of Franchere's book, published in French in 1820, nothing at all is said about a plan to fight the British being considered by the Astorians. In the English translation of his work,

The furs which were sold with Astoria were worth no less than $100,000 at the mouth of the Columbia. They would have brought at least four times that amount in Canton or London. A reasonable assessment of the entire property of Astoria would have been no less than $160,000, and perhaps as much as $200,000.

It was on November 30, 1813, that H.B.M. sloop-of-war *Raccoon*, mounting twenty-six guns, came into the Columbia River. Captain Black was in command. Aboard was John McDonald of Garth, a distinguished partner of the North West Company. The weather was very bad, and no landing was attempted for twelve days.

The *Raccoon* had been in the convoy in which the North West Company's ship *Isaac Todd* and Astor's ship *Forester* had sailed from England. The *Isaac Todd* had become separated from the others somewhere after rounding Cape Horn, and her whereabouts were unknown. She had failed to appear at an appointed rendezvous, and after waiting a reasonable time, the *Raccoon* had continued on to the Columbia. The other warships of the convoy set out to engage the American commodore, David Porter, who was reported to be inflicting heavy damage on British ships in the Pacific.

On December 13, Captain Black landed, and enjoyed a good dinner at the fort, but he was unable to conceal his disappointment. He and his men had been led to believe that a valuable prize awaited them on the Columbia, and all they had found was a cluster of huts surrounded by a stockade, and a group of dirty Indians lounging about the gate.

This disreputable conglomeration of log hovels was what he had been sent halfway around the world to capture. He stared about with mounting contempt. "Damn!" he growled. "I could batter it down in two hours with a four pounder!"

---

issued thirty-four years later, Franchere enthusiastically described such a plan. Between the publication dates of the two editions, he had had ample time to read Washington Irving's *Astoria*, in which McDougal and others are condemned for their "perfidious" and "cravan" acts. The plan to put up a fight for Astoria seems to have originated in Irving's mind.

John McDonald of Garth had no such feelings. "The force was sent to fulfill a duty to the North West Company," he said. "It was no government measure. They were under my directions as a Partner of that company, and acted accordingly."

Despite his disappointment, Captain Black carried out his orders. He took formal possession of Astoria and all the immense Columbia River country for Great Britain. The grubby buildings he rechristened Fort George.

He need not have been disappointed or ashamed. In taking possession of Astoria, he had saved an empire for his country.

10

When he reached the Marquesas in the *Albatross*, Hunt found Commodore Porter there in the American frigate *Essex*, and with several British vessels as prizes. Hunt tried to persuade Porter to send an armed ship to the Columbia, or to sell him one of the prizes so that he might return and rescue the Astorians and the furs. Porter refused, but he promised to try to intercept the British warships en route to capture Astoria. He sailed away. Hunt was forced to remain in the Marquesas until late in November, when the *Albatross* continued on her way to the Hawaiian Islands. Oahu was reached December 20, 1813. It was then Hunt learned that the *Lark* had been lost off Maui.

Captain Northrup of the *Lark* had been saved, and from him Hunt received the information that Astor wanted the property of Astoria taken to New Archangel in the event it was necessary to save it from the British.

Hunt bought the *Pedler*, a 225-ton brig, manned it with survivors of the *Lark*, and late in January sailed for the Columbia, not quite thirty days behind schedule. He reached Astoria on the last day of February, only to see the British flag flying above it.

Hunt was indignant at the low price received for the Astor furs, and swore he would make every effort to recover them. Mc-Tavish is alleged to have offered them to Hunt at an increase of 50 per cent. Hunt did not recover the furs, but if he declined to buy them at an increase of 50 per cent, he was not living up to his reputation as a good businessman.

McDougal had gone over to the North West Company, so Hunt took charge of winding up the affairs of the Pacific Fur Company on the Columbia. He turned over all papers to McKenzie, who was going to Montreal overland, to be delivered to Astor.

On April 3, Hunt sailed away in the *Pedler*, taking several clerks with him. Instead of setting a course for Hawaii and New York, he turned north, bound for New Archangel. He was determined to make a last attempt to conduct a successful trade, and recover some of Astor's great investment.[11]

On the next day the North West Company brigade started overland for Montreal. With them went McKenzie, carrying Astor's papers, and the partners Stuart and Clarke. Franchere also had chosen to return home by land. The other potential authors, Cox and Ross, chose to remain on the Columbia in the employ of the victorious North West Company.

One day in the vicinity of Walla Walla, members of the brigade were startled to hear a child crying out, "*Arretez donc! Arretez donc!*" They turned their canoes into shore, and found the squaw of Pierre Dorion and her two children.

[11] From New Archangel the *Pedler* took supplies to Russian settlements in California. The Spanish seized her on a charge of smuggling, but were unable to prove a case. She went to Hawaii, then again to New Archangel, with supplies. There she was seized by the Russians for selling gunpowder to natives, but was released. She sailed again to Hawaii after trading on the coast, then went to China. Some two years after Hunt had taken her out of the Columbia, she unexpectedly sailed into New York with a heavy cargo of Chinese teas, silks and other products, much to the delight of Astor. As a businessman, Hunt turned out to be a good trader and sea rover. Astor was always his friend, and later helped to get him appointed postmaster at St. Louis.

The distinguished historian of the western fur trade, Hiram Martin Chittenden, told of Squaw Dorion's terrible experiences with more accuracy than did Irving. He wrote:

"On the 5th of July, 1813, John Reed left Astoria with the large party that set out for the interior that day, his destination being the country of the Snake River, where he was to trap during the winter and collect as many horses as possible for the overland expedition [of the Astorians in defeat] the following spring. With him were Giles, Leclerc, François Landry, Jean Baptiste Turcot, André La Chapelle, Pierre Dorion and family, and Pierre Delauny. Late in September he was joined by those hardy hunters, Hoback, Robinson, and Rezner, who here come to sight for the last time.

"Reed finally located for the winter on what is now Boise River, Idaho, long known to fur traders as Reed's River. During the autumn three men were lost from one cause or another. Delauny left the party and was never again heard from, and was probably killed by the Indians. Landry fell from his horse and was killed. Turcot died of King's Evil. Late in the year Rezner, Dorion, and Leclerc went about five days' march from Reed's house, where they put up a hut and commenced a prosperous trapping campaign. One evening, about January 10th, Leclerc staggered into the house desperately wounded, and told Dorion's squaw that her husband and Rezner were killed. She at once caught two horses, put Leclerc on one of them, and herself and two children on the other and started for Reed's house. On the third day Leclerc died. When the Indian woman reached Reed's house it was only to find that the rest of the party had likewise been slain. She at once summoned all her energies and started for the Columbia. She forded the Snake River and got as far as the Blue Mountains, but could not cross at that season. With marvelous resource she maintained herself and the children during the winter, but the imminence of starvation at length compelled her to move. She made her way with great suffering to Walla Walla, and was on her way down the Columbia when she was met by the Northwest Brigade."

Squaw Dorion's tale of horror was an appropriate finale for the epic drama of Astoria.

11

When he heard of the capture of Astoria, Astor's fury was greater than either his friends or his family had ever known it. He wrote McKenzie, who was still in Canada: ". . . while I breath & so long as I have a dollar to spend I'll pursue a course to have our injuries repair'd & when I am no more I hope you'll act in my place . . . we have been sold, but I do not despond."

In informing Astor of the affairs on the Columbia, McKenzie had made out a good case for himself. Astor did not yet know the extent of McKenzie's disloyalty to him, but he was soon to learn the truth.

If Astor's anger subsided, his determination did not, but the end of the war brought a drastic change in the course of his thinking. He gave up plans for retaking Astoria with military force, and he began to look for peaceful, not necessarily legal, means of recovering the settlement.

Perhaps for the first time in his life Astor thought less about his financial losses than he did about the injury done to his prestige and his pride. He had set out to accomplish the boldest and most significant venture ever conceived and executed by an American. It had embodied more than a dream of wealth. It was built upon a dream of power, of empire, of unprecedented accomplishment.

And it was more than that.

On May 24, 1812, Thomas Jefferson had said that he "hoped

for the establishment of an independent nation on the Pacific Coast, bound to the United States by ties of blood, language and friendship."

The statement was reflective of plans which Astor had confessed in confidence to the great statesman. Astor wanted to found a new nation, to be named Astoria, and he wanted to be its king.

Early in 1815, Astor wrote his nephew, George Ehninger, who was in Canton: "By the peace we shall have a right to the Columbia River & I rather think, that I shall again engage in that business."

Astor had good reason to make the statement. His overtures to Washington had brought him some encouragement. The Administration was attempting to formulate a course of action that would have been highly favorable to him. In July, Secretary Monroe put some flesh on the skeleton by informing "Mr. Baker, the chargé d'affaires of Great Britain at Washington, that the president intended immediately to reoccupy the post at the mouth of the Columbia." This determination was made "partly at the instance of Mr. Astor, who was anxious, if possible, to recommence operations on his former plan in North-West America."

But then, as always, the wheels of progress turned slowly in Washington. For a year Astor waited, but the President made no move to carry out his announced intention. Astor considered sending a strong force of his own to the Columbia, not to oust the North Westers by military force, but to establish a rival post. The possibility of bloodshed was too great. Already the western frontier was aflame with a murderous struggle between the North West Company on one side and Lord Selkirk and the Hudson's Bay Company on the other. More internecine warfare would have been costly in life and money, and would not have accomplished the desired results.

Astor waited more than another year. Then his hopes rose again. Monroe, now President, asked that "Mr. Astor, of New York, be informed of the measure contemplated in relation to the Columbia River."

The measure was the commissioning of Capt. James Biddle and J. B. Prevost to proceed in the sloop-of-war *Ontario* to the Columbia and there "to assert the claim of the United States to the sovereignty of the adjacent Country, in a friendly and peaceable manner . . ."

Astor wrote to the commissioners, telling them of the intrigue by which he had lost Astoria. He also warned them not to trust representatives of the North West Company, and to be careful crossing the Columbia bar.

Prevost got off the ship in Valparaiso, Chile, to conduct some other Government business, and Biddle went on alone. On August 9, 1818, he took "temporary" possession of the Columbia River country in the name of the United States, then sailed away to the South Pacific.

Meanwhile, discussions between Great Britain and the United States were revolving on a new question. It was whether Astoria had been taken as a prize of war or merely through its purchase by the North West Company.

In time the negotiators came to the conclusion that Captain Black had taken Astoria after it had been sold. This resolution placed the United States in a superior position, but it helped Astor not at all.

On October 6, 1818, Astoria was restored to the United States, and the American flag was raised over the fort, but by the treaty of October 20, between the United States and Great Britain, the right of the North West Company to the possession of the post was confirmed. They had bought it from Astor.

The result was that although the United States owned Astoria, the North West Company owned the fur trade that was conducted there.

The treaty also proclaimed: "All territories and waters claimed by either power, west of the Rocky Mountains, should be free and open to the vessels, citizens, and subjects, of both for the space of ten years."

Astor could send his ships there to trade, just as could any other citizen of either nation, but the great dream was destroyed.

The great venture had met disaster on political reefs far more dangerous than those guarding the mouth of the Columbia.

But Astor's fortitude was not destroyed.

On the evening of the day he had first heard of the loss of the *Tonquin,* Astor had attended the theater. A friend had expressed surprise at seeing him in his usual seat at such a time. "What would you have me do?" Astor demanded. "Would you have me stay at home and weep for what I cannot help?"

When his last hope of recovering Astoria was gone, his attitude was the same. He never forgot, he never forgave, but he did not weep.

There was, in fact, no time for weeping. His eyes were regaled by a great vista. It was the vista of an immense western wilderness, a land of limitless distances, a land still unconquered.

Part Seven

Beaver, Bribes and the Northern Department

1

In 1815 John Jacob Astor was fifty-two years of age. He had been in America thirty-one years. He was in the prime of life. His commercial genius was recognized and feared on three continents. He was a power behind the Washington political scene. He was a shipping tycoon, a merchandising magnate, the owner of more real property than any other person in New York, the undisputed leader of the world's fur trade, and a multimillionaire.

It wasn't enough to satisfy him. When he sent Robert Stuart and Ramsay Crooks, the former Astorians, to the Great Lakes and the Mississippi Valley after the war, the dies for their operations had been cut. He had great confidence in Stuart and Crooks. After their return from the debacle on the Columbia, they had served him well and had demonstrated their ability. Now he had greater things for them to do.

In the beginning, when he first traded some penny sugar cakes for a pelt on the New York wharves, Astor's ambition had been simply to be successful. To remain in America he had to make enough money to maintain himself. As he began to reap fantastic profits in the fur trade, the scope of his ambition widened like ripples caused by the dropping of a pebble in water.

But more than a pebble had gone into the pool of American commerce. Into it had gone a latent force composed of an incomparable shrewdness, an indestructible fortitude, an irrepressible determination. Ambition which had been normal and commendable in the beginning soon became adulterated by lust, by greed, by an ungovernable craving for domination and power. The world soon knew what Astor was, and what he could do. His goal was no longer only financial security. It was monopoly. And motivating it was an obsession so great that not even severe monetary losses could destroy it.

He was driven by an overriding dream, and he took the first step toward fulfilling it with the incorporation of the American Fur Company in 1808. Next, in 1810, came the creation of the Pacific Fur Company. The destruction of the Montreal Michilimackinac Company and the establishment of the South West Fur Company followed in 1811.

War disrupted progress, even brought disaster to him on the Northwest Coast of America, but only individual battles were lost, and wounds inflicted soon began to heal.

Even while the conflict raged, Astor was planning the new offensive with which he would drive beyond the Great Lakes and up the Missouri River, the campaign in which he would capture the rich St. Louis trade. When he sent John Day to Montreal in 1813 to direct his illegal wartime fur-importing operations, he told him: "Do not forget to sound them of, how they would like to sell me their Interest in the Indian Country." At the same time, when he dispatched Crooks on a mission to Ohio and Detroit, he told him that he intended "to take hold of the whole." He meant that he intended to take over the South West Fur Company from his Canadian partners, and all the trade of the Great Lakes region.

"If we get peace," he said to Crooks a little later, "we shall make as much money as you want by the Indian trade."[1]

Peace would mean that the difficulty in obtaining trade goods from Europe would be ended. It would mean that the Indians would return to their trap lines and hunting, which they had

---

[1] Astor's first steps to gain a foothold in the St. Louis trade were taken almost simultaneously with the launching of his drive to monopolize the trade of the Great Lakes wilderness. To avoid confusion from overlapping events occurring in the two areas, and to present clearer and more dramatic narratives, the Northern Department and the Western Department are dealt with separately.

deserted for the more exciting warpath. Astor knew what he would do, and his program was ready for launching the moment the tomahawks and muskets were supplanted by the skinning knives and the beaver traps.

The articles of agreement under which the South West Fur Company had operated would become void when the trade of 1815 was completed. Astor summoned Stuart to New York to discuss matters, and Stuart wrote Crooks excitedly: "I have only time to give you the purport of a short tête-à-tête I had with the old Cock this morning Viz:—That he digesting a very extensive plan for establishing all the Indian Countries with the line demarkation between G. B. and the U. S. . . . a considerable time may elapse before that object can be brought to full maturity, as he wants an exclusive grant or privilege &c.&c. he added that it would be a pity, we should in the meantime be altogether inactive, therefore he expects a parcel of Indian goods out in the spring . . . You can very readily draw your own conclusions regarding his views, which I really believe are as friendly toward us all, as his own Dear interest will permit, for of that you are no doubt aware, he will never lose sight *until some kind friend will put his or her fingers over his eyelids.*"[2]

Crooks, too, hurried to New York in response to Astor's guarded message: "I wish you to be here to see if we cannot make some arrangements for something more important."

The last outfit under the original South West Fur Company agreement went into the wilderness in the spring of 1815. Studying the situation, Astor concluded there was nothing to be gained as yet by entering into open competition with the Canadians. His reasoning was clear. Even though the war had ended, the Canadians were not in a much better situation than they had been in 1810 and 1811, when he had forced them to compromise and become his partners. He saw no reason for spending the money to buy them out when they were not in a position to fight him to their own advantage.

[2] Stuart's italics.

Besides, he had been urging his high-ranking friends in Washington to secure passage of a bill that would deny foreigners the privilege of trading with the Indians in the United States, and he had heard from a confidant in the War Department that "it is the intention of the Government to prevent altogether the British Indian traders from coming within the United States."

It was, indeed, cheering news. Astor bided his time, waiting for the Canadians to come to him, and they did.

Once again, as he had done five years before, William McGillivray went to New York in the interests of peace. He proposed that the articles of the South West Fur Company be continued for another five years (until after the 1820 outfits had completed their trading), and Astor agreed. With the scratch of a pen, Astor once more held 50 per cent of the immense trade which would be conducted throughout the Great Lakes region by the South West Fur Company. The other 50 per cent was held by McTavish, McGillivray & Company; Forsyth, Richardson & Company; and Pierre de Rocheblave, all partners of the North West Company which had defeated Astor on the Columbia.

In a cleverly worded letter, Astor was to inform Secretary of State Monroe why he had made a new agreement with the Canadians. It revealed the scheme by which he intended to drive them from the company, after which he would take it over for himself. "Soon after the late War," he told Monroe, "I found that the Canada traders had pretty well established themselves in the Indian Country within the Boundary of the United States and that a trade could not be carried on by Americans without an Opposition from the Canada Traders and that a heavy loss would probably be the result of such opposition. to prevent which I made an agreement with the Principles of them to carry on that Trade for the joint acc for the Term of Five years, *unless the Government of the United States should in the meantime pass such Laws or Regulations, which would render it incompatible for me or the American Fur Company to be so interested with them.* I agreed to this in Order to get a hold in part of the *Trade and under the firm belief that such a law or Regulation would be passed by Our Government,* as soon as We are in a situation of carrying on the Trade to the full extent, *and which I think we are now prepared to do, provided we can have the use of Canadian Boatmen,* as Our Citizens will not submit to the hardships and habits of living [which the Canadians] have to endure."[3]

Astor had made a new agreement with the Canadians which he believed would never go into effect. At the time he had scrawled his signature to the document extending the life of the South West Fur Company, he had authoritative word that the Government soon would close the doors of the Indian trade to all foreigners.

2

On April 29, 1816, Congress struck a mortal blow at the interests of Canadian traders who conducted their business within the territory of the United States. It passed a law which provided that "licenses to trade with the Indians . . . shall not be granted to any but citizens of the United States." Severe penalties were established for violations. Goods taken by an unlicensed foreign trader into the United States were subject to confiscation.

All the forces of the Government stood in support of Astor's scheme to eliminate the British and Canadians from the American fur trade, but he was not quite satisfied. Swift application of the law might interfere with his plans to gain an advantage over his American rivals. For this reason he wrote to Monroe expressing his approval of the stringent act, and declaring that it

[3] Author's italics.

should have been passed "some years ago," but adding that without "some few Canadian traders" it would be impossible to supply the Indians with enough trade goods that first year. This
would cause "great distress" among them. He said nothing about
it causing a financial loss to him. The situation could be relieved,
Astor told Monroe, if the President would grant him (Astor) "six
to nine licenses" for his exclusive use. The licenses should be
blank. They could be sent to him at Michilimackinac, and he
would be glad to have them filled out.

Monroe transmitted the brazen request to the President. Madison ignored it.

Astor was not to be easily thwarted. He knew that Presidential
policy decreed that the power to grant licenses in the Indian
trade was to be vested in "the Governor of the Michigan Territory, and in the agents for Indian affairs at Michilimackinac,
Green Bay and Chicago." These officials were under the direction
of the War Department.

Astor persuaded Secretary of War W. H. Crawford to instruct
George Graham, the department's chief clerk, to write a letter on
the matter to the commanding officer and the Indian Agent at
Michilimackinac. The letter requested them to give Astor's representatives, Crooks, W. W. Mathews and Joseph B. Varnum,
"every possible facility and aid in the prosecution of their business, that may be compatible with your public duties."

Next Astor wrote his old friends and associates in Canada to
tell them how surprised and sorry he was that Congress had seen
fit to cut them off from the lucrative trade they had enjoyed for
so many years in United States territory. It was a letter well calculated to pave the way for a step he had in mind.

William H. Puthuff, the Indian Agent at Michilimackinac, an
honest and sincere public official, made known his displeasure
with the War Department's subservience to Astor. He did not
care for the methods in which Astor conducted his affairs in the
Indian trade, and he made this clear in a letter to Governor Lewis
Cass, of Michigan Territory.

Puthuff told Cass that he had "seen a letter addressed by J. J.
Astor to a Mr. Franks a British trader now at this place in which

Mr. Astor expresses surprise and regret at the passage of a law forbidding British subjects from trading with the Indians, within American limits etc. but [Mr. Astor] observes that the power is vested in the President to grant special licenses for that purpose, and that he dispatched a messenger to the President from whom he entertains no doubt that some may be procured and will be immediately forwarded to Mr. Franks and Mr. Astor's friends in the North west trade."

Puthuff had no way of knowing that Governor Cass, who was to become Secretary of War, was in the pay of Astor.[4]

"I wish to God," Puthuff wrote Cass, "the President knew this man Astor as well as he is known here. Licenses would not be placed at his discretion to be distributed among British subjects, Agents or Pensioners. I hope in God no such license will be granted, his British friends here calculate confident on his success in this matter, that they may be disappointed is my most sincere wish, should they succeed incalculable evil will assuredly grow out of the measure."

Puthuff was not advised that President Madison had ignored Astor's request for "six to nine licenses," and he began a fight of his own to prevent the "evil" he believed would ensue if Astor received them.

When Crooks applied to Puthuff for licenses on behalf of the

[4] Some letters and account books of the American Fur Company are owned by the Public Archives of Canada and by the Detroit Public Library. Some of them were put on display in a New York gallery in 1909. The *New York Times* reported: "An entry, May 3, 1817, shows that Lewis Cass, then Governor of Michigan Territory . . . took about $35,000 of Astor money from Montreal to Detroit, in consideration of something that is not set down."

Gustavus Myers wrote that he had "personally inspected these ledgers. One entry showed that $35,000 had been paid to Lewis Cass for services not stated. Doubtless Astor had the best of reasons for not explaining that payment. Cass . . . became the identical Secretary of War to whom so many complaints of the crimes of Astor's American Fur Company were made."

A catalog of the Anderson Gallery, in which some of the ledgers were displayed, stated: "On May 13, 1817, an entry shows that Lewis Cass took about $35,000 of the Astor money from Montreal to Detroit in consideration of something not set down."

Note the conflict in dates: May 3 and May 13.

The Astor account books in the Canadian Archives do not contain such an entry. In a ledger in the Detroit Public Library a page is torn out after the entry of May 12, 1817.

South West Fur Company, which were to be used in trade west of the Mississippi River and north of Prairie du Chien, Puthuff told him he would grant them only to persons whose "characters were unobjectionable," and on condition that they would not be used in any territory in which Americans were already established. Puthuff understood very well that 50 per cent of the South West Fur Company was owned by British subjects.

In Puthuff's view, at least, the first of these two conditions precluded Astor and his men from qualifying for licenses. He was not stupid enough to believe that the second condition would restrain them from trading where they pleased, and he was infuriated by the thought of Britishers hiding behind the Astor flag and taking business away from native-born Americans on American territory.

When Crooks found the "conditions to be inadmissable," Puthuff referred him naïvely to Governor Cass. Puthuff may have known Astor's character, but he apparently had little understanding of Astor's political power. He did not know, for example, that when George Graham became Acting Secretary of War, Graham wrote to Cass requesting him to afford Astor "every facility in your power consistent with the laws and regulations."

That was all Cass needed to take action. He advised Puthuff, "it is the intention of the Government that Mr. Crooks as the agent of Mr. Astor should have the selection of such persons to enter the Indian country and conduct the business as he may require. To such persons therefore as Mr. Crooks may designate you will please grant licenses . . . On mature reflection on this subject I would recommend that as few licenses as may be consistent with those regulations be granted, rather reducing than exceeding the number."

Puthuff needed no interpreter to tell him that what Cass was saying was to give Crooks all the licenses he might desire, and grant few to others.

Crooks had written Astor: "the Canadian Boatmen . . . are indispensible to the successful presecution of the trade, their places cannot be supplied by Americans, who are for the most part are [sic] to independent to submit quietly to a proper controul, and who can gain any where a subsistence much Superior to a Man of the interior and although the body of the Yankee can resist as much hardship as any Man, tis only in the Canadian we find that temper of mind to render him patient docile and perservering in short they are a people harmless in themselves whose habits of submission fit them peculiarly for our business and if guided as it is my wish they should be, will never give just cause of alarm to the Government of the Union. *It is of course your object to exclude every foreigner except those for whom you obtain licenses.*"[5]

Astor got in touch with Cass, with the result that an order granting him permission to employ foreign boatmen was issued.

Cass's interpretation of his instructions from the War Department was so liberal that even Crooks was surprised. So was Puthuff, and he was also discouraged, but he was not completely beaten yet in his struggle for fairness and justice. By early August of 1816 he had awarded licenses to only three of Astor's men, and he rejected requests made by Crooks for licenses for others, whom he declared had been in "the British Indian Department during the war." Puthuff had not forgotten how these British Indian agents, with the aid of unlimited liquor and gifts, had stirred up the redskins to kill Americans.

But Puthuff was not strong enough to defeat for long the will of Astor and his political supporters. Enough licenses were obtained for agents of the South West Fur Company to permit the conduct of a successful trade during the 1816 season. At that time Astor let it be known that he had sent goods valued at $150,000 into the Great Lakes area. An estimated $600,000 worth of furs were secured in exchange.

Late in the 1816 season, Astor agents, through no fault of their own, became involved in the bitter war between the North West and the Hudson's Bay Companies. The Earl of Selkirk looked upon the South West Fur Company as an adjunct of the

[5] Crooks's italics.

North West Company. Defying United States regulations, he sought to drive the North Westers out of Wisconsin and adjacent territory, and take over the trade of that area for the Hudson's Bay Company.

A Selkirk brigade invaded the Fond du Lac Department of the South West Fur Company and seized goods valued at several thousand pounds from the company agent, James Grant. This raid took place on United States soil. Selkirk's men arrested Grant and his clerk, William Morrison. At Fort William, they detained another Astor clerk, Eustache Roussin, and seized seventy kegs of liquor and various other articles of merchandise. As a result, not only the goods and the trade of this department were lost, but the South West Fur Company was obliged to pay the wages of eight clerks and forty Canadians.

Astor demanded that Washington send a military force against Selkirk from Michilimackinac, Prairie du Chien or Green Bay, and recapture the seized goods. He offered to furnish Indian guides and Canadian *voyageurs* to assist the expedition. But Washington did not choose to become embroiled in a serious international incident only because of the loss of some merchandise, and a row between bandits. It would be difficult to justify an invasion of Canada on such grounds, especially when a large part of the goods lost was liquor that was not supposed to be there. Nothing official was done to aid Astor in securing satisfaction.

With Canadian traders forbidden by law from operating in American territory, Astor was at last in a good position to take over the entire South West Fur Company. He might have forced his Canadian partners to withdraw and suffer the consequent losses, but he realized the resentment such a move would engender. By it he would lose some of his oldest and staunchest Montreal friends, and the Montreal market might very well be closed to him. The good will of certain Canadian houses was worth far more than the few dollars he might gain by the forceful seizure of the company.

Although he was in a position to name his own terms, he paid something more to the Canadian partners than the mere value of the company's buildings and equipment. The exact amount of the purchase price was not disclosed, but it approximated $100,000.

Astor was now by far the largest and strongest fur trader in the region of the Great Lakes and the upper Mississippi. He began at once to secure his position and to increase his strength. Crooks and Stuart were promoted and given three-year contracts. In addition to annual salaries . . . $2,000 for Crooks and $1,500 for Stuart . . . each of them was to receive the profits on five shares "out of the hundred shares in said business."[6] All their expenses while they were "absent on business of the company" were to be paid by Astor, and they were to give their "whole time and attention to said business, and not to trade for account of themselves or any other person whatsoever." They were to have full command of field operations. Crooks held the highest rank, next to that of Astor himself. William W. Mathews was named the company's Montreal representative. His chief duties were to purchase furs for Astor in the Montreal market, obtain Spanish dollars for use in the China trade, and have goods manufactured in Canada for the Indian trade, such as "6000 ear boobs round."

The name South West Fur Company gradually disappeared. It was supplanted by the most famous name in the trade . . . the American Fur Company.

Between 1808, when it was incorporated, and 1817, the American Fur Company had been hardly more than a paper entity. Now it became a living, breathing, physical organization. Astor was the American Fur Company. He owned almost all of its stock. He supplied all capital. He personally directed all operations. He sold the furs received. He gave all orders.

The South West Fur Company and the ill-fated Pacific Fur Company were laid to rest, but no one mourned their passing, no one placed flowers on their graves.

The American Fur Company stood alone, and no one, least of all its shareholders, looked into the past. They only looked ahead.

[6] Possibly only three shares for Stuart.

3

The wisdom of Astor's policy of keeping the Montreal door open became apparent. Canada was the greatest source of competent men. Without access to this manpower market Astor would have been badly handicapped.

In the spring of 1817, Mathews sent a large number of clerks and *voyageurs* out from Montreal over the water route to Michilimackinac. On Mackinac Island the brigades were organized. At the head of each was an experienced trader. He was assisted by two clerks, a complement of *voyageurs* and *engagés*, and an interpreter. Each brigade was sent to a specific region, such as the south and west shore of Lake Superior, the upper Mississippi, the Wisconsin, the head of St. Peters, Prairie du Chien, Fond du Lac and Green Bay. According to one contemporary report, Astor "fitted out two hundred and forty boats, each one containing two traders and from four to six hands." This was an exaggeration, but that Astor's operation in the Old Northwest at the time was enormous was without question.

In 1817 Astor acquired by purchase the interests of the North West Company at Fond du Lac on Lake Superior, and William Morrison was sent there to handle the business. John Johnston, with goods for which he was charged nearly $15,000, traded west from St. Mary's. Another Astor brigade went into Canadian territory east of Lake Huron, although trading in this area by Americans was soon to be prohibited by Canadian law. Other outfits appeared on the Illinois, the Kankakee and Wabash Rivers. John Kinzie was the Astor trader at Chicago. James Abbott, an experienced trader, was in charge at Detroit. Russell Farnham led his men to the Mississippi to trade below Prairie du Chien as far as St. Louis. He and Joseph Philipson were to ask Governor Clark for a license to trade west of the river.[7] Other traders working for Astor were Reaume, Antoine Deschamps, Pierre Connes's Outfit, Darling's Outfit, and Louisignan.

Astor was well organized for the 1818 season. Crooks ordered Mathews in Montreal to "engage 80 men for three years." Governor Cass's order permitting licensed American traders to employ "foreign Boatmen and Interpreters" made it easier to secure full outfits of competent men. French names predominated in most crews. The Illinois River outfit had eleven boatmen, all with French names, and their wages were almost the equivalent of those paid the clerks . . . indicating the value placed on the ability of veteran *voyageurs*. Clerks received $360 a year, and some of the interpreters received almost as much. In some cases, interpreters got more than the clerks under whom they worked. Samuel Lashley, clerk for the St. Joseph Outfit, got $300; his interpreter, François Page, $333.33. Morrison, at Fond du Lac, received $1,000 a year, and had two clerks with non-French names who got $240 and $220, and three interpreters with French names whose annual pay was $333.33, $400 and $300. In addition, Morrison had fifty boatmen, all with French names. Many of the French-Canadian boatmen and interpreters were married to squaws, and most of them, like the proverbial sailor, had their Indian girls in every tribe.

At the beginning of his offensive in the Old Northwest, Astor's competition from independent traders was large and strong. Canadian traders continued to trap in certain parts of the region in violation of the law. At Detroit, David Stone & Company, enterprising and well financed, was a major threat. Crooks and Stuart wrote Astor that Bostwick, Stone's agent at Mackinac, was doing business wtih the independent traders "Franks, Dousman, Berthelot, and half a dozen others." Bostwick slashed the prices of his goods, and Crooks complained that he "seems determined to ruin either us or his associates." Strouds were "cut 25% . . . irresistable baits have been exhibited in the most attractive manner."

[7] The license was refused.

Charles O. Ermatinger operated a house near St. Mary's, and presented serious opposition. Crooks and Stuart accused him of being an agent of Lord Selkirk, "who so abused and insulted the laws & dignity of the United States." The Astor agents, British subjects themselves, suddenly seemed to be deeply concerned about the good name of the United States. They plotted to keep Ermatinger from sending "a single trader into the country," and they soon succeeded.

Michilimackinac was, as it had been since the earliest days of the French explorers, the trade center of the great arena. Its geographical location made it the most accessible market for trappers, traders and Indians, and they went to it from the south, west and north.

Astor himself mapped out the various localities in which his brigades operated. All . . . with the single exception of the country east of Lake Huron . . . were south of the border. What furs came into his Mackinac headquarters from north of the line were generally unsolicited. From Fond du Lac on Lake Superior, near the present city of Duluth, he sent traders up the St. Louis River through the Minnesota wilderness. Two portages brought them to the Sandy Lake source of the Mississippi. There they came in touch with the Sioux. Going on, with easy portages, they could reach the Red River of the North. On this route were Fort Snelling and Traverse des Sioux, both prominent outposts of the trade.

Another route of the Astor brigades ran up Green Bay from Lake Michigan, utilizing the Fox River. A portage put them on the Wisconsin River, which ran into the Mississippi. Winnebago Indians, whose trade was important, lived in the vicinity of the portage. Near the mouth of the Wisconsin was the old post of Prairie du Chien.

Astor bateaux and canoes also traveled down Lake Michigan to Milwaukee, the Chicago River, and other points . . . the land of the Chippewas. They moved down the Des Plaines and Illinois rivers through the domains of the Foxes, the Peorias and the Potawatomies, all good hunters.

Boasting of Mackinac's great influence and importance, the

Detroit Gazette said: "When the persons engaged in this trade are assembled at Michilimackinac, men can be found acquainted with every foot of the country, and with every influential Indian on this side of the Mississippi, including the heads of that river, the river St. Peters and the heads of the Wabash and the Illinois."

As the furs poured into Mackinac, they were baled and loaded on the great cargo canoes and taken down Lake Huron, across Lake Erie, to Buffalo. There they were loaded on wagons and transported to Albany. Once more they were placed on boats and carried down the Hudson to New York.[8]

Detroit also was a major trading center. Into it came furs from Ohio, Indiana and southern Michigan. This was one of the most productive areas in the Old Northwest. On its numerous streams and in its thick forests, trappers for many years took countless thousands of mink, raccoons, opossums, skunks, otters, beaver, wildcats, wolves, muskrats, deer and foxes. Pelts also came into Detroit from the Canadian territory east of Lake Huron, but this trade was halted in 1821, when Americans were at last barred from operating on Canadian soil.

Astor watched with great interest the developments in Canada as the Hudson's Bay Company and the North West Company waged a desperate and relentless war for control of the country west of the Great Lakes. Old enemies, old friends and former partners of his were engaged in a death struggle. The outcome would have a significant effect on his own future. He fully understood that when he moved his own forces into the trade of the upper Missouri River, he would have two powerful antagonists . . . unless one of the Canadian companies was destroyed.

[8] After the Erie Canal was completed, in 1825, canal boats carried the furs from Buffalo to Albany, a cheaper form of transportation that immeasurably increased the profits of the American Fur Company. A news item in the *Buffalo Gazette* on September 2, 1817, illustrated the size of the fur traffic through that transfer point. Speaking of shipments arriving by schooner and sloop, the newspaper said: "They consisted of beaver, otter, muskrat and bear skins and buffalo robes. Three hundred and twenty-two packs . . . were owned by John Jacob Astor, of New York, and one hundred packs were consigned . . . to several owners. The value of these furs is figured at one hundred and fifty thousand dollars."

Every effort of the North West Company to break up the monopoly of the Hudson's Bay Company had failed. Nor had the North Westers been able to obtain security in any other form for themselves. All attempts to establish areas of trade had been futile. Bitterness increased with the passage of each month. Both companies sought to employ the most violent traders. Murders were frequent. Wages were greatly increased to the detriment of profits, and prices paid to the Indians for furs were raised until severe losses resulted. It was obvious that both companies were headed for financial disaster.

The partnership agreement under which the North West Company operated was due to expire in 1822. Some of the partners, dissatisfied with small profits, or none at all in some cases, gave promise of a revolt. They directed their complaints chiefly against the Montreal agents, McTavish, McGillivray & Company, and McTavish, Frazer & Company. These concerns, they said, took any profits that accrued from the business, and they nominated two of their number, Dr. John McLoughlin and Angus Bethune, to make another attempt to reach a compromise with the Hudson's Bay Company.

The Hudson's Bay Company, wrote the historian, P. C. Phillips, was not endangered by any kind of insurrection. Its stockholders were "timid investors, many of whom had inherited their stocks . . . none of them knew anything about the business or had any alternative to accepting the policies developed by the governing board. Under these circumstances, the officers of the Hudson's Bay Company were in a stronger position than were the agents of the North West Company."

Simon McGillivray feared the complete destruction of the North West Company, and he proposed an unqualified merger. Hudson's Bay officials eagerly grasped the opportunity. In March, 1821, the consolidation was completed.

A great name, North West Company, died. The new organization would operate under the name of Hudson's Bay Company.

Now Astor had a single Canadian opponent, and he soon felt its great power.

4

The brutality with which the humble *engagés* were treated in the fur trade was often incredible. Many Government officials and Indian Department Agents . . . not the least in rank among them Governor Lewis Cass and Superintendent William Clark, the famous explorer . . . protested to Congress about the fraud and mistreatment practiced on the "human mules."

As a clerk, son of a trader, grandson of an Ojibway chief, and brother-in-law of Henry R. Schoolcraft, the noted Indian Agent William Johnston was fully qualified to speak on the subject. The *engagés*, said Johnston, ". . . perform all the menial services . . . their labour is very hard for in a few years they are completely broken down in constitution, they have to work more like beasts of burden than men, and when they can procure the means they will go into all kinds of excesses; exposed constantly to change of heat and cold; which soon brings them to an untimely grave."

As Crooks had so bluntly stated, no American could be employed for such work, for Americans, although physically strong, refused to suffer the indignities and cruelty inflicted on the docile French-Canadians. The *engagés* were usually employed for three to five years. There was no limit to the hours of their working day . . . they simply worked as long as there were tasks to be performed. At the time the American Fur Company secured "nineteen twentieths" of the trade in the Northwest, the standard wage for *engagés* was about $100 a year. A small advance was given them when they were hired, but the employer was not required to pay the balance until after the expiration of their term of service. Small perquisites usually were allowed them. As Astor became dominant, Johnston stated, "at present they are seldom allowed perquisites, formerly it was an indispensible rule; but it is gradu-

ally losing ground. Some now get a few triffling articles of clothing; tobacco, soap, salt, etc."

Astor was soon able to dispense completely with the "indispensible rule." The only perquisite allowed company *engagés* was
a ration of "blé d'Indi" . . . Indian corn. It was the only food the
company, under its contracts with *engagés*, was required to furnish them. In the woods they often were reduced to supporting
themselves on wild game alone.

Astor also succeeded in reducing the wages of the *engagés* from
$100 a year to $250 for three years, but as if that did not satisfy
his greed, he condoned the practice of cheating them out of
money due them. If a company trader could by any device avoid
paying an *engagé* his full wages, in the eyes of Astor that was
much to the trader's credit. Any goods which an *engagé* might require to survive, or anything he might desire to break the hardship
and monotony of his life with a few moments of pleasure, such as
tobacco or spirits or a bright ornament, was sold to him at a
markup even higher than that charged Indians.

In the season 1823–24, Astor's post at Mackinac Island made
on goods sold at retail to *engagés* a net gain of $7,200 on mer-
chandise invoiced at $8,300, a markup approaching 90 per cent.
It was not unusual for an *engagé* to end three years of backbreaking labor heavily in debt to the company, and thereby be forced
to re-engage for another term.

Wrote Chittenden: "It is difficult to exaggerate the state of affairs which at times prevailed . . . the American Fur Company
was thoroughly hated even by its own servants . . . Many an em-
ploye, it is said, who had finished his term of service with a letter
of credit for his pay fell by the way and was reported as killed by
the Indians."

Astor's monopoly had created an evil pyrimidal system. The
company furnished goods to the traders at an enormous profit,
which made it impossible for it to lose money, even though disasters, such as the destruction of shipments, occurred. To break
even, the trader had to resort to all manner of deceit and trickery.
The temptation to cheat his *engagés*, therefore, became irresist-

ible. Some traders were so desperate under their inescapable burdens of misfortune and debt that they would kill an obscure
engagé to save two or three hundred dollars.

This was Astor's system. He created it, and he approved it in
operation. Some entries in the moral ledger, however, might have
appeared to redound to Astor's credit, but in a strict analysis this
would have been found to be deceptive. He made a fight to keep
liquor out of the Indian trade, and he insisted that Indians receive good merchandise for their furs, even when the cost was
exorbitant.

Hercules L. Dousman, who managed the Astor post at Prairie
du Chien for a number of years, declared "that if by accident a
gun, a blanket, or any other article sold to an Indian was not up
to standard, the policy, regardless of trouble or expense, was to
replace it with a perfect article as soon as possible. This was a
strict rule within Astor's dealings with the Indians and to it is
undoubtedly due much of the success which rewarded his enterprise in the wilderness."

Dousman's statement implied that consideration for the welfare of the Indians was inherent in this policy. Nothing could
have been less true. Astor was forced to follow it simply because
of competition from the British, who, however else they might
have mistreated and debauched the Indians, never failed to
supply them with superior and dependable merchandise.

As he studied the history, economics and peculiarities of the
fur trade through the years, Astor had not neglected to familiarize
himself with the liquor problem. This phase of the trade, in fact,
had been given his special attention, for he understood its importance. Long before he had set out to monopolize the trade of the
Old Northwest, he recognized alcohol for the evil it was, realizing
the deleterious effect it had on the commerce with the Indians.
He had on numerous occasions let it be known that he stood
against its use, and he had clearly expressed the conviction that
not only was it not needed but that the trade would be greatly
benefited if it were prohibited.

Samuel de Champlain, in the seventeenth century, was one of

the first officials to attempt to halt the sale of liquor to the Indians. He issued orders forbidding the importation of spirits, and he joined with the Jesuits in their efforts to convince the Indians that only harm could come to them from strong drink. But if Champlain and the Jesuits could achieve even a moderate success in their struggles, they were in no position to prevent English traders from supplying the Indians with unlimited quantities of rum, and neither their police power nor their political influence was great enough to stop the *coureurs de bois* from trafficking in it.

To begin with, the *coureurs de bois* objected to the fathers' trading with the Indians, and the Jesuits' firm stand against the use of liquor served to increase their complaints against the order. The missionaries, they declared, enjoyed unlimited freedom, while they were subject to stringent regulations. To be sure, they didn't always obey the regulations . . . and least of all did they obey the Crown's prohibition of the sale of intoxicants to the natives . . . but they resented them just the same.

It had not been easy to induce the Indians to drink. In the beginning, they had been unwilling to exchange their furs for the unfamiliar fiery liquid, but both the French and British had persisted, and at last had succeeded in making alcohol a requisite of the trade. The French and British knew what they were doing. An Indian who could be induced to take a few drinks became wild for more. Those who developed a craving would give anything they had for it. Returning from a successful hunt, an Indian who had known the delights of intoxication would trade his season's catch for a few bottles of raw, impure liquor.

"It is useless," wrote a Jesuit, "to forbid the trade in wine and brandy with the Savages. There is always found some base person who, to gain a little beaver fur, introduces by moonlight some bottle into their Cabins."

When the Indians with whom they were conducting a trade became impoverished and began to degenerate, with the result that they were unable to hunt, the *coureurs de bois* simply pushed farther out into the wilderness until they found unspoiled tribes to debauch.

That was the pattern, and it was not to change as long as there were new territories to be conquered, although kings, Parliaments, Presidents and honorable individuals never ceased in their attempts to halt the destructive practice. On innumerable occasions Indians themselves sought to stop the traffic that was ruining their people. As early as the middle of the seventeenth century, many Algonquins and Hurons avoided traders who offered alcohol, and they petitioned the French Governor to forbid traders to give or sell it to them. The Governor granted the petition, but it had no effect.

The problem became so acute and disruptive that the French Crown ordered the leading traders of New France to meet and settle upon a definite policy. Comte de Frontenac, then Governor, and members of the Council met with twenty of the largest colonial traders in what was dubbed the "Brandy Parliament." Robert Cavelier de La Salle and the famed explorer Louis Jolliet were present, and they stood on opposite sides. La Salle argued that it was impossible to keep liquor from the Indians, that if the coureurs de bois were not allowed to sell it, unscrupulous individuals would smuggle it into the Indian country, and he insisted that the Indians would not trade with those who did not furnish them with drinks. He cited a case in point: three hundred Iroquois were en route to Montreal with furs, but when told they could not obtain liquor there, they turned about and went to Albany, where the Dutch willingly supplied them with all the drink they desired. If the French forbade the use of liquor in the trade, the English and Dutch would continue to hold the alliance of the Iroquois and secure the loyalty of the western tribes. As it was, the French drinks were more delicious, the Indians liked them better than the English drinks, and this advantage should be maintained.

Others attending the "Brandy Parliament" argued that brandy was helpful in saving the Indians' souls. If the English and Dutch held the Indians through drink, they also would convert them to heresies which would send their souls to perdition. It was asserted that the Indians could not afford to purchase enough alcohol to hurt them.

Taking an opposing view, Jolliet pointed out the violence of the Indians when intoxicated. They would run deeply into debt to get brandy, he declared, and their deterioration, caused by strong drink, made them poor hunters. So extreme were Jolliet's views on the matter that he urged the death penalty for those who used liquor in the fur trade.

The conference voted to continue the liquor traffic. Accepting the will of the majority, the Crown amended it by limiting the sale to the French settlements and allowing only a small number of permits for transporting liquor into the wilderness. The edict meant less than nothing. It was ignored, and the Indian country was in reality thrown wide open to unlimited traffic in alcohol.

The Jesuits continued their strenuous fight, but only with moderate success, and when the first war between France and England began in the New World, a Government official reported that drink had brought ruin to all the Indian missions.

The pattern was maintained as the years passed, the troubles did not lessen, and the British, winning control of all of North America above Florida, were no more successful in halting the destructive traffic than their French predecessors. Most of the Indians preferred to trade where they could obtain spirits, and always there were intelligent, sincere chiefs who sought to abolish the evil liquor that was ruining their people.

In 1734 British authorities received a letter from some Indian leaders pleading that no trader be allowed to "bring more than 30 gallons of Rum twice a year and not to hide it in the woods." If this were done, they promised that debts would be paid. In 1738 an Indian council resolved "that whatever Rum is in our Towns shall be broak and spilt, and nott Drunk." But a few years later the same Indians were demanding more rum from the British.

The situation was the same in the South as it was in the North. The Carolinians were accused of using a particularly detestable trick on the Indians. After purchasing all the skins in a village, they would produce a quantity of rum. When the Indians had become drunk, they would give back to the traders the goods they had received in exchange for their pelts so that they might continue their drunken revel. The traders would then depart for the next village, taking both furs and trade goods.

Conditions to be met in a given area, however, affected policy when it came to selling liquor. In northern Canada, the Hudson's Bay Company . . . before learning better from bitter experience . . . sold spirits to the Indians. Widespread impoverishment was the result.

French traders, in deadly competition with the gargantuan British monopoly, well understood the error the British were making, and took advantage of it. The Indians of the Far West had not yet been corrupted by liquor, and the French, wise in the ways of the trade through decades of experience, realized the advantage to be gained by refraining from its use.

The French traders moved out to the headwaters of the Moose and Albany Rivers, at Lake Winnipeg, an enormous, virtually untouched wilderness fur empire, and cut off much of the trade that would otherwise have gone north to the posts of the Hudson's Bay Company. The Frenchmen were more adroit than the Englishmen. They lived with the Indians, won their affections, supplied them with guns, traps, axes, brilliantly colored, warm clothing and luxurious trifles. But they offered no liquor, and the Indians with whom they traded, there in the remote far northwest country, were sober and vigorous, and brought in great quantities of fine furs.

As the French had done, the victorious British forbade the usage of alcohol in the fur trade, to no avail. England's "Imperial Plan" for the fur trade in its American colonies contained provisos against the use of liquor in transactions with the Indians. They were seldom obeyed. Canadian merchants complained that large quantities of spirits were smuggled into the Indian country, and the Indians themselves complained that traders were offering them "quantities of Brandy and other spiritous liquors in exchange for their Peltries." The Lords of Trade ordered that justices of the peace cancel licenses of all traders "who retail spirits to the Savages."

The merchants and traders of Montreal, seeking a conservative and sane policy, petitioned the Government to control the traffic. Stating that they had been grievously injured by it, they pleaded that no canoe for Mackinac, Detroit and other posts be allowed to carry more than "4 bbls. of strong Liquors of eight or nine gallons each." General Guy Carlton sent troops to "stop the sale of rum," but they had no success.

General Thomas Gage wrote that quarrels between "drunken Indians and licentious whites" were common. "The most general complaint at present about the Trade is," he said, "of the vast Quantitys of Rum carried amongst the Indians." It was so "Easy to smuggle it past Posts and profits so great that it will likely continue."

Gage thought the Indian trader was "generally a pretty Lawless Person," and he ordered his officers to prevent the sale of rum at the posts. He suggested to Sir William Johnson, Superintendent of Indian Affairs, that the Indians be allowed to police themselves and take on the responsibility of preventing "Spirits being carried into their villages and hunting Grounds." Johnson thought such an experiment might be "too dangerous, and it would give Pretence for plundering, and if they began to seize one article, it's uncertain where they would stop."

General Gage was right. The liquor trade would continue. And when the Americans were at last victorious over the powers of Europe, it remained the most complicated, controversial problem having to do with the Indians and the fur trade.

The United States Congress had no more than assembled in the new capital city of Washington when it passed an act which authorized the President "to take such measures, from time to time, as to him may appear expedient to prevent or restrain the vending or distributing of spiritous liquors among all or any . . . of the Indian tribes."

It was a weak, vacillating measure. If it put Congress on the side of righteousness and good sense, it did nothing more. All action was left to the discretion of the President, and he had many other important burdens to bear. For the next twelve years no President used his powers to halt the trade in alcohol. It was a fact, of course, that the sale of corn whisky to traders brought welcome revenue to Western farmers, and only a careless politician would have ignored the growing strength of the western electorate. It was also a fact that British traders trafficked in alcohol, and it would have been unfair to deny the same privilege to Americans.

The horrors, the crimes, the terrible debauchery and suffering taking place on the frontier in the ensuing years, however, stirred Congress to give brief attention to the problem once more, and in 1815 it forbade the setting up of a still in the Indian country under pain of a fine of $5,000. If Congress had deliberately set out to pass a law which would have little or no effect on the situation, it could not have done better.

There the matter stood. Some territorial governors believed the vague regulations gave them jurisdiction to control liquor traffic, and they took steps to do it. The governors were also superintendents of Indian affairs for their respective territories. Governor Ninian Edwards of Illinois wrote a proviso into trading licenses forbidding traders to deal in spirits. His sincerity was indicated by the unusual penalty established for violators. It authorized Indians to seize the goods of traders who attempted to give liquor for furs. But the authority of Governor Edwards was restricted ... there was a great deal of Indian country outside the boundaries of Illinois Territory.

When Astor sent his historic expeditions, by land and by sea, to the Columbia River, he gave them explicit instructions that they were not to supply the Indians with liquor under any circumstances. The orders were obeyed, but in those cases compliance was without difficulty, for there were no competitors.

He maintained the same attitude and the same policy at the time he launched his drive into the Great Lakes region, and even if an effective blockade against all liquor, except that belonging to him, had been enforced, he would not have taken advantage of such a favored position to use intoxicants. Unfortunately his theories could not be put into practice.

The reasons were simple. Liquor had been used in the Indian trade of the Northwest Territory for more than a hundred years when the American Fur Company launched its major operations there. Moreover, honorable traders who held the same views as Astor soon found out that only by the use of alcohol could they prevent him, with his unlimited resources, from driving them out of business.

It became a vicious circle. Astor had no need for whisky, if no other trader used it. When competing traders resorted to the use of alcohol, he understood that price-cutting would not suffice alone as a weapon for destroying his opposition.

Crooks and Stuart bluntly informed Astor that unless the American Fur Company was permitted to use alcohol in the trade without restraint, it could not hope to compete successfully with either the Hudson's Bay Company or the independent traders who dispensed it to the Indians.

There was no such thing as a moderate drinker among the Indians. They were either teetotalers or sots. Said Governor Cass: "Their attachment to ardent spirits is a moral phenomenon, and to it they sacrifice every consideration public or private." Said United States Superintendent of Indian Affairs Thomas L. McKenney: "The trader with the whisky, it must be admitted, is certain of getting most furs."

Despite the situation Astor found facing him when he began his northwest drive, he and his agents were able to bring about some temporary curtailment of the liquor trade.

When Illinois was admitted as a state in 1818, the northern part of it was cut off to form the Territory of Wisconsin, and it was wide open to traders vending liquor. Alarmed at the prospect, Crooks wrote Secretary of War John Calhoun urging that the 1817 regulations restricting the use of liquor in the trade be extended to include Wisconsin and the upper Mississippi areas, as well as the Great Lakes region. Crooks also persuaded George Boyd, Indian Agent at Mackinac, to grant William Morrison, the

American Fur Company trader, authority to "destroy all spiritous liquors . . . introduced within the American limits in the neighborhood of the Fond du Lac and Red Lake Settlements." This order was aimed at foreign traders as well as American rivals.

"Liquor secretly introduced has hurt our trade," Crooks wrote Astor. "If government agents will not stop it, although the proof of guilt is easy, I sincerely hope the opportunity will not be lost of punishing such miscreants. If the Government permits the sale of this pernicious liquid we can have no hesitation of availing ourselves of the privilege although we are convinced its total prohibition would benefit both the Country at large and the natives who are its victims. But to succeed in the trade when our opponents set the law at defiance and we implicitly follow its dictates is wholly impossible."

In June, 1817, Crooks and Stuart were at Mackinac. They wrote Astor: "The first thing we learned . . . [on arriving there] was the injury our outfits had sustained at Sagina Bay on Lake Huron, and at Grand River, on Lake Michigan, from the clandestine introduction of Spiritous liquors . . ."

The Canadians, making a last desperate stand, sent a flood of alcohol over the border. Crooks complained bitterly, but told Indian Agent Boyd: "We wish to do the same." So bad was the situation that even Governor Cass, liberal in his views on the trade in alcohol, was moved to write Secretary Calhoun of the revolting conditions resulting from the distribution of intoxicating drinks to the Indians.

To the impossibility of guarding a wild and lengthy border was added the uncertainty of the regulations. No official knew exactly what he could do, what power he possessed, or how far he might go, to curtail the smuggling. The Indian Agent at Green Bay "prohibited the landing of every description of spirits in this agency, for the purpose of trade or Barter." His superior, Governor Cass, opined that while "there is no treaty or law which extinguish the Indian title in the vicinity of Green Bay," the district could not be classed as "Indian country," and therefore "the sale of such liquors to the Inhabitants of the Country ought not to be

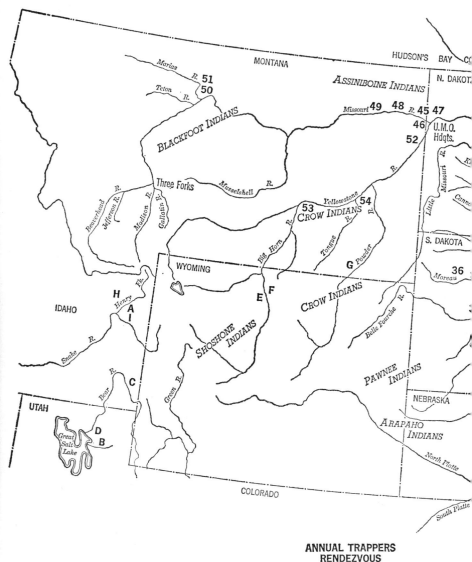

ANNUAL TRAPPERS
RENDEZVOUS
1825-33

A — 1825 — Henry's Fork
B — 1826 — Weber River
C — 1827 — Bear Lake
D — 1828 — Weber River
E-F — 1829-30 — Big Horn River
G — 1831 — Powder River
H — 1832 — Snake River
I — 1833 — Snake River

WESTERN DEPT. OF
THE AMERICAN FUR CO.

Location of posts shown in relation to
present state series and cities

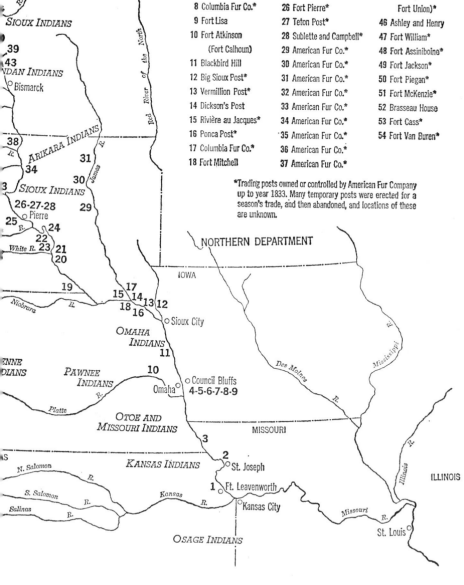

MAIN TRADING POSTS

1 Chouteau's Post (Kansas Post)*	19 Handy's Post	38 Fort Manuel
2 Blacksnake Hills*	20 Cedar Fort (Fort Recovery)	39 Fort Clark*
3 Nishnabotna*	21 Fort Brasseaux	40 Lisa's Fort
4 Crooks and McClelan	22 Fort Lookout*	41 Sublette and Campbell*
5 Bellevue*	23 Fort Kiowa*	42 Tilton's Fort*
6 Pilcher's Post*	24 Loiselle's Post	43 Kipp's Post*
7 Cabanne's Post*	25 Fort Tecumseh*	44 Kipp Post*
8 Columbia Fur Co.*	26 Fort Pierre*	45 Fort Floyd (later called Fort Union)*
9 Fort Lisa	27 Teton Post*	46 Ashley and Henry
10 Fort Atkinson (Fort Calhoun)	28 Sublette and Campbell*	47 Fort William*
11 Blackbird Hill	29 American Fur Co.*	48 Fort Assiniboine*
12 Big Sioux Post*	30 American Fur Co.*	49 Fort Jackson*
13 Vermillion Post*	31 American Fur Co.*	50 Fort Piegan*
14 Dickson's Post	32 American Fur Co.*	51 Fort McKenzie*
15 Rivière au Jacques*	33 American Fur Co.*	52 Brasseau House
16 Ponca Post*	34 American Fur Co.*	53 Fort Cass*
17 Columbia Fur Co.*	35 American Fur Co.*	54 Fort Van Buren*
18 Fort Mitchell	36 American Fur Co.*	
	37 American Fur Co.*	

*Trading posts owned or controlled by American Fur Company up to year 1833. Many temporary posts were erected for a season's trade, and then abandoned, and locations of these are unknown.

HAGSTROM CO., N. Y.

wholly prohibited, but only limited or guarded in such a manner as to prevent their subsequent transfer to the Indians." Cass was thinking of the few white people who comprised the Green Bay colony . . . the eternal politician . . . and advocating action that was obviously impossible.

Once again the Federal Government, horrified by the continuing tales reaching Washington of murder, arson, rape, stabbings and plunderings, was moved to action. In 1822, Congress passed a law forbidding traders to take ardent spirits into Indian territories under penalty of forfeiting all their goods. This was nothing more than a reaffirmation, in statute form, of the regulations which had been in force since 1817. It made it no easier for the authorities to enforce the law. And it left many questions unanswered. What was and what was not Indian territory? Maj. Willoughby Morgan, the commanding officer at Fort Crawford on the Mississippi River, wrote his department in an effort to find out whether Prairie du Chien, located in the heart of the Indian country and "resorted to by some powerful tribes of Indians," was itself actually "Indian country."

Another question Morgan wanted answered was whether American citizens who were not Indian traders could pass through Indian country with ardent spirits. If the answer to the first question was *no*, and the answer to the second was *yes*, the new law was dead in Prairie du Chien as well as in all the Indian country supplied from it. Morgan held the view that only by prohibiting all persons from transporting liquor for any purpose whatsoever could the law be enforced. But no one cared very much what Morgan thought.

All reticence on the part of Astor to engage in supplying liquor to the Indians vanished, and by 1822 the American Fur Company became the largest supplier of all. To say, as some persons did, that Astor was in Europe much of this period and did not know what his agents were doing was a palliation ridiculous in the extreme. Astor not only was fully apprised of the actions of his agents, but he formulated every policy and ordered every action they carried out.

The gates were down, as far as Astor was concerned, but even as he ordered his posts and outfits to use liquor as freely as they deemed necessary, Crooks was dishonestly proclaiming that the American Fur Company would comply with the regulations of 1822. He openly instructed Astor traders to conduct the sale of whisky "with decency," and added: "Our people must do nothing against the law." Shortly afterward he sent a circular to the company agents directing them to take "no ardent spirits into the Indian country."

Crooks's next move was against the Hudson's Bay Company. It was utterly impossible to close the Canadian border against the traffic, and the Hudson's Bay agents brought whisky across in large quantities without difficulty. To combat them, Crooks arranged with Governor Cass to suspend American regulations at all points on the border and west of Lake Superior where Hudson's Bay Company posts were located.

American Fur Company liquor was sent into the Indian country from its posts at Chicago, Milwaukee, Green Bay, Mackinac, Fond du Lac, and from points on the Mississippi.

"Mr. Kinzie, son of the sub-agent at Chicago, and agent for the American Fur Company, has been detected in selling large quantities of whiskey to the Indians at and near Milwaukee of Lake Michigan," the Indian Agent at Green Bay wrote to his superior in Washington.

Superintendent McKenney reported the seizure by the Indian Agent at Fort Wayne (in Indiana) of a large supply of liquors en route to the Indians with an American Fur Company outfit. "The forbidden and destructive article, whiskey, is considered so essential to a lucrative commerce, as not only to still those feelings [of repugnance] but lead the traders to brave the most imminent hazards, and evade, by various methods the threatened penalties of law," McKenney stated. "There are many honorable and high-minded citizens in this trade, but expediency overcomes their objections and reconciles them for the sake of the profits of the trade."

Adam D. Steuart, U. S. Collector at Mackinac, a "servant" of

Astor, cleared a large shipment of American Fur Company whisky for Wisconsin. Maj. John Biddle, Indian Agent at Green Bay, stopped it. Steuart at once protested to the War Department on the ground that Prairie du Chien was not in Indian country. Secretary Calhoun dutifully complained of Major Biddle's action to the Treasury Department. The shipment was released, and Prairie du Chien was thereupon established as the "center of lavish sales of liquor to the Indians."[9]

This incident brought from the noted William Clark, Indian Superintendent at St. Louis, the comment: "Permit me to observe, that in relation to the scenes of intoxication at Prairie des Chiens, neither the Agent at that place, or the Officer in command, has the power to prevent the sale of spirits to the Indians; that being a Town and settlement without the Indian limits, over which the Government and Laws of Michigan Territory are extended, and where the Laws in relation to that subject are but little regarded by the civil authority . . ."

Astor's great influence in Washington, and his many powerful friends there, encouraged Government agents and company traders in open defiance of the liquor regulations and in some instances to inspire and condone violent tactics.

From 5,000 to 8,000 gallons of Astor liquor passed through Mackinac alone each season. Collector Steuart appeared to have been afflicted with spasmodic blindness.

Col. Josiah Snelling, famed frontier commander, made a valiant effort to halt the liquor traffic. He wrote the Secretary of War: "The neighborhood of the trading houses where whiskey is sold presents a disgusting scene of drunkenness, debauchery and misery; it is the fruitful source of all our difficulties, and of nearly all the murders committed in the Indian country . . ."

Major Tipton, a zealous Indian Agent in the Wabash region, seized a quantity of liquor and a cargo of merchandise being taken to the Indians by Astor traders, one of whom was William

[9] Steuart was collector at Mackinac from 1818 to 1833, but on occasion during this period he also acted as the American Fur Company's representative in Washington.

H. Wallace, a former clerk with the Astorians. Said Tipton: "From the time of my comeing into the agency complaints were frequently made to me of the improper conduct of the Clerks of the American fur Company . . . as soon as they arrived among the Indians of this agency . . . I was informed of their selling liquor . . . of which I have ample proof."

On this occasion, William B. Astor, by this time working with his father in New York, took action, writing to Tipton to assure him that there must be some mistake. William demanded an investigation. Tipton made no reply. Young Astor sought to secure the release, on bond, of the merchandise among which the liquor had been found. Tipton countered by seizing another shipment of Astor whisky and goods. William then wrote angrily to the Secretary of War accusing Tipton of being "more actuated by a desire to injure our Company than to discharge his duty to the public faithfully." But the Secretary of War stood by Tipton, and the goods were condemned.

Astor had been in Europe at the time the Tipton seizures were made, but when he returned, a change in the War Department's attitude soon took place. James Barbour had become Secretary of War, and upon Astor's application to him, the goods were returned in bond to the American Fur Company "to prevent their complete destruction." Astor's overtures to Barbour were accompanied by a letter from Gallatin, praising Astor's patriotism.

Maj. Lawrence Taliaferro, agent at St. Peters, also made an effort to enforce the law. He seized whisky in the possession of Joseph Rolette and other Astor traders. Scurrilous attacks were immediately launched against him by Robert Stuart.

Robert Stuart was a man of violent temper. He was often brutal in dealing with the simple laborers, the *engagés,* who worked under him. On one occasion he felled with a club two drunken and insolent *voyageurs,* fracturing the skull of one of them. He was known as a man who struck first and spoke afterward.

Later he appeared to undergo a mysterious change in his attitude and nature. He halted his violence toward defenseless employees, and he gave orders in a quiet voice. The men with whom he worked reasoned that he had either "got religion" or had contracted some wasting disease.

Stuart, himself, had begun to wonder what had happened to him. He was not sick, so he came to the conclusion that he had been "reborn," and he held grave doubts that as an elder of the Presbyterian Church he should engage in debauching the Indians with liquor.

One obviously prejudiced writer said that Stuart's "conscience troubled him. He felt that it was inconsistent for a temperance man and Christian to send whiskey by the barrel to the Indians. The company would put this branch of the trade into other hands and relieve him; but then the evil would be increased four-fold. His best friends persuaded him to hold his position, even if he was reproached, and lessen the evil he could not cure. He finally consented . . ."

Stuart salved his conscience for a time, not only by refraining from breaking the skulls of his workers, but by forbidding all Sabbath work for the company on Mackinac Island, much to the bewilderment of the maltreated *engagés*. But when it came to debauching the Indians with liquor, his conscience appeared, in the end, to be disturbed not at all. Instead of lessening the evil he could not cure, he pleaded with the War Department for permission to increase the supplies of whisky to Company posts near the border, and he increased shipments of liquor to Mackinac alone 50 per cent in two years.

5

Forced to obey the instructions of the corrupt Governor Cass, Puthuff suffered condemnation by departmental colleagues who were outside of Cass's jurisdiction. Severe criticism came especially from the factors in charge of the Government trading houses. John W. Johnson, the Government agent at Prairie du Chien, complained that Major Puthuff was licensing "the blackest of characters" to trade in that area. Maj. Mathew Irwin, the Green Bay factor, wrote to Col. Thomas L. McKenney, Superintendent of the Indian Service, that British traders licensed by Puthuff were ruining independent American traders and Government factories by their opposition. Nearly all of these Britishers, he declared, had been active in stirring up the Indians against the Americans during the War of 1812. "It was not expected," said Irwin, "that Mr. Astor would engage to do business with the Indians with none but British subjects, and those, too, so exceptional in every particular." Two of the most "exceptional" were Crooks and Stuart.

American military officers supported the complaints of the Indian Agents, and on at least one occasion took violent action against Astor. Russell Farnham and Daniel Darling were leading an outfit to trade on the Des Moines River when they were stopped by Lt. Col. Talbot Chambers, the commanding officer at Prairie du Chien. Chambers refused to recognize the licenses given to Farnham and Darling at Michilimackinac, and he ordered them to proceed to St. Louis without trading en route and obtain new licenses from Governor Clark, who had jurisdiction in that area west of the Mississippi.

Farnham and Darling disobeyed. They were arrested and their trade goods were seized. When Astor was informed of the incident, he complained bitterly directly to President Monroe. The

American Fur Company filed a suit against Chambers, which resulted in an award to it of $5,000.[10]

At times, independent fur buyers invaded what Crooks considered "company territory," and offered higher prices than Astor was willing to pay. They met with some success on a few occasions, but in each instance Crooks was soon on their trail and found means of stopping them. Traders who were tempted to deal with the "intruders" were persuaded to remain loyal to the American Fur Company with bribes in the form of an annual stipend or by a share contract. Trader James Crofts was an example. Crooks gave him a salary of $1,000 for a year. An enterprising young clerk, Gordon S. Hubbard, was paid $400 to assist Crofts.

Not all new competitors, however, were easily bought off. William Farnsworth arrived in Wisconsin in 1820 and began to deal directly with the Indians. He was warned that a man who attempted to compete with the American Fur Company was risking both his property and his life. An Indian chief was paid to threaten Farnsworth by lighting a candle on a keg of powder. But Farnsworth was courageous and he remained for a number of years a small but stubborn thorn in the Company's hide.

Jacob Smith was another defiant and troublesome independent trader. He competed boldly with Astor agent William H. Wallace near Fort Harrison, on the Wabash. Crooks reported that Smith was smuggling liquor into the area, but the complaint went unheeded by authorities.

Regarding the problem of "interlopers," Crooks told Astor: "The best of the traders have little or no capital, still we are more secure by selling [them goods] than engaging them as clerks, for they give us all they collect and in a bad year we have no wages to pay. You are aware no doubt that we must send Goods to several places where little or no profit is expected, as furnishing one tribe and not their neighbors would occasion a war & the plundering of our people. There are likewise frontier posts where we expect but small gain, yet must create barriers to prevent the encroachment of interlopers upon our interior and more valuable posts."

[10] It was never paid, however.

Crooks sent a constant stream of advice to the company's traders, repetitiously cautioning them to "buy cheaply," telling them to practice "rigid economy," "Do not give credit," "Do not allow any trade except with Indians." He gave minute instructions about prices to be paid for skins, and informed them about market conditions in New York and Europe, which generally he reported as poor. Frequently he wrote of the "prospect that all furs will fall much in price," and spoke of "gloomy prospects." He insisted that traders free themselves from the obligation of supporting employees with "large families of women and children," admonishing them not to "employ men with families unless necessary."

Crooks was, of course, merely parroting orders he received from Astor.

Stuart and Crooks had made several attempts to "win over" Puthuff, but had failed. Puthuff went no further in accommodating them than he was forced to do by Cass. They launched a scurrilous attack on him, writing Astor that he was charging $50 apiece for licenses, was favoring competitors of the American Fur Company, and was failing to check smuggling and the sale of liquor to the Indians. Astor took the matter up with Washington.

Puthuff's associates and superiors did not realize how greatly he had been forced by Cass to favor Astor. Nor was Puthuff given a chance to defend himself. He was removed from office.

George Boyd succeeded him, and Astor hardly could have asked for more. Boyd was a brother-in-law of John Quincy Adams. He was highly sympathetic to the policies of the American Fur Company, and was eager to see it defeat its British competitors. Soon after taking office he issued a unique bit of propaganda in an effort to throw a good light on Astor's traffic in liquor. "Whiskey is allowed in small quantities to each Outfit for the use of the *Engagés* or men employed in the laborious part of the Trade," he said, "with the explicit assurance that no part of the same be given under any pretences to the Indians."

One of Boyd's early acts was to authorize the Astor trader William Morrison to seize the goods of competing traders which assertedly had been "illegally introduced" in the Fond du Lac and Red Lake districts. Morrison also was authorized to "destroy all spiritous liquors." Thus, Morrison held powers equal to those of the Government.

Boyd also revoked all licenses granted to one of Astor's strongest competitors, Charles O. Ermatinger, and declared that Ermatinger would get no more licenses until a "lawless trader" whom Ermatinger had discharged was "brought back." Crooks wrote triumphantly to Astor that Ermatinger's post had been closed.

Ermatinger may have been forced to close his post, but he had not lost his nerve. He continued to trade without a license, much to the annoyance of the American Fur Company. However, the strength of his competition had been drastically weakened.

With these victories behind them, Crooks and Stuart became bolder. They boasted that they had got Puthuff removed, and they threatened the Government agents at Green Bay and Prairie du Chien with a similar fate.

The attitude of the Government toward Astor had convinced the British and Canadians that the American Fur Company had been awarded an official status. "Ever since the peace," wrote a British officer, "the Americans have been bestowing uncommon pains to perfect and complete their plan of entirely gaining the western Indians—They are aware of its vital importance in the event of another war—as one great means of effecting this whole Trade of Michilimackinac is to be monopolized by the House of John Jacob Astor who will soon distance all competitors in consequence of being enabled by the favor of his Government to send his goods to the Indian country free of all duties whatever."

The British officer was mistaken in asserting that Astor was permitted to import goods duty-free, but he was correct in his statement about Astor receiving uncommon favors from the Government.

Cass stood behind Crooks and Stuart, with no fear of being criticized by his superiors. He commissioned Crooks, a British subject, to visit Mackinac, Green Bay, Prairie du Chien, and St.

Louis on behalf of the American Government and examine the conduct of American agents in those places.

Superintendent of Indian Affairs McKenney fought back with exceptional courage. His factors had kept him well informed of the way foreign traders, most of them in the employ of Astor, were ruining the trade of American citizens, selling large quantities of liquor to the Indians, and committing other illegal acts injurious to the trade of the Government houses.

McKenney at last was able to prevail on the President to issue an order forbidding the granting of licenses "to any foreigner to trade with the Indians," and prohibiting "an American Citizen licensed to trade to take with him or to send into the Indian Country any foreigner."

Had it been allowed to stand, the order of the Chief Executive would have been a severe blow to Astor. The American Fur Company, being the largest in the field, employed more foreigners than all other houses combined.

Government factors and Indian Agents hailed the new ruling, but the outlawed foreigners, knowing Astor's strength, were not unduly apprehensive. Jacob Franks, a British subject who operated out of Green Bay, conferred about the matter on a trip to Montreal with David Stone, one of Astor's main competitors. Franks then reported: "Mr. Stone is of the opinion that we can go on with the fur trade. Mr. Stone also says if Mr. Astor has any advantage with the American Government he is sure he [Stone] will be entitled to as much from the Interest of his friends who are Members of the Congress." This information, Franks added, "has in some measure made my mind more easy."

Michael Dousman, also of Green Bay, entertained a similar opinion to the effect that "J. J. Astor and D. Stone" would make some satisfactory arrangements.

Franks and Dousman were right. Astor and Stone got busy in Washington. In a few weeks the Presidential order was revised to state that "permits may be granted to American traders, to employ in their trade with the Indians Foreign Boatmen and Interpreters."

The situation was the same as it had been before the executive order was issued. All Astor had to do was to engage British and Canadian traders as boatmen. Once in the wilderness, they could not be prevented from functioning as traders. McKenney's efforts had borne fruit, but it had turned out to be sour.

Astor had been a close friend of President Madison's, but he was much more intimate with President Monroe. He felt free to write directly to Monroe, and to expect Monroe to give special attention to his problems.

The basis for Astor's attitude was not a mystery. It was the result of certain financial transactions between himself and Monroe. In 1820, Astor wrote from Europe to Monroe: ". . . understand that landed property in the U. S. is at present not very saleable. I presume you have not sold any of your estates, and therefore it may not be convenient to repay me the sum lent to you, nor am I particularly in want of it. It will, however, be agreeable to have the interest paid, and I have taken the liberty to draw on you for £2,100, favor of my son at 90 days, being equal to three years interest."[11]

The letter showed that Astor had loaned Monroe money some time prior to 1817. It was after the War of 1812, in 1815, that the American Fur Company began its great offensive to capture the fur trade of the Great Lakes region and the upper Mississippi country.

The amount and circumstances of the loan were disclosed in a letter written some time later by Monroe to his old friend, former President Madison, "I have sold my slaves," Monroe told Madison, ". . . to Col. White of Florida, who will take them in families, to that territory. He gives me for them . . . five thousand dolrs., which are paid for obtaining for me a release in that amount from J. J. Astor, for a loan obtained of him in the late war, offered by himself, on hearing that I was pressd for money."

This letter made it clear that for a number of years Monroe had owed Astor at least $5,000, which, despite the fact that he

[11] The spelling and punctuation have been corrected to the extent that the letter may be understood by readers. It apparently was clear to Monroe, however.

held the highest offices in the Government, he had been unable
to pay until he had sold his slaves. Quite understandably, Monroe
was more inclined to grant favors to Astor than he was to someone . . . say, an Astor competitor . . . to whom he did not have
the same sense of obligation.

The views and loyalties of Boyd, who was such an unqualified
partisan of the American Fur Company at the beginning of his
career as an Indian Agent, underwent a change as time passed.
He became critical of the company's cold-blooded policies and
business tactics, and he spoke of it as a "great monied Aristocracy."

Astor often had brought independent traders into his spreading monopoly by guaranteeing them trade goods at the comparatively reasonable markups of 35 or 40 per cent. Once he had them
in his debt, the markup was increased, and Boyd stated that in
the mid-1820's the "traders for the Company generally receive
their goods at an advance of 75 per Cent on the Sterling cost . . .
with the full understanding that the Company shall have the refusal of the Returns."

The company, in other words, reserved the right to reject any
furs offered in payment.

Boyd estimated that in one period of four years the company
sent an annual average of approximately $68,000 worth of trade
goods through Mackinac alone, but this was an extremely conservative figure. The extent to which Astor dominated the Mackinac trade was shown by Boyd's statement that "the Amount of
furs & peltries brought yearly to this Island, are supposed to be
worth 250 to 300,000 dollars—nineteen twentieths of the same
being for and on account of the American Fur Company."

In a sharp criticism of the American Fur Company, Boyd declared: "Suffer the Indians, in particularly cases as in Robbery
or Murder, to give testimony in our courts, and it will go far to
do away with many of the Evils they at present suffer from our
violence & our avarice—at the same time give the poor Canadians, hirelings for a term of years to hard taskmasters, an assurance that there is a power vested somewhere in the Government,

to Call this great monied Aristocracy to account, not only for aggressions practiced on the red man, but for any maltreatment of any free man trading by their permission within these limits, and under the sanction of their laws, and you will at once divest them of a great portion of that power, which is but too often used to grind down & oppress all within the Circle of their influence: '

"To effect this let a Board of Comptrol, or of accounts, be established, under the authority of the War Dept., composed, say of the principal agent of the American Fur Co., the Ind. Agent, & the Commanding officer of post; whose duty it shall be, to see that justice is rendered to all & Every Canadian employed by the Company, & receiving his discharge . . ."

The insuperability of Astor's financial strength and political power, and the competency, shrewdness and unscrupulousness of his agents were bringing disaster to the oldest trading firms in all the immense area between Detroit and the Mississippi, Mackinac and the Wabash. Crooks wrote exuberantly to his chief: "Berthelot of Mackinac has quitted the trade. Ermatinger of St. Mary's is crippled and D. Stone & Company appear wavering." Should Stone, Astor's strongest competitor, withdraw, said Crooks, "the smaller importers must soon give in to our views . . ."

The "views" were cold, diabolical and easy to learn.

An independent trader had only one alternative under the pressure of Astor's power. He could accept the proposal made by Astor's agents, or he could face Astor in open competition. Actually he had no alternative, for by engaging the insuperable Astor forces he opened the gate to his own destruction.

6

The Tiber was a dirty little creek that ran across the foot of Capitol Hill and along the Mall. On its banks were shacks and hovels harboring persons of such ill-repute that it was called "Murderer's Bay." To get to the unfinished Capitol Building, one had to cross the Tiber on a rickety bridge. Often in winter the bridge was washed away. On such occasions the dignity of Senators and Representatives and other high officials suffered severe blows. They were obliged to tie their horses on the bank and wade through the cold muddy water, or make perilous crossings on logs.

In February, 1818, the Washington newspapers reported that John Jacob Bentzon, eight-year-old grandson of John Jacob Astor, had been drowned in Tiber Creek.

It had been with great pride and pleasure that Astor had taken the boy to the capital. He returned to New York almost prostrate with grief.

John Jacob Bentzon had been his first grandchild, the son of his eldest daughter Magdalen. Her second child, a daughter, had died in infancy. Shortly after the tragedy in Washington, her husband, Adrian Benjamin Bentzon, deserted her.

Magdalen lived alone for a time in her New York mansion, but this situation seemed not to weigh as much on her as it did on her father. She obtained a divorce from Bentzon on grounds of adultery, and shortly afterward married John Bristed, a literary lawyer and physician from England. Less than seven months after the wedding, Magdalen gave birth to a healthy, fully developed son. About the same time this momentous event took place, Bristed also deserted her. Her cousin, Henry Brevoort, was to explain that Bristed simply found it "impossible to bear the matrimonial yoke any longer with that Lamb of Bellzebub . . . She is certainly a maniac."

Astor's grief was enduring, and the antics of Magdalen did nothing to relieve it. He wrote his old friend Peter Smith in Utica, "It is a long time since I had the pleasure of receiving a letter from you—the last you wrote me I was sorry to see you were in bad or low spirits—this indeed has been my case for these 13 months past and tho' I cannot recover mine I would willingly recommend my friends to endeavor to recover theirs—the best is to travel about and attend to business—to keep body and mind engaged & not reflect too much on our afflictions which we must all have at some period . . . we must support ourselves as well as we can . . ."

Smith was having family troubles of his own, and in another letter to him Astor said: "I regret very much your distressed situation, yet I cannot but think that it is greatly in your power to alleviate it . . . you had the misfortune to lose an affectionate wife but you have yet several fine children . . . your happiness must more or less depend on theirs and theirs on yours . . . remember my dear friend how soon you may have to leave this world . . . forgive your children as you wish our Father in Heaven to forgive you—Let them come to you and support them . . . all your wealth will do you no good in your grave . . . See them happy and comfortable and you will be so yourself . . . don't tell me that it is easy to give advice . . . I say to you that I do divide with my children . . . I worked for them & I wish them to have all the good of it—the more they enjoy it, the more happy I am."[12]

Astor practiced what he preached.

After his second son, William Backhouse, had received a careful preparatory education in the United States, he had been sent to Europe to study. William was a rather shy and silent young man with a profound love and appreciation for literature and art. He might have become a writer had not he received a summons from his father in 1818 to return home.

Astor loved William as much as he was capable of loving anyone. When he bade him *bon voyage* on a trip to Europe in 1815

[12] Spelling corrected where necessary to make letter comprehensible, but text unchanged.

. . . William made several trips abroad as a youth . . . he had given him permission to spend as much money as was necessary. William had returned at the end of a year, and Astor had expressed surprise that he had spent so little. "He spent only ten thousand dollars," Astor told a friend. "I thought he would certainly spend fifty thousand."

Hearing such a statement from a man who so greatly frowned on any type of extravagance, those who knew Astor best understood that what he meant to say was that he was proud of William's inherent frugality. Well might they have wondered what Astor's attitude would have been had William not demonstrated his knowledge of the value of money. Of course, it would have been difficult to imagine a son of Astor's and Sarah Todd's in the role of a spendthrift. Had such been the case, William never would have been given the opportunity to move his nose from French classics into the Astor ledgers, and he would have pursued his literary career on a small annual allowance begrudgingly sent him by a disappointed father.

The family tragedies, the great business load he carried and the belief that the time had come when a young and trustworthy hand should assist at the helm had prompted Astor to ask William to become his partner. But there was another, and not insignificant, reason for the proposal. It was the refusal of former Secretary of the Treasury Gallatin of an offer to become associated with the Astor enterprises.

Astor had been very eager to have Gallatin as an associate. He had long been close to him, and he was fully aware of the Swiss's remarkable ability as a financier. Gallatin's distinction as a diplomat and politician was unsurpassed . . . as great as Astor's rank in the world of commerce and trade.

Astor had offered Gallatin a fifth interest in his business . . . real estate excluded . . . but Gallatin had politely declined. Rumor had it that Astor had attempted to lure Gallatin by methods ordinarily ascribed to Cupid. He had suggested that Gallatin's son James, marry his daughter Eliza. In such an event, Astor would not only make Gallatin a partner, but would find a post for young James.

If such a proposition was advanced, neither Eliza nor James was attracted by it. Astor's wealth appeared to impress James less than the great fur trader's table manners, and Eliza seemed to make no impression on James at all.

Gallatin's refusal of the "most generous offer" assertedly was based on the absence of any desire to engage in private business. He expressed the opinion that he "must not die rich" after holding so many Government posts. He preferred to continue in the public service in diplomatic roles.

These excuses may have been sincere, but they did not comprise the whole reason why Gallatin rejected Astor's offers. He knew Astor only too well, and he feared that his Calvinistic conscience could not endure the methods and tricks he would be obliged to condone as Astor's associate. He had not forgotten such episodes as the Chinese Mandarin, nor had he forgotten the equivocal orders he had been obliged to issue in Astor's behalf during the war.

James Gallatin gave his own opinions of the matter, and whether they were based on fact or were purely imaginative, they were unrestrained. Although his father respected Astor, said James, "he could never place himself on the same level with him. I am not surprised, as Astor was a butcher's son at Waldorf—came as an emigrant to this country with a pack on his back. He peddled furs, was very clever, and is, I believe, one of the kings of the fur trade. He dined here, and ate ice cream and peas with his knife."

James confided to his diary: "Really Mr. Astor is dreadful. Father has to be civil to him, as in 1812–1813 he rendered a great service to the Treasury. He came to *déjeuner* today: we were simply *en famille*, he sitting next to Frances [Gallatin's young daughter]. He actually wiped his fingers on her fresh white spencer. Mamma in discreet tones said, 'Oh, Mr. Astor, I must apologize. They have forgotten to give you a *serviette*.' I think he felt foolish."

Either Astor had suffered a relapse to the days when he sat about campfires in the wilderness on his fur-trading trips, or the snobbish young Gallatin was lying. No such complaints were heard when Astor was being lavishly entertained in the fine homes and clubs of the wealthy Montrealers.

When his father sent for him, William dutifully abandoned his artistic pursuits in Europe and returned home to become the junior partner of a new firm . . . John Jacob Astor and Son.

If outwardly William reflected little of his father's personality, he was in reality no less than a second edition of the masterful merchant, landowner and fur trader. He was quieter than his father, spoke well and did not eat with his knife, but he was no less bold, no less shrewd, no less thorough and competent, and he was far more thrifty and much colder. He went to work in the company office at 8 Vesey Street as if he had never desired to pursue a scholarly life, but had thought only of preparing himself to occupy a high position in the business world.

Within a few months after his return from Europe, he had so fully demonstrated his ability to command that Astor felt free to absent himself from the president's chair as the occasion required.

William soon married Margaret Armstrong, the daughter of Madison's Secretary of War. The first of the seven children they were to have was named John Jacob Astor II.

William was tall, and in time he was to be described as "ponderous." His eyes "were small, contracted, with a rather vacuous look, and his face was sluggish and unimpressionable."

Gustavus Myers wrote that William "took delight in affecting a carelessly dressed, slouchy appearance as though deliberately notifying all concerned that one with such wealth was privileged to ignore the formulas of punctilious society. In this slovenly, stoop-shouldered man with his cold, abstracted air no one could have detected the richest man in America."

A contemporary of William declared that he "knew every inch of real estate that stood in his name, every bond, every contract, every lease" held by the Astors. "He knew what was due when leases expired, and attended personally to the matter" of terminating them. "No tenant could expend a dollar, or put in a pane of glass without his personal inspection . . . He was somber and solitary . . . mixed little with general society, gave little and abhorred beggars."

William lived in a fine mansion in Lafayette Place. Myers stated that the "sideboards were heaped with gold plate, and polyglot servants in livery stood obediently by at all times to respond to his merest nod. But he cared little for this show, except that it surrounded him with an atmosphere of power. His frugality did not arise from wise self-control, but from his parsimonious habits. He scanned and revised the smallest item of expense. Wine he seldom touched, and the average merchant spent more on his wardrobe than he did . . . No scruples of any kind did he allow to interfere with his constant aim of increasing his fortune."

William had been on the quarter-deck only a year when Astor became convinced that the destiny of the company was in good hands and he could go to Europe for a badly needed rest. He did not, however, close all gates behind him. On the contrary, he left orders that he was to be constantly informed by mail . . . and special courier if necessary . . . of the condition of the business and all events bearing upon it.

Astor retained the right to issue all important orders. He wrote long and detailed instructions for William, especially regarding the affairs of the American Fur Company and the prospective drive on from the victories in the Old Northwest across the Missouri River to the Rocky Mountains. Nothing was to be permitted to stand in the way or alter the course of that vast undertaking.

There were other areas in which Astor felt that only a man of his experience and knowledge could carry on with the required efficiency. These included the purchase in Europe of the immense quantities of manufactured goods needed for the Indian trade, the direction of his fleet of ships, and the sale of furs sent from New York to London. He would interrupt his vacation and rest to perform these important duties.

Another problem which he took with him across the Atlantic had to do with opium-smuggling.

7

During the War of 1812, the British had succeeded in crippling American shipping with a powerful blockade. This resulted in sharp declines in the prices of vessels. Astor took advantage of the situation, and in 1815, when the conflict ended, he was the owner of four ships, four brigs, and a schooner. The treaty of peace found them sailing in various parts of the world, either outbound with cargoes of furs and specie, or homebound with Oriental and European merchandise.

Before 1816 no Astor ship had carried opium. At that time, however, his vessels were touching with some regularity at Near East and Mediterranean ports. Some returned from these areas to the United States and Europe, but others continued on around the Cape of Good Hope to India and China.

On July 15, 1816, the Astor brig *Macedonian* had reached Canton with, among other things, $110,000 in specie, 450 piculs of ebony, 133 piculs of quicksilver, and 40 piculs of opium. It was the first time an Astor vessel had gone to China without furs.

His ship *Seneca* sailed into Canton on February 26, 1817, with $54,000, 160 piculs of quicksilver, 832 piculs of lead, and 95 piculs of opium. The lead and quicksilver had been picked up in Gibraltar, the opium taken aboard at Smyrna, in Turkey.

With these two shipments Astor was one of the pioneers in the introduction of Turkish opium into China.

During the next two years the Astor vessels *Boxer, Alexander, William and John, Pedler* and *Seneca* carried opium cargoes to Canton. Forty piculs of opium amounted to about 5,000 pounds. Some of his ships carried as much as a hundred piculs on a voyage.

The value of the unrefined Turkish product at Canton was more than $500 a picul.

Turkish opium was greatly inferior to that produced in China or that imported from Bengal. It was contemptuously called "foreign mud" by the Chinese, and its importation was forbidden by law. Dealers surreptitiously used it to adulterate the high grade products.

Astor, therefore, was not only engaging in an illegal trade, but he was selling his smuggled opium to peddlers who defrauded the poor wretches addicted to the habit of smoking it.

Astor's excuse was that other shippers were smuggling opium, and inasmuch as "everyone else does it," he saw no reason why he should not profit from the illicit business. One American firm, Olyphant & Company, did refuse to transport opium in its vessels, and this squeamishness won it the nickname of "Zion's Corner." Astor did not care to suffer such embarrassment. Anyway, old Olyphant was a Quaker or something, with stupid religious beliefs.

The extent of Astor's participation over a period of four years in the opium trade was indicated by a letter from the Boston firm of J. & T. H. Perkins to its agent at Leghorn, Italy. It showed that Astor's position as a narcotics smuggler was pre-eminent. Said the letter: "*We know of no one but Astor we fear.* It is our intention to push it as far as we can . . ."

After he had gone to Europe, Astor suddenly halted his opium-smuggling.

Opium-smuggling was not only a vicious, evil trade, but its illegality added an enormous burden of concern to the many difficult problems of operating a fleet of ships. The chief reason for Astor's decision to abandon the trade was simply that there was not enough money in it to justify facing the dangers involved.

Astor was not a hypocrite. Some shippers of opium, retreating behind a screen of false piety, claimed that the main reason they sent the drug to China was to aid in the conversion of the heathen Chinese to Christianity. Astor made no such dishonest claim. He had smuggled opium only because he thought it would increase the profits of his China trade. When he decided the game was no longer worth the risks it presented, he quit.

Although they carried no more opium, his ships continued to sail around the world, his sea trade expanded, and from New York countless thousands of furs poured out to Europe and China in a never-ending flood. Into New York came the millions of dollars in cash, credit and merchandise from European ports, from China and India and South America.

And in New York, William counted the till and balanced the ledgers with unflagging care and no end of satisfaction, never failing to keep an eye on the horizon for more wealth.

8

Persistent poor health caused Astor to maintain a pessimistic attitude toward the fur trade, even though the American Fur Company was enjoying unprecedented progress and prosperity. From Europe he sent a stream of letters warning against buying more merchandise than could be readily sold. He intimated on several occasions that he might wish to dissolve the company. Monotonously he admonished his agents to "pay less for skins," because the outlook was "not good."

The outlook had never been better, but during a siege of sickness that made him unusually gloomy, he wrote, ". . . the more I see of it, the more I am convinced that we have ever imported too many goods and been induced to give them too freely to people who are not able to pay for them . . . It appears to me that even the last year you had too many goods. I hope this year you will not order so many rather fall short than to have over . . . I repeat don't order too many and be not too sanguine in so loosing a trade as that in which we are engaged." Yet, no order was placed in Europe without Astor's approval. If he was convinced that William, Crooks and Stuart were ordering too much, he had the means of cutting their requests.

William was given the title of acting president. Robert Stuart, with offices at Mackinac and Detroit, was in command of the Northern Department, the Greak Lakes and the upper Mississippi country. Crooks was giving most of his attention to the job of forming a new Western Department, under which the trade would be expanded in the Missouri River territory.

The energetic Stone, who had been forced out of the Northern Department, was again in the picture at St. Louis, but Crooks had succeeded once more in bringing him into the Astor camp by an agreement to trade on joint accounts. Things were going extremely well in both divisions. The prospects for the Missouri River trade were most promising. The outfits in the Northern Department had become larger and better organized through consolidations, and they were returning good profits.

In 1824 Congress passed an act requiring "Indian agents to designate from time to time Certain Convenient & Suitable places for Carrying on trade with the different Indian tribes, and to require all traders to trade at the place thus designated and at no other place." In spite of his remoteness and illness, Astor was highly influential in getting the law enacted. It favored the American Fur Company, "for if a license was granted to some adventurous trader not connected with that Company he was only permitted to trade at some designated point already occupied by that opulent and formidable company; and the consequence was, that the company would sell goods at half their real value, and thus drive away the new opposition trader who could not compete with them, and then the company would again put up their goods to the old prices, and soon make up for the little loss sustained while performing the necessary process of breaking down all show of opposition."

So a discouraged independent trader saw the situation, but Astor also was dissatisfied. In some cases the government failed to enforce the new licensing law as the American Fur Company desired, and William wrote to Superintendent McKenney protesting against locations assigned to some company traders. McKenney instructed Superintendent Clark at St. Louis that any locations requested by Astor were to be assigned to him. This order brought some favorable adjustments, and the company was successful in "breaking" most of the weaker competitors.

With achievement of the desired results, the Northern and Western Departments sent a joint letter to Secretary of War James Barbour in which they petitioned for repeal of the location law.

The request was predicated on the claim that uncertainty "made the assignment of definite trading stations a distinct disadvantage to those engaged in the business, and also that the regulations worked to the advantage of the Hudson's Bay Company along the border and the lawless trader everywhere."

Governor Lewis Cass sponsored the appeal, but McKenney insisted that the location law was necessary in the campaign against the liquor trade with the Indians. The law remained in effect, but the company was not bothered by it. Cass saw to that. When an American Fur Company trader was ordered out of a district assigned to an independent trader, Stuart merely got in touch was Cass. Cass at once revoked the order with the excuse that the American Fur Company previously had made plans to trade in the disputed district. No independent could stand up against Astor's political influence.

The Astor lobby also was busy in 1824 in Washington with a drive to lower tariffs on certain imports, and to raise duties on imported furs. Stuart wrote Crooks, who was in the capital, "You will of course make every exertion to get a duty laid on Neutra Skins, Cony Wool, Russia Hares, &c." These were pelts that came into competition with Astor's beavers and muskrats in the hatmaking industry. Stuart also urged Astor to induce Superintendent McKenney and other Washington friends to work on Congress to "lessen the duties on at least Strouds, Indian Blankets & Guns." These, Stuart pointed out, could be brought in from Canada at a price 20 to 30 per cent below the American costs. Stuart advocated a nauseating plea for "the poor red children of the Forest," suggesting that this might stir the sympathies of Congressmen.

In October, 1824, the company announced that the "greatest quantity of furs ever before offered for sale at one time in the United States, will be put up at auction, in the city of New York on the 11th instant . . . It consists of 12,500 lbs of beaver, 120,000 muskrat skins, 72,000 Racoon ditto, 60,000 hare and nutria ditto, and 10,000 buffalo robes from different regions, and will be sold in lots to suit purchasers."

Astor continued to advocate retrenchments, telling Crooks, ". . . you have always been too sanguine as to the result of our trade, I am sure that to this day it has not paid interest for the money."

This, of course, was palpably untrue. When the same message was sent to Stuart, he took sharp issue with Astor, seeing the trade in anything but an unpleasant picture. He told Astor: "You intimate a wish that we should contract our business: to this Sir, I can have no *personal* objection, but rest assured of its being bad policy, unless you mean *imperceptibly*, (if I may use the expression) to withdraw altogether."

Even while Astor was issuing his stock admonitions "to contract the business, order less goods, buy fewer skins at lower prices, keep out of debt," he was controlling the New York market by buying all of certain types of furs offered for sale. Whenever his health took a turn for the better, he became optimistic, and on one occasion he even admitted that the year 1824, of which he had complained so bitterly, had been "a good year."

It was at this time he sensed that his pessimism might have an adverse effect on his two most valuable lieutenants, Crooks and

Stuart. He realized that without them his operations would have been far less profitable and successful. Worriedly he wrote Crooks: "With regard as to whether I continue in the trade I really cannot now tell . . . but whether I do or not I never had any other thought than that I did retire, I would like you and Mr. Stuart to be fully satisfied. I must say that I never intended to make an arrangement contrary to your interest. Quite otherwise, nor did I contemplate that you or Mr. Stuart would ever separate from the concern while I continued . . ."

Astor's periodic complaints that the company was not making sufficient profit and was in danger of suffering severe reverses did not stir fears in Crooks and Stuart, nor even in William, for all of them knew its strength and true condition.

Astor was not being true to facts. For all practical purposes, he was the Company. Crooks and Stuart had shares, but when the Northern Department was organized, it was Astor who got 90 per cent of the profits. The structure was somewhat different in the Western Department, where some capital was furnished by partners. Nevertheless, in both cases Astor received interest on all money he supplied, and at one time this amounted to more than a million dollars. In addition, Astor paid himself a large salary, the amount of which he kept a secret. He also furnished all merchandise. The articles of agreement governing the branches forbade him to make a profit on selling goods to them, but there was no way to prevent him from doing it. Chittenden, an admirer of Astor, declared that he did make a profit on them, writing: "They were generally furnished by Mr. Astor at a fixed advance upon cost and charges."

Although William saw fit to destroy many of the records in the New York office, others survived, and letters and accounts were preserved by traders and Government officials. They evidenced the unjustness of Astor's pessimism and revealed his inordinate greed.

It was estimated by Indian Service officials that in the Northern Department $125,000 was expended annually for trade goods and wages, and furs valued at $250,000 to $300,000 were received in return.

The conservativeness of this estimate was made clear by William's statement to the Secretary of War that "The capital we employ in the trade in the interior . . . is upwards of one million dollars . . . You may estimate our annual returns at about half a million dollars." This was hardly a discouraging condition.

Yet, Astor wrote Senator Benton: "I very much fear, that unless a duty is imposed on foreign furs, the American Fur Company, the only respectable one of any capital now existing in the country, will be obliged to suspend their operations. I believe I am safe when I say that all our Indian traders for these 20 years past, with very few exceptions, have been losing time and property in that trade . . . The American Fur Company have for years past, and do now employ a capital of a million or more dollars. They have not yet been able to declare a dividend . . . The Hudson Bay Company divide ten per cent. per annum, and have a large surplus on hand. Their stock is at a premium of 150 per cent. above par."

Astor was employing the plea of poverty customarily made by one asking for government assistance, but its falsity did not rest alone on that ground.

Shortly afterward he wrote Stuart: "On settlement in April 1830, a dividend was paid you on that concern (the one known as *no. 3, running from April 1, 1823, to April 1, 1827*) of $450 per share profit, being an estimated profit of $450,000, on the Capital."

Therefore, a dividend was paid on profits for the very years in which Astor complained the company was not making money, and in which he prognosticated an unpromising future. This dividend amounted to approximately 10 per cent of the actual capital employed, the same amount which Astor declared was being paid by the Hudson's Bay Company. A dividend paid for the years 1827–34 was approximately the same.

The "blotters," "journals" and "ledgers" of the Mackinac agency provided reliable indications of the size of the business in that area, and the immense profits which accrued to Astor in the Northern Department.[13]

Imported goods were sent to the Northern Department at a markup of 75 to 85 per cent, and goods purchased in New York at 13 to 16 per cent. By far the larger part of the trade goods sent out came from Europe.

To these markups was added a commission of 5 per cent, which went to Astor. When furs were sold, regardless of how much profit was made, Astor also received a commission of 2 1/2 per cent on all sales. Astor frequently made additional profits by buying furs from his own company and holding them for higher prices, a mere bookkeeping transaction. If company furs were exported in his own ships, he made money by charging the company for the freight.

Few traders who worked for or with the American Fur Company, under any type of an agreement, made money, and the majority of them remained deeply in debt. Astor frequently obtained mortgages on the property traders owned, thereby holding them in virtual bondage. Referring to prices charged by Astor, the trader William Johnston wrote: "At these exorbitant charges, the traders were through necessity compelled to take the merchandise, the consequence was, and still is, that for them to pay for the goods, and barely to obtain a livelihood, they are in part

---

[13] Entries in the Mackinac books showed that in July, 1817, Astor was credited with having advanced $154,739.49 worth of equipment and goods. Three months later, interest credited to Astor amounted to $19,528.73, indicating an interest rate approximating 40 per cent per year.

Entries in 1820, apparently a very good year, showed Astor's credits as $504,393.12. The next year in June a balance was due him of $435,907.99, and he was paid in full in September through the sale of furs. The interest he received varied from as little as 10 per cent up to 40 per cent. He set the prices, and he also set the interest rate.

Other entries showed that in one period furs valued at $536,000 were purchased at Mackinac. A profit, after deductions for costs and expenses, was estimated at $136,000. This was the profit at Mackinac. What the same furs brought on the markets of Europe, China and New York could only be conjectured by outsiders. If they went to New York bearing a profit of $136,000, however, it could be reasonably assumed that they brought a gain of four to five times that amount.

These figures applied only to Mackinac. Furs also poured into Astor's New York warehouses from numerous other areas.

compelled to use fraud and deceit towards the men they have in their employ. . . ."

Astor callously admitted in a letter to Senator Benton that ". . . all our Indian traders, with very few exceptions, have been losing time and property in that trade."

9

Astor returned from Europe in the fall of 1821, having been gone approximately two years. A number of important events had taken place in Washington and on the western frontier during his absence, and he reviewed the situation thoughtfully with William.

Holding his attention especially was the campaign he had launched to force the Government out of the fur trade. Progress had been made toward that goal, but he was far from satisfied.

From the time of the first Federal factory in the Indian country, before the turn of the century, Astor had been opposed to the program. He had denounced the Government houses to DeWitt Clinton in 1808, when the American Fur Company was incorporated. The 1811 agreement for the South West Fur Company had provided that in the event the Government posts were abolished, Astor would be entitled to an interest of two-thirds instead of one-half in the company. In 1817, when the American Fur Company was well into its drive to monopolize the trade of the Old Northwest, an attack on the factories had figured prominently in its plans.

During the operations directed out of Mackinac Island, headquarters for the Northern Department of the company, Crooks

and Stuart had informed Astor that unless the Government factories were abolished "it will in our opinion be imprudent" for
him to continue in the trade in that area. As plans were evolved
for expansion west of the Mississippi, the destruction of Government competition had, in their opinion, become even more imperative.

As Chittenden so aptly pointed out, the Government's trading
system had been created with unquestionably noble motives. It
was the desire of officials to protect the Indians from the evil
designs and wicked practices of private traders. Goods the Indians wanted were to be sold to them at cost, and it was hoped
that through fair dealing the victimizing of the natives and the
traffic in liquor could be halted. There could be no argument
with the assertion that the policies of such men as Washington
and Jefferson and numerous other high officers were designed
for the highest good of the Indians. Criticism could not be justifiably leveled at the men who established the Government posts
and organized the Indian Bureau. They had acted on the highest principles. If they had been blind to realities, it had not been
because they were insincere, but because they had no precedent
by which to gauge their actions, no experience to help them shape
their decisions.

The proper targets for censure were: the system under which
the government posts were obliged to operate, the rules decreed
for them, and the unscrupulous men who, because of the system's weaknesses, were able to twist the program to their own
advantage.

High principles could not be carried out by a Government
which was essentially weak when it came to controlling its citizens, and that was the condition of the American government
when the system was inaugurated, and for some time afterward.
Not only was it unable to control the forces which brought about
the destruction of Indian institutions, customs and way of life,
but it hesitated to interfere in what, by every popular conception
of democracy, seemed to be the inalienable rights of all Americans.

Monopolies were practiced and encouraged by European nations. That was reason enough for the American individualist to despise them. But there were other reasons why they were anathema to him. They were in conflict with every belief and theory contained in the fundamental concepts upon which the United States had been founded, and not the least of these was the privilege of every man to build for himself with all the ability God gave him, and without interference, competition, restraint or coercion on the part of his national government.

Yet, the only way in which the Federal authorities could have protected the Indians, the only way in which the Federal factories could have succeeded in achieving their admirable goals, would have been through the strength of an impenetrable monopoly.

The early administrations facing the complicated Indian problems were aware of this truth, but they did not have the courage of their convictions. If the Government had taken over the Indian trade the way it had taken over the handling of the mail or the coinage of money or the making of war, the crimes against the Indians would not have been committed, and Americans would not have been obliged to look back with shame on a vital chapter in their history.

The weakness of the Government, Chittenden declared, "showed itself particularly in those details of administration by which its human and benevolent purposes were to have been accomplished. The prostitution of the Indian Service to mere personal or partisan advantage, and the placing of those delicate and vital questions at the mercy of political adventurers, were crimes which must ever leave a stain on the American name.

"Herein, whether avoidably or not, the government has been irredeemably at fault. It has sinned knowingly—sinned with the consequences patent to its eyes—and from the paltriest and basest of motives that can guide the policy of a nation."

Deserting its own ideals and purposes, the Government granted licenses to private traders to compete with its own posts. It degraded itself to the level of a competing trader among a horde of lawless and irresponsible rivals. At the same time, Congress forbade its Indian Agents from leaving their posts to go into the wilderness to trade. It forbade them to allow credit to any Indian. It prohibited the use of liquor in the trade. Even the possession of alcoholic spirits on a Government post was a violation of the law. It fixed prices at which goods were to be exchanged for furs. It required its houses to handle merchandise produced by American industries.

In the face of preordained results, the Government persisted in its stupid, if not criminal, program.

British manufactured goods used in the fur trade were invariably superior to those made in America. The Indians came to understand that soon after the first American traders pushed their way over the eastern mountains with articles made in the cities of the Atlantic Coast. From the time he first entered the trade, Astor was fully aware of the great disparity in the qualities of American and European goods. American blankets and cloth were shoddy. American manufactured articles were poorly made of inferior materials. American gunpowder was generally second quality. American whisky was not only raw but was highly diluted. American traps and axe heads were sometimes brittle.

Yet the prices charged by American traders were always as high, and frequently higher, than prices charged by the Canadians for superior goods. American scales could be depended upon to register dishonest weight, always in favor of the trader, of course.

Until the Government factory at Green Bay was opened, reported Indian Agent Irwin, private American traders received "as much as one dollar and fifty cents . . . for a brass thimble, and eighteen dollars for one pound of tobacco."

The Indians were fully aware of the superiority of British goods, and sought them. Astor made every effort to supply them.

The government factories forced prices down, but they didn't put the private traders out of business any place. Many Indians wanted, and often needed, credit, and they could get it only from the private traders.

It was remarkable that the Government factories did not fail quickly from bad business practices alone. Yet they survived . . . and some even made a little money . . . for almost a quarter of a century. When the American Fur Company set out to secure the monopoly which the Government feared to take for itself, the doom of the Federal posts was written on the wind. No system, public or private, could have stood before the onslaught of Astor's capital, brains, experience and political influence.

The Government traders were salaried employees with nothing to gain through personal initiative. Most of them had got their jobs through political patronage, knew nothing at all about dealing with Indians, and cared little about learning the business.

Moreover, Government officials seemed unable to grasp the fact that in the Indian trade they were not dealing with experienced businessmen, but with children. Their customers were only a hop, skip and jump out of the Stone Age.

There was one issue on which Astor and the St. Louis traders who hated him could stand firmly together. They might be the bitterest enemies in every other respect, but when it came to opposing the Government factory system they were in complete accord. Astor, Crooks and Stuart took full advantage of this situation.

Crooks was the field marshal of the attack. Astor sent him orders, and also gave his attention to the Washington front. It was a formidable combination, and action soon occurred. By design it began on the western frontier. Congress received a petition from the St. Louis traders for the abolishment of the system. Supporting this move was a swiftly rising Missouri politician, Thomas Hart Benton. Crooks's voice was heard in behalf of the American Fur Company. Governor Ninian Edwards of Illinois Territory was in the chorus. The Astor stooge, Governor Lewis Cass of Michigan, dutifully appealed to Secretary of War John C. Calhoun to shut the factory doors.

Calhoun did not appreciate the policies of the American Fur Company. He stood with Indian Superintendent McKenney in favor of the factories. Also, Calhoun wanted very much to move all Indians from the southern states to lands west of the Mississippi River, and he felt the Government should attempt to control the trade in the new reservation areas to protect the Indians from exploitation by private individuals or companies. The Government's system, he declared, was essential in the difficult task of teaching the Indians to live under the inescapable requirements of civilization. Together Calhoun and McKenney were able in 1817 to persuade Congress to continue the Government houses.

As a result, the attacks by Astor and his men were increased. Newspapers carried criticisms of the system inspired by Astor agents. More appeals were sent to Congress. Government factors were falsely accused of trading surreptitiously on their own accounts, in violation of Federal law. Attacks were made on the characters of Government employees, and the Federal posts were charged with selling inferior goods to the Indians, thereby making them enemies of the United States.

Crooks and Stuart reported to Astor, "we cannot check the extensions of the system lately pursued by the public trading-houses in situations affecting our commerce most materially and which on the most mature deliberation, gives every reason to fear, and but little to hope from even the most active exertions on our part." This was gross exaggeration of the aggressiveness of the factories, but it was the kind of report Astor needed in Washington. It gave support to the charge that private enterprise was being destroyed by the government.

Congress saw the need of a move to stem the rising tide of complaints, and in 1818 it directed that not only superintendents of the Indian trade but all "agents and assistant agents of Indian trading houses and the several agents of Indian affairs" were to be "appointed by and with the advice and consent of the Senate." Rigid Congressional control, it was hoped, would eliminate the evils which were bringing public condemnation of the Federal program.

The House of Representatives, getting into the act, directed Calhoun to prepare "a system providing for the abolition of the existing Indian trade establishments in the United States and providing the opening of the trade with the Indians with suitable regulations."

Congress was doing nothing more than sticking its head in the sand to keep from facing reality.

Calhoun attempted to obey the House's order, but its very vagueness made the task difficult. No one seemed to know exactly what the Congressmen had in mind, if anything, or what they actually wanted. The best Calhoun could do was to point out that it would be difficult to plan a trade by individuals. However, if that was what Congress desired, a superintendent should be appointed to issue licenses and enforce regulations. Under such a system, Calhoun maintained, it would be necessary to raise the license fee to $100, or perhaps $500, and establish a penalty of $1,000 for trading without a license. Licenses should be issued for specific areas, and traders must be prevented from either selling or giving away liquor. The Government's superintendent should have the power to control prices.

Calhoun pointed out that this scheme would reduce the number of traders by eliminating the smaller ones. He believed the traders with large investments would be careful to obey regulations.

Calhoun's report further stated:

(1) The trade should be concentrated under strict laws in a few sections. This would make it easier for the Indian Bureau to prevent fraud and maintain peace with the Indians.

(2) Actually, two programs were necessary, with the Mississippi River the dividing line between them.

(3) If a system was to be formulated under which the trade would be carried on by licensed individuals, it should be carried on only in areas east of the river. The tremendous slaughter of wild animals in the Old Northwest was swiftly reducing the trade to the point where it would become inconsequential. Indians who continued to live there would be forced to become farmers, or turn to some other means of livelihood.

(4) The future of the trade was west of the river, and for that enormous territory an entirely different kind of plan should be established.

(5) All foreigners should be excluded from the West. Posts should be built along the Mississippi and up the Missouri to its headwaters. An organization strong enough to compete with the British to the north, and the Spaniards to the southwest, should be formed with the sanction of the Government. This would bring the trade completely under American control. Individual private traders would be unable to inaugurate such a program, nor could they make it effective. The Western trade, therefore, should be invested "in a company with sufficient capital," and this company should have "a monopoly of the Indian trade for twenty years." Such a company not only would eliminate all foreigners, especially the British, and insure peace on the frontier, but would be able in a few years to push over the Rockies to the Pacific. "The most profitable fur and peltry trade in the world would be ours."

(Although Calhoun was known to dislike the manner in which the American Fur Company conducted its business, the program he advocated for the Far West sounded as if it had been prepared in that company's office by a man named Astor.)

While Calhoun had been writing his report, the Senate appointed a committee to work out a plan for abolishing the factory system. Its chairman was Senator Walter Leake of Mississippi. However, after making an investigation, the committee decided that the Government system wasn't as bad as it had been painted. It expressed a fear of independent traders, regarding them as of bad moral character. It found . . . certainly no discovery . . . that private traders played dirty tricks on each other, stole each other's furs and debauched the Indians with liquor. For these reasons it recommended that the Government factories be continued, even though they didn't make much money, and in some cases operated at a loss.

Calhoun did not wait for Congress to act on his suggestions. He struck a blow at Governor Cass by ordering that licenses be refused to French-speaking inhabitants of Michigan Territory who had previously considered themselves British subjects until they became naturalized American citizens. The order applied even to such persons who had been born on American soil, and any licenses previously granted to men who came within these categories were to be revoked.

It was hardly an astute or realistic order. Crooks warned Astor that if Calhoun's proposals were carried out, there would be so few licensed traders that the Government factories would be completely revived and have a clear field. Employees of the American Fur Company, he declared, probably would not be able to obtain licenses. He appealed to Astor to "interest some of your numerous friends to obtain if possible the abolition of the Factory system."

Astor needed no urging, nor did he need more ammunition. His power in Washington . . . even though he carried on his lobbying from Europe at times . . . was so strong that in February, 1820, the Congressional Committee on the Indian Trade reported that the factories were "productive of very serious injuries." It advocated that the Government either take over the entire trade or grant it to a single company which could be held responsible for all violations of law or mistreatment of the Indians.

Officials of the War Department and the Indian Bureau vigorously opposed all such proposals, maintaining that the Government houses were influential in controlling the Indians. Ramsay Crooks hurried to Washington to give support to the suggestion that a single company be awarded a monopoly. The name of the company he thought should be selected was not concealed from his listeners. But the Government officials had considerable support in both public and private quarters, and their influence outweighed that of Crooks and Astor, at least at the moment. Less than two months after advocating the abolishment of the factories, the committee reversed itself and recommended that they be continued.

Thomas Hart Benton was elected to the Senate by Missouri in 1820. Astor promptly put him on his payroll. It was not an accident that Crooks and Benton were quartered in the same Washington hotel during the winter of 1820–21. Together they mapped out the fight to be made during the next Congress, al-

ways keeping in touch with Astor in Europe. Benton also numbered among his clients several prominent St. Louis traders. He
was an unrelenting advocate of private initiative, and he had gone
to Washington leaving no doubts as to how he stood on the issue
of Government factories.

The Astor forces received unexpected support from a most
unlikely source. Calhoun had expressed his conviction that the
Government houses had prevented Indian wars and had improved
the way of life for the red man. In this belief he was joined by
eastern groups who were interested in bringing cultural advantages to the American Indian. It was upon the commendation
of these well-meaning easterners that Secretary Calhoun sent
the Reverend Jedidiah Morse on an extensive tour of the Indian
country to report on conditions. Morse was the author of several
widely used textbooks on geography, in addition to being a highly
respected and influential Congregationalist.[14]

On his tour the Reverend Morse visited factories and talked
with many Government employees and private traders. He
learned to his astonishment that the Government agents had no
authority to prevent independent traders from selling whisky to
the Indians, and moreover, at exorbitant prices. This prompted
him to ask what the value of the factories was if they could not
prevent the evil debauchery and robbery of the Indians.

If he never got a good answer to that question, he did get
enough evidence to convince him that the Government's program
left a great deal to be desired. He found out that Indians were
suspicious of Government agents and friendly to private traders.
This was, of course, he realized, the result of the malicious work
done by British traders in the employ of Astor and other Americans.

The private traders poured tales into Morse's ears of how the
Government houses cheated the Indians by selling them inferior
goods. As proof of their charges they displayed both British and

[14] He was the father of Samuel Finley Breese Morse, noted artist and inventor of
the electric telegraph and the Morse Code.

American goods. Even the untrained parson could see the difference.

Morse was principally interested, however, in finding out how the Government houses had contributed to the cultural improvement of the Indians. The knowledge was soon obtained.

The Indians on the frontier were as savage as they were at the time the first Government house had been built. In fact, the factories had done nothing whatever to aid them in adopting the ways of civilized Christians. On the contrary, the factories had done much toward keeping the Indians on wilderness hunting trails. The picture was simply drawn for him. The factories gave the Indians goods for pelts. If an Indian had turned to farming or some craft, he would not have been able to secure a single pound of flour in exchange for his products at a Government house. They accepted only furs.

In addition, Morse could discover no qualities in the political appointees who worked in the factories which might have assisted the Indians in improving either their mode of living or their culture. He was astonished to learn that the Indians had never been told what the Government's program was designed to do for them. Therefore, they didn't understand it at all, and they had no respect for the men in charge of it.

Morse returned to the East disillusioned and much wiser. He submitted a report advocating the abolishment of the factory system. It was excellent ammunition for Benton and Crooks, and they fired it in resounding salvos with telling accuracy.

A letter Astor wrote to the President of the United States from Paris in January, 1821, was notable for its implications. It was addressed to "James Manrae Eq' President."

Astor, keeping in the closest possible touch with developments in the fur trade, had been informed that President Monroe had directed Congress to give its attention to the trade with the Indians.[15]

---

[15] It must be presumed that Monroe understood what Astor was saying, but the punctuation and spelling in the letter are so atrocious that it was deemed advisable to correct them, but only to the extent that they would not require deciphering by the readers of this book.

Astor told Monroe that if he was contemplating any change in the Government's fur trade policies, "I hope it will not be to operate against Citizens who are at present engaged in that trade under the System which government adopted Some years ago." Astor obviously was speaking of the system under which he had obtained licenses and which permitted him to engage foreigners as boatmen and interpreters.

"I may confidently assert," he continued, "that the trade has been much extended, & Chiefly so by the american furr Company of whom I am principle. Relying on that we shall be permitted to trade under that System we have made many and extensive engagements, Some of which will not expire for Some years to come. In fact our men for the conducting of that trade are generally engaged for 4 to 5 years & whether the trade is good or bad they must be paid & must be fed at a great expense. Our property too becomes So engaged that it takes years to retire. I have at present not less than $400,000 engaged in this particular trade. No favor is asked, but I trust that no new measure will be adopted by government to the Injury of us or other Private traders & that if congress who perhaps may not bee fully Informed as to the nature of the trade pass any act that will Leave it to the Discression of the executive to Carry the Same into effect as the good of our Country may Require."

Astor added: "You friends here all will Speeck of you with muish cordiality & good feeling, I have the Hanner to bee most Respctfully Sir you H Sert."

Crooks decided that circumstances in Washington demanded that he make a rush trip to Europe to confer personally with Astor. He had in mind, however, not only talks about the trade and plans for the months immediately ahead. For some time he had been dissatisfied with his own personal situation. This stemmed, simply enough, from the conviction that he should be receiving more money for the good work he was doing. As Astor's field general he was responsible for all operations outside of New York City. He looked upon William B. Astor as hardly more than a parrot repeating the commands sent across the ocean by his father. In this view, of course, Crooks was making a serious mistake. William was a parrot, but while he dutifully carried out the policies and the strategy his father formulated, he was quite capable of thinking for himself, and his talents as financier and businessman were equal, if not in some ways superior, to those of the commercial genius who had sired him.

Crooks held no such confidence in William. Also, he was fully apprised of William's parsimoniousness, and he did not propose to be put off in his demands on the excuse that any increase in expenditures would have to be sanctioned by the president of the company. William might have delayed a decision indefinitely in such a way, and Crooks wanted the matter of his own position settled before he gave more of his energy and ability in behalf of the American Fur Company.

It was Crooks's opinion that he was entitled to a substantial increase in income. He had directed the successful campaign to destroy other independent traders in the Old Northwest. Even the strongest competitor of all, David Stone & Company, after a period of "wavering," had been brought into the Astor camp. Crooks had secured an agreement under which Stone was to keep out of the Mackinac trade for five years. In return, Crooks had bought out Stone's goods and supplies, allowing him a profit of 50 per cent.

Crooks also had got Astor's foot in the St. Louis door by trade agreements with John P. Cabanne and Berthold & Chouteau, and he could anticipate victory in the fight against the Government factories. Under his direction in the field the American Fur Company had become the largest and strongest company in the trade east of the Mississippi River, and the invasion of the Far West was in the offing.

Crooks's original agreement with Astor expired on March 16, 1821, just about the time Crooks reached Paris. In less than a week he and Astor had come to terms. Crooks obtained a new agreement that was to last five years, a sizable increase in salary, and the privilege of enjoying the profits . . . or suffering the losses . . . on twenty of the American Fur Company's one hundred shares instead of the five originally set aside for him.

To Crooks's credit he did not think only of his own welfare while he was with Astor in Europe. He also took up the matter of Stuart's salary, with the result that he obtained for Stuart a $1,000 raise and the profit of seven and a half shares of stock. Crooks also arranged with Astor to re-employ Benjamin Clapp, his fellow Astorian. Clapp had worked for the company a brief time before the War of 1812. Astor had sent him to the West Indies to spy on his errant son-in-law, Bentzon. Now Clapp was to receive a salary of $1,200 a year and the profits from five shares of stock.[16]

All these arrangements were to become null and void in the event of Crooks's death, an indication of the great reliance Astor placed on him.

Crooks did not tarry in Paris. Rushing on to London, he paused to study the fur market, writing Astor that the leading fur houses "expressed to me great anxiety that you would consent to make London the general place of sale for all your Furs." The London houses were confident that if Astor would send all his furs to them, eliminating shipments to Continental ports, all European buyers would come there with confidence. The result would be greater competition, and Astor would get better prices.

Reaching Montreal, Crooks hurried on to Michilimackinac. He spent the summer directing the operations of the numerous Astor outfits in the field, where they were now in supreme command of the trade. When he received orders from Astor to rejoin Senator Benton in the fight against the Government factories, he replied: "I shall follow your advice in again visiting Washington, and will use every fair means to obtain a decision on the Public Trading House system."

Astor had paved the way for him, and, fair means or foul, the battle against the factories was resumed with new fury. Benton's powers had been increased immeasurably by his appointment to the chairmanship of the Senate Committee on Indian Affairs.

Early in 1822, Benton introduced a bill calling for the complete abolishment of the Government houses. In the debate on

[16] Clapp turned the offer down, much to Crooks's regret, and went into business for himself.

it Benton argued erroneously that the system had been established because Jay's Treaty allowed British traders to operate in the United States at a time when American traders were not numerous enough or strong enough to hold their own. Since then, he declared, independent American traders had acquired the resources and the ability to serve all the needs of the Indians. He charged that the Government program had been badly managed, and that it had failed to furnish the goods which the Indians most desired. He was violently sarcastic when he stated that the Government houses carried stocks of such things as jew's-harps.

Most of the material Benton presented to the Senate came from Ramsay Crooks. The Government was accused of selling goods bought for the Indian trade to soldiers and private white citizens, even to competing traders, in violation of the law. The superintendent of the Indian trade was charged with ignoring the statutes which required that furs from Government factories be sold at public auction. They were sold instead, Benton declared, by private contracts at less than market prices.

Senators Van Buren and King, of New York; Johnson, of Louisiana; another Johnson, of Kentucky; and Lowrie, of Pennsylvania, challenged the veracity of Benton's charges. Lowrie, however, made a strong speech in favor of abandoning the system, saying: "Nothing but individual enterprise, individual industry and attention, is equal to such a business. In every competition, individual interest is always too sharp-sighted where the government is a party." He advocated that the trade be opened to free but carefully regulated competition.

Benton's bill passed the Senate on May 2, 1822, and the House two days later. It was approved on May 6.

The measure provided that the President should take over all the property of the factories "to be used to extinguish the treaty obligations on the part of the United States to keep up trading houses with the Indians, payment of annuities due or to become due to the Indian tribes and for customary presents to individuals in amity with the United States." The Indian trade was to be carried on by private traders licensed by the Federal Government.

Exuberantly Crooks wrote Benton: "I . . . hasten to congratulate you on your decisive victory . . . The result is the best possible proof of the value to the country of your talents, intelligence, and perseverance, and you deserve the unqualified thanks of the community for destroying the pious monster, since to your unwearied exertions and sound practical knowledge of the whole subject is indebted for its deliverance from so gross and unholy an imposition."

Since Benton was Astor's "legal representative," and had been paid to accomplish exactly what he had accomplished, Crooks's letter was a little flowery, if not hypocritical.

Refuting the attacks on the decline in the trade and on the evil influence of government posts, stressed so strongly by Benton, Superintendent McKenney told Senator Henry Johnson: "no man knows better than Mr. Crooks the causes of this decline and the means it is necessary to adopt at any time to produce the same results elsewhere."

The Government factories were all but buried, but the American Fur Company had no intention of being a gracious victor and letting them rest in peace. The Indian Department had planned to keep the posts open until the goods on hand had been sold. When he learned of this, Stuart wrote Crooks indignantly that the factory at Prairie du Chien was in full operation, and declared: "Would it not be well for Mr. Astor to communicate with Mr. Graham [George Graham, chief clerk of the War Department] on the subject—and if he does not order it to be closed, Benton ought to give them another rap . . ."

Crooks agreed, and he sent Senator Benton a strong message objecting to the policy of letting the factories sell out their stocks of goods. Crooks had the effrontery to demand that these goods should be inherited by the American Fur Company.

The doors of the factories closed one by one.

Chittenden wrote a fitting epitaph for them:

"Thus ended in failure a system fraught with possibilities of great good to the Indian—a system, which, if followed out as it should have been, would have led the Indian to his new destiny by easy stages and would have averted the long and bloody wars, the corruption and bad faith, which have gained for a hundred years of our dealings with the Indians the unenviable distinction of a Century of Dishonor."

Crooks, knowing no dishonor, but only the joy of victory, was hurrying to St. Louis as stage manager of another great Astor drama . . . the invasion of the West by the American Fur Company. He had orders from Astor in his pocket.

Part Eight

The Long River and the Western Department

1

Long before any of the Frenchmen, pushing westward from the St. Lawrence into the region of the Great Lakes, saw the big rivers, they knew of their existence. The Indians spoke of them, one on each side of the great mountains, and sometimes the Indians talked vaguely of a third river that lost itself in the southwestern sky. The Frenchmen dreamed of seeing them.

It was very unfortunate that few of the men who gave reality to the old dreams kept any records, or even made reports of their exploits and discoveries. But it was established in time that some of them had found a great river, and some of them had traveled up it. Nicholas de La Salle wrote that unnamed *voyageurs* had gone up the Missouri for three or four hundred leagues, and they had found "the most beautiful country in the world." An *Exacte description*, written about 1712, said that *voyageurs* traded with Indians on the big river in a country filled with bison, deer, wolves and beavers, and there were people called Omahas who traded in peltries, and farther up were people as white as Europeans, and who were the handsomest of all people on the continent.[1] And near them were the Arikaras in three large villages. And six hundred leagues from the mouth of the river dwelt a nation of nomads. All of these people had for a long time known *voyageurs* who had wandered among them.

In 1726, the great trailbreaker and trader, Pierre Gaultier de

[1] The Mandans, often thought to be Caucasians by early explorers.

Varennes, Sieur de La Vérendrye, listened to an old Indian speak before his fire at Nipigon. As he talked, the old man drew a crude map on the ground, and it showed a wide river running straight toward the setting sun. La Vérendrye's blood raced with excitement.

He never had an opportunity to go himself in search of the western river, but he never ceased to dream of going. At last, in 1742, he sent his two sons, François and Louis Joseph, to find it, and they set out with a company from the Mandan Villages . . . well-known places now . . . in July, traveling west and southwest.

The La Vérendryes found the Little Missouri, and they passed through the Badlands, and they crossed a stream that was to be called Powder River, and on January 1, 1743, they stood on a height and they saw far to the west of them a great range of mountains . . . the Big Horns.

No passage through the range could be discerned, and the Indian guides were frightened by ghosts and by whispers that came on the wind which told them that enemies waited ahead, and the company turned back. They found the Belle Fourche River and they circled the Black Hills, and they came to the Arikara Village of Little Cherries. In a hillside they buried a metal plate to record their passage.[2]

The river which led to the Vermilion Sea was still shrouded in mystery, the mystery that lay beyond the Shining Mountains, but the "riviere longue" which poured its snowwater flood from those mountains was no longer a mystery or a dream. It had become a great highway to the West, and the hunters, the traders, the mountain men pushed up it, not for the purpose of discovery . . . although there still remained vast areas nearby which had never been seen by a white man . . . but for the furs which abounded in the great plains, the hills, the ranges, through which it had torn its tortuous course for thousands of miles.

Long before the fateful year of 1804 had arrived, the Canadians were solidly established in the northern part of Louisiana Terri-

[2] The plate was buried where the city of Pierre, South Dakota, was to rise, and it was found on February 16, 1913, by some schoolchildren.

tory, and they had carried their trading enterprises clear out to the Little Missouri, the Powder and the Yellowstone. That far western country would be closed to them by the cession of Louisiana . . . at least theoretically . . . but they had no intention of surrendering the trade, of which they held the larger part, eastward from the Missouri and as far south as the Des Moines River. Several important North West Company posts stood on soil that would belong to America, and they proposed to find means of keeping them in full operation.

The leading St. Louis traders, men like Auguste Chouteau, Gabriel Cerre and Charles Gratiot, had never manifested more than a casual interest in the northern country. They had left it to the Canadians, being satisfied with conditions nearer home. They had always made money trading with the tribes of the lower river.

Suddenly the entire way of life St. Louis had known so long, all social and economic conditions, were changed. On March 10, 1804, Louisiana Territory became part of the United States, and the Stars and Stripes were raised for the first time west of the Mississippi River.

The St. Louis traders were Americans. The upper Missouri was American territory. The Canadians would have no rights in it, and their places would be taken by American traders.

The St. Louis traders began to think of moving with speed and energy to which they had never been accustomed.

2

There were few more important or impressive incidents than the meeting by Lewis and Clark, when on the way home from their great journey across the continent, with parties of American fur

traders pushing up the Missouri River. It marked the beginning
of a new era, an era that was to end as abruptly and as unosten-
tatiously as it had begun with another incident . . . one not always
accorded the importance due it . . . occurring thirty-seven years
later. That was the building of a trading store by James Bridger
on a tributary of Green River, a stream of the Pacific watershed,
for the convenience of emigrants. Not only because it was the first
built in the mountains for that specific purpose was Bridger's
store celebrated. Its establishment marked the beginning of the
era of emigration, and so it marked the end of the great days of
the fur trade.

Several years before the return of Lewis and Clark, Astor had
given serious thought to the St. Louis trade, and in the ensuing
years, as he expanded his activities through the Old Northwest
Territory, he became increasingly attentive to it.

In 1799, he had assumed the task of collecting some debts . . .
at a substantial discount, of course . . . which the St. Louis traders
Chouteau and Gratiot owed a London fur house. He did not
press strongly, however, for payment. In letters to Gratiot and
Chouteau, he suggested that inasmuch as he had to go to Montreal every year to buy furs, many of which came from St. Louis, it
would be to their mutual advantage to ship their catches directly
to him in New York. He suggested also that through his connections in Europe he could not only dispose of their furs at the best
prices, but he was in a good position to supply them with trade
goods they required.

In this quiet way were his first feelers cautiously extended
across the Mississippi River.

Chouteau ignored the offer, being suspicious of Astor's motives. Gratiot was more open-minded about the matter. He replied that he would be pleased to do business with Astor, and
expressed the belief that Astor was better able to hold fur prices
high and buy merchandise cheap than any other trader. Gratiot
forwarded his note for £1,000 sterling, payable to Astor in New
York in April, 1804. Eager to begin the association, he advised
Astor to ship St. Louis furs to Europe out of New Orleans, asked

him to secure debentures on trade goods sent out of the United States by land across the Mississippi, and submitted a list of items he needed.

But Astor shied away, believing it would not be worth his while to have a connection with only one St. Louis house.

Although his initial overtures to St. Louis traders had not borne fruit, Astor's interest in the Missouri River trade was not diminished. He maintained a friendship with Gratiot, meeting him once in Philadelphia when the trader was on a pleasure trip to the East. When Gratiot's note became due and he was unable to pay it, Astor did not demand a settlement. It was to his advantage, he reasoned, to have one of the leading citizens of the West under obligation to him. Gratiot was deeply appreciative of Astor's kindness, and he wrote a friend: "I am indebted to Mr. Jacob Astor who has treated me with great indulgence. I wish to satisfy him with all the means in my power."

Chouteau, Lisa and others thought more about preparing an opposition to Astor than they did about satisfying him. The annexation and the expedition of Lewis and Clark had opened gates they knew would never again be closed. There was nothing at all to prevent the prosperous and cunning New Yorker from crossing the river and engaging them head-on.

The concern which troubled their sleep had its roots in indisputable facts. The fur trade, in which Astor had gained such prominence east of the Mississippi, was the foundation upon which the economy of Louisiana rested. Money was valued in terms of furs. Deer skins, for instance, were the unit of value for small purchases. A good one was worth forty cents a pound. Three dollars was the value of a bear skin, and a good buffalo robe brought six. A pack of beaver skins weighing one hundred pounds was priced at $180; a pack of marten, $300; a pack of otter, $450; and one of the highly prized lynx, $500.

The St. Louis traders had good reason to worry, as well, about how the advent of the American Government would affect their relations with the Indians. During the Spanish regime there had not been a major Indian war. In the few years the United States had been independent, it had fought many. Tribes which had lived from time immemorial east of the Mississippi River had migrated west of the river, and they all were enemies of the United States.

The situation in which the Chouteaus and Lisa found themselves was typical. The Chouteaus held a monopoly of the trade with the Osages on the Arkansas, and Lisa traded with the same Indians on the Osage River and near the Missouri. The Grand and Little Osage tribes annually purchased $20,000 worth of merchandise at an advance of 125 per cent above cost at St. Louis. Other St. Louis houses generally respected these trading rights, and the Indians themselves preferred to deal with men whose policies were dependable.

The established patterns would be destroyed by the intrusion of any number of Americans, and the Indians would be influenced to turn to new sources of supply. Americans were not above employing violent tactics in competing with each other, nor were they above stirring up tribal wars if by so doing they could gain commercial advantages. Americans cared nothing for human life.

The Sioux would be a lucrative source of furs. They were generally friendly to the British, although some of their trade, amounting to $60,000 worth of merchandise, came down the river. This trade was a plum that would be irresistible to Astor. But whether Astor or some other American went after it, the Sioux would be stirred up, and blood would run on the upper river.

The same results would occur among the smaller tribes along the Missouri . . . the Kansas, the Otoes, Pawnees, Loups, Arapahoes, Omahas, Poncas, Arikaras . . . and all of them were bitter enemies of the Sioux. Farther up lived the Mandans, the Minnetaries and the Gros Ventres. Trade with them had been small, but its potential was large. The Americans would go after it, and by so doing would clash with the British on other fronts. The Indians would be forced to take sides, and would war among themselves.

Far out toward the mountains, or in them, were the Cheyennes, the Kiowas, the Crows and the formidable Blackfeet, all rich in furs, all waiting for the arrival of the Americans.

It was a distressing outlook. Chouteau the younger studied the regulations Congress had written when it organized a new government for Louisiana, and he hurried to Washington, where he obtained interviews with President Jefferson and Secretary of the Treasury Gallatin.

Jefferson thought Chouteau "well disposed, but what he wants is power and money." It was an accurate analysis. Chouteau proposed that "he should have a negative on all Indian trading licenses, and the direction and all the profits of the trade carried on by the government with all the Indians of Louisiana, replacing all the capital." Gallatin was familiar with Astor's clever manipulations and boldness, but the scope and brazenness of Chouteau's requests astounded him.

When Jefferson stated that the demands were inadmissible, Chouteau countered with a request "for the exclusive trade with the Osages, to be effected by granting licenses only to his agents." This also was found to be inadmissible, but Jefferson did not reject it. The President wasn't quite certain whether Chouteau would be "useful or dangerous." At least, he did not want to incur the trader's enmity, and he advised Chouteau to submit his second request in writing to Secretary of War Dearborn. General Dearborn did not grant it, but in time he did award Chouteau licenses that permitted him to trade extensively along the river, and Chouteau prospered.

Astor might well have taken cognizance of Chouteau's methods. Indeed, it appeared that he had, and that he had recognized Chouteau's unusual ability.

When Gen. James Wilkinson was made Governor of Louisiana Territory in 1805, he formed an alliance with Chouteau to conduct trade with a number of Missouri River tribes. Wilkinson was unscrupulous enough to refuse to give licenses to other traders to operate in any area he and Chouteau controlled. These included the larger part of the adjacent country, in which there was high fur production. Wilkinson further sought to protect his own and Chouteau's interests by issuing a proclamation forbidding British traders to enter Louisiana for any reason at all.

The Government rejected the British protests with the statement that privileges granted British subjects under Jay's Treaty could not be extended to territory subsequently acquired. But while supporting Wilkinson's proclamation, it looked with disfavor on some of his other acts, and he was removed from office. The loss of his henchman did not injure Chouteau. He continued to hold his trade rights, and he shipped his pelts to Montreal, still refusing to deal with Astor. His business increased to such proportions that most of the furs exported from St. Louis to Canada passed through his house.

Astor kept abreast of Chouteau's operations through friends in Washington and correspondence with Gratiot. He also studied thoughtfully all reports available on the expedition of Lewis and Clark. These proffered the first dependable information on the fur resources of the Missouri.

Lewis and Clark reported in some detail on the trade already existing, and made estimates of the trade that might be developed. They recommended the establishment of posts at certain points, among them Council Bluffs, the Mandan Villages (to counter the British), and at the confluence of the Yellowstone and Missouri rivers. They mentioned the importance of the Marias River, which "abounds with animals of the fur kind, and most probably furnishes a safe and direct communication to that productive country of furs exclusively enjoyed at present by the subjects of his Britannic Majesty." The Yellowstone, they said, would "afford a lucrative fur trade & will hold in check the N W Co on the upper Missouri which we believe it is their intention to monopolize if in their power." Lewis thought the Yellowstone provided every natural advantage for an establishment "both in regards to the fur trade and the government of the natives."

3

After the return of Lewis and Clark, Manuel Lisa, the only Spaniard prominent in the St. Louis trade, had gone swiftly into action on the upper river. Lisa was bold, restless, shrewd, but his true character was an enigma his associates had never been able to understand. Often cursed and always hated, he was at the same time recognized as one of the most competent river traders.

Lisa, like Astor, quickly recognized the value of the information Lewis and Clark brought back about the resources of the Far West. He formed an association with William Morrison, an experienced and successful trader from Kaskaskia, and Pierre Menard, who had for years been connected with St. Louis companies. They prepared to send a strong expedition to the headwaters of the Missouri, an extremely hazardous undertaking, for it involved a journey of more than two thousand miles through Indian country in which several of the tribes were unfriendly and always treacherous.

Lisa left St. Louis in the spring of 1807 with a keelboat heavily loaded with trade goods. At the mouth of the Platte River the expedition met a lone white man descending the Missouri in a canoe. He was the famous American mountain man, John Colter.

Colter had been a soldier with Lewis and Clark. He had been given permission to remain on the upper Missouri with two other American trappers. Lisa could have asked for nothing better than to have Colter as a guide and adviser. Colter agreed to turn his back on civilization once more. He was to perform great feats of exploration, traveling alone into countries never before seen by a white man. Among his discoveries was the mountain wonderland to be called Yellowstone National Park. When Colter returned at last to St. Louis and told about seeing geysers and colored springs and smoking cones, men grinned and tapped their heads. Colter had been too long alone in the wilderness. They called his great discovery "Colter's Hell."

Lisa led his company to the junction of the Yellowstone and Missouri rivers, then proceeded up the Yellowstone as far as the mouth of the Big Horn River, where he began his trade.

Lisa, for all his knowledge of the wilderness and the Indians, made a serious mistake. He had announced his intention to establish a trade among the Blackfeet, but he began in the heartland of their greatest enemy, the Crows. Perhaps Colter had advised him to go first to the Crow Nation. Colter had been there, and he knew that it was an excellent fur country. Colter also knew that the Blackfeet were not to be trusted. In any case, the Blackfeet concluded that Lisa preferred to deal with their bitterest foe rather than them. They never forgave him, and they applied the same damning brand to all Americans.

At the junction of the Big Horn and the Yellowstone, Lisa built the first post on the waters of the great upper Missouri system. It was variously called Fort Lisa, Fort Manuel, and Manuel's Fort. His trade with the Crows was highly successful, and in the spring of 1808 he and his trappers descended the Missouri with their keelboat low in the water with valuable furs.

Lisa thereupon began the organization of the Missouri Fur Company, and the activity was duly noted and considered by Astor in New York. He was at that time busily engaged in organizing a fur company of his own, was negotiating with the New York Legislature for a charter, and was seeking from President Jefferson official approbation of his plan.

In the spring of 1809, Lisa led his second expedition up the Missouri. At this time, Crooks and Robert McClelan were operating a trading post near Council Bluffs. Both men had been trading individually on the river for several years. In 1807 they had formed a partnership, and with a company of eighty men, financed on shares by Sylvester and Auguste Chouteau, they had set out for the upper river. Reports that Sioux and Arikaras were on the warpath caused them to turn back. They had remained near Council Bluffs.

After Lisa's expedition of 1809 had passed, Crooks and Mc-Clelan decided to follow it. They started with forty men, but shortly afterward were halted by a war party of 600 Sioux. The Indians forbade them to proceed, but offered to trade with them. Faced by such a formidable force, Crooks and McClelan had no alternative. While most of the Indians left for their villages to procure furs, they commenced the construction of a post. At the first opportunity they suddenly stopped their building and fled down the river.

In their talks with the Sioux, Crooks and McClelan had formed the conviction that Lisa had schemed to stop them from going to the upper river. They swore revenge.[3]

Lisa returned to St. Louis from his 1809 expedition in the fall, and soon afterward set off on a business trip to Montreal. The British stopped him at Detroit, and he was obliged to turn back. He made another journey up the river in 1810, and in the spring of 1811 set out once more. In addition to bringing down furs collected during the winter by his trappers, he hoped to learn the fate of a contingent that had been left up the river in 1809 and had vanished into the mountains.

That contingent was led by Lisa's partners, Pierre Menard and Andrew Henry. In the spring of 1810, it had left Fort Lisa on the Big Horn and had gone out to the Three Forks of the Missouri.

There a post had been erected. Trapping surpassed all expectations. Furs had never before been taken in the country by white men. Beaver were thick in many of the streams, and there was every prospect of acquiring 300 packs during the season.

Then the dreaded Blackfeet appeared. They struck from the forest on the morning of April 12. So swift was the attack, that before the trappers could organize an adequate defense five of them had been killed, and their horses and furs were in the hands of the Indians.

Thereafter the men trapped in groups, but the Blackfeet con-

[3] In the winter of 1810-11, when Crooks and McClelan joined the overland Astoria expedition, their anger had not abated. As previously recounted, they were able to pursuade Hunt not to wait for Lisa to overtake him.

tinued to harass them with telling effect. At last Menard and some of the men elected to give up and leave the country. They started back to St. Louis, taking with them thirty packs of skins.

Henry refused to quit, and the majority of the trappers remained with him, but it was a futile fight. Before fall had come, more than a dozen other men had been slain in surprise attacks.

With no hope of negotiating with the elusive Blackfeet, and with trapping impossible under the conditions, Henry still refused to go home in abject defeat. He led his men westward across the mountains, passed over the Continental Divide, and into the valley of a stream that flowed into the Snake River. Where the village of Elgin, Idaho, was to stand, he built several log houses. The stream was named for him . . . Henry's Fork.

By the spring of 1811, Henry and his little band were facing starvation. Throughout much of the winter they had existed on horseflesh. Completely dispirited, the men separated. Some of them set out for the Spanish possessions, far south and west. Some set out eastward. Some never were heard of again.

They had collected along Henry's Fork some forty packs of beaver, and the intrepid Henry determined to take them back to St. Louis. With a few companions, he set out, descending the Yellowstone to the Missouri. At the Arikara Villages he found Lisa looking for him.

Lisa's 1811 voyage up the Missouri was notable in another respect besides the reunion with Henry. It was the trip on which he had sought to overtake Hunt and the Astorians, so that the two companies might pass together through the Sioux.

The strength of the original Missouri Fur Company was indicated by the roster of its partners. In addition to that of Lisa, it contained the names of almost every prominent businessman in St. Louis . . . Benjamin Wilkinson, Pierre Chouteau, Auguste Chouteau, Reuben Lewis, William Clark, Sylvester Labadie, Pierre Menard, William Morrison, Andrew Henry and Dennis Fitz Hugh. The *Louisiana Gazette* remarked of the company: "It has every prospect of becoming a source of incalculable advantage not only to the individuals engaged but to the community at large. Their extensive preparations, and the extensive force with which they intend to ascend the Missouri, may bid defiance to any hostile force they may meet with. The streams which descend from the Rocky Mountains afford the finest of hunting, and here, we learn, they intend to build their fort."

Strong men, shrewd men, veteran traders, money . . . some $40,000 capital . . . and force . . . 150 trappers in the first expedition . . yet these assets could not dispel disastrous losses, such as that of Henry at the Three Forks. Other incredibly brave company men died in fights with Indians along the river. "The Gros Ventres of the Prairie fell upon a party of Americans whom they confess that they murdered, and robbed of considerable booty in utensils, beaver skins, etc. Some of the beaver skins were marked Valley and Jummell . . ." Valle and Immel were free trappers working with Lisa. "The Bloods were at war on the Missouri . . . They also fell on a party of Americans, murdered them all, and brought away considerable booty . . . From the description the Bloods gave of the dress and behavior of one whom they murdered, he must have been an officer or trader; they said he killed two Bloods before he fell. This exasperated them, and . . . they butchered him in a horrible manner and then ate him partly raw . . ."[4]

The man was the Lisa trapper George Drouillard, who had been an interpreter and hunter with Lewis and Clark.

In his New York office, great burdens weighed on Astor . . . the expeditions to the Columbia, the difficulties of his ships, the impending war which threatened the loss of his furs and his trade . . . yet he found time to study the reports he received from St. Louis. Most interesting were the accounts of the disasters being suffered by the Missouri Fur Company. He concluded that it might be well to delay any decisive move, and see what else befell Lisa.

---

[4] From the Journals of Alexander Henry.

4

The original agreement between the partners of the Missouri Fur Company was due to expire in the spring of 1812, and in November of 1811, Gratiot wrote Astor about the matter. Gratiot was the only St. Louis trader who advocated bringing Astor into the Missouri River trade in a substantial way. It was as if he were able to read Astor's thoughts, and by this remarkable power discern the secret plans harbored by the great trader. He seemed to understand that it would be best for all concerned if Astor could be counted a friend rather than an antagonist.

It was his suggestion that Astor might wish to join the new Missouri Fur Company that was to be organized, the articles of which he had assisted in preparing. Perhaps Astor might be willing to take five of its fifteen shares at $3,000 each. The capital of the new company would be about $50,000, of which $27,000 would be funds and property of the old company. If Astor purchased five shares he would be in a position to sell trade goods to the company, and handle the company's furs in New York and Europe, on a commission basis.

Gratiot revealed his shrewdness with the remark that such an arrangement would be advantageous to Astor's desire to "draw the furr trade into your hands," and it would also "facilitate the operations of Mr. Hunt, as you could by that means have a Communication open from this place to the Columbia." However, Gratiot stressed that he could only speak for himself, and he frankly admitted that some members of the new company doubtlessly would oppose Astor's inclusion.

The truth was that at the time Gratiot wrote, the partners of the new company were determined that Astor would not be allowed to join them. Despite Gratiot's counsel, they decreed that shares would not get out of the hands of St. Louis traders. Their confidence in themselves and the faith they held in their own power were indestructible, and led them to the determination to keep the incredibly rich trade of the Missouri to themselves. They bluntly spurned Gratiot's proposal. It was a mistake that long haunted them.

They had not needed to concern themselves with the problem, however, for Astor had no intention of investing in the new company. He had at once seen the weaknesses of its structure. Capitalized at only $50,000, it contained almost every trader of note in St. Louis, and all of them were allowed to participate in the administration of its affairs, both at home and in the field. Astor understood that the result would be confusion and dissension that could lead only to serious difficulties. He wanted no part of an organization that did not have a single capable individual in control of its management. He would, of course, have been quite suitable for such a capacity, but obviously the hostility of the St. Louis traders precluded the possibility of such an arrangement.

"I Do Not knaw that I would be interested even if the company wishd it," he wrote Gratiot, "if hawever I can by any means be of use to tham I shall be happey in So Doing."

His kind offer to be of service had not come from the goodness of his heart. The War of 1812 had started, and he understood very well that the St. Louis traders were stopped from bringing goods in from Canada. Merchandise they owned had been held up at St. Joseph just as his own had been. He was then struggling for permission from Washington to bring in his own goods, and if he could accomplish that he might well be in a position to be of similar service to the houses of St. Louis . . . a very profitable service.

The war brought havoc to the Missouri trade, just as it did in all other areas. Communications with the East were disrupted. The Great Lakes were closed. The mouth of the Mississippi was blockaded. Indian tribes under British influence were warring on Americans.

The Missouri Fur Company's expeditions of 1812 and 1813, smaller than in previous years, brought little profit. A number of the partners withdrew. Lisa was the only active St. Louis trader on the river, and the company became known as Manuel Lisa & Company. The posts on the upper river were closed or abandoned.

Word reached Federal authorities in St. Louis that British agents had become active among the upper Missouri tribes, and were endeavoring to persuade them to attack American posts on both the Missouri and Mississippi. No man in the Missouri River trade had more influence with the Indians than Lisa, and he was induced to accept an appointment as subagent for nations living above the Kansas River. His assignment was to hold them as allies of the United States. Lisa went up to the post of his company at Council Bluffs. He succeeded beyond all expectations in controlling the Indians. Not only did he organize war expeditions against tribes on the Mississippi who were loyal to the British, but he secured pledges of friendship with nearly all the river tribes. In the spring of 1815, he brought with him down the river to St. Louis forty-three chiefs and headmen authorized by their people to sign treaties of alliance with the United States. It was because of his extraordinary accomplishments that the upper Missouri Indians were prevented from aligning themselves with the British. His reward was the payment of $548 in salary, and a State Department notation: "Lisa . . . has been of great service in preventing British influence the last year by sending large parties to war."

When at last the conflict ended and conditions returned to normal, Lisa once again gradually extended his fur-trading operation toward the upper Missouri. At this time his competitors were both smaller and weaker than he. Chief of them was Berthold & Chouteau, in partnership with Robidoux & Papin, and having altogether a capital of only $12,000, who sought to share with him the trade with the Pawnees, Omahas, Otoes, Sioux and Iowas. Pratte & Vasques, with a capital of $7,000, traded above Council Bluffs. Closer to St. Louis several groups traded with the Osage and Kansas Indians. One of these was Cerre & Chouteau, with an investment of $4,000. Another was composed of several other members of the big Chouteau clan, with a capital of $6,000.

All these outfits were too insecure financially . . . if not too timid and cautious . . . to undertake dangerous expeditions far up the river, and Lisa looked once again with covetous eyes toward the Yellowstone and the great mountains beyond it.

During the war, while he was busy smuggling furs in from Canada and other places, Astor conceived the idea that peltries might also be obtained in St. Louis. He sent a letter to the dependable Gratiot in the summer of 1813, inquiring if deer skins might be purchased there. Transactions of any sort were slow under the circumstances, transportation was precarious at best, and numerous tribes who normally sent deer skins to St. Louis had turned from hunting to the warpath, but by August, 1814, Gratiot had obtained 120 packs. They were sent by keelboat to Astor representatives in Pittsburgh, whence they were forwarded to others in Philadelphia, and in turn sent on to New York. Astor paid Gratiot 5 per cent commission, but instead of sending the money he deducted it from Gratiot's debt to him.

In the year that peace came, 1815, Gratiot bought for Astor all the deer skins in the St. Louis market, amounting to 133 packs, and sent them to Pittsburgh. Under orders to continue his purchases, and increase them if possible, Gratiot, in 1816, sent Astor 189 packs of deer skins, 26 packs of red deer skins, two packs of bear skins, and one pack of assorted furs.

The outbreak of the war had caught two St. Louis traders en route to Mackinac with a large quantity of furs. It was their purpose to obtain Canadian goods and attempt to bring them into the United States in violation of wartime restrictions. They were caught by American soldiers, charged with violating the Nonintercourse Act, and the furs, amounting to 602 packs, were confiscated. It was fortunate for the traders, John P. Cabanne and one Chenie, that some of the furs impounded were the property of the South West Fur Company. This brought Astor into the picture. He at once began to pull strings in Washington. Both men were acquitted, but before Astor could save the furs, 200 packs were stolen, and the balance were arbitrarily sold at auction for $8,000, from which the Government deducted $2,000 for expenses. Astor got his proportionate share from the balance. It was a severe loss, but he philosophically shrugged it off as an exigency of war. He was doing quite well in other efforts along the border.

Cabanne, an enterprising merchant-trader, took advantage of his unexpected association with Astor by arranging to have Astor sell him a quantity of merchandise. This was not a difficult accomplishment, for Astor was always ready to sell anything he had to anybody who wanted it, but the arrangement inspired grandiose ideas in Cabanne. The year following the war, he proposed that Astor refrain from selling goods to any other St. Louis house. Under such circumstances, Cabanne declared, he would be in a position to buy large quantities of Astor merchandise and profitably distribute it.

Astor must have smiled. Goods suitable for the Indian trade, prevented from coming into the United States from Europe for nearly four years, had not yet become readily available. It would have, indeed, been an advantage for Cabanne to be the only trader in St. Louis to have recourse to Astor's enormous resources.

It was Astor's reply to Cabanne which disclosed that he had quietly taken the first step toward establishing his own traders among the Missouri River Indians. He wrote Cabanne that he had supplied Stuart and Crooks with merchandise "for the purpose of trading with Indians & & in your quater of the Cauntry. Sorry to say that I am under Several Engagements . . . which must be complyd with on my part . . . I will make no more which can possibly tend to Injure any of my friends."

Astor had sent Stuart and Crooks across the Mississippi for a very special reason, and it had nothing to do with the welfare of his "friends." The move was prompted by the forthcoming action of the Government by which all Canadian traders would be forbidden to operate in American territory. The effect of such a regulation on the fur houses of St. Louis would be severely detrimental. Trade goods could not be sent there, nor into the valleys of the Missouri, Mississippi and Illinois rivers by foreigners . . . not even those with whom Astor was associated in the South West Fur Company.

Next Astor wrote Gratiot suggesting that he persuade Cabanne to take over the goods furnished Stuart and Crooks, giving them "Some Compensation for time Lost."

The deviousness with which Astor customarily approached a major undertaking was never better illustrated than in this case. Stuart and Crooks had not even reached St. Louis when he suggested that they sell their goods, not in the Indian trade, but to Cabanne. He further revealed his hand by telling Gratiot at the same time: "I have tought a good Deal on the proposition made me Some time Since by your frinds to make Some genral arrangement for the Indian Trade & if our Government Do exclude Canada traders from aur Cauntry as I believe they will the trade will become an object & I would Licke to cam to the arrangement of which I will thank you to Inform tham."

An uncomplicated interpretation of this letter would be that Astor was using Gratiot to pave the way for negotiations he had secretly instructed Stuart and Crooks to carry out. If that was his strategy, it was succesful. Gratiot loyally went to work.

Stuart reached St. Louis first, but Crooks was not far behind him. He arrived in July, 1816. Stuart was not well known, but Crooks, a former Missouri River trader, had many friends in St. Louis, and he was well qualified to carry out the assignment.

He did.

Crooks fashioned agreements with Cabanne & Company and the house of Berthold & Chouteau. The two companies were bound to trade exclusively with Astor, and there was an understanding that Astor would not send his own outfits to trade on the Missouri as long as the agreements endured.

Gratiot wrote Astor, somewhat coyly, perhaps: "it appears to me that all rivalls for the Indian Trade will soon be over, & fore see a disposition in all those who are concerned to come together to Some understanding. I mean with Cabanne, Berthold & Chouteau &c."

Crooks had got what Astor wanted, but it had not been easily accomplished. The St. Louis traders' hatred of Astor had not decreased. Gratiot wrote Astor that "the difficulties he [Crooks] met with were almost insurmountable, but his indefatigable activity conquered most every difficulties."

Gratiot wanted more orders for deer skins and furs, but Astor informed him: "I have made Some arrangement with aur frinds in your plaise . . . and as they seem to be excallent men I wish to please them . . . it is on this account that I Do not now Give you an order for Skins."

With those words Astor kicked his old friend out into the cold. Gratiot died before another year had passed.

Astor had permitted Crooks to do in St. Louis what he had refused to do himself before the war . . . that is, to agree to supply certain persons with trade goods to the exclusion of all others, but Astor's strategy was influenced by new factors which had appeared suddenly in the St. Louis situation.

Not the least of them was the significant news that reached New York in the summer of 1817. On July 27, the first steamboat to reach St. Louis had tied up among the keelboats, canoes and barges of the waterfront. The *Pike* had pushed its way up the strong current of the Mississippi, writing history with every turn of its paddle wheels. It was an event that caused men to hold startling and sobering thoughts, even as they cheered. Trade with the sea would be completed in a small part of the time that barges drifting downriver and keelboats rowed and poled upstream had consumed. The use of steamboats meant that furs brought down the Missouri and Mississippi could be speeded on their way to the waiting ships at New Orleans and could reach world markets before the year was out. Merchandise could be brought up the Mississippi in the early spring, instead of the previous year, in time to be loaded on keelboats which were to be sent up the Missouri on their annual spring journeys. Of course, as one newspaper said, common sense told one that while steamboats might be able to travel on the Mississippi and the Ohio, which were broad and deep, they would never be able to fight the raging muddy torrent of the shallow, treacherous Missouri. Yet, having them reach St. Louis was advantage enough to satisfy any man.

Astor suddenly thought it necessary to assure people in St.

Louis that the opening of steamboat traffic would not in any way affect the agreements, that he intended to abide fully by every provision in them. If Crooks was less inclined to adhere to such high scruples, he had no alternative but to follow Astor's injunctions. Crooks, therefore, was obliged to censure the American Fur Company trader Russell Farnham, for entering the country of the Sac Indians by way of the Missouri and Grand Rivers instead of by the Mississippi and Des Moines route. He wrote Farnham that "although no agreement exists between us and Messrs. Cabanne & Company, to prevent our going into that river or they into the Mississippi, still, as Mr. Astor supplies their goods, they partly calculated on our not opposing them."

Actually it was not the advent of the steamboat that was to bring about a change in Astor's actions as much as it was the ill-advised campaign of slander conducted against him by some St. Louis firms.

By 1818 the Missouri River traders were seeing a full-dress demonstration of Astor's immense power. His drive to monopolize the Great Lakes trade was in full swing through the unequaled facilities and resources of his Northern Department. If the St. Louisans wondered at Astor's reticence to throw more brigades and unlimited money into the Missouri River trade, they were thankful for the mysterious reasons that kept him out of their territories, whatever those reasons might be.

Yet, this reaction had little therapeutic effect upon the concern that persisted in them. They could see what was happening in Michigan, Wisconsin, Illinois, Indiana, and the valley of the upper Mississippi. The Astor juggernaut was rolling steadily onward in those vast regions, crushing all that stood in its way, and they could see its shadow, a shadow that came closer as they watched.

5

It was amazing news. A steamboat had fought its way up the Missouri as far as Franklin. On May 16, the *Independence* had steamed northward from St. Louis, not for the falls of St. Anthony, not even for Prairie du Chien, but for Franklin. It had thrashed its way directly into the Missouri, defying the spring flood, and gone clear to Franklin. If this bordered on the inconceivable, the thoughts it stirred were even more startling and unbelievable. Next, some reckless captain would try to go on up river . . . but that was impossible.

The *Missouri Gazette* reflected the wonder of it all by crying: "In 1817, less than two years ago, the first steamboat arrived at St. Louis. We hailed it as the day of small things, but the glorious consummation of all our wishes is daily arriving . . . Who could, or would have dared to, conjecture that in 1819 we should have the arrival of a steamboat from Philadelphia or New York. Yet such is the fact!"

The cheers and the wondering had not subsided before the *Western Engineer*, belching its smoke and spitting its sparks over the endless plains and shattering the silence of the wild with new and terrifying noises, had battered its way on to Council Bluffs. Now men began to believe that nothing was impossible. They began to believe . . . oh, but no steamboat, no matter how great its power, could defeat the mad currents, break through the snags and bars, and pass on the low water of the upper river.

"A species of civil war has already been too long waged by the St. Louis interests against those of the Lakes. Our rights to the Indian trade are precisely the same . . . We ask nothing for ourselves, from either the civil or military authorities of the country, which we would for a moment wish to be withheld from others. We are full entitled to equal privileges with our opponents, and we can never consent to have them abridged or in any manner impaired."

Thus Crooks wrote a business associate in the summer of 1818. The words were significant. Not only was Astor resentful of the campaign of vilification being waged against him by the St. Louis traders . . . and in some cases by the authorities . . . but the urge to enter the Missouri River trade was mounting to a point where he would, regardless of conditions, he obliged to give way to it.

By 1818 the western trade had fully recovered from the devastating effects of the war, and its revival gave every promise of bringing unprecedented prosperity.

Lisa planned to send large Missouri Fur Company expeditions to the mountains and beyond. He also had taken over the management of Cabanne & Company, but he soon concluded it was not in a position to progress, and liquidated it. This had the effect of eliminating one of the concerns with which Astor had an agreement, but it soon became apparent that Lisa had not closed Cabanne & Company in the hope of injuring Astor. He immediately formed an association with Dennis Julian, and they applied to Crooks for merchandise with the intention of sending a company upriver.

Crooks refused the request with the excuse that goods were not available, but Lisa soon learned that Astor's policy of supplying St. Louis houses had been quietly revised. It was apparent that Astor was no longer willing to restrict his own position in such a way. Lisa spread the word that big events were in the wind.

At once Lisa began the reorganization of the Missouri Fur Company, greatly strengthening its management and financial structure, a move thoughtfully noted by Astor and Crooks. Lisa was the only one of the original partners remaining, but among the new partners were a number of experienced and able men . . . Thomas Hempstead, Joshua Pilcher, Joseph Perkins, Andrew Woods, Moses Carson, John B. Zenoni, Andrew Drips, Robert Jones.

The refusal of St. Louis Indian Department and military authorities in several instances to recognize licenses issued to Astor traders at Mackinaw incensed Crooks. He made a trip to Washington in connection with the problem, accusing officials of conniving with influential St. Louis houses to keep the American Fur Company from operating between the Mississippi and the Missouri. The mission . . . with some assistance from Astor . . . was successful, and in March, Crooks wrote Russell Farnham: "You may ascend the Missouri with your Mackinaw men in perfect confidence. Governor Clark [at St. Louis] has the order about respecting your licenses, and so has Colonel Chambers. I met with Mr. Benjamin O'Fallon in Washington. He is appointed agent for the Missouri, and is, I believe, convinced that all reports so industriously circulated about Mr. Astor and his agents, which created such unheard-of prejudices against us, and did us so much injury with the officers, were invented and propagated by people who feared us, and labored to drive us by this means from the country . . . On the whole we have no reason to believe that this reign of persecution is, if not at an end, at least very nearly so . . . There is nothing to prevent your going into the Missouri now with your Canadians."

In this instance Crooks was not speaking of Farnham's entering directly into competition on the Missouri River itself, but in country between the Missouri and the upper Mississippi. However, this was country the St. Louis houses considered theirs, and they had gone to great lengths to poison the minds of the Indians dwelling in it against Astor.

In a sarcastic vein Crooks admonished Farnham not to listen "to the thousand stories and perhaps threats you will hear, for such things will be attempted with a view to checking your activities and enterprise . . . Be extremely cautious in giving vent to the hard things you may and will feel inclined to say of some people you will have to deal with . . . for, be assured, every word affecting *these great men* will be treasured up against you. And beware of others who will try to insinuate themselves into your confidence the better to betray you."

Farnham's journeys up the Missouri took him only as far as the Grand River, up which he turned to visit the Sac Indians, but to him belongs the distinction of being the first trader to carry the business of the American Fur Company into the Missouri Valley. He was a native of Vermont's Green Mountains, was intelligent, daring and industrious. Both Astor and Crooks considered him one of the most able and dependable men in their service.

Soon after Astor agreed to furnish Berthold & Chouteau with merchandise, Chouteau had indicated he would like to buy a number of shares in the American Fur Company. It was his thought that if his firm could become partners with Astor the evil day when Astor would enter into open competition with them might be postponed. Berthold was not enthusiastic about the idea. Talk and more talk resulted in no definite agreement, and Crooks became irritated by the situation. He wrote Astor in Europe in July, 1820, that "To address Messrs. Berthold and Chouteau on a subject so often canvassed, appears to me more than useless, as their conduct has hitherto betrayed such indecision that small hopes ought to be entertained of their determination now. Perhaps the appearance of David Stone and Company at St. Louis may rouse them from their fancied security and turn their attention seriously this way. Lest that should be the case, and to clear myself from all blame, I shall in a few days write them and request an immediate and specific reply at New York."

Stone, whom Astor had, after a strenuous battle, finally driven from the field in the Northern Department, had moved into the Missouri River trade with such rapidity and energy that St. Louis traders had become alarmed. Stone's expeditions drove relentlessly into territories in which the older houses had long enjoyed dominant positions. A group of Boston traders also had entered the trade with a great show of strength. It was clear that all the houses could not prosper on the amount of business then in sight, and Astor and Crooks carefully weighed the idea of stepping into the picture, and by effecting consolidations through purchases, attaining an advantageous position.

The sudden death of Lisa in August, 1820, presented new complications. Although the Missouri Fur Company was in poor financial condition, instead of being dissolved it was again strengthened with new money and manpower. Joshua Pilcher, a man of great ability and tireless energy, became president, and he began at once to enlarge upon the plans for developing the upper river trade which Lisa had harbored. Within a short time he had sent more than three hundred men up the Missouri, and he had established a strong post, called Fort Benton, at the mouth of the Big Horn River.

Crooks delivered his promised ultimatum to Berthold and Chouteau, demanding that they either come to terms with the American Fur Company at once or abandon the idea. ". . . I neither advise you to join nor dissuade you from the undertaking," he told them. "You know enough to enable you to decide on what you ought to do, and I cannot consent to be blamed should my anticipation and the result prove at variance . . . I am permitted to say, we will with pleasure pursue the same path with you, but if you will not be of our party, we are determined on traveling, as heretofore, by ourselves."

Berthold and Chouteau were still unable to reach a decision, and Crooks advised Astor forcefully that to delay longer in entering the Missouri River trade would be folly.

Astor issued an order for Crooks to proceed in establishing a Western Department. The decision, however, was not based alone on his faith in Crooks's judgment. Since Crooks had urged prompt action, another new and strong competitor had suddenly appeared. It was the Columbia Fur Company, and it at once presented an exceptionally formidable front.

Founder of the new company was Joseph Renville, a Canadian trader who had been thrown out of employment by the 1821 amalgamation of the Hudson's Bay and the North West Companies. He had invited a number of other traders who also had been injured by the merger to form an association with him. They were for the most part wilderness veterans. Among them were Kenneth McKenzie, William Laidlaw, Honoré Picott and James Kipp.

Federal statutes forbade foreigners from engaging in the fur trade within the boundaries of the United States, and to circumvent this barrier the new company took into partnership two Americans, Daniel Lamont and an obscure trader named Tilton, and registered the legal name of the concern as Tilton & Company.

The Columbia Fur Company, by which name it was always called in the trade, did not have a large capital, but it made up for this deficiency by the superabundant energy and experience of its members. They not only plunged into the Missouri trade, but they launched a fierce opposition to American Fur Company posts in the upper Mississippi and Wisconsin regions. Major posts were soon established between the headwaters of St. Peters and the Red River of the North; at Prairie du Chien, on the Mississippi; and Green Bay, on Lake Michigan.

Astor not only recognized the Columbia Fur Company as a serious threat to his monopoly in the Northern Department, but realized that it would become a severe antagonist in his future trade on the Missouri. He lost no time planning its destruction.

Generally Astor had displayed two policies in dealing with rivals. Individual traders and small, weak companies had been ruthlessly crushed. Often the more efficient of the vanquished had been employed by him, or permitted to trade for him on shares. If he determined that a competing company could not easily be eliminated, he set about buying it out or merging it with the American Fur Company. In either instance he wasted no time. Business was business, and though he often enjoyed his struggles with opponents, he never regarded trade as a game in which a victory was in itself the principal end.

In the case of the Columbia Fur Company he correctly judged that crushing it in a trade war would be costly and time-consuming. Either outright purchase or amalgamation were the sensible and economic courses to be pursued, and he ordered Crooks to investigate the possibility of bringing about the necessary negotiations.

Late in 1821, Crooks gave his main attention, however, to matters in St. Louis, and before the year ended he was able to report to Astor that: "Preliminary arrangements are made for prosecuting the Trade of the Missouri & St. Louis next season . . . Berthold and Chouteau with all their advantages has suffered the Concern of Stone & Co. to get the better of them more effectually than could have been believed, and as there is no injunction to the contrary we may as well come in for a share of the Business . . . you now do no business with them worth attending to, and any scruples we have heretofore entertained in regard to embarking in their portion of the Trade ought not to be indulged in any longer. Besides, their apathy or bad management in opposing Stone begins to enlarge *his* views . . ." Pointing out that because of the weakness of Berthold and Chouteau, Stone had opened competition with Astor posts on the Mississippi, Crooks declared that "independent of other considerations, self defense will lead us into the field against him."

However, Crooks informed Astor, "I shall not . . . for the first year attempt much. My intention is merely to supply our . . . Mississippi and Illinois River outfits from St. Louis, and tamper with the Missouri traders on a moderate scale, in order to secure them for the following year . . . Without being very sanguine, I feel so favorably toward the undertaking as to make me enter it with great confidence of success."

Astor's confidence equaled that of Crooks. If it had not, he would not have been willing to move into the Missouri trade. If he did not approve of Crooks's policy of moderation, he made no effort to change it at the moment. He soon demonstrated, however, that while he never failed to display cautiousness, once he had adopted a program moderation affected his actions little, if at all.

Samuel Abbott was the manager of the important American Fur Company post at Prairie du Chien, and Crooks wrote him in the fall of 1821, "Unless it is absolutely necessary for you to remain at Prairie du Chien it is our wish that you proceed this fall to St. Louis, there to remain until you obtain a *complete* list of the goods usually found in the retail establishments of that place. Ascertain everything that may be of advantage to us, and, as soon thereafter as may be convenient to yourself, pursue your journey to New York."

Abbott carried out his assignment. In the spring of 1822, Crooks opened a warehouse and store in St. Louis. He put Abbott in charge of it, and wrote Astor, "I regret beyond measure that our fastidiousness about interfering with our St. Louis friends induced us to postpone until the present time any attempt to participate in the Missouri trade."

The Astor juggernaut had crossed the Mississippi.

6

The fortunes of David Stone's firm, sometimes known as Stone, Bostwick & Company, were on the ascendancy. Stone, as Crooks had stated, had got the better of Chouteau. Astor saw the need for drastic action. Back in New York from Europe in 1822, he not only guided the launching of his Western Department, but sought once again to bring Stone under his wing. He had been successful in driving Stone out of Mackinac, but now he changed the method of his attack. He proposed to absorb Stone instead of destroying him. Stone, benefiting from experience, realized the folly of resisting. A consolidation was effected. It included the Stone affiliate, Munson & Barnard, and was to run three and a half years, from April 1, 1823 to October 1, 1826.

From Mackinac Stuart wrote Stone: "Permit me to welcome you as a member of the American Fur Company & I think you have all acted wisely, but if the junction had been formed five years ago there would have been cause of mutual congratulation."

Astor, feeling that things were progressing satisfactorily, bestowed the title of president on William, and went back to Europe, taking his very attractive daughter, Eliza, with him.

Trouble with the new associates in the Western Department broke out almost at once. Munson violated the terms of the agreement . . . probably with the knowledge of both Stone and Bostwick . . . by buying some furs on his own account. Astor, in a way known only to himself, differentiated between dishonesty and disloyalty, and he appeared to consider the latter the worse of the two crimes. He wrote that he did not "consider the act of buying the skins as a dishonest act," but he was profoundly irritated, and he told Crooks, "I think this will afford a good reason for displacing Bostwick and even Mr. Stone." He was willing to forgive them if they would "indemnify the Company . . . but they must indemnify the Company first, and if this can be done to mutual satisfaction, so much the better, you are on the spot and can judge better than I can."

His anger cooled, however, for shortly afterward he wrote Crooks, "I presume nothing has been got from Munson. I only wish these gentlemen may act with strict integrity and economy . . . From Messrs Stone & Co. I see as I expected we got nothing for the supposed great damage done by Mr. Munsons contract . . . it is now done with . . . I rather suppose you will find Mr Stone a useful member and I hope Mr Bostwick will turn out better than we expected."

Astor's kindly attitude toward Stone and Bostwick and Munson was not simply a reflection of big-heartedness. When he entered the St. Louis trade, Stone had begun to trade in buffalo robes obtained from Indians on the lower Missouri River. Astor had not handled these skins, and after his merger with Astor, Stone had continued to buy them as a subsidiary venture, finding his own customers.

Astor's uncanny perspicacity suddenly created the suspicion that Stone . . . and undoubtedly Bostwick and Munson . . . had stumbled onto a good thing. His suspicions were well founded. Stone had sold large quantities of buffalo skins to eastern buyers who appeared in St. Louis. This was the beginning of an American fashion that was to endure for years . . . that of using buffalo hides for floor coverings, carriage and sleigh robes, and overcoats for men. Profits on them were high.

Astor got rid of Munson, who had carried his extracurricular activities beyond an endurable limit, and he no longer considered Munson a threat. He saw danger, however, in releasing Stone and Bostwick to carry on a lucrative trade in buffalo hides, so he recanted and Stone was forced back into line. The traffic in buffalo hides went to the Western Department.

That Astor had not intimidated all St. Louis traders became fully apparent with the appearance of an advertisement, early in 1822, in the *Missouri Republican*. It said: "To enterprising young men. The subscriber wishes to engage one hundred young men to ascend the Missouri river to its source, there to be employed for one, two, or three years. For particulars enquire of Major Andrew Henry, near the lead mines in the county of Washington, who will ascend with, and command, the party; or the subscriber near St. Louis."

The subscriber was William H. Ashley, and both his record in business and his political prominence indicated to Astor and Crooks that his competition in the river trade would be nothing less than formidable. Ashley had been elected the first Lieutenant-Governor of the new State of Missouri. He held the rank of general in the state militia. He was one of the organizers of a bank. He had been engaged in real estate, in the manufacture of gunpowder, and in lead-mining.

The man Ashley had chosen to command his first expedition, Andrew Henry, was already famous as a trader. He had been a partner in the Missouri Fur Company, and it had been he who, in 1810, had borne the brunt of the terrible struggle with the Blackfeet at the Three Forks of the Missouri. He had led his intrepid trappers over the Continental Divide, and had built a post on a tributary of the Snake River . . . Henry's Fork; he was the first American to carry his trade up the Missouri and over the mountains to the Pacific slope.

Through the eyes, ears and written reports of Crooks, Astor

closely watched the formation of Ashley's Rocky Mountain Fur Company, knowing that the time would come when he would have to move against it. Indeed, this was not a new situation. He had smashed bigger companies, destroyed stronger men. In accomplishing each of these victories, he had waited patiently for the moment when his prey would be in a vulnerable position, when its power to resist would be in a weak condition. He adopted the same tactics toward General Ashley, watching with the silence and stealth of a cougar waiting to spring on a deer in the tall grass of a prairie meadowland.

The plans of Ashley and Henry were unique. They did not intend to rely entirely on the Indians as trappers. Instead, they would take white men into the upper river country and the western mountains to obtain beaver and other furs. No posts were to be established. Experience had shown them to be expensive, and often useless for a large part of the year. Also, the problem of keeping them adequately supplied involved great difficulties.

Astor was intrigued by this departure from the historic pattern of the fur trade. Crooks informed him that Ashley and Henry, in order to avoid the danger and expense of maintaining permanent posts, planned to establish an annual rendezvous. Each year the partners would agreed upon a meeting place, and to it at an appointed time the trappers, both Indian and white, would bring their furs to trade for merchandise that would have been brought out from St. Louis. The rendezvous could be changed without cost, it precluded the danger of mass attack by Indians, and it could always be established in what appeared to be the most advantageous place for the season.

Astor understood that the system could have a vital effect on the fortunes of the western fur trade, and sought means of turning it to his own advantage. He had no pride in being the inventor of an idea. It was enough for him that he could find the products of other men's brains useful to him, and he willingly gave credit where it was due as he profited. Results were all that mattered to him.

General Ashley's advertisement had rallied to his banner some of the most able and courageous traders and trappers on the river, intrepid young men such as Jedediah S. Smith, David E. Jackson, William L. Sublette, Milton Sublette, Robert Campbell, Étienne Provost, James Clyman, James Bridger, and Thomas Fitzpatrick, and in the spring of 1822, just as Crooks was getting things in order in the new office of the Western Department, Henry and Ashley set out with their first expedition. The plan was to ascend to the Three Forks. Henry knew it was rich fur company, but now it was believed to contain a "wealth of furs not surpassed by the mines of Peru." The brigade would be absent three years, but General Ashley did not plan to remain with it. He would go only as far as the mouth of the Yellowstone, and then return to St. Louis.

Two large keelboats had been equipped and heavily loaded. Enthusiasm and dreams filled the young recruits who comprised the majority of the company. Many of them "had relinquished the most respectable employments and circles of society for the arduous" life of the wilderness.

The high spirits of the trappers were soon heavily dampered. About twenty miles below old Fort Osage one of the keelboats was torn apart by a snag and vanished quickly beneath the muddy waters of the Missouri. Supplies and merchandise valued at $10,-000 were lost, and it was with difficulty that the crew was saved.

In one overcrowded boat the company defiantly went on. Horses were obtained near the Mandan Villages, and were driven along the bank. Henry had developed a plan to ascend to the Falls of the Missouri, and establish winter headquarters there, but the Indians had other plans for him. Suddenly a band got hold of the horses by a ruse and drove them off.

Instead of continuing to the Falls, Henry halted the company at the mouth of the Yellowstone and built a wintering post. By spring he had obtained a new supply of horses from the Indians, and with a small company he set out for the Great Falls. There four of his men were killed by Blackfeet, and he was forced to retreat. By June, 1823, he was back at the mouth of the Yellowstone.

When he had returned to St. Louis in the fall of 1822, General Ashley had advertised for another hundred men. An adequate number responded, and while Henry was fighting the Blackfeet, Ashley started upriver with the second expedition of the Rocky Mountain Fur Company. It was marked for disaster.

Ashley reached the Arikara Villages without trouble and received a friendly welcome. He planned to send a company overland while his boats continued on up the river, and he soon obtained the horses he needed.

On June 1, he gave orders for both expeditions to start the following morning, but at dawn of June 2, the unpredictable and treacherous Arikaras poured a devastating fire into both the boats and the horse camp.

Thanks to the traders of the Hudson's Bay Company, most of the attackers were armed with London fusils, which fired a ball with great accuracy and force. Within fifteen minutes, so fierce was the Indian assault, that half the men with the horses on shore were either killed or wounded. Some of the survivors were drowned in attempting to reach the boats.

Ashley was forced to retreat twenty-five miles downriver. A camp was established. One of the boats was unloaded and sent downstream with the wounded and men who refused to remain. Ashley sent a message asking for military assistance.

It was important that word of the situation be sent out to Henry. That would be an extremely hazardous mission, and Ashley called for volunteers. To his astonishment, a mere youth named Jedediah S. Smith stepped forward. Ashley was able to induce a veteran French-Canadian to go with the brave young man.

Smith and his companion, traveling by any means available, had several narrow escapes before they found Henry at the mouth of the Yellowstone. They descended the river with him, rejoining Ashley at the confluence of the Missouri and the Cheyenne in July.

The military, commanded by the distinguished Col. Henry Leavenworth, arrived in August, and some sporadic fighting occurred. As a punitive campaign it was worthless, but it brought a temporary peace.

Ashley had to get back to St. Louis. He was a candidate for Governor of Missouri.

Having obtained a new supply of horses from the Indians, Henry set out overland with eighty men for the Yellowstone. He erected a post at the mouth of the Big Horn, and sent out a party under Étienne Provost toward the southwest.

It was during the next winter and spring that American mountain men entered the rich beaver country of the Green River Valley and the area of the Great Salt Lake for the first time since the suffering Astorians had passed through them. It was Provost and his little band who discovered the invaluable South Pass which Stuart had missed on his journey to St. Louis.

Despite the disaster at the Arikara Villages and other violent interruptions, the 1823 operations of the Rocky Mountain Fur Company were profitable. When the various trapping parties met in the mountains in 1824 . . . the first of the famous annual rendezvous which were to follow . . . it was found that large quantities of beaver had been collected. Henry took the catch back to St. Louis, and no red ink appeared on the company's books for that year.

Henry, highly encouraged, felt justified in starting upriver again in the fall, instead of following the usual custom and waiting for spring. He set out from St. Louis with a large expedition in October, but suddenly he abandoned the fur trade for reasons he did not disclose, and returned.[5]

Ashley was defeated in his campaign for Governor, and he plunged with even greater vigor than he had previously displayed into the fur trade. In the fall of 1824, he was at the head of an

---

[5] Henry reportedly was living in St. Louis some years later, and was reputed to be well-to-do. There was no substantiation of a report that he lost his fortune by becoming surety for defaulting debtors. Urged to put his property in his wife's name to prevent its confiscation, it was alleged that he indignantly refused, preferring to live a poor man rather than a dishonest one. The story may have had some foundation in fact. His obituary, published in January, 1832, referred to him as "a man much respected for his honesty, intelligence, and enterprise . . ."

immense overland expedition up the Platte River on his way to the mountains.

In their close observation of Ashley's operations, Astor and Crooks had taken cognizance of several significant factors. They had noted especially that Ashley had been unable to carry out his plans as he had originally intended. He had been obliged to conduct at least a part of his business from established trading posts. Ashley had built two, one at the mouth of the Yellowstone, and one on the Yellowstone near its confluence with the Big Horn. Ashley also had let it be known that he intended to construct two more, on the Marais and at the Three Forks.

But like all his predecessors, Ashley had failed in his attempts to open trade with the Blackfeet, and he had found that methods which worked so well on the lower river were inadequate and unsatisfactory in the mountains. These facts Astor and Crooks filed away for possible future reference.

They noted other things: The explorations of Henry, Smith and Provost had shown that the mountains, especially in the areas east and north of the Great Salt Lake, abounded in beaver. The Missouri Fur Company was pushing its operations with great enterprise toward the headwaters of the Missouri. These considerations were influencing Ashley's plans. There were indications that he intended to abandon the Missouri River Valley altogether, and send his brigades to the western slope of the mountains. It seemed reasonable to Astor and Crooks to assume that Ashley's chief purpose was to escape from all strong competition by going beyond the reach of other organizations. He had been unable to conduct his trade on the river without posts. Therefore, by going beyond the mountains he would be able to revert to his former scheme of operating with itinerant trading parties. Mobility had great advantages, and not the least of them was that by being able to leave a country quickly a company might well avoid clashes with Indians, which inevitably resulted in death and losses of furs and supplies.

Strength in numbers and mobility . . . in that combination Astor saw possibilities that fascinated him.

7

Crooks advised against plunging headlong into a clash with Ashley. Lurking in his mind was the thought . . . if not the hope . . . that a final disaster would strike the Rocky Mountain Fur Company, and put an end to its daring expeditions.

He held the same attitude toward the Missouri Fur Company and the upper river trade. Joshua Pilcher was reaching out for large bites, perhaps more than he could chew. If he continued to send Missouri Fur Company expeditions into the Blackfoot country, he was inviting serious trouble.

In essence, Crooks suggested to Astor that it might be wiser to advance slowly and with security up the river. Even in the event both Ashley and Pilcher won absolute control of the Rocky Mountain and the upper river trades, respectively, it might well be to the advantage of the Western Department. Let Ashley and Pilcher do the hard work of opening the country, let them suffer the heavy losses of men, merchandise and furs that were inescapable in overcoming the Indians. After that was done, the Western Department could step in and either buy them out, absorb them, or destroy them by sheer weight of superior resources.

If he had any reservations about such strategy, Astor did not voice them at once. He held great respect for Crooks's judgment, and Crooks's ability had been demonstrated in the successes of the Northern Department. He told his son not to reject any proposals Crooks made without conferring with him, whether he was in Europe or New York.

Crooks made numerous trips to New York, and when Astor was there he held long conferences with him. William participated in some of them, but William was more interested in the company's real-estate holdings on Manhattan Island and the collecting of interest and rents than he was in the problems of a smelly and hazardous business in the remote reaches of the Missouri River.

Astor and Crooks spent hours going over reports and studying maps. For a man who had never been as far west as the Mississippi River, Astor's knowledge and understanding of the country and the trade were nothing short of phenomenal. No detail seemed to be too small for his consideration, and his mind was like a file in which every fragment of information gathered through the years remained in its proper place, always quickly available. Crooks, however, was not Astor's only source of information. Far from it. The accurate and thorough material Crooks submitted in an endless stream was duly noted and catalogued, but it was supplemented by a constant supply of intelligence which came to Astor from his agents in Washington, from his friends in the administration and from such men as Senator Benton. The American Fur Company lobby was far more efficient and larger than any espionage service to which the Government had access.

Each year since the return of Lewis and Clark, maps had improved. John Colter, breaking his amazing trails through the mountains and discovering Colter's Hell about the falls of the Yellowstone, had made a major contribution. The wanderers who followed him brought back bits of new knowledge. Ashley's mountain men, as well as the general himself, had thrown light on great areas of darkness.

Every mile of the Missouri had been visited and charted, at least mentally, by trappers, notably the mountain men of the Missouri and the Rocky Mountain Fur Companies. Red Rock Creek was known. It was the upper course of Jefferson Fork, and it was a distance of approximately four hundred miles from its headwaters to the Three Forks. At Three Forks the Jefferson was joined by the Madison and the Gallatin, and the Missouri was born. From that junction to its confluence with the Mississippi was slightly more than 2,500 miles.

Between Red Rock Creek and the Missouri's terminus were the vast domains of the nomadic red people, who, although only a few generations beyond the Stone Age, were swiftly adapting themselves to the use of the white man's marvels as they fell victims to his diseases and his vices. How many of them there were, no one could say. The mountain men talked of the Blackfeet, Piegans, Bloods, Gros Ventres of the Prairies, Arapahoes, Cheyennes, Crows, Minnetaries, Assiniboines, Mandans, Arikaras, Pawnees, Yanktonais, Tetons, Brules, Sans Arcs, Minneconjous, Oglalas, Hunkpapas, Poncas, Omahas, Kansas, Osages, Iowas, Otoes, Missouris. If their numbers were unknown, they differed in no essential particular from their brothers of the Old Northwest Territory, and that was an important thing to remember. It meant that trade with them could be carried on in much the same manner as had been done east of the Mississippi. Only distances, the task of transportation, would be greater.

As they analyzed their reports and studied their maps, Astor and Crooks understood that Lisa, the men of the Columbia Fur Company and Ashley's lieutenants had chosen wisely in selecting sites for their posts. Each one stood at or near a confluence of rivers, such as the junctions with the Missouri of the Marias, the Yellowstone, the Teton, the Little Missouri, the Rivière au Jacques, the Platte, the Kansas and numerous others. These were natural centers of trade, reachable over courses of least resistance, accessible from several directions, just as were Michilimackinac, Detroit, Green Bay, Grand Portage, Chicago, Prairie du Chien and St. Louis itself.

It was only good sense to go where the trailbreakers had gone in the territory of the Western Department, just as had been done in the region of the Great Lakes. Astor gave the order. When Crooks moved, he was to go to these places first, but was not to overlook the possibility of finding advantageous unoccupied locations.

The next steps were obvious, no different than those taken when the American Fur Company forces moved westward through Michigan, Wisconsin, Illinois and along the shores of Lake Superior toward the headwaters of the Mississippi. Lower prices, superior merchandise, credit, alcohol, minimum expenses

... the weapons and resources that Astor possessed in quantities no other organization could hope to match. Drive out, buy out, or destroy ... Crooks was free to employ the methods he deemed best for any situation, and they were to be used without regard for consequences. There was no place in business for personal feelings or sentiment.

As for the caution which Crooks advocated, it, like any other habit or quality, had its sensible and its practicable limits. A man might be overly cautious just as he might be careless. The advisable, the reasonable, course had to be determined, and followed. Certainty was paramount, for there could be no turning back without loss of profit.

Astor had no fault to find with the moves Crooks had made. In the drive for supremacy in the Northern Department he had found it advantageous for a time to buy furs from other traders instead of sending out his own brigades. This policy had been followed with the establishment of the Western Department. Stone, Bostwick & Company had been taken over and used as agents. They had made enormous purchases of pelts brought into St. Louis by other houses, sometimes taking all offered of certain kinds and controlling the market. Immense quantities of merchandise had been sold to expeditions going into the mountains or up the river. The system had enabled Astor to gain knowledge of the size of the trade and of its potentialities. In that respect it was good, but there were drawbacks he did not want to continue.

The chief disadvantages were two, and they were the same ones that Astor had eliminated as soon as possible in the Northern Department. Selling goods to other traders brought a profit, but it was much smaller than the profit to be made by selling goods directly to the Indians. Buying furs from other houses was profitable, but again the return was considerably smaller than it was on furs obtained at the source. In each case the middleman was eliminated.

In the first two years after the establishment of the Western Department, Crooks had dispatched a dozen traders up the Missouri on seasonal journeys to buy furs, but he had opened only three permanent posts. All were in excellent locations. The first American Fur Company shingle was displayed over a log structure on the left bank of the river about halfway between the present cities of St. Joseph, Missouri, and Omaha, Nebraska. This was the territory of the Otoe and Missouri tribes. The second, called Cabanne's Post, was constructed just above the mouth of the Platte River.[6] Several other companies maintained houses in the area for years. The third post, Fort Kiowa, was much farther upstream, just beyond the mouth of the White River.[7] It stood within a pistol shot of the Columbia Fur Company's post, Fort Lookout. Also nearby was Fort Recovery, owned by the Missouri Fur Company.

Crooks knew the river. If he was proceeding slowly, he was doing so with the certainty that Astor wanted. The first post was at the mouth of the Nishnabotna, to which Indians came downriver with pelts. They came with furs from as far west as the Big Blue. The confluence of the Platte and the Missouri had been for half a century one of the most important trade centers. The Omahas, the Pawness and some of the lower Sioux tribes brought their pelts there. Lewis and Clark had met the Indians nearby at a place called Council Bluffs. It had been near there . . . at Papillon Creek . . . that Crooks himself had built one of the earliest posts in the area at the time he and McClelan were in partnership. That had been in 1810, a year before they had joined the overland Astorians.

Crooks understood why Kenneth McKenzie and Joshua Pilcher had chosen the sites for Fort Recovery and Fort Lookout. Furs came to the Missouri from the Sioux along the Rivière au Jacques on the east, and from the tribes on the White River to the west. He had seen these furs come down to St. Louis, and he had built Fort Kiowa to get some of them.

In each instance he had adhered to his policy of going where others had gone first, where it was shown that furs were to be regularly obtained, fearing no competition. It was Astor's policy,

[6] About nine or ten miles from the old Union Pacific Bridge.
[7] On the right bank about ten miles above Chamberlain, South Dakota.

part of the scheme which had worked so well in the Northern Department . . . invade, undersell, and destroy.

Astor was hardly in a position to disapprove. He indicated that he thought Crooks might be waiting too long before taking other strategically important steps, but he refrained from over-riding any of Crooks's decisions. His confidence in Crooks was too great for him to do that. In the end, he did no more than admonish his gifted lieutenant to move with all reasonable speed, and went back to Europe.

Astor was soon to know that he had been right. Crooks's hesi-tation to meet their main competitors head-on in power drives to the upper river had cost the American Fur Company money. Yet, when Crooks did, at last, begin to advance on a large scale, Astor said nothing of his past feelings. He saw nothing to be gained in recriminations.

Meanwhile, it had begun to appear that Crooks's plan of let-ting others do the hard and dangerous work of opening doors, would pay dividends. Early in 1822, Crooks had watched . . . admittedly not without some envy . . . an immense Missouri Fur Company expedition leave for the upper river. In command were two famous mountain men, Robert Jones and Michael Immel. The 180 "adventurers" in their brigade brought the total of Mis-souri Fur Company men trapping on the headwaters of the Mis-souri and in the mountains to more than three hundred . . . a formidable force.

Early in 1823, Jones and Immel set out with a large party for the headwaters of the Missouri from Fort Benton, at the junc-ture of the Big Horn and Yellowstone rivers.[8] Their purpose was to carry out Joshua Pilcher's plan to open trade with the Black-feet, a thing no trader had succeeded in doing.

Reaching the Three Forks, the company trapped while wait-ing for the Blackfeet to appear. By May 16, more than fifty packs of beaver had been taken, and Jones and Immel concluded that the Blackfeet were avoiding them. The next day they started

---

[8] Not to be confused with the famous Fort Benton built years later at the head of navigation on the Missouri.

down the Jefferson Fork on their way back to the Yellowstone. Suddenly they met a party of thirty-eight Blackfeet. One of the Indians produced a letter written on the sheaf of a notebook. It stated that the bearer was a principal chief, felt no enmity toward the white man and possessed a large quantity of furs. On the bottom of the letter was written in a bold hand: "God Save the King."

The Blackfeet seemed greatly pleased to learn that Jones and Immel wished to establish a post at the Great Falls of the Missouri; they chatted amiably through the night. Jones and Immel were, however, too experienced to be lulled into carelessness by the outward attitudes of the Indians. The next day they pushed on as fast as their heavily loaded packhorses could travel. By May 31, they had almost reached Crow territory, and considered themselves safe. They were traveling on an age-old buffalo path along the bank of the Yellowstone when they were suddenly set upon by a horde of Blackfeet.

Jones and Immel and five other men were killed, and four were wounded. All the property of the company, including horses, traps and furs valued at $15,000, was lost. The survivors succeeded in constructing a raft and escaping across the river.

If he felt compassion for the trappers who had been slain, Crooks could review the misfortunes which had beset the companies with the satisfaction of knowing he had expected them to occur. The correctness and wisdom of his policy had been made apparent to Astor by at least half a dozen tragic incidents.

Crooks could agree that in every case the Indians had been induced to attack by British traders who gave them handsome presents, but that did not alter the situation. The important consideration was that not a man in the employ of the Western Department, nor a dollar of Astor's money, had been lost. As for the British stirring up the Indians to attack Americans, that was a problem for Astor to take up in Washington. Nothing could be done about it in St. Louis.

Others on the frontier held a different opinion. Official reports and strong complaints were being received in the War Department. A letter from Maj. Benjamin O'Fallon typified their tone: "I was in hopes that the British Indian Traders had some bounds to their rapacity. I was in hopes, during the late Indian War, in which they were so instrumental in the indiscriminate massacre of our people, that they were completely saturated with our blood. But it appears not to have been the case. Like the greedy wolf, not satisfied with the flesh, they quarrel over the bones. They ravage our fields and are unwilling that we should glean them. Alarmed at the individual enterprise of our people, they are exciting the Indians against them. They furnish them with the instruments of death and a passport to our bosoms. Immel had great experience of the Indian character, but (poor fellow!) with a British passport they at last deceived him and he fell a victim of his own credulity; and his scalp, and those of his comrades, are now bleeding on the way to the British trading establishments."

Astor's men thundered with their fists on Washington desks. It was an outrageous situation. Something had to be done to stop the British fomenting attacks upon Americans.

Something was going to be done, but it would be slow in coming. The State Department was interested in the matter, for the accusations were aimed at a friendly power. The War Department was advised to move with caution. The traders in the British posts north of the border smiled.

The Jones and Immel tragedy was a terrible blow to the Missouri Fur Company and to the hopes of Joshua Pilcher. He wrote pathetically to Maj. Benjamin O'Fallon, the Indian Agent: "This, our second adventure to the mountains, had surpassed my most sanguine expectations; success was complete and my view were fulfilled in every respect . . . The flower of my business is gone; my mountaineers have been defeated, and the chiefs of the party both slain."

Pilcher's prostration was duly reported by Crooks to Astor, and with it went the encouraging news that Pilcher . . . which meant the Missouri Fur Company . . . had withdrawn from the upper river trade. Pilcher himself had retired to the company's main post at Council Bluffs.

Ashley was still going strong in the mountains, and meeting with considerable success. It was Crooks's opinion that nothing should be done in the way of opposing him on an extensive scale. Pecking at him would suffice for the time being.

Under the circumstances, the same view should not be taken with regard to the Missouri Fur Company. It was staggering, its operation restricted to the lower river and out toward the mountains in the direction of South Pass. Pilcher was a thoroughly discouraged man. A few strong blows now might send the Missouri Fur Company down beyond recovery.

Astor made no comment. He ordered Crooks to keep in close touch with him through the New York office, and to pursue the course in the field that would be in the best interests of the company.

Crooks needed to strike no blows against the Missouri Fur Company. It vanished from the stage, and in the last act Pilcher wandered off to the Columbia, lost his horses, and was rescued and brought back across Canada by the British. Crooks gave him a job.

8

Astor's trips to Europe during the early 1820's were not taken entirely for reasons of health. He had other troubles. With his youngest daughter, Eliza, a retinue of servants and a trained nurse, he took his mentally incompetent son to Paris to be examined. A small fortune was spent in efforts to discover treatments that would restore the sanity of John Jacob Astor, Junior. The efforts were in vain. Washington Irving wrote to Henry Brevoort that young Astor, who was then in his thirties, "seems in a state of mental stupor . . . there appears but little prospect of his recovery." Refusing to give up hope, Astor brought his son back to the United States and placed him in expensive care in Cambridgeport, Massachusetts. He also engaged a young man named Dexter Fairbanks to be his son's companion.

The family was reported to be split over a romance Eliza had entered into with a young dentist who was also a mushy poet, named Eleazar Parmly. Sarah Astor seemed to favor Parmly, but Astor could not stomach him. He induced Eliza . . . it was rumored that he forced her, but that would not have been in keeping with the soft attitude he displayed toward all his children . . . to go back to Europe with him in the hope of making her forget the dentist-poet.

If that was Astor's scheme, it was successful. In Paris, Eliza met Count Vincent Rumpff, a Swiss acting as minister of the Hanseatic Free Cities of France, fell in love with him, and was soon the Countess Rumpff.

Back in New York, Parmly made a public fuss, and turned out a flood of verses about aching hearts and broken flowers. However, his own wounds seemed to heal quickly, for within a short time he had found another love and had married.[9]

Although Astor's sojourns in Europe were marked by periods of feverish activity in the fur markets, as well as family problems and sieges of illness, none of these burdens prevented him from keeping in the closest possible touch with affairs on the American frontier. Reports came to him with every mail ship crossing the Atlantic from William, Stuart and Crooks, and he studied them with great care.

Certain situations stirred profound concern in him. He con-

[9] But Parmly considered his brief affair with Eliza too useful to abandon . . . possibly her money and name influenced his feelings . . . and he claimed that she had died after grieving for him for eight years. The story was widely believed, but the truth was that Eliza enjoyed a happy marriage for thirteen years before she died.

tinued to chafe at Crooks's inexplicable slowness to enter the trade of the upper Missouri. He felt the purchases of furs made by his St. Louis agents were inadequate and less profitable than they should have been. It was apparent that both Ashley's Rocky Mountain Fur Company and McKenzie's Columbia Fur Company . . . as well as some smaller houses . . . were reaping harvests in which the American Fur Company might well have shared.

Astor was especially irked by the increasing success of a previously little known house, Bernard Pratte & Company. In 1825, it and the Columbia Fur Company obtained control of nearly all the buffalo hides and beaver skins brought into St. Louis. They held the price so high that the Western Department agents could not buy them, ship them to New York, and hope to make a profit. This was an intolerable situation, and Astor's blood pressure mounted.

His agreement with Stone, Bostwick & Company to act as agents for the Western Department was due to expire in October, 1826. Also, the contracts he held with Stuart and Crooks would terminate in the same month. Obviously, in view of conditions, some new arrangements were in order, and he proposed to see that they were created.

His letter to Crooks regarding Stone was unusually blunt, stating: ". . . I will order goods for 1826, for be the agreement [with Stone] extended or not, the trade will be carried on by some one, and be it who it may they must have goods . . . what will be prudent if not necessary [is] to make no agreement beyond Oct. 1826, if it can be avoided of which you and the other Agents can judge better than me."

Astor expressed the belief that Stone "will prefer to sell out, and excepting Stone, I should as leave be without them, though I may also wish to sell out, but whether I do or not, it will be of great satisfaction to me to see the Company's affairs in a good state . . ."

Astor was disappointed and dissatisfied, but the fear that his attitude might prompt his two valuable assistants, Stuart and

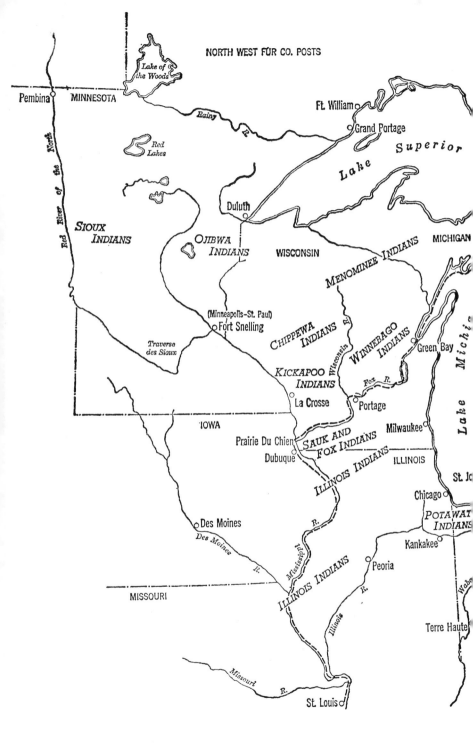

NORTH WEST FUR CO. POSTS

Lake of the Woods

Pembina   MINNESOTA

Red River of the North

Rainy R.

Ft. William

Grand Portage

Red Lakes

Lake Superior

Duluth

SIOUX INDIANS

OJIBWA INDIANS

WISCONSIN

MICHIGAN

MENOMINEE INDIANS

(Minneapolis-St. Paul) Fort Snelling

CHIPPEWA INDIANS

Wisconsin R.

WINNEBAGO INDIANS

Green Bay

Traverse des Sioux

KICKAPOO INDIANS

Fox R.

Portage

Lake Michigan

La Crosse

IOWA

Prairie Du Chien

SAUK AND FOX INDIANS

Milwaukee

Dubuque

ILLINOIS INDIANS

ILLINOIS

St. Jo

Chicago

POTAWAT INDIANS

Des Moines

Des Moines R.

Mississippi R.

Kankakee

Peoria

Illinois R.

Waba

MISSOURI

ILLINOIS INDIANS

Terre Haute

Missouri R.

St. Louis

HAGSTROM CO., N.Y.

CANADA

NORTH WEST FUR CO. POSTS

Ottawa R.

Sault Ste. Marie
St. Joseph Island   HURON INDIANS   French R.

To St. Lawrence River
and Montreal

Georgian Bay

Michilimackinac

Lake Huron

Lake Ontario

MICHIGAN

OJIBWA
INDIANS

Detroit

Lake Erie

OHIO

Wayne

SHAWNEE INDIANS

DELAWARE INDIANS

NA

**NORTHERN DEPT. OF
THE AMERICAN FUR CO.**

Hdqts: Michilimackinac

Principal Trading Posts shown to year 1833

— — — — Trading Route from Montreal to St. Louis

Crooks, to terminate their services with him was made clear in the letter he wrote Crooks in August, 1825, at a time when he was a very sick man: "I think I have already replied to your letter of the first July, that it is my intention to come home this coming Autumn, providing my health will permit the same," he told Crooks. "If not attended with danger for my health be that as it may, I shall set out from this very soon. With regard as to whether I continue in the trade I really cannot now tell. Much will depend on situation of matters when I get home, but whether I do or not I never had any other thought than [if] I did retire, I would like you and Mr. Stuart to be fully satisfied. I must say I never intended to make any arrangement contrary to your interest. Quite otherwise, nor did I contemplate that you or Mr. Stuart would ever separate from the company while I continued."

Crooks, aggravated by Astor's criticisms, was also becoming increasingly dissatisfied with what he felt to be the insufficiency of his own contract, but he had no thought of quitting. That would have been most unwise at a time when he was very busy carrying on a romance with Miss Emelie Pratte. The Pratte family was hardly less prominent than the Chouteaus, to whom they were related by blood ties. Nor were the Prattes any less successful than the Chouteaus in the fur trade, and they were, in fact, associated with them in various trading enterprises.

If Astor entertained the ungallant notion that Crooks's choice of a spouse had been influenced by such circumstances, he never revealed it. There was every indication that Crooks was deeply enamored of Miss Emelie, and that her choice of a swain was dictated only by her heart.

It was not a misfortune, however . . . and certainly not for Astor . . . that through his marriage Crooks would become a member of the old, distinguished and influential Chouteau-Pratte clan. In St. Louis, Crooks couldn't have done better.

Astor did not get home in the autumn of 1825. It was early in 1826 before his health would permit him to undertake the voyage to New York. He arrived to find that his son and Crooks had seen fit to extend the agreement with Stone, Bostwick & Company for another year, until October, 1827.

Admirably concealing his displeasure, Astor set about rectifying what he considered a wholly inacceptable situation. Before he made any decisive moves, however, he summoned Stuart and Crooks to his office to discuss new contracts for them.

Stuart and Crooks were not as amenable as they had been on similar occasions in the past. They made it clear that they were disgruntled by the way in which their respective departments, from which they were obliged to take their profits, were milked by what they felt to be excessive expenses, commissions and charges levied by Astor.

Nevertheless, Astor succeeded in bringing Stuart to terms with a salary of $2,500 a year, and 15 per cent of the net profits of the Northern Department. Crooks was harder to deal with, and at one time he blurted to a friend: "If Mr. Astor maintains the ground he took with me five days ago, we will part as sure as the sun shines on the poor as well as on the rich."

Crooks's position in the commercial and social circles of St. Louis had been made secure by his marriage, and he understood that Astor was fully aware of that fact. Grounds acceptable to both, however, were reached, and Crooks returned to St. Louis and his loving bride with a substantial increase in salary and a greater share in the profits of the Western Department. Neither he nor Astor divulged the terms of their agreement. Crooks obviously had been satisfied enough to sign his new contract, but it was noted that his attitude toward Astor thereafter was somewhat colored by antagonism.

9

The master was back at the helm. The course he charted in the early months of 1826 was irrevocable. The first order he issued was for full steam ahead.

Astor had crossed the Mississippi with a single purpose in mind. It was to win control of the fur trade of the Missouri River, as he had monopolized the trade of the Great Lakes. Nothing less than that would be satisfactory. Four years had passed since the Western Department had been established, and progress had not been to his liking. He was not finding fault with what Crooks had done. Crooks was the most competent executive in the entire fur trade. His dissatisfaction stemmed from what Crooks had not done. It was a picture which had strange overtones, but if he did not understand them, he knew how to eliminate them. He had become convinced that for some peculiar reason Crooks needed prodding . . . certainly a reversal of the situation in previous years. In the drive through the Great Lakes, restraining Crooks had been a greater problem than persuading him to advance.

Crooks had worked for him for the greater part of fourteen years, and gazing back through those years Astor came upon a consideration that held his interest and raised a question in his mind. It was that in the face of adverse conditions and mounting opposition, Crooks, unlike Hunt, had thrown up his hands on the Columbia and had started back to St. Louis. Crooks had made no fight to salvage any part of the great investment in Astoria.

Yet, Astor could find mitigating circumstances in Crooks's behavior. Crooks was shrewd and practical, and he was not a man who would waste time belaboring a dead horse. Crooks had realized that Astoria was a lost cause, beyond redemption. Nor was

Crooks a man to engage in heroics. Astor had expressed regret that Crooks had thrown up his partnership in the Pacific Fur Company, but he had not condemned him for it, and he had put him back on the payroll at the first opportunity after the War of 1812.

His faith in Crooks as a loyal associate equaled his recognition of Crooks's ability, and he had never suspected Crooks of being in any manner a coward. He held no such suspicion in 1826. What Crooks needed was direction, just as every man, no matter how great his ability, needed it at times.

Astor wanted first of all to get rid of Stone, Bostwick & Company. Stone, as he had remarked on several occasions, was a most able trader, but the others in the agency he considered distinct liabilities. In the face of his advice, William had chosen to agree to a year's extension of the agreement with Stone, Bostwick. That roadblock had to be removed, and standing idly by until October, 1827, when the agreement would die a natural death, was not to be considered.

In studying the matter, Astor analyzed the structure, financial strength and personnel of the various St. Louis houses. He realized at once that the Rocky Mountain Fur Company was beyond the reach of the moves which had to be made with urgency. There was no reason why Ashley, who was enjoying such apparent success, should agree to withdraw. Ashley's price would be exorbitant. Besides, the greater part of Ashley's trade was being carried on in and beyond the mountains. It would be injudicious to consider investments in that remote trade before matters on the Missouri River had been settled. The proper time to engage Ashley would come, and when it did, he would give Ashley the attention he demanded.

The Columbia Fur Company was the most desirable target, but both its size and enterprise made it a formidable antagonist. A clash with it was inevitable, but either absorbing it or destroying it would require considerable time and necessitate large expenditures. The Columbia Fur Company could not be considered in the light of the present situation and in the face of a need for drastic and immediate action.

Crooks had signed an agreement with the small house of Menard & Valle. It was similar to the first agreements made with traders when Astor was looking forward to securing a foothold in St. Louis. That is, Menard & Valle were to buy all their merchandise from the American Fur Company . . . or John Jacob Astor & Son . . . and Astor was to be given the first right to purchase their furs. Astor believed Menard & Valle reliable, but soon after the agreement had been signed with them, certain actions of Valle's had aroused suspicions in Crooks. At any rate, Astor checked Menard & Valle off his list of possible candidates to succeed Stone, Bostwick. Their company was too small. Besides, he already had them in the fold.

Size eliminated several other houses, and at last Astor's eyes were fastened on the name Bernard Pratte & Company. Actually, he had selected Bernard Pratte in the beginning, but his inherent thoroughness had prevented him from making a final decision before thoughtfully examining every possibility.

The shrewdness of Astor was never better illustrated than by his selection of Bernard Pratte as the chief agency of the Western Department. The house itself was not old, but its record was comparable to that of any other, and its prestige was without compare. Pratte was the leader of one of St. Louis' wealthiest and most distinguished families, outranked, perhaps, only by the Chouteaus. In this instance, however, rank, either social or financial, was not a significant factor, for one of the chief partners of Bernard Pratte was Pierre Chouteau, Junior.

A grandson of Auguste Chouteau, one of the founders of St. Louis, Pierre was reared in the atmosphere of the fur trade, and as a youth showed an unusual aptitude for business. He became clerk to his father before reaching the age of sixteen. In 1806, when only seventeen, he accompanied Julien Dubuque to the lead mines of the upper Mississippi. In 1809 he went with his father up the Missouri in the service of the Missouri Fur Company. Soon after he was twenty-one he went into business for himself, and in 1813 formed a partnership with B. Berthold, a prominent trader of many years' experience. This partnership was continued even after Chouteau and Berthold joined Bernard Pratte & Company.[10] Chouteau also had invested in the Rocky Mountain Fur Company, although he had no voice in directing its field operations.

Although he could anticipate the results of Astor's projected advance, Chouteau did not hesitate to make plans for the future of Bernard Pratte & Company, and by so doing not only brought Astor to attention but demonstrated his own shrewdness. He wrote to Kenneth McKenzie of the Columbia Fur Company at the very time it was known that Astor was contemplating approaching Bernard Pratte & Company with an offer. "I have the satisfaction," Chouteau told McKenzie, "to inform you that our mountain expedition in connection with General Ashley has been successful in its trade by closing at once the outfit and fortunate by having reached the settlements in safety with the whole returns; which terminates our arrangements with the General. It therefore becomes necessary to learn from you with the least possible loss of time what is to be done to prosecute the business in the Rocky mountains, which is intended to be carried on through the medium of your Upper Missouri Outfit."

If he did not have factual information, Chouteau suspected the trend of Astor's thinking. It had become a matter of trade gossip . . . probably revealed by Crooks in his associations with his new relatives . . . that Astor intended to abandon Stone, Bostwick. But Chouteau was well informed about sales in St. Louis and New York, and it would not have been difficult for him to deduce that Astor was far from satisfied.

Once Astor had reached a determination, the instructions he sent to Crooks were simple and unequivocal: arrange to terminate the agreement with Stone, Bostwick, Munson and Bernard, and begin negotiations for an association with Bernard Pratte &

[10] Chouteau later became interested in railroads and various industrial enterprises, and for many years lived in New York City, where he was recognized as a skilled financier.

Company. The success of the second assignment was dependent on the consummation of the first. Bernard Pratte & Company would not consider becoming agents of the Western Department as long as Stone, Bostwick was in the picture.

Crooks dutifully attacked the problems energetically and with pleasure. Not only was the prospect of having two distinguished kinsmen as associates pleasing to contemplate, but the power, prestige and enterprise of such a company could do no less than open the way to greater profits. Astor, needless to say, had given thought to both of these considerations. He was way ahead of Crooks.

Stone, once again recalling his futile efforts to fight Astor, promptly announced his willingness to sell out and terminate the agreement. Crooks put the matter into Astor's hands. The details could be worked out between Stone and him while he continued his talks with Pratte and Chouteau.

Astor quickly came to terms with Stone, Bernard and Munson, but O. N. Bostwick balked, and complained to Crooks, who wrote Astor that Bostwick ". . . says his partners sold out too cheap; and as long as he retains his interest I cannot (unless he behaves improperly) deprive him of his agency . . ."

No time was wasted by Astor in bringing the recalcitrant Bostwick into line. He offered to give Bostwick some stock for his interest. If that was not satisfactory, the matter was settled. Bostwick had no wish to be a small stockholder with no voice in the management of the company. He sold out as the others had done.

Astor bought what furs Stone, Bostwick had collected, repurchased all merchandise he had sold to them, took over their accounts with other traders, and made a settlement to compensate them for the abrogation of the agreement before its date of expiration. It was an expensive transaction, and Astor thought he had been cheated. Angrily he told Crooks, ". . . make Bostwick account for all. Have his books examined. We have been robbed." Stone, Astor declared, "has, I fear, not acted fairly."

Crooks determined that Bostwick had not been dishonest, but careful examination of the books did reveal that Bostwick had borrowed more than eight thousand dollars from the company till, and without authority had loaned Michael Dousman, a trader, another thousand. Astor would have to assume these debts.

Disregard for his opinion had been costly, but Astor blamed himself for the situation. He had been careless in leaving the final decision to William and Crooks. That, he promised himself, would not happen again.

In his reaction to the proposal to appoint Bernard Pratte & Company agents of the Western Department, Pierre Chouteau demonstrated his ability as a good businessman. He had no illusions about Astor's power, no foolish hopes that the spreading tentacles of the American Fur Company could be avoided. Astor had more resources . . . money, brains, affiliations, political power . . . than all the other St. Louis traders combined. Astor had agents in Europe who purchased manufactured goods for him at the lowest possible cost, directly from the factories. He was the largest fur dealer in the world, associated with the best houses of England, France, Germany, Belgium and other countries. His own ships carried his furs across the seas, and returned with his merchandise. Astor could put British goods on the waterfront of St. Louis at a lower cost than any other merchant.

Chouteau had wanted some years before to buy shares in the Western Department, but he had been dissuaded from doing it by his colleagues. He had felt then that an association with Astor would be wise and profitable, and he had never relinquished that view. He reminded his partners that they might long before have enjoyed the advantages of Astor's world-wide organization. Now they were being given a second opportunity. Continued defiance of Astor would be folly on the part of Bernard Pratte & Company. He saw it as sheer good fortune that they had a chance to become affiliated with a machine which, once it started, would roll up the Missouri Valley crushing all before it. In the beginning he had wanted Astor. Now Astor wanted him. That meant that Astor would make concessions. The alternative, in Chouteau's opinion, was bitter and costly fighting, perhaps even disaster.

Chouteau's partners acquiesced. The agreement was soon completed. It was to run for four years, and under it Astor was to furnish all trading goods at a fixed advance over New York and London prices. He was to have the opportunity of taking all furs collected, the price to be agreed upon, and he was to receive a commission on all sales. He was to advance all money needed for operations, and on this money he would receive interest. Bernard Pratte & Company and the American Fur Company were to share equally the profits and losses of the trade conducted on the Mississippi below Prairie du Chien and all of the Missouri River and its tributaries. The Mississippi above Prairie du Chien remained in the domain of the Northern Department.

The agreement became operative in January, 1827. For a few months things ran smoothly. Crooks was occupied with organizing expeditions to open a number of small posts above the Platte. Three were to be established on the Rivière au Jacques, one at the Forks of the Cheyenne, and another at the confluence of the Cheyenne and the Missouri. Men were being engaged, equipment and supplies were being purchased, and keelboats loaded in preparation for departures as soon as the Missouri was reported to be free of dangerous ice floes.

In New York, Astor plunged vigorously into those routine chores of the business which were no less important than the more spectacular tasks of forming coalitions and crushing opposition. It had been his belief for some time that retrenchment, even withdrawal, from certain of the less productive areas was essential, but the burden of work and his ill health had not permitted him to accomplish these desirable maneuvers. Now he gave his attention to them, his thought being that as the American Fur Company pushed up the Missouri and westward to the mountains, the trade farther east, in the Great Lakes region, might gradually be curtailed and more emphasis put on the activities of the Western Department. He wrote Stuart: "in comparing your order of this yeare with that of last the amount Dos not Differ mush & I have some toughts of ordering about 10 pct Less an the whole than Your order but Will not Determine till I See Mr Crooks who has ben ill at St. Louis & is not yeat arrivd I exspt him in 15 Days."

Astor especially desired retrenchment at Detroit, the eastern-most post of the company. In proposing this action, he was once again demonstrating his understanding of the trend of the national economy. The Erie Canal, which he had advocated more than thirty years before, had been completed. It had opened eastern markets to the products of the Great Lakes region, such as grain and timber, and had spurred emigration to the Old Northwest. Settlement meant the destruction of wild animals. He told Stuart, "about our Detroit concern it must be lessond or Giveng up I presum to Lesson will be best."

Stuart did not share such a view, and he registered a strong protest, declaring: "Your intention of curtailing the order for our next year's supplies will not I trust be put into execution for rely upon it that for every per Cent you take off; at least a proportionate diminution of percentage on the profits will be the consequence; and it may involve a much more ruinous result."

Unconvinced of the correctness of Stuart's analysis, Astor ordered Abbott, who had been the company agent at Detroit but had been transferred to St. Louis, to return to his former post and study the situation. Next Astor sought the opinion of Crooks, writing: "I am quite at a loss about our matters at Detroit, as I can give no directions about outfits or what to do with our goods there . . ."

Crooks, recovered from a bad cold, declared: "It will never do to abandon Detroit altogether for if you leave our opponents there free to act as they please, they will annoy the Northern Department most seriously in the district of Chicago particularly and make enough in their own country to balance the loss they may sustain in Stuart's territory. I would not do much at Detroit but still enough to hold our adversaries in check, and keep them busy nearer home."

Astor compromised, instructing Stuart to continue operations at Detroit, but to attempt to sell out, "provided it can be done to safe people." With this escape hatch in his orders, Stuart appeared unable to find any "safe people."

The Western Department, with new blood in its veins, was giving every indication of conducting a highly profitable trade for the year, yet Astor became increasingly pessimistic, and he told Crooks that "buffalo robes, muskrats, beaver, raccoons, martens, and deer skins were depressed" on the markets. Otters were the only skins that he had been able to sell at a good profit, and "on the whole Prospects for furrs is Bade."

Prices rose with the spring trade of 1827 in New York, but remained depressed in London. "We have no good accounts from Europe," Astor wrote to St. Louis, "not for any one article."

Astor's superb commercial instincts, however, indicated to him that a general rise was in the offing. While he maintained a pessimistic attitude, he began to make heavy purchases. He bought large quantities of muskrats from the Hudson's Bay Company, and sent orders to Crooks to buy all types of furs. Within a few months he held corners on beaver, buffalo, muskrat, bear and otter. His dominant position, worth a good million dollars to him, was shown by a sale of one type of fur. Jubilantly he wrote Crooks ". . . you will be surprised to learn the quantity of Muskrats I sold in less than 24 hours by Private and Public Sale. Say at Public Sale 200,000 at Private Sale 350,000 altogether 550,000, so many in the world have never been sold in one day. We still have 200,000 on hand the average price is about 36 cents . . . This year I had to arrange as to have nearly all in our own hands, as I bought some lots and made a good profit on them."

The prospects for a big year on the Missouri had suddenly become somewhat clouded by "such disturbing factors as Indian wars," said Crooks, but he was making every effort to carry out Astor's orders for heavy purchases. He offered to take all the muskrats and buffalo hides collected by the Columbia Fur Company, but McKenzie raised the price beyond reason. Crooks suffered another rebuff on his home grounds. Bernard Pratte also demanded such high prices for buffalo, beaver and otter that Astor ordered Crooks not to buy them. Crooks wondered if Pratte, Chouteau and McKenzie were reading his personal mail from Astor.

The truth was that even though they were Astor's agents, Pratte and Chouteau were not of a mind to assist him in cornering the entire St. Louis market without substantial benefit to themselves. McKenzie was just as astute, and if he saw an opportunity to hold up Astor, he would grasp it with pleasure. Columbia and a smaller firm, Collier & Powell, which operated above the Platte and on the upper Mississippi, held half the buffalo robes that were for sale, and they had large inventories of beaver, otter and other furs. Bernard Pratte & Company held the other half of the buffalo hides, and they also owned large quantities of otter and beaver.

When Astor refused to pay the prices asked, Pratte found other buyers for his buffalo, and went to New York to sell his beaver and otter under Astor's nose. All Crooks had managed to do was to buy the muskrats offered by small concerns, and moderate quantities of beaver, otter, deer and raccoon from independent traders. Astor was profoundly irritated, but he did not criticize Crooks. His wrath was turned on Bernard Pratte in New York.

He had, Astor informed Crooks, made Pratte "the first offer for the Beaver at 4 1/8$, on his promise that unless he could get more I was to have it. I am now told that he sold it at the same price, contrary to what he stated." Another thing that raised Astor's blood pressure was that Pratte had thrown his beaver on the market only a day before Astor had scheduled a large sale.

Astor frankly admitted that by failing to secure Pratte's beaver he had been unable "to keep up the price . . . Had I gotten it I would have sent it out of the country to China . . . I am quite at a loss to account for the conduct of Generl. Pratte, he did everything to prevent our getting his Beaver . . . he has forfeited everything with me, and even those who bought his fur think no better of him . . . Had Mr. Pratte acted candidly with me, it would have been greatly to our mutual benefit. I am sorry to say I lost all confidence in him."

Crooks could understand, as could everyone else who knew Astor well, that he was not sincere in resting his protests against Pratte's actions on unfriendly or disloyal grounds. Astor was mad because of the money he had lost by not obtaining Pratte's beaver. Pratte had not sold the furs at the same price Astor had offered him. He had sold them at $5 to $5.12½ per pound. If Astor had been able to buy them at $4 to $4.12½, he would have, in the course of a few days, made an extra profit of about a dollar a pound.

Astor raged against Pratte in three successive letters to Crooks . . . it seemingly did not occur to him that Pratte's daughter Emelie was Mrs. Crooks. Crooks probably would have ignored a single burst of vilification, but three were more than he could bear in silence.

The pride and clannishness of the typical Highlander, to whom ties of kinship, if only by marriage, were of greater strength than any commercial bonds, rose in him, and he delivered a stinging rebuke to Astor. "I cannot close this letter," he wrote, "without adverting to your remarks on the conduct of Mr. Pratte, and must be permitted to say that whatever reason you may have to find fault with him as relates the sale of his beaver, which he did not dispose of at $4.12½, I do think you might have recollected he is my father-in-law and not have forced the subject upon me in all of your last three letters."

It would not have been Astor's way to take offense at such plain language from a man he so greatly respected. He did not apologize, or even make any reference to the matter, but his next letter to Crooks was full of solicitude for Crooks's health and the welfare of "your good family." This was the equivalent of a formal expression of regret, and Crooks so considered it.

His failure to outwit McKenzie and Pratte had made clearer than ever to Astor the need for drastic steps to eliminate such strong and skillful opponents in the St. Louis market. He had no means of forcing Bernard Pratte & Company to sell him their furs. Even though they were the agents for the Western Department, they were not obligated to accept his offers if they thought they could obtain higher prices elsewhere.

In his search for a way to obtain greater control, Astor's cunning mind turned in another direction. His thoughts were concentrated on the Columbia Fur Company and Collier & Powell. He had the impression, which seemed to come to him out of the air, that Columbia might be agreeable to some sort of an understanding that would lessen the competition in St. Louis. The only basis he had for such a feeling was a statement allegedly made by Kenneth McKenzie that a division of the trade in the upper Mississippi country would be beneficial to all parties . . . certainly in itself a vague premise on which to rest hope. He instructed Crooks to learn if possible what was in McKenzie's mind.

Crooks carried on a cautious correspondence on the matter with both McKenzie and Daniel Lamont, another Columbia partner. The letters revealed that McKenzie did think a division might be worked out. He tentatively suggested St. Croix as a dividing line, Columbia having rights to the trade in the northern area. That would have meant the abandonment by Astor of the valuable St. Peters area from Traverse des Sioux upward.

Astor considered the scheme wholly unacceptable. Crooks, however, left the door open by suggesting a conference at Prairie du Chien or Fort Snelling at some future time, and he asked McKenzie and Lamont to avoid making commitments to other firms if they felt there was any chance of an understanding being reached.

Although this door stood no more than slightly ajar, it kept hopes alive in Astor. He was somewhat surprised to learn that Crooks had suddenly become completely discouraged. The basis for Crooks's dejection was a letter from McKenzie containing exorbitant demands. He wrote Astor that McKenzie's "expectations are too unreasonable to permit me to hope that we can make an equitable arrangement with them . . ."

Then, as suddenly as he predicted failure, Crooks found a new reason to be encouraged. "I heard," he wrote Astor, "that the house which supplies his [McKenzie's] concern is sick of the business and somewhat cramped in its means, but whether this be true or otherwise, it will not prevent my offering him fair terms, and if we do not agree, the negotiations will only be broken by his unreasonable pretentions."

Astor urged Crooks to continue his efforts. If an agreement could be made for the Northern Department, it might pave the

way for discussions about St. Louis and the Missouri River. Mc-
Kenzie's contract with the other eight partners of the Columbia
Fur Company was due to expire late in 1827, and this gave rise to
the belief that McKenzie might be induced to enter the American Fur Company's service. Crooks warned Astor that McKenzie
was not the kind of a man who would desert his partners and
leave them to struggle with a disorganized company. "To secure
even Mr. McKenzie," he wrote, "would be very desirable for he is
certainly the soul of his concern: but I would prefer taking with
him such of his partners as are efficient traders, and might continue to annoy us so as to annihilate their opposition entirely, for
it is the only sure way of improving our affairs if we arrange with
them at all."

Obtaining a man of McKenzie's ability would be extremely
costly, but Astor resigned himself to meeting the expense, and he
told Crooks, "I still hope you will succeed in arranging with Mc-
Kenney [sic], as it will be better than to carry on one opposition
after another."

Crooks soon sent an encouraging dispatch: "The business with
McKenzie & Co. is drawing to a close, and the negotiation will
terminate in 2 to 3 days at the fartherest when you will be advised
of the result."

The result was a complete breakdown of negotiations. Despondently Crooks informed Astor there was no possibility of
reopening them. McKenzie's demands were beyond all reason.
Chouteau and Pratte, he said, agreed with him that peace under
such conditions would be worse than war.

War it was to be then, declared Astor, and a fiercer war than
Columbia had ever known. Stuart was ordered to launch unlimited attacks on Columbia "above the falls of St. Anthony . . . not
suffer them to triumph on the River of St. Peters . . . we must
now fight harder than ever."

As to Collier & Powell, Astor remained unconcerned. He would
hurt them by making inroads on their importing business at St.
Louis, and he felt that if he could destroy Columbia in the North-

ern Department, Collier & Powell would fold their tents and fade away rather than attempt to compete with him.

Columbia accepted the challenge, strengthened its lines in the upper Mississippi country, and continued its expansion toward the west. It succeeded in establishing trade with northern tribes friendly to the British. This led to charges being published in St. Louis and elsewhere that McKenzie was either a British agent or a representative of the Hudson's Bay Company. Who instigated the newspaper articles was not disclosed, but suspicion rested on Astor. The articles were signed "Iverist." Astor may well have instigated them, but he obviously did not write them himself.

McKenzie sent Tilton and Kipp to the upper Missouri, and they built a post in the Mandan country. Columbia also established posts on the Big Knife, in the Assiniboine country, at Teton River, on the Rivière au Jacques, the Niobrara, the White, the Vermilion, and the Big Sioux. It was in a position to secure trade from an enormous area, running not only westward to the mountains but eastward to Lake Michigan. It opened an office in St. Louis to facilitate the purchasing of supplies, and it began to ship its furs by steamboat down the Mississippi to New Orleans, whence they were shipped in deepwater vessels.

The success of Columbia in competition with the British along the northern border and in its trade with the Crows demonstrated the ability of its traders. This trade was extremely profitable. Enormous quantities of buffalo robes, muskrats and beavers were obtained. Two years after its organization, Columbia had been as much as $50,000 in debt, largely due to the violent competition with the Northern Department. But after becoming established on the upper Missouri, the trade of a single season had enabled Columbia partners to pay off debts, "leaving much money for themselves."

The door which had for more than a year stood slightly ajar was now tightly closed. Across the northern lakes and forests the war raged with unprecedented fury. Collier & Powell allied themselves irrevocably with McKenzie, but still Astor wasted no ammunition on them. McKenzie was the man to beat, and Astor ordered Crooks to build a post beside every Columbia post on the Missouri. Expeditions, heavily armed, moved up the river to do the work.

Suddenly, and without apparent reason, a whisper that McKenzie was not averse to resuming discussions with Astor was heard in St. Louis. Crooks did not believe it, but he kept his ears cocked, and soon he heard the whisper again. Astor ordered him to knock once more at McKenzie's door.

Now Menard & Valle began to jump over the traces. Under the early arrangement Crooks had made with them, they were to buy their merchandise from Astor, and he was to have the first opportunity to buy their furs each season. A further provision stipulated that Astor would not furnish supplies to their competitors . . . largely along the Illinois River and the lower Mississippi. It was the latter provision that offered temptation they could not resist. With Astor prohibited from selling to their competitors, they made efforts to secure goods at prices beneath those he demanded. The transgression was quickly noted, but in the press of more important affairs Astor had not had time to inflict punitive measures.

It was not a matter of great consequence. Astor wrote Crooks that Menard & Valle's seasonal order would amount to only £400, such a "triffling order" that he hardly considered it worth handling. He presumed that Menard & Valle were securing the balance of the goods they would need "by other means," and he instructed Crooks to "judge whether they play fair with us and act accordingly."

Crooks, busy planning his approach to McKenzie, had not the time to conduct more than a cursory investigation, and he replied that "I am not quite able to give an opinion whether or not they treat us fairly, or make this triffling demand merely to cover their requisitions elsewhere."

The mystery was soon explained. Astor discovered that Valle was in New York "shipping his deer skins." He advised Crooks: "I find this moment that Manard & Valle shipped furs and skins to Gillespie here and ordered goods from them. You will know what to do, and that we ought at once to oppose them in this country [their trading areas] . . . by accident I saw a letter from Gillespie & Co. to them in which they stated that they received his letter and some skins which they were to sell for them & ship goods for the Indian Trade . . ."

Crooks reminded Astor that he had always been suspicious of the firm, and declared: "I am truly glad you have detected Valle at last, and shall not fail to bear in mind your orders . . . We are not left in doubt of the final result of Menard & Valle's attempt to befool the company."

Suddenly Western Department traders invaded the territory of Menard & Valle, paying high prices for furs and selling merchandise far below prices they could meet. In three months Menard & Valle were bankrupt and out of business. The efficiency, swiftness and ruthlessness of Astor's assault was duly noted in the trading houses of St. Louis.

To his complete amazement, when he appeared, hat in hand, on McKenzie's doorstep, Crooks was courteously invited into the parlor. McKenzie readily admitted that his high demands had been a bluff. He had simply been trying to see how much he could squeeze out of Astor, whether Astor wanted peace badly enough to sacrifice for it. He had found out. He had got war, and war had not been what he wanted. Neither Columbia nor Astor, McKenzie told Crooks, could make money fighting each other. All anyone ever got out of a trade war was bloodshed, financial disaster and unpleasant memories.

Besides, said McKenzie, he and his partners had known all along that they could not continue to fight Astor. His resources were a hundred times greater than theirs. They would be gradually beaten down, until at last they would fall, broken beyond recovery. What, McKenzie wanted to know from Crooks, did Astor have in the way of a new proposition to make?"

The question was answered as soon as letters could be exchanged between Crooks and Astor. It was to Astor's credit that he did not attempt to take unfair advantage of the situation. But he was too clever to do that. He wanted McKenzie and the other

Columbia partners to work for him, and he could not achieve that by alienating their affections.

The Columbia men considered Astor's offer eminently fair, and they hesitated only briefly before accepting it.

On July 6, 1827, Crooks triumphantly wrote Astor that the Columbia Fur Company had been absorbed by the Western Department.

This was the most important trade victory in Astor's career, greater by far than any of his victories in Canada or the Old Northwest. Moreover, it had come with comparative ease, and the terms of the agreement were advantageous beyond any degree he had hoped to secure.

Astor was to repay Columbia for all "goods on hand in the Indian Country at their cost and transportation." "It affords me great pleasure," wrote Crooks when he informed Astor of the details. Columbia was to withdraw altogether from the region of the Great Lakes and the upper Mississippi. This left the Northern Department without major opposition.

Into the Western Department came some of the most able and experienced traders in the West, men like McKenzie, Laidlaw, Lamont, Kipp and Mitchell. The Indian Agent at St. Peters, Lawrence Taliaferro, an avowed enemy of Astor, wrote bitterly that the American Fur Company had "purchased out, and given places to a number of the late Columbia Fur Company—tho confining these exclusively to the Naturalized Scotchmen, whom they have villified and abused ever Since they entered the Indian Country."

This was not the truth. The Columbia partners had wrought a tight, efficient and profitable organization that had brought them as much as $300,000 in profits in a single year, and Astor was too shrewd to destroy it. He made every effort to keep it intact, to bring it whole into the Western Department, and he thought not at all about "naturalized Scotchmen." He cared not what nationality a man was, but only what he could do.

As a consequence, with the Columbia partners who chose to work for Astor came many of their clerks, trappers and *voyageurs*.

Astor gave orders that they were to be disrupted as little as possible, that they were to continue working together. Only the name on the banner under which they operated was to be changed. All the great valley above the Big Sioux River was to be their territory, and there were to be no limits set on expansion. Kenneth McKenzie would be the lieutenant in charge of that vast northern region.

Through the amalgamation Astor acquired seven more major posts that had been built by Columbia. They were located at Council Bluffs, Vermilion River, Rivière au Jacques, White River, Niobrara River, Teton River and the Mandan Villages. The Astor name also would appear on a dozen smaller stations in the upper valley.

Collier & Powell, as Astor had expected, ran up a white flag. Crooks wrote that he had completed an agreement with them under which they were to "desist from all interference whatsoever in the trade with the Indians for four years. We have to pay Collier & Powell ½ per cent profit on the importation of this year, the English part of which was bought for cash, and most of that from Philadelphia also." It was a far cry from the arrogant attitude displayed by Collier & Powell during the original negotiations between Crooks and McKenzie. At that time they had demanded that Astor buy their goods at an advance of "25 per cent on the English importations and 20 per cent on the goods bought in the United States!!!" The exclamation marks were written by Crooks, who was appalled by the demand.

Columbia, Menard & Valle and Collier & Powell in the course of a few months had vanished from the St. Louis scene. At once Astor, never resting on his laurels, inquired of Crooks as to the situation of General Ashley and the Rocky Mountain Fur Company.

General Ashley was marching on with extraordinary success. Far out in the western mountains his brigades were opening new countries, trading where no Americans . . . with the exception of a few wandering mountain men . . . had ever traded. Ashley himself had gone up the Platte River and crossed the ranges. He and a few companions were the first white men to attempt to navigate Green River, which was thought to flow into the Gulf of Mexico. But Ashley had not floated down the Green to find out where it went. He was looking only for new fur territory. The experiment had been disastrous. Ashley had made his way at great peril through Brown's Hole to the point where the Green suddenly abandoned its easterly course. On he floated to the southwest until his boat was destroyed at the junction with a stream that was to be known as the Ashley River.[11]

Undaunted, Ashley and his men had set out on foot for the valley of the Great Salt Lake. Luck favored him, and shortly he met another of his expeditions led by Étienne Provost. Together the parties traveled on westward across the Wasatch Range to the great lake, thence southward until they reached Sevier Lake before they turned back.

Once more their destination became the Green River valley. It was there that the annual rendezvous was to be held. On the way they entered a beautiful mountain park that was well named . . . Cache Valley. Accidentally they discovered an enormous cache of furs which belonged to the Hudson's Bay Company and had been left there by the noted trader, Peter Skene Ogden.

When Ashley, Provost and their men moved on, their horses were loaded with beaver valued at $200,000. They had looted the immense cache on the grounds that the British had no right to trap in American territory and were not entitled to the furs.

Following the rendezvous on Green River, Ashley crossed the mountains with a fortune in skins, and reached St. Louis by way of the Yellowstone and Missouri Rivers.

He was back in the mountains again the following summer with a large company. On this journey he traveled through South Pass, taking with him a six-pounder cannon, the first wheeled vehicle that crossed the plains north of the Santa Fe Trail.

It was Ashley's last journey to the mountains. Once again he

---

[11] Ashley carved his name on a rock at the site. It was found forty-four years later by the great explorer, Maj. J. W. Powell, on his famous journey through the Grand Canyon of the Colorado.

became absorbed by his political ambitions. He sold out, ran for Congress, and was elected. His buyers were three of his ablest lieutenants, Jedediah S. Smith, David E. Jackson and William L. Sublette.

Ashley's triumphs had stirred the blood and aroused the envy of Astor, but with his customary methodicalness he had followed the principle of "first things first." Ashley and his men had returned from the mountains each season with no less than two hundred packs of beaver, each weighing a hundred pounds, and having a market value of $4 to $5 a pound. Ashley went to Washington a well-to-do man.

It had been difficult for Astor each year to refrain from attempting to emulate Ashley and sending out large expeditions to compete with him, but he had controlled his impulses and his jealousy. Also, Chouteau and Crooks warned him that to engage Ashley would be costly and hazardous. He was constrained to agree, although willing to make the investment, that it should not be attempted without assured supply lines and established posts. Ashley simply had been lucky.

Perhaps that was true, Astor told Crooks, but the time would come when Ashley's successors would feel his hand, when he would drive against them in a full-scale offensive under propitious conditions.

He felt that time had come with the absorption of the Columbia Fur Company. The Western Department had acquired at least twenty-two permanent posts on the waters of the Missouri River system. They stood in strategic places, between Council Bluffs and the Mandan Villages, more than 1,500 miles above the mouth of the Missouri.

Astor was the largest fur trader in America before he moved across the Mississippi in 1822. By 1828 he was not only the largest but by far the most powerful. From Detroit on the east to the upper Missouri on the west he was without an equal. He made more money in a single hour of each day than any of his hunters made in an entire year. His private income from furs alone was nearly a million dollars every twelve months. His resources in property and money in the western wilderness and his power were greater than those of the Federal Government.

He was not satisfied, not content. As he had done in the Northern Department, he set out to achieve an absolute monopoly of the Missouri River and the mountain trade.

The efficient organization he had acquired from Columbia not only was kept intact as far as possible, but it was given *carte blanche*. McKenzie, made the chief, was free to drive on, subject only to the best interests of the Western Department.

McKenzie selected the name for the immense subdepartment over which he ruled. He called it the Upper Missouri Outfit.

Part Nine

The Upper Missouri
Outfit

1

The bars were down. Competition on the Missouri River was all but nonexistent. What remained was inconsequential, and might have been likened to a terrier yapping at a bear. The bear lumbered on, ignoring the noise until it became aggravating. Then with the sudden swipe of a paw, the yapping was forever stilled.

It was nothing less than an inexorable conquering army that rolled up the great river. The departure of each company was signaled by gunfire, wild shouts and howls, the shriek of steamboat whistles. This followed days of carousing, drunken stupefaction, mad fornication with Indian and half-breed sluts. Men staggered toward the waterfront, falling down, bleeding from smashing their heads on barroom floors and cobbles, from depraved fighting. Those unable to stagger were carried aboard and dropped on decks like sacks of potatoes, and there they lay in pools of puke until revived by buckets of water dashed over them.

The keelboats were marvels among the conglomeration of river craft, products of an evolution that was colored by bitter experience and the blood of the adventurers who had devised them. Some were seventy-five feet long, eighteen feet wide, drew four feet of water, and had a heavy stout keel from bow to stern. The cargo hold was in the center, a twelve-foot deck at each end of it, but in some of the boats freight space was sacrificed to staterooms in which prominent passengers could be quartered.

The chief means of propulsion was the *cordelle*, a long line attached to the top of a high mast so that it would clear brush. Twenty to forty men toiled with it along the bank. When the *cordelle* could not be operated because of stream mouths or cliffs, poles were used. The poles had knobs on their upper ends that were to be placed under the shoulders of the pushers. Planting his pole on the river bottom, a *voyageur* pushed against it as he walked toward the stern along the *passe avant*, a narrow passage only fifteen inches in width on each side of the cargo box. In deep water, where neither the *cordelle* nor the poles could be used, long oars were brought out, and six or eight men on each side of the bow strained against them. Wide water and a strong favorable wind came together on occasion, permitting the use of a sail, and at such times the men sprawled about, chatting, singing, laughing, enjoying the luxurious respite.

A thousand, perhaps two thousand, miles of unpredictable muddy current lay ahead after the mouth of the Missouri was passed, weeks of backbreaking labor through storms, terrible heat, numbing cold, rain, snow and hail; weeks during which every hour brought its perils, the treachery of the river, its boils and eddies, crumbling banks, snags and bars; and the vicious whims of the red people, the arrows and gunshots that might come without warning, the inexplicable capriciousness and inconstancy of the Indian mind, qualities as inherent as the skin pigmentation and the physiognomic characteristics which distinguished him.

There was no government, no law, no civil authorities, no sheriffs, only a few powerless Indian agents and a handful of troops at Cantonment Leavenworth . . . that was all. If the Government was there in theory . . . the land did belong to the United States of America, a sovereign nation . . . it was not there in reality. If the laws were written, they were meaningless, for they could not be enforced.

The law was the *bourgeois*, the partner, who reigned supreme in the trading post or was in command of the brigade in the wilderness. But if the *bourgeois* was the absolute authority, if he conducted his business with military discipline, he was little protection for the individual trapper, the meat hunter, the *voyageur*, the *engagé*, the stupid *mangeur de lard*. The *bourgeois* could wear a military uniform, dine alone in splendor, sleep with his squaw concubine between freshly laundered linens; he could beat a man, cast him out alone, rob him of his wages with dishonest bookkeeping, shoot him. Or he could, if he so desired, be kind, considerate, understanding, fair. The *bourgeois* could be anything he wanted to be, be nothing he did not wish to be. Still, he had the responsibility of guarding the company's investment, and that came first. Furs were more important than men. Even horses ranked above them. The furs had to get back to St. Louis. The agreements signed by the men said they had to go out, but no agreement said anything about coming back.

Even the protection of God was not to be relied upon, and certainly it could not be expected two or three thousand miles from the nearest church cross. All that stood between a man and an unmarked grave were his own superstitions, his own knowledge of ghosts, his own ability to sense the presence of danger, smell it in the wind, see it in the markings of the dust, hear it in the whispers of the grass.

The bars were down. The Astor juggernaut rolled on. The men in the keelboats, at the posts, on the animal trails of the great plains, in the Indian villages, spoke of the "company's" furs, the "company's" property, the "company's" expeditions. After the year 1827, when a man in the Missouri River trade used the word *company*, it had only one meaning. It meant *Astor*. If the man wished to speak about anyone else, he used the word *opposition*, and he smiled knowingly as it passed his lips.

In the spring of 1828, Kenneth McKenzie, filled with new enthusiasm and ambition, went down to St. Louis from his command post among the Mandans. The successes of Ashley, Smith, Jackson and Sublette, stirred an almost uncontrollable envy in him. He submitted plans for an expedition to the mountains. Crooks, fired up by Astor's orders to drive ahead without limit, would have approved it had not Pierre Chouteau voiced objections.

The performances of the Rocky Mountain Fur Company, in

Chouteau's opinion, were too extraordinary to be easily imitated. Even if they had met with good fortune, it did not mean that others, following in their wake, could do the same. Conditions changed overnight in the far western country, just as they did along the river. A sudden Indian war, an unexpected cold period, reprisals by British agents, a dozen other things, could mean disaster. It was Chouteau's conviction that a slow advance would be most advisable. He advocated the establishment of a strong post at the mouth of the Yellowstone, the terminus of half a dozen trails from the mountains, where conditions could be observed and preparations made that would insure the success of companies sent out to compete with Ashley's men.

When the issue was placed before Astor, he agreed with Chouteau. With "great gentleness and consideration," Chouteau dissuaded the dynamic McKenzie from "his cherished mountain enterprise." But Chouteau promised that mountain expeditions would be sent in time, and he would have no objection to McKenzie going with the first one. A man of McKenzie's hardness and diplomatic ability would be needed in such a situation

"For three years," Chouteau declared, "these enterprises have succeeded well with General Ashley, but with him alone. Many others, and even before his time, have met with great disasters. I believe that there is a great deal to gain if such an expedition succeds, but there is also great risk to run. One of the principal dangers is loss of horses at the hands of Indians. It is necessary to be prudent, firm, and especially to exact obedience from the *engagés*, who are generally very insubordinate. The least negligence in the care of the horses may entail the ruin of the party."

McKenzie, not a little disgruntled, obeyed orders and returned to the Mandans. On September 15, 1828, despite the lateness of the season, he dispatched a company in the keelboat *Otter* up the river. In command was the veteran James Kipp.

The undertaking illustrated the efficiency and determination with which the ex-Columbia Fur Company men operated. Kipp reached the mouth of the Yellowstone, more than 250 miles above his starting point, "in sufficient time to build a fort and have all necessary preparations made for security" before winter set in.

The post was named Fort Floyd, and it was the first built by the American Fur Company above the Mandans.

McKenzie's eyes were still gazing far out toward the western mountains. Stopped from going there, he did not stop planning for the time when the checkrein on him would be removed. That time came sooner than he had expected, not in the way he had hoped it would come, but under circumstances which permitted him to make his first moves directly against Ashley's men.

Étienne Provost, an Ashley lieutenant, suddenly appeared at Tilton's Fort, McKenzie's headquarters in the Mandan Villages. Provost and Ashley had fallen out. Hurrying to St. Louis, Provost had attempted to secure backing which would let him enter into competition with his former partner. He failed to get the backing, but he did get a job with the Western Department, and Chouteau had assigned him at once to the Upper Missouri Outfit.

McKenzie recognized the opportunity Provost offered. He sent him with a small group to find the independent trappers who customarily sold their furs to the Rocky Mountain Fur Company. Provost's mission was to persuade them to bring their catches into Fort Floyd, where they would be given unusual consideration and high prices. The assignment was most acceptable to Provost, and he and his little band vanished into the prairie, in the face of advancing winter, toward the western mountains.

Provost had not been gone long when old Hugh Glass, a famed mountain man, arrived at Fort Floyd. Almost a legendary figure, Glass had traveled thousands of miles through the mountains. He had been with Henry and Ashley, and he had wandered alone or with a few companions where white men had never before gone. His miraculous fight with a grizzly bear and her two cubs was one of the greatest tales on all the frontier.

Glass brought word to Fort Floyd that he had been deputized by a number of free trappers to ask McKenzie to send goods to a rendezvous and trade for their furs after the spring hunt of 1829. McKenzie wasted no time in getting the good news to St. Louis.

The spring found McKenzie moving up to Fort Floyd, while 1,800 miles down the river on the waterfront of St. Louis hundreds of men were preparing to depart on the greatest series of expeditions ever known in the western fur trade up to that time. Almost all of them were "company" expeditions. The others, permitted to exist mainly by the sufferance of Crooks and Chouteau, had good reason to fear that they might be making their last independent trading journeys. The single exception to this general apprehension was the overland brigade going out to the annual rendezvous of the trappers serving Smith, Jackson and Sublette, General Ashley's intrepid and enterprising successors. They had never found reason to fear the Western Department or the Upper Missouri Outfit, and they saw none now.

This was overconfidence they were to regret.

It was April when Henry William Vanderburgh, who had been educated at West Point, set out with thirty men and a pack train of twenty-five heavily loaded horses to meet the free trappers somewhere in the mountains beyond Wind River. His company was small, but it brought a new phase to the mountain trade. The Western Department had at last entered into direct competition with Smith, Jackson and Sublette. Vanderburgh, although only thirty, was experienced. He had worked with Joshua Pilcher in the Missouri Fur Company, fought in the battle with the Arikara Indians, and trapped on the upper river.

Two more companies, led by men equally as daring and experienced, were preparing to follow Vanderburgh. Andrew Drips, who also had served with Pilcher, would ride at the head of one. He was a Pennsylvanian who had gone west to the frontier as a youth. In command of the other would be the handsome, dashing Lucien Fontenelle, born in New Orleans of noble parents. At the age of fifteen he had run away, disappearing into the wilderness beyond the outpost of St. Louis.[1]

---

[1] Fontenelle's sister, Amelia, grew up to marry wealth and maintain the high social position the family had always enjoyed. For twenty years she presumed her brother to be dead. One day a fine-looking man, roughly dressed, browned and swarthy from life in the wilderness, knocked at her door in New Orleans, and asked for her. She refused to receive him. When the man claimed to be her brother, she sent an

Crooks and Chouteau continued to draw the most experienced and able men into the ranks of the Western Department. In the spring of 1829 these partisans led more than two hundred men up the river. The Astor flag waved over thirty posts between St. Louis and the Yellowstone.

McKenzie was pushing on. He had sent a company two hundred miles up the Missouri above the Yellowstone, and they had built Fort Union. McKenzie's eyes were toward the Blackfoot country in which no American had ever succeeded in trading. He intended to be the first to smash the influence of the British, but he moved with the patience and caution of an old wolf. His salary had been increased to $2,000 a year, but it would be through profits on his shares in the Western Department that he would make money. There was no land richer in beaver than that of the Blackfoot, and he would pierce the barrier that stood before it . . . but not even the thought of growing wealthy could spur him to carelessness.

2

The ten-pound keg of gunpowder cost Astor $2.00 in London. It traveled in one of his vessels to New Orleans. There it was placed aboard a steamboat which carried it up the Mississippi River to St. Louis.

Transferred to a keelboat, it was taken on up the Missouri to

---

old family nurse who had known Lucien as a child to see him. The nurse identified him by a birthmark on his foot. But Amelia was a snob, and she resented her un-polished brother. Once more Lucien Fontenelle returned to the fur trade of the Missouri. He married an Otoe woman, and raised a family. He never went home again.

the post at the Yellowstone. On a packhorse or in a canoe, it was transported to the Big Horn country. Somewhere in that vast empty land it was parceled out, pound for pound, across a trading blanket to Indians. The price to the Indians was $4 a pound, or $40 for the contents of the keg.

The Indians did not give money for the gunpowder. For each pound of it they exchanged a prime two-pound beaver skin . . . ten beaver skins with a combined weight of twenty pounds for the keg.

The beaver skins traveled to London over the same route. There they were sold at $7 a pound, bringing Astor $140.

On the original investment of $2, there was a gross return of $140.

Astor deducted 2 per cent commission for buying the gunpowder, or four cents of $2, leaving a gross of $139.96.

He deducted 5 per cent commission for handling the sale of the furs, or $7 of $140, leaving a gross of $132.96.

Next, 25 per cent was deducted for transportation, wages and other expenses. This amounted to $35.

The remainder, $97.96, was considered net profit.

Fifty per cent of the net was divided between partners in the Western Department, according to the number of shares each held. The other 50 per cent went to Astor.

Astor's profits on his original investment of $2 in the keg of gunpowder were:

> Commission on the purchase.........$ .04
> Commission on the sale of furs....... 7.00
> Fifty per cent of net................ 48.00
> _____
> Total....................$56.02

Actually, his profit was greater. He charged interest on the money he advanced to make the purchase, and in using his own vessel between London and New Orleans, round-trip, he made money on freight charges. But these figures were concealed behind the haze of Astor bookkeeping.

Similar enormous profits, some of them even larger, were multiplied thousands of times in the course of a single trading year.

After Astor's brigades had won almost absolute control of the Missouri River trade, Secretary of War Lewis Cass, perhaps at the request of some Congressmen, asked his agents in the West to file reports on the state of the commerce with the Indians.

It was the report submitted by Thomas Forsyth that placed in official records prices and costs that indicated the immensity of Astor's profits.

The fur trade, Forsyth told Cass, "continues to be monopolized by the American Fur Company, who have divided the whole of the Indian Country into departments as follows . . ."

In listing some of the chief traders of the company, Forsyth omitted a number of important subdivisions. He stated: "Farnham & Davenport have all the country of the Sauk and Fox Indians, as high up the Mississippi River as Dubuque's mines, as also all the Winnebago and other Indians who reside on the lower parts of Rock River; also the Iowa Indians who live at or near the [Black] Snake Hills of the Missouri. The division of Mr. [Joseph] Rolette includes all the Indians from Dubuque's mines to a point above the Falls of St. Anthony, and up the St. Peter's River to its source, as also all the Indians on the Wisconsin and upper parts of Rock River. Mr. [J. P.] Cabanne, a member of the American Fur Company, has in his division all the Indians on the Missouri as high as a point above Council Bluffs, including the Pawnee Indians of the interior, in about a southwest direction from his establishment. Mr. Auguste P. Chouteau [a brother of Pierre, Junior, and associated with him in Bernard Pratte & Company] has within his department all the Indians of the Osage Country and others who may visit his establishment, such as Cherokees, Chickasaws, and other Indians. Messrs. McKenzie, Laidlaw & Lamont have in their limits the Sioux Indians of the Missouri, and as high up the river as they choose to send or go."

Forsyth made a strong appeal to Secretary Cass for measures

to improve relations between Americans and the western Indians. He had been on the frontier for forty years, and in that time he had seen conditions deteriorate until the Indians, debauched, robbed, cheated and brutally treated, had lost all respect for Americans.

This was not a new appeal for Forsyth. More than ten years before he had gone to Washington, where he had laid the "lamentable" problem before one of Cass's distinguished predecessors. "I had several long conversations with Mr. Calhoun on Indian affairs," he recounted to Cass. "I told him that it must appear strange to many people to perceive that we, as Americans, speaking the same language with the British, whose manners and customs were the same, exceeding them perhaps in our Indian expenditures, and having all the Indians residing in our own territories, still had not the same influence over them that the British had. Therefore said I there must be a fault somewhere. To which Mr. Calhoun replied, that I ought not to point out an evil without showing a remedy for it."

Forsyth gave the only remedy he knew. It was "to follow the same policy . . . towards the Indians that the British pursued with success." Calhoun didn't think much of the idea.

Forsyth spoke with some bluntness in his report to Cass, saying, "The British government have a well-regulated Indian Department. No person is eligible for an Indian agency under that government unless he can speak some one of the Indian languages; for it is natural to suppose that a man understands at least the general manners and customs of all Indians if he has been among them long enough to learn any one of their languages, and the British have brought their Indian affairs to a perfect system."

Forsyth deplored the intelligence of American Indian Agents and their lack of training, declaring indignantly that "our government appoints young men to Indian agencies . . . who, in all probability, have never seen more than three or four together in the course of their lives, and those Indans perhaps civilized. When the old chiefs and warriors hear of the arrival of their new father (as they term the new agent) they call at the agency to see him, but the agent does not know what to say or do to them and perhaps does not give them a pipe of tobacco, or even a good or bad word. The Indians then go away dissatisfied, and consequently in cases of this kind, everything depends on the interpreter. If the interpreter is an honest man he may teach the agent something in the course of years; but on the contrary, if he is a designing man, and wishes that no one should share his influence, he will keep the agent and the Indians in continual broils and quarrels, and nothing being rightly done, the public service must suffer. Instead of trying to heal the old sores that have existed for the last fifty or sixty years between the American people and the Indians, the breach is made wider and fuel is added to the flame . . . a young man who was appointed an Indian agent on the Missouri River cut off the ears of a halfbreed who resided among the Sioux Indians because, being in a state of intoxication, he made use of some extravagant language disrespectful to the American people. Another agent on the Mississippi turned out of the guard-house an innocent Indian to other Indians, his enemies, who shot him down and butchered him in a horrid manner, in the presence of an American garrison of soldiers. Another Indian agent also invited some chiefs to a council, when a number of their enemies . . . organized themselves . . . attacked the chiefs and others who were invited, and . . . killed nine and wounded three of sixteen persons."

Astor wanted no efficient and intelligent Indian Agents assigned to the tribes. If there was anything Astor despised it was a government official who was sincerely concerned with the welfare of the people. What man ever made money by raising the living standards of the impecunious and the ignorant, be they red or white? Interest was not paid on investments in social improvements.

Let the stupid Government officials propound laws that theoretically gave the Indian some rights, if that amused them. When at last there were no more fabulous profits to be made in trading with the savages, the naïve and impractical public hacks could have the West, and pursue their ridiculous schemes to improve and develop it.

Astor knew his own strength, and he knew that in the West he was stronger than the Government. The record was clear. Indian tribes had produced evidence to show the dishonest practices and brutality of the "company," but neither the War Department nor the courts had made a move to protect them. To the contrary, both had been "quick and generous in affording the greatest protection and the widest latitude" to the American Fur Company.

Astor could point out dramatically that in fifteen years more than 150 traders had been killed by Indians. No count of the number of Indians killed by traders was available, but it was obvious that if 150 traders . . . "hardworking men simply trying to conduct a legitimate business and help the Indians" . . . had lost their lives defending themselves, their attackers had suffered a much greater loss, probably five times as great. Traders could not be expected simply to go about letting Indians kill them. Certainly not, said official Washington.

Astor showed his political sycophants how the record graphically illustrated the hardships and problems . . . the losses of goods, horses and men . . . with which he was faced in keeping the British out of the fur trade on United States soil, and carrying on the trade for the benefit of Americans. It was very difficult to make a profit under such penalties and unfavorable conditions.

Secretary Cass made so bold as to inquire how much profit the American Fur Company was able to squeeze out of its operations under such adverse circumstances. Astor had arranged with him to ask the question. William previously, apparently suffering a mental lapse of some sort, had said the company made half a million dollars annually on an investment of one million. Astor wanted to correct that. It wouldn't do to let the Congress know the truth, and so he replied to Cass that in some years the company made nothing at all, and in certain of its operations had suffered heavy losses. Astor did not hesitate to state that he thought he was performing a great service to his country by his efforts to develop the economy of the West. And that had always been his desire. One had only to recall the disastrous events of Astoria to understand how he had fought to open the West for Americans.

If the Government had wanted to probe deeper into the matter, and to take steps to halt the bloodshed and slaughter, it had the material before it. The files of the War Department stated in simple language that numerous tribes not only were forced to trade their entire catch of furs at Astor's prices each year, under threats of being punished by force, but that some of them were so deeply in debt to him that they could never hope to escape. In 1829, the Winnebagos, Sacs and Foxes owed Astor $40,000, and two years later the debt had risen to $50,000. The Cherokees, Chickasaws and Sioux each owed him similar amounts.

These debts did not mean that Astor was in danger of losing money to these nations. Not at all. The profits were so enormous that he could well afford to extend them that much credit. If the debts were never paid, he would still net 400 or 500 per cent gain on every transaction that had been completed. Also . . . and here he could obtain ample protection from the courts, if necessary . . . the debts obligated the tribes to trade with him and no one else. Some laws came in handy at times.

The War Department reports contained other facts that might have been weapons in the hands of conscientious members of Congress . . . if they had dared to oppose Astor's mouthpiece, Senator Benton, who came from the very State of Missouri in which St. Louis was located, and in which many of the Indians lived.

In the reports could have been found "a terrifying commentary to which men are forced to go in quest of a livelihood," and "the benumbing effects on their sensibilities." Astor had no difficulty finding a host of men ready to cheat and rob the Indians, only to chance being killed in return. For ten or eleven months of the year, Astor's *voyageurs*, hunters, trappers and traders faced the dangers of the wilderness. They did not rob because it benefited them. It was what they were paid to do . . . paid from $130 to $400 a year. But they seldom got their wages in cash. They were obliged to buy the clothes and personal supplies they needed in the American Fur Company posts, at an increase of 300 to 400 per cent, and when the year was done few had any wages due them, and the majority were in debt to the company.

That wasn't due entirely to Astor's unconscionable method of dealing with them. It was in part their own fault. Habits of thrift among them were virtually unknown. They were improvident by choice, spurning the idea of frugality and economy. "Scarcely one man in ten of those employed in this country," said the trapper Zenas Leonard, "ever thinks of saving a single dollar of his earnings, but all spend it as fast as they can find an object to spend it for. They care not what may come to pass tomorrow, but think only of enjoying the present moment." The trader, Nathaniel J. Wyeth wrote: "Almost all the men take up their wages as fast as they earn . . . and would faster, if I would let them . . . in goods at about five hundred per cent on original cost."

Chittenden thought that it "was a sort of mountain pride, a convention of the business, to squander wages as fast as earned."

It was something else, too. It was the understanding that death lurked in the tall grass nearby, that the next moment might not come for them. There was no justification for the hope or the supposition that they would live to spend their money in civilization.

The evidence was in the reports, all the evidence the Congress needed to bring government, law and at least a semblance of justice, to the Indian country beyond the wide Missouri.

There were these words from Agent Andrew S. Hughes:

"The traders that occupy the largest and most important space in the Indian country are the agents and *engagés* of the American Fur Trade Company. They entertain, as I know to be the fact, no sort of respect for our citizens, agents, officers of the Government, or its laws or general policy . . . The capital employed in the Indian trade must be very large, especially that portion which is employed in the annual purchase of whiskey and alcohol into the Indian country for the purpose of trade with the Indians. It is not believed that the superintendent is ever applied to for a permit for the one-hundredth gallon that is taken into the Indian country. The whiskey is sold to the Indians in the face of the [Government] agents. Indians are made drunk, and of course, behave badly."

Congress moved cautiously, beset by pressures from both sides. A law forbidding the use of liquor in the Indian trade was on the books. Apparently it was not enforceable, but finding the means to halt violations posed difficult problems. Great expense, international relations, and politics . . . all severe headaches that did not come out of a bottle . . . had to be given thoughtful consideration. One did not simply crack down on men as powerful and influential as Lewis Cass, Thomas Benton and Jacob Astor.

3

The successful operations of Smith, Jackson and Sublette weighed constantly on McKenzie's mind. He feared they would find a means of establishing a trade with the Blackfeet ahead of him. So agitated was he that in the spring of 1830 he went down to St. Louis to discuss the problem again with Crooks and Chouteau.

In addition to enjoying profitable hunts, the successors of General Ashley had performed some notable feats of exploration. Smith, who carried a Bible in his pocket and read it assiduously, had gone twice to California. Most of his company had been killed in a fight with Indians in Oregon, and a large quantity of furs they had collected had been stolen. Deserted by the survivors, Smith had made his way alone to the Hudson's Bay Company station at Vancouver.

Dr. John McLoughlan, the factor at Vancouver, was most solicitous and generous. He dispatched a force to punish the Indians. Almost all of Smith's furs were recovered. Although he considered Smith an interloper in Hudson's Bay Company territory, McLoughlan made only a small charge . . . the wages of his men sent on the punitive expedition . . . for his services, and then purchased Smith's furs for $20,000, giving him a draft on a London bank.

In the spring of 1829, with $20,000 in his pocket, Smith and a companion named Black ascended the Columbia. Late in the summer, on the Snake River, Smith met Jackson, who was looking for him, and a little later, on Henry's Fork in the Tetons, they found Sublette.

While Smith had been wandering on the West Coast, Jackson and Sublette had been doing well in the mountains, going back to St. Louis each year with large catches of beaver. Reunited, the partners moved into a beautiful valley known in the fur trade as Pierre's Hole.

After recuperating from their hardships, the brigade started on its fall hunt, moving northeasterly toward the Yellowstone with the intention of swinging around into the Big Horn Basin, where they planned to meet Milton Sublette and his trappers.

The journey was completed after great suffering and a severe fight with marauding Blackfeet. Picking up Milton and his furs, they moved southward to the Wind River. It being too late in the season to take their catch on to St. Louis, they cached it, and set Wind River for the rendezvous of 1830. William Sublette and one companion set out for St. Louis to bring out packhorses and supplies. It was Christmas when the two men started on the perilous journey. They reached St. Louis, February 11, 1830, having crossed the great plains in the dead of winter.

On April 1, Jackson led his men on a spring hunt to his old stamping ground, Jackson Hole. Smith, with a youthful guide named James Bridger, took a company north for the headwaters of the Missouri. He did exactly what McKenzie feared would happen . . . successfully penetrated the edges of the Blackfoot country. Although Smith was fortunate and met no Blackfeet, he had a successful hunt, and he was back on Wind River in July. Jackson also had enjoyed success, and together they awaited the arrival of Sublette and the supply train.

Sublette left St. Louis, April 10, with eighty-one men mounted on mules; ten wagons loaded with merchandise, each drawn by five mules; two dearborns pulled by a single mule; twelve head of beef cattle and one milk cow. These were the first wagons on the Oregon Trail. He reached the rendezvous on the 16th of July. It was reported that "here the wagons could easily have crossed the Rocky Mountains, it being what is called the Southern Pass, had it been desirable for them to do so."

The first peal of the bell that was to toll the end of an era had sounded, and the mountain men who had been the first to penetrate the great unknown western wilderness clearly heard it.

Now Smith, Jackson and Sublette emulated their great mentor, General Ashley. They sold out to younger men in their company . . . Thomas Fitzpatrick, Milton G. Sublette, Henry Fraeb, Jean Baptiste Gervais and James Bridger. The new organization revived the name Rocky Mountain Fur Company.

Smith, Jackson and Sublette reached St. Louis in October with 190 packs of beaver, valued conservatively at $76,000 on Wind River, in ten wagons. They also brought back a trail-weary milk cow.

Much to the satisfaction of Astor, they announced their intention to enter the Santa Fe trade. But while this removed three able veteran competitors from the mountain trade, it in no way lessened the threat of the new and energetic Rocky Mountain Fur Company. Word soon came that Fraeb and Gervais and their men were trapping in the Colorado mountains. Fitzpatrick, Milton Sublette and Bridger, with two hundred men, had moved north through the Big Horn basin, crossed the Yellowstone, and had set their sights on the Great Falls of the Missouri . . . the Blackfoot Country.

The Blackfeet had been afraid to attack such a strong force, and Fitzpatrick, Sublette and Bridger returned south to Ogden's Hole, on the northeast shore of Great Salt Lake, with an enormous catch of beaver. There they found Peter Skene Ogden of the Hudson's Bay Company, and a large quantity of furs. It was Ogden whom Ashley had robbed, or swindled, and Fitzpatrick set out to repeat the dishonorable performance.

The Hudson's Bay Company did not permit the use of liquor by its traders, except in operations along the Canadian border. Ogden, a partisan who scrupulously obeyed company regulations, therefore had none with him. Fitzpatrick had a sizable stock of whisky, and he proceeded to bestow it on Ogden's thirsty men in generous drinks. The result was that they became thoroughly debauched, and failed to resist when Fitzpatrick demanded that Ogden sell him his furs at a ridiculously low price. Ogden, defenseless, had no choice but to accept the offer.

After completing this discreditable deal, the men of the Rocky Mountain Fur Company started eastward. They reached the valley of the Powder River, where a good supply of buffalo and other game always could be found, before winter set in, rich from their season's labors.

McKenzie in St. Louis demanded action, requesting that he be permitted to lead a large expedition to compete with Sublette, Bridger and Fitzpatrick in the mountains, but once again less sanguine counsels prevailed. Chouteau reminded McKenzie that Vanderburgh, Drips and Fontenelle were somewhere out in the far country for the very purpose of launching the competition McKenzie wanted. It would be best to wait until they were heard from before investing any more money in such costly and precarious ventures. McKenzie, burning with anger and disappointment, went back up the Missouri.

He decided that Fort Union, which was on the Missouri two hundred miles above the Yellowstone, was not strategically located, and he ordered it abandoned. The name was preserved by being transferred to Fort Floyd.

Under its new name, McKenzie's headquarters at the junction of the Yellowstone and Missouri was enlarged and improved until it became not only the best post on the entire Missouri but the strongest, most comfortable and most spacious. Only

Bent's Fort on the Arkansas might have been compared with it.

Fort Union was 240 feet in length and 220 feet in width, the shorter side facing the river. It was guarded by a palisade of square-hewn pickets, each a foot thick and twenty feet in height. Bastions rose at the southwest and the northeast corners. They were square, twenty-four feet in length on each side and thirty feet in height, built entirely of stone and surmounted with pyramidal roofs. Each bastion contained two levels, the lower pierced for cannon, the upper used for observation. The usual *banquette*, or raised way, ran completely around the inside of the palisade, except at the main gate, which was of double thickness and heavily secured by crossbeams.

McKenzie's private house stood on the opposite side of the open square from the entrance. It was a well-built structure, two stories in height, with glass windows, stone fireplaces and the rare convenience, an inside commode. The "modern" touch was greatly appreciated by such distinguished guests as the artist George Catlin, John James Audubon and Maximilian, Prince of Wied.

Barracks for employees ranged around the square, interspersed with storehouses, workshops, stables, a council room for Indians, and a cut stone magazine capable of holding 50,000 pounds of powder. A tall flagstand from which the Stars and Stripes flew each day rose in the center of the main court, and around it were the buffalo-hide tents of the half-breeds in the service of the company.

McKenzie was born of educated and distinguished parents at Rosshire, Inverness, Scotland, in 1801. He was a close relative of Alexander McKenzie, the intrepid explorer. As a youth he made a pleasure trip to Canada, and never returned home. After several years of service with two or three British fur houses, he went to work for the North West Company. When it was merged with the Hudson's Bay Company, he had little seniority, and lost his job. At the age of twenty-one he joined with Joseph Renville in forming the Columbia Fur Company, and he was its president when the amalgamation with Astor took place.

McKenzie affected a kind of military uniform, polished belt and holster, shiny metal buttons, silver and gold adornments, and at times he wore a hat over which flowed a plume. Only a select few were permitted to sit at his table, but he was lavishly hospitable to his invited guests. Delectables and fine wines were served . . . to the astonishment of those privileged to share his food. Servants maintained a vegetable garden, shepherded flocks of chickens, geese, ducks, and herded cattle, sheep and swine. To this sumptuous fare was added the wild game of the northern plains . . . venison, antelope, partridge, rabbit . . . all delightfully prepared by a talented French-Canadian chef.

When a canoe came downriver with news that a party of his hunters had been attacked by Blackfeet, and that their horses, furs and equipment had been lost, the men narrowly escaping death, McKenzie swore angrily:

"Damn the men! If the horses had been saved it would have been something!"

4

On a fall day in 1830, while McKenzie was brooding over his inability to establish trade with the Blackfeet, opportunity walked out of the wilderness. It came in the form of a wizened old mountain man in tattered buckskin that smelled of bear grease and the smoke of a thousand campfires.

Jacob Berger could scarcely remember how many years he had wandered in the northern mountains, or where he had been, but he knew the ranges that struck the sky, the country Going-to-the-Sun, and he spoke of rivers in which no American trapper had ever taken beaver, the Cut Bank, the Milk, the Marias, and they ran deep in the Blackfoot country.

He knew the British posts, he knew their strength and the number of furs they bought. But he knew the Indians better, because he had lived longer among them than he had among white men, and some of the chiefs were his friends. He had slept in their lodges, and he had ridden with them on long hunts and even on horse-stealing forays, and they thought of him as their brother. He spoke the Blackfoot tongue as well as they did . . . almost as well.

McKenzie was suspicious, and when he asked why Jacob Berger suddenly had arrived at Fort Union the reply he got was unsatisfactory. Berger merely had shrugged his bony shoulders . . . he had heard it was there, and he had just wanted to have a look at it.

McKenzie was inclined to dismiss Berger, but something, some strong impression which came to him without recourse to inference or reason, made him hesitate. He sat down with Berger before his fire. When they had finished their conversation, the Upper Missouri Outfit had been launched on its greatest adventure.

After hearing McKenzie's plan and thinking about it a bit, the men at Fort Union shook their heads. There was no hope of its succeeding. Only an army could enter the Blackfoot country and return alive. As for trading, it was useless to try.

But Berger was willing to try. He had no loyalty to the Hudson's Bay Company. Actually, he had no loyalty to the Americans either. He would go and attempt to open negotiations with the Blackfeet as an emissary of McKenzie simply because the mission attracted him. It would be an interesting assignment, and he had nothing better to do. Besides, the emoluments McKenzie offered would be most welcome. He needed a new gun and some tobacco.

Berger smiled when McKenzie was able to obtain only five volunteers to go with him, but once more he shrugged. They would be enough. He gazed toward the west. The Moon of the

Falling Leaves usually brought fine clear days. They had better go at once.

McKenzie watched the six men and their packhorses pass over a rise beyond the river and vanish under the immensity of the blue fall sky. Misgivings rose in him. If they did not come back . . . Now it was McKenzie who shrugged. He had many other things to think about, and one of them was a steamboat.

It was while he was in St. Louis the last time that McKenzie had brought up his scheme to take a steamboat up the river to Fort Union. Crooks and Chouteau had been unreceptive to the idea, labeling it impractical if not impossible. The expense involved would be great. No steamboat had succeeded in going farther than the mouth of the Kansas River, below which the Missouri in normal years carried sufficient water for such traffic. Above the Kansas, bars, snags, rocks and narrow channels made it a perilous and unpredictable gauntlet. Loss of a steamboat that was heavily loaded with furs or supplies might wipe out the profits of a season.

McKenzie insisted the feat could be accomplished. Just because it had not been done, there was no good reason for refusing to try. Admittedly it would be hazardous, but if it succeeded profits would be increased. Fewer men would be needed, thus the payroll would be decreased. A small powerful boat, one that was specially built for the attempt, would cost no more than a mere $7,000. It could leave St. Louis in April, after all ice was out, and be back with the catch of the previous winter and spring by the end of June.

This, McKenzie argued, would let him hold keelboats and barges up the river, and they could be sent down with furs late in the fall. They also would be available in case the steamboat met with an accident. As he saw the matter, the greatest problem would be a breakdown in the machinery far up the river, but that could be overcome by sending up spare parts. Blacksmith shops could be established at strategic points.

McKenzie had returned to Fort Union without convincing Crooks and Chouteau that the experiment was worth trying. He wrote letters reiterating his arguments, and warning that if the

American Fur Company did not carry out the scheme, someone else would beat them to it. He was unaware that Chouteau had undergone a change of mind, and had written to Astor advocating the plan and letting it be believed that he had been the first to think of it, although he did state that McKenzie was in accord.

Astor's approval came by return mail. A contract for the boat was given in October, 1830, to a Louisville firm. It was to be delivered at St. Louis on the following 1st of April, and its name was to be the *Yellowstone*.

Ignorant of all this, McKenzie brooded and watched the rim of the western plain for the appearance of a messenger bringing bad news of Berger. His thoughts also were occupied by the problem of a new threat which had arisen.

Some time before he had received a letter from Chouteau warning of impending trouble in the area of the Teton River. "It now remains for me to tell you," Chouteau had said, "of the new company which is lately formed here, consisting of eight partners, who are Messrs. Papin, Chenie *fils*, the two Cerres, Delaurier, Picotte, Denis Guion and Louis Bonfort, with an equipment of $16,000, of which each partner contributes an equal share.[2] These gentlemen have done, and are still doing, everything in their power to debauch all our clerks . . . You cannot but see how important it is for our future interests to make every effort this year to arrest this opposition from the start."

The American Fur Company's post, Fort Tecumseh, stood on the Missouri at the mouth of the Teton. In command was the capable and energetic William Laidlaw. McKenzie promptly placed the problem in his hands, accompanied by instructions to take whatever measures were necessary to stop the intruders. He had no doubt that it would be done. Most of the partners of the French Fur Company were known to him. They were competent traders, but they were subject to the weaknesses that marked all associations of the type, that is, they were equal partners, and without subordinating themselves to a leader who had absolute authority to make decisions they could not hope to succeed.

[2] It was called the French Fur Company.

The French Fur Company set up its headquarters across the river from Fort Tecumseh. This was bravado which both McKenzie and Laidlaw saw through. They had permitted the interlopers to acquire a sizable quantity of pelts, then, on McKenzie's orders, Laidlaw delivered an ultimatum: sell out or be driven out.

The bravado vanished. Laidlaw purchased the company's furs, and closed its posts. Papin, Picotte and one of the Cerres agreed to work for him. The other partners disappeared down the river, glad to escape with their lives.

The Moon of the Popping Trees brought deep snow and bitter cold to the valleys of the Yellowstone and the Missouri, and by his fire McKenzie thought often of Berger, wondering what fate he and his men had met. Had he been able to project his gaze beyond the western horizon into the emptiness of the country that swept in its winter whiteness against the peaks, he would have witnessed scenes that surpassd every good hope he had dared to harbor.

From Fort Union, Berger and his men had ridden steadily for four weeks up the Missouri without meeting an Indian. One of them at all times carried an unfurled flag so that any Blackfeet who saw them would know at a distance that they were white men.

Half a day's ride above the Marias, a large village was sighted some distance ahead. Berger had difficulty preventing his men from turning about and fleeing. He convinced them at last that flight would bring the Indians down on them, for they probably were already surrounded by warriors they could not see. Their best hope of surviving was to remain with him.

As he led his little group on, a number of mounted Indians rode out of the village toward them. Berger ordered his men to stand still, and taking the flag he advanced alone. This curious maneuver caused the Indians to stop. When Berger got close enough to them, he called out his name. With a yell of delight they descended on him, clapped him on the back and shook his hand. He and his astounded men were escorted into the village with shouts of joy, and welcomed into the lodge of the chief.

During the long winter and well into the spring the six men remained as guests in the village. Berger was held in high esteem, and headmen from other villages made cold journeys to smoke a pipe and converse with him. Their respect, however, did not reach such proportions that they were ready to accept his proposal that McKenzie be permitted to open a trade with them. The hatred and distrust of all Americans which they had harbored so many years could not be easily quelled. Yet, they were willing to discuss the matter. They did trust Berger, they admired his wisdom, and they did not propose to be discourteous by refusing to open their ears.

The councils were long, wearying and repetitive, but Berger never gave up, and when the Moon of the Grass Turning Red arrived, he was victorious. The Blackfeet agreed to send a delegation of forty warriors, including several headmen, to talk with the great McKenzie at Fort Union.

The Indians moved slowly, and there was more talking to be done about the council fires, and there was a need for dancing and a careful analysis of the route to be taken. Scouts had to be sent ahead to listen to the wind and the whisperings of the grass. Enemies could be waiting.

The Moon When the Ponies Shed passed, and the Moon of Making Fat had come before the band was well on the trail. More weeks slipped away, for the headmen chose to travel unhurriedly, always watching for unpropitious signs. The way was long, and some of the delegates began to complain. The Moon of Black Cherries came and they stopped, and some demanded that the mission be abandoned.

Berger knew where they were. Triumph was almost within his grasp. Not a little desperate, he made a forceful speech. If the headmen would go on one more day, the fort would be reached. If it was not reached in that time, he would give them his scalp and all his horses.

They went on. It was three o'clock on the afternoon of the next day when the flag of Fort Union came into their view.

McKenzie was overjoyed. He showered the delegates with expensive gifts. He set bottles of good wine before them. He swore eternal friendship, honest trade and generous prices for their furs.

Again the councils were long and exhausting. Often they were delayed for several days while the delegates recovered from their drunkenness. But at last marks, scratches and names were affixed to a document that opened the gates of the immense, rich Blackfoot country to the American Fur Company. Berger had accomplished a diplomatic feat that no American trapper thought possible.

McKenzie had sent no official word to St. Louis about Berger's journey, but now he wrote with immense satisfaction to Chouteau: "On my arrival at Fort Union last fall I fortunately found a Blackfoot interpreter, Berger, and by this means have been enabled to make those Indians acquainted with my views regarding them."

This selfish and unfair statement was typical of McKenzie. It was not his way to give praise to subordinates, and he saw to it that he, and he alone, got full credit for the successes of the Upper Missouri Outfit. But the story of Berger's incomparable accomplishment was carried to St. Louis by trappers and *voyageurs*, and it steadily became more vivid and astonishing with each telling. In the end Berger received the credit due him.

"I sent him with four or five men to their village," McKenzie told Chouteau, "where they were kindly received and well treated. On their return to the fort they were accompanied by some of the principal chiefs."

Nearly a year's perilous mission was summed up in that casual statement.

McKenzie had a little more to report. According to him, the Blackfeet "expressed great satisfaction and pleasure at having a post in their village, which I promised and assured them that they should have this fall; and in order to strengthen my promise I have sent a clerk, with four or five men, to trade what they may have. It is impossible to say what may be the result of this enterprise, but I am very sanguine in my expectations."

McKenzie also took the credit for preparing a treaty that

brought a temporary peace to the Blackfoot country, telling Chouteau with serene deceptiveness, "I have lately negotiated a treaty of peace between the Assiniboine and the Blackfoot Indians, which I expect will be ratified. Exchange of tobacco has been made and all requisite ceremonies observed. If firm and durable it will be of great importance to this district."

Men wise in the ways of Indians who read the treaty knew that only a man with an extraordinary knowledge of both Blackfoot and Assiniboine customs and a penetrating understanding of their minds could have written it. That man was Jacob Berger.

"We send greeting to all mankind!" proclaimed the treaty. "Be it known unto all nations that the most ancient, most illustrious, and most numerous tribes of the redskins, lords of the soil from the banks of the great waters unto the tops of the mountains, upon which the heavens rest, have entered into a solemn league and covenant to make, preserve and cherish a firm and lasting peace, that so long as the water runs, or the grass grows, they may hail each other as brethren, and smoke the calumet in friendship and security.

"On the vigil of St. Andrew in the year 1831, the powerful and distinguished nation of the Blackfeet, Piegan, and Blood Indians by their ambassadors appeared at Fort Union near the spot where the Yellowstone River unites its current with the Missouri, and in the council chamber of the Governor, Kenneth McKenzie, and the principal chief of the Assiniboine nation, the Man-that-Holds-the-Knife, attended by his chiefs of council, *le Bechu, le Borgne,* the Sparrow, the Bear's Arm, *La Terre qui Tremble,* and *l'Enfant de Medecin,* when, conforming to all ancient customs and ceremonies, and observing the due mystical signs enjoined by the great medicine lodges, a treaty of peace and friendship was entered into by the said high contracting parties, and is testified by their hands and seals hereunto annexed, hereafter and forever to live as brethren of one large, united, and happy family; and may the Great Spirit who watcheth over us all approve our conduct and teach us to love one another."

5

The expedition McKenzie dispatched up the river to carry out the provisions of Berger's agreement with the Blackfeet consisted of twenty-five men under the command of James Kipp. They left Fort Union late in August in several cargo canoes. Low water made progress extremely difficult, and the mouth of the Musselshell was not passed until mid-September. In one period of eleven days they were able to advance only eight miles. About the middle of October they reached the Marias and commenced the construction of a post.

To their surprise, word of the signing of the pact already had reached the British, and a trader of the Hudson's Bay Company, known only as Fisher, had sent a message to the Piegan Nation in the hope of halting the trade with the Americans before it got started. Fisher promised that if the Piegans would bring their furs to him they would receive high prices for them, the chiefs would be well dressed at no expense to themselves, and the needs of all would be supplied. The Hudson's Bay Company, declared Fisher, was rich but the Americans were poor and often could not afford to pay their debts.

McKenzie's astuteness here was well demonstrated. Anticipating some such move on the part of the British, he had sent emissaries to the various nations, and they proved to be quite as influential as "the smooth-tongued Englishman." In approaching the Piegans, Fisher had made a mistake, and his plea was wasted. They fully intended to abide by the treaty. Moreover, they had decided that neither Englishmen nor Americans would be permitted to enter their country. This was an advantage for the Upper Missouri Outfit for it was spared the expense of sending traders there.

Kipp selected a site for his post in the angle between the Marias and the Missouri. Indians came in throngs to watch the work of construction. Without protection, Kipp and his men were extremely uneasy. At last Kipp was able to prevail on the Indians to leave by counting off seventy-five days on his fingers, and promising that if they would return at the end of that period the post would be ready to receive them.

Exactly at the end of seventy-five days a horde of Blackfeet appeared. Kipp had kept his promise. The post, named Fort Piegan, was completed and open for business.

Business was good. In the first two weeks, 2,400 beaver skins passed over the trading counter, and before the winter ended 4,000 more had been brought in. These were prime furs from the rivers flowing out of the northern Rocky Mountains, and their value in St. Louis would be in excess of $50,000.

The enormous success had not been accomplished without serious difficulties, however, and had it not been for Kipp's courage, as well as his thorough knowledge of the fur trade, the result might have been quite different.

The British, greatly angered by the invasion of the Americans in territory they considered theirs by right of being first on the ground, set out to make trouble. They managed, by the use of lavish gifts, to induce a tribe of Bloods to attack Fort Piegan. Advised of the impending assault, Kipp laid in a supply of ice for water, and closed the gate. For some days the Bloods maintained a seige, but did not launch a major attack. Kipp, deducing that their hearts were not in the fight, invited the headmen to a council. Those who came were sent back reeling drunk on good whisky and heavily loaded with gifts. In a short time all the attackers were at the gate, suing for peace and clamoring for similar treatment. They got it. At the end of a wild orgy that continued for several days, the Bloods staggered toward their homeland, vowing eternal friendship to the Americans. Never had men they intended to kill treated them so well. When it came to dispensing gifts and alcohol, the British were amateurs.

Early in the spring of 1832, Kipp decided to take the fortune in furs down to Fort Union. The Indians had requested that

Fort Piegan be kept open during the summer months, but Kipp's men refused to stay without him. The post was closed, and the company set off down the river. They had no more than got out of sight before it was burned to the ground by Blackfeet who were angered because their request that it remain in operation had not been met.

Kipp and his company arrived at Fort Union to find the place in a state of great excitement. The steamboat *Yellowstone* was expected any day.

In the previous year, the *Yellowstone*, having been delivered on schedule, had started north from St. Louis on the 16th of April. This was the first attempt ever made to transport a fur-trade cargo by steamboat to the upper river. On board, sharing the quarter-deck with Capt. B. Young, was a proud Pierre Chouteau.

For six weeks in that spring of 1831, the sturdy little side-wheeler had battled the raging muddy current, and on May 31, passed the mouth of the Niobrara. History already had been made, for no steamboat had ever gone that far, but it had fought on, feeling its way between the shoals and bars, narrowly escaping disaster on numerous occasions. Then suddenly the river, in keeping with its capriciousness, fell. The *Yellowstone* could not go on.

Days passed. Each morning Pierre Chouteau, impatient and fearing the great experiment was to fail, went ashore and paced back and forth on some high ground, watching the brassy sky for signs of rain, praying for more water. The place was christened Chouteau's Bluffs.

At last he sent an express upriver to Fort Tecumseh with orders to bring barges down to the stranded boat. A large part of the heavy cargo was placed in them, and this lightened the *Yellowstone* enough to let it proceed. Fort Tecumseh was reached on the 19th of June.

"*Ce ne fut donc qu'à la faveur de trois berges,*" Chouteau wrote Astor, "*que j'envoyai chercher au Petit Missouri, et qui recurent une grande partie de la charge, qu'il m'a été possible de me rendre avec le bateau le 19 Juin au Fort Tecumseh."*

It was too late to go farther, but this disappointment was offset by the knowledge that steamboat traffic on the upper river was practicable. Experience was required, but Chouteau had no reason to believe that the *Yellowstone* could not reach the far-off stream after which it was named. The spring of 1832 would bring the great test.

At Fort Tecumseh the boat was turned around and sent back down the Missouri. It traveled fast and came into the wharf at St. Louis, to the accompaniment of gunfire and whistle blowing, on the 15th of July, carrying "a full cargo of buffalo robes, furs, besides ten thousand pounds of buffalo tongues."

Word of the great feat of the *Yellowstone* was sent by express up the river to McKenzie. Little wonder that when Kipp and his men came down the Missouri in the spring of 1832, with their great haul of beaver, they found excitement reigning at Fort Union.

The *Yellowstone* was on the way. Any day it might come into sight. Any day its whistle might shatter the silence with a noise signaling the beginning of a new era in the western wilderness.

6

Astor had not been abroad since 1826. He had remained in New York, except for an occasional trip to Washington, directing the western expansion of the American Fur Company, and keeping abreast of the affairs of his immense real estate empire.

Cholera in Europe had prevented him from crossing in 1831.

The epidemic had been world-wide, and it was expected to strike New York in the summer of 1832. Once more he made plans, this time for an extensive trip, but his reason for going was not only to avoid the dread disease.

He was sick. For several months he had suffered from a dull pain which at times spread over most of his heavy body. Although he said little about it to Sarah, he knew that something was seriously wrong with him, some internal organ was failing him. His New York physicians had been unable to diagnose the trouble, and he was anxious to consult French specialists.

The depression caused by the state of his health was suddenly increased by the death of his daughter Magdalen. He took her twelve-year-old son, Charles, into his home, and his affection for the boy was boundless. He immediately established a fund that would make Charles wealthy for life, and he bestowed on him the utmost loving care and kindness, although he often found it necessary to reprove him for taking too much butter and leaving it on his plate.

Astor was cheered by the successes of the Western Department under Crooks and Chouteau, and he was especially appreciative of the work of McKenzie, whom he warmly congratulated for the good management of the Upper Missouri Outfit and for advocating the use of a steamboat on the river. Things were going so well in the West that he felt no hesitancy in leaving. William was fully capable of managing affairs in New York. Yet he knew a profound concern as a result of the apparent growing power of persons in Washington who wanted to halt the use of liquor by Americans in the fur trade.

Astor made a trip to the capital to confer with his friends and representatives about the question. He found strong agitation for passage of a law forbidding the use of alcohol in any form, or for any reason, in dealings with Indians.

Ever since his drive into the Old Northwest Astor himself had been opposed to the use of liquor in the fur trade. He had never believed it to be a necessary adjunct of success, and he always had been confident that he could overcome his competitors without it. But that could not be done as long as they were free to use whisky in opposing him.

When it had first appeared to him that Congress might make moves which would place unfair restrictions on him, he had made some attempts to solve the problem. Nothing could be done, of course, to halt the destructive traffic unless the Hudson's Bay Company also agreed to forbid its traders to dispense liquor. In the hope of achieving such an agreement, Astor had ordered William to make an effort to open negotiations with the British monopoly.

William wrote to James Keith, a chief factor of the Hudson's Bay Company, stating that the American Fur Company would "not in the future, either directly or indirectly, carry in, or in any way give ardent spirits to the Indians . . . provided the Honorable The Hudson Bay Co., pledge themselves to the same effect."

The letter was sent to the Hudson's Bay Company governor in London, and shortly William received a rather cold reply which said: "The Governor and the Committee have this season confirmed and repeated the orders given last year by Governor Simpson, that in the event of the American Traders discontinuing the practice, those in the Service of the Company should do the same; But the Governor and Committee do not feel justified in leaving their trading Posts on the Frontier totally deprived of Spirits, at the same time I am directed to assure you, that the Governor and Committee have the means of strictly enforcing the instructions given to their Traders; the discontinuance of the Practice will therefore entirely depend on the conduct of the American traders, to which I am to call your attention."

Astor felt that placing the responsibility for stopping the liquor traffic entirely on Americans . . . actually in this case largely on his own shoulders . . . was unfair, and the uncertainty of the reply was too great to risk an attempt to carry out such a program. This was not a justified attitude. The British well understood both the strength of Astor and the weakness of the American Government in the Indian Country. The Hudson's Bay Company could obtain obedience from its traders, the American Government could not. There was no reason why the British should believe that either Astor or Washington would keep a promise when it came to the fur trade.

In Washington, Astor gave orders to oppose any restrictive bill with all possible force. He told Representative Ashley, the noted former fur trader, that if the "Hudson's Bay Company did not employ ardent spirits against us, we would not ask for a single drop. But without it competition is hopeless."

Astor summoned Crooks to a conference. The essence of the instructions he gave him was that if a stringent new liquor law was passed by Congress, it was to be ignored. Until the Hudson's Bay Company had stopped its traders from selling and giving liquor to the Indians, the American Fur Company would continue to use it.

Astor went back to New York. He sailed for Europe on June 20, arriving at Le Havre "after a short passage of 19 days." At once he consulted physicians in Paris, planning to go on to Genthod, his villa on Lake Geneva, later in the summer. This plan was disrupted by a severe fall which confined him to his room.

The summer waned, and he remained in Paris, a sick and depressed man.

7

The fight to stop passage of a new prohibition law was vigorously waged by Astor lieutenants.

Agitation for enactment of a drastic new statute, however, was carried on not only by "drys" but by politicians in high office. Congress was flooded with reports of tragic conditions on the frontier. The administration took cognizance of the growing public resentment of them.

Driving the Astor lobby from Capitol Hill, Congress passed the most stringent prohibition law written up to that time. It provided that "no ardent spirits shall be hereafter introduced, under any pretense, into the Indian country."

It placed on the American Fur Company greater hardships than it did on other organizations. The Western Department shipped its merchandise in immense cargoes up the Missouri, and avoiding inspection by the authorities was virtually impossible. The small trader, who went overland with a few packhorses or made his way stealthily up the river in a small craft, could easily escape detection.

Astor made it plain that he had no alternative, if he wanted to stay in business, but to violate the law. His traders would be confronted in the Indian country by competitors, both British and American, well supplied with liquor. In self-defense he would be forced to become a smuggler, placing himself on the same level with "lawless adventurers who had little investment to lose in the event of arrest."

As long as he was obliged to become a violator, he told Crooks, he would not hesitate to become the largest of all. Nothing could be accomplished by half-measures.

Astor was especially disappointed by the stand of his old friend and recipient of his favors, Secretary of War Lewis Cass. Cass, of course, had played politics to his own advantage. He had announced his great interest in the welfare of the Indians, a role he had studiously avoided as Governor of Michigan. He had deserted Astor and had urged passage of the new law.

Immediately after the law's enactment, Crooks made strenuous efforts to secure exceptions to it along the Canadian border, pointing out that the posts of the Western Department were obliged to compete with British traders who carried liquor to the northern tribes. "I explained fully to Governor Cass that our sole and only wish for a partial supply was to enable us to cope

with our Hudson Bay opponents at our new posts above the
Mandans, relinquishing it voluntarily everywhere else as advantageous both to the natives and to ourselves . . . I pointed out
the pernicious tendency of its exclusion on our side, while they
enjoyed the privilege to an unlimited extent; and the absolute
certainty of the country being deluged by a larger supply than
usual, purposely to show their superiority over us, degrading us,
and with us the government, in the eyes of the Indians, by our
withholding from them a gratification which was abundantly
and cheerfully furnished by the British . . . I presumed upon
his [Cass's] attention the efforts we had made at the risk of the
lives of our people, and much pecuniary cost, to open an intercourse with our mortal enemies, the Blackfeet, who had on every
occasion waged an exterminating war upon our citizens for upwards of twenty years . . . the great value of the trade we had
already gained, and the prospect of a large increase we might
calculate upon, when, by our peaceful relations with the savages
of the Falls of the Missouri and Maria's River, we could extend
our intercourse to the Flatheads, and other tribes—and lastly,
the loss of influence which the government must sustain in the
belief that they would entertain its poverty, when contrasted
with the affluence and liberality of the British, who supplied
every want, while we denied them the greatest of all gratifi-
cations . . .

"To all this the secretary replied, that the law was imperative,
and the executive had no discretion but to see it executed to the
letter."

Although he refused to grant the American Fur Company any
special privileges, Secretary Cass did agree to ask the President
and the Secretary of State to open negotiations with the British
for the purpose of having similar regulations enforced north of
the border. Having lost faith in Cass, however, William Astor
began his own campaign to cut off the flow of British liquor into
the United States, writing to both the White House and the
Department of State. There were no immediate results.

A major loophole in the new law was soon found. It was the

provision which permitted traders to carry a certain amount of liquor with them into the Indian Country "for their boatmen." Congress had no desire to deny a white boatman, who might have a vote, a relaxing drink at the end of a hard day.

Stuart was quick to take advantage of the opening. In the year after passage of the law the Astor post at Mackinaw alone received more than 5,500 gallons of whisky, "for its *voyageurs* and *engagés*." Diluted in the customary manner, it made no less than 20,000 gallons for use in the Indian trade. The boatmen got precious little of it.

Chouteau wrote Astor that the law "will do us incalculable injury at all posts above the mouth of the Yellowstone," but gave Astor assurances that this would not be permitted without every effort being made to prevent it.

Chouteau was as good as his promise. He wrote McKenzie, ". . . it is permitted to take one gill per day for each boatman during the period of their absence—that is, for twelve months. It is on this ground that I have obtained permission to take an amount corresponding to fifty men . . . I took the names of those . . ." recently sent to you ". . . without knowing whether you will keep them or send them back. That makes no difference, however, for I explained the matter to General Clark."

In this single instance, Chouteau submitted a list of twenty-three men who had already been sent up the river to work for McKenzie. By using their names he was able to add more than 300 gallons of whisky to a cargo destined for river posts.

At the same time, Sublette was preparing to send a supply train to the mountains. He was given permission to take 450 gallons of liquor "for the special use of his boatmen." Sublette's outfit was going overland to Pierre's Hole. It had no use for either boats or boatmen, and there were none with it.

On a business trip to the East, Crooks wrote bitterly to Chouteau, "I truly regret the blindness of the government in refusing liquor for the trade of the country in the vicinity of the Hudson's Bay posts, because the prohibition will not prevent the Indians from getting it from our rivals, to our most serious injury. It might have been possible last winter at Washington to accomplish some modification had we been there together. I have, however, some very strong doubts on the subject, because Gov. Cass is a temperance society man in every sense of the word, and it was with his full consent and approbation that the law . . . was passed . . . the chairman of the Indian committees were made as fully acquainted with the subject in all its hearings as if I had detailed all the facts to them in person. Had [Congressman] Ashley opposed the bill, his presumed knowledge of the Indian trade would probably have been more than a match for the influence of the Secretary of War. But it was got up as one of the *government* measures of the session, and your representative [Ashley] as a good Jackson man, gave it his unqualified support, and secured its passage."

Posing as a temperance society supporter was, indeed, a new role for Cass, but following Administration orders was not. Neither he nor Ashley honestly favored the bill. They had merely supported an Administration measure. But Crooks seemed to view this as a traitorous act. His attitude was all the more strange in view of the fact that Ashley had no love for the American Fur Company. Ashley's good friends, to whom he had sold out, were Astor competitors.

Despite widespread usage of the "boatman" loophole and smuggling, shipments of liquor up the river by the Western Department were curtailed. Indian Bureau authorities, although handicapped by insufficient manpower, strenuously attempted to inspect all cargoes, and their efforts had an effect. This was soon made apparent by appeals from upriver for more liquor. In one instance, Honoré Picotte, the Western Department's manager at Fort Pierre, wrote desperately that invading competitors ". . . have the advantage and that is liquor. We know of a certainty that they have five barrels of alcohol at Cedar Island, seventeen at Fort Morrison . . . and three at Fort Clark. Mr. Laidlaw writes me that he has no doubt they will open their liquor as soon as the trade commences, and he says he has not wherewith to oppose them in that article . . . With their liquor on one side and the Hudson Bay Company's on the other we are sure to lose the trade of that part next season."

Other traders, declared Picotte, had "twelve kegs *en cache* at the head of the Cheyenne which they will trade in the spring if they are not closely watched, and every day some one comes up from the St. Peter's River [in Minnesota] with that article . . .

"Under these circumstances you see plainly that we must lose the Blackfeet and Assiniboine trade next year *unless we have liquor.* I therefore request you to use all your influence to send us some of that article next year, say four or five hundred gallons in canteens, kegs, even in bottles, if no other way . . . At all events *we must have it."*

The American Fur Company had never been in the habit of leaving its traders in any way at the mercy of rivals, and Picotte's case was to be no exception. Chouteau got the "article" out of St. Louis and on the way up the river, writing Picotte: "The quantity of A— sent is somewhat short of what you asked for, but we think it sufficient. In regard to this article it has been highly necessary that every possible care be taken, both to prevent its abuse and to lessen the quantity distributed. Information respecting this matter has already reached the Department of the Attorney General, and if our Mr. Sanford [an Astor lobbyist] had not been at Washington this winter most opportunely, we should unquestionably have been prevented from sending any at all this season."

The Western Department, and especially the Upper Missouri Outfit, were to receive assistance in fighting British competitors, not from a windfall of liquor or successful smuggling, but from an unexpected source . . . the little sidewheeler *Yellowstone.*

8

Far out in the mountains, Vanderburgh and Drips were pursuing courses that were not a credit to either their ingenuity or their ability as traders. They had decided that the best way to find the good trapping grounds was to spy on Fitzpatrick, Bridger, Sublette and their associates.

Early in 1832, Fitzpatrick and the other partners set out from the Powder River, on which they had spent the winter. Their trail lay by way of the Snake, through the valley of the John Day, and over a high range to the Bear River. There, to their disgust, they were met by Vanderburgh and Drips. They decided to strike off at once in another direction. Unfortunately Sublette was badly wounded in a fight with an Indian, and had to be left behind. Joseph Meek remained to care for him.

The others left and soon believed they had eluded the American Fur Company men. The rendezvous had been set for the year at Pierre's Hole, and arriving there after a successful spring hunt, they once more found Vanderburgh and Drips waiting for them.

William L. Sublette had agreed to bring out the year's supplies from St. Louis and take the winter and spring catches back with him. It was essential that the convoy arrive before Vanderburgh and Drips could enter into trade with Indians who would attend the rendezvous. In order to urge Sublette to travel fast, Fitzpatrick set out to meet him.

Fitzpatrick found Sublette at the Platte River, 400 miles from Pierre's Hole. Traveling with Sublette was a party of eighteen inexperienced New Englanders, led by Nathaniel J. Wyeth, who were en route to trap in the Oregon country. The train was further enlarged by a party of men working for the small firm of Gant & Blackwell. They had met with little success during the

winter, and Fitzpatrick engaged them to work for him. The
united groups pushed on with all possible speed toward Pierre's
Hole. When the Sweetwater was reached, Fitzpatrick went ahead
alone to apprise his waiting partners that the goods were approaching. It was an extremely reckless thing to do.

Fitzpatrick made good progress until he reached Green River.
There he fell into a running fight with some Blackfeet. He escaped by hiding for three days. Believing he was safe at the end
of that time, he started on, only to meet the same Indians again.
His horse was shot and his equipment was lost. Once more he
saved himself by crawling among some rocks. After lying in
concealment for several days, he emerged and started on foot for
the rendezvous. When he arrived at Pierre's Hole his feet were
bloody masses of torn flesh, and he was so emaciated that he was
scarcely recognizable. The supply train had arrived safely nearly
a fortnight before. Milton Sublette also had appeared, having
recovered from his wounds.

Vanderburgh and Drips had found themselves at a decided
disadvantage. They had expected that Fontenelle would come in
with a pack train of trade goods, but he had failed to arrive, and
his whereabouts were unknown.[3] Their own supplies were soon
exhausted, and they were obliged to stand idly by while their
competitors enjoyed a brisk and profitable trade.

Pierre's Hole was a valley of rare beauty. On the east was the
great range of the Tetons. Across the floor of the Hole, which
was for the most part level, ran several streams, marked in their
courses by shimmering green cottonwood groves. The rendezvous
was held in the upper part of the valley, about twelve miles from
Teton Pass. There in early July were camped more than a hundred lodges of Indians who had brought furs to trade, the ninety
men under Vanderburgh and Drips, the Rocky Mountain Fur
Company's hundred men, the contingents of Wyeth and Gant
and Blackwell, and several score free trappers.

About the 17th of July, the rendezvous began to break up.

---

[3] Fontenelle had set out from Fort Union with the goods, but at the time of the
rendezvous was still far away in the Big Horn Valley.

Milton Sublette and his men started for the main Snake, and
Wyeth elected to travel with him. They camped the first night
only eight miles from Pierre's Hole. As they were starting out
the next morning, they saw two large parties of Blackfeet, containing 150 warriors, approaching. A rider at the head of one
party carried a British flag. Sublette immediately dispatched two
men for assistance, and began to retreat toward Pierre's Hole.
He did not know then that a vicious battle already was raging
there.

Another large band of Blackfeet had arrived in the valley with
full intentions of attacking, but finding the force of white men
there larger than they had thought it would be, had made signs
of peace and sent a chief forward under a white flag.

There were at the rendezvous two men who possessed an uncontrollable hatred for the Blackfeet. One was Antoine Godin,
a trapper whose father had been murdered by them. The other
was a Flathead chief whose nation had suffered terribly from
Blackfeet raids. It was these two men who advanced to meet the
Indian bearing the flag of truce.

In accordance with an agreement they had quickly made between them, the Flathead shot the Blackfoot chief dead as Godin
pretended to grasp his hand in friendship. Godin seized the
Blackfoot's scarlet robe, and both he and the Flathead ran back
to safety.

"Joab with a vengeance!" cried the shocked New Englander,
Wyeth. "Art thou in health, my brother?"

The battle of Pierre's Hole began. The Blackfeet entrenched
themselves in some willows. Throughout the day the fighting
continued, but some time during the night the Blackfeet stole
away, leaving nine dead. Seventeen others were reported to have
died of wounds. Five white men had been killed, and six were
badly wounded, among them William L. Sublette. Seven of the
Indians who had fought with the whites lay dead on the field,
and six were wounded.

Fitzpatrick, Bridger and their partners, feeling there were
enough furs in the Rocky Mountains to satisfy both themselves

and the American Fur Company, sought to establish peace by offering to divide certain areas with Vanderburgh, Drips and Fontenelle. The offer was rejected. Fitzpatrick and Bridger thereupon hatched a scheme to lead their antagonists into the Blackfoot country and lose them. They slipped away, but not without leaving spoor.

Vanderburgh and Drips did not pick up the trail at once. Somewhat desperate for supplies, they set out to find the tardy Fontenelle. Early in August they came upon him on Green River, gave him the furs they had collected, took on fresh goods and then set out in pursuit of Fitzpatrick. Fontenelle turned about and started back to Fort Union.

Foolishly Vanderburgh and Drips rode on as Fitzpatrick and Bridger hoped they would do . . . into the Blackfoot country. Reaching the Jefferson, they turned downstream, leaving part of their equipment in a cache so that they might travel faster. At the end of another ten days, they found Fitzpatrick and Bridger busy trapping on the headwaters of the Missouri.

On September 17, Fitzpatrick and Bridger started down the Jefferson. Vanderburgh let Drips pursue them while he took his company to the Madison to take advantage of the good trapping there.

Drips soon realized that he was being decoyed out of the good trapping country, and he turned back up the Jefferson. The wily Fitzpatrick and Bridger vanished toward the valley of the Gallatin. A few days later, crossing over into the Madison valley, they were disgusted to run into Vanderburgh.

Once more Fitzpatrick and Bridger started up the Madison, but Vanderburgh surprised them by remaining where he was. His men were taking many beaver, and he let Fitzpatrick and Bridger go on. They had led him to good trapping grounds, and he would take all he could in the area before setting out again in pursuit. He was unaware that Fitzpatrick and Bridger had picked up Indian sign, and were moving in a manner to assure their own security.

It was October 12, when Vanderburgh started up the Madison.

Two days later they were on Alder Creek. They did not know
that they were treading on millions of dollars worth of gold . . .
the world-famed placer mine that was to be known as Alder
Gulch. They continued on to the Stinking Water River, a tributary of the Jefferson to which Lewis and Clark had given the
name Philanthropy. There they too came upon Indian sign. Vanderburgh and six men left the main group to reconnoiter. After
traveling some six miles they were suddenly attacked by a hundred Blackfeet.

Vanderburgh and a *voyageur*, Alexis Pillon, were slain. The
other five, all wounded, fled and managed to get back to the
company.

A swift retreat was started. Near the Beaver Head, a famous
landmark on the Jefferson, they fortunately fell in with a large
band of Flathead and Pend d'Oreille Indians. A strong party
was sent to bury the two men. Pillon's body was found untouched, but because Vanderburgh was known as a chief the
Blackfeet had stripped his corpse of all flesh, thrown it into the
river, and left his bones on the bank.

The men resumed their retreat and found Drips at Horse
Prairie, where the equipment had been cached, late in October.
A few days later the united parties started for the Snake River
to establish winter quarters.

9

While the ill-fated mountain expeditions of the Western Department were being led through the wilderness to death and
disaster by the cleverer men of the Rocky Mountain Fur Com-

pany, an event of great importance had taken place on the Missouri River at Fort Union.

The *Yellowstone* had left St. Louis on March 26, 1832. The celebrated artist Catlin was a passenger, as was Pierre Chouteau. To both of these men . . . but not for the same reasons . . . the heavily loaded, crowded little craft was a beautiful sight as she fought the muddy flood of the great river. Her lofty twin chimneys poured out clouds of wood smoke, signals that Indians could not read but which brought closer their manifest destiny. The blasts from her whistle sent wild game fleeing in terror across the prairies. Sparks from the funnels were carried by the wind to start the grass burning, and she left a trail of churned water and fire to mark her historic journey.

For nearly eight weeks she toiled before she stopped to rest. It was May 31 when she reached Fort Tecumseh. Six days were given over to making repairs and cleaning the machinery. A new fort was being built there, and during the respite in the journey ceremonies were held and it was christened Fort Pierre.

Leaving Fort Pierre on June 5, the *Yellowstone* advanced upon waters through which a steamboat had never passed. In the amazingly short time of twelve days it came into sight of Fort Union.

The most modern mode of water travel on earth had reached the heart of the West. In a few weeks the keelboat had become obsolete. The Missouri had been conquered by steam. Never again would men break their bodies toiling against the river. Furs would come down to St. Louis in a matter of days.

It was Astor's money that had made the great feat possible, but it was to Kenneth McKenzie, who had always believed the trip possible and had first advocated the attempt, and to Pierre Chouteau, who had carried out the plan, that the credit belonged.

Chouteau received it, but McKenzie was officially ignored.

From New York Crooks wrote Chouteau: "I congratulate you most cordially on your perseverance and ultimate success in reaching the Yellowstone by steam, and the future historian of the Missouri will preserve for you the honorable and enviable distinction of having accomplished an object of immense importance, by exhibiting the practicability of conquering the obstructions of the Missouri considered till almost the present day insurmountable to steamboats even among those best acquainted with their capabilities. You have brought the Falls of the Missouri as near, comparatively, as was the River Platte in my younger days."

From Bellevue, France, Astor wrote Chouteau: "Your voyage in the *Yellowstone* attracted much attention in Europe, and has been noted in all the papers here."

Kenneth McKenzie, the general on the front line, was no more interested in receiving personal congratulations, however, than he was in the effect which the arrival of the *Yellowstone* would have on the wild people who inhabited the immense empire over which he ruled. No amount of adulation from Chouteau or even Astor could have gratified him more than what he saw taking place before him.

Indians, many of whom had never appeared before at a white man's fort, traveled hundreds of miles to stare at the monster who walked on the water. To them, and to all the others, it was more than an astonishing product of the Great White Father's magic. It was a supernatural phenomenon beyond all possible understanding. It struck terror in the hearts of the great warriors, and it sent them, and all their women and children, as it had the animals, running in panic.

Long before the outside world realized the full meaning of the *Yellowstone*'s journey, McKenzie read the signs prognosticating the change that was to come to the savage, boundless territory over which ranged the Blackfeet, the Gros Ventres, the Bloods, the Piegans, the Crows. He read the signs in their faces, in their eyes, in their hushed words and their gestures.

That day the *Yellowstone* had created a respect for the Upper Missouri Outfit, and for him, the king of the river, that could never have been won in a hundred years of giving presents and smoking pipes about council fires.

The *Missouri Republican* was to reflect McKenzie's understanding in a brief editorial about the voyage, saying inadequately,

"Many of the Indians who had been in the habit of trading with the Hudson Bay Company, declared that the company could not longer compete with the Americans, and concluded thereafter to bring all their skins to the latter; and said that the British might turn out their dogs and burn their sledges, as they would no longer be useful while the *Fire Boat* walked on the waters."

Wasting no time, McKenzie sent David D. Mitchell to take charge of the post Kipp had abandoned at the mouth of the Marias, and a company led by Samuel Tulloch was dispatched to build a new post at the confluence of the Yellowstone and the Big Horn, in the heart of the Crow country.

Mitchell found Fort Piegan burned to the ground. He went on six miles up the Marias to what he considered a better site, and began to construct a new post while several hundred Indians watched. On several occasions braves, driven by inherent savagery, were on the verge of attacking Mitchell and his men to rob them, but were restrained. The stockade was erected first, and the men withdrew within it and closed the gate. Most of the Indians wandered away. The post was named Fort McKenzie.

About the same time Tulloch and his men completed a post on the Big Horn, christening it Fort Cass, in honor of the Secretary of War and former Governor of Michigan who had been such an Astor stalwart.[4] Now McKenzie had three strategically located permanent bases. In less than five years he had won for Astor almost complete domination of the upper river trade, and, even more important, he had won footholds in both the Blackfoot and Crow countries from which he could not be driven.

As sovereign of an empire larger than Western Europe, McKenzie felt that he should have the privilege of bestowing distinctive honors and gifts . . . not merely commonplace presents such as tobacco and a bottle of rotgut rum . . . upon loyal and deserving Indians. His gratification, as well as his egotism, was immensely stimulated by the knowledge that his position in the royal lineage was considered by his subjects to be second only to

---

[4] They didn't know how Cass had deserted Astor in the fight over the prohibition law, or they might have selected a different name.

John Jacob Astor . . . third, of course, if one included the President of the United States. On the practical side of the matter was his thorough knowledge of the Indian's nature, and he understood that nothing was more appreciated than a showy, glistening piece of metal, unusual in design and not easily obtainable.

Out of these considerations evolved the decision that medals were the answer, burnished, large, official-looking medals that would ring impressively when dropped on a rock, and of a kind that one might expect to see adorning the chest of an admiral, general or ambassador.

He prepared a design, but he did not go so far as to ask that President Andrew Jackson permit his likeness to appear on it. He did, however, pause to consider the probable results of such an achievement. A chief would have given a dozen of his best horses for an imitation gold medal bearing the head of the Great White Father. McKenzie also found it pleasant to envision his own handsome profile on the face of such a valuable adornment, but he quickly realized the futility of such a proposal. Astor would have to do. Yet, he did not intend to neglect completely his own kingdom.

Astor, beaked nose, tight mouth, and numerous chins, would occupy the face, encircled by the words: "President of the American Fur Company." On the back would be two sets of crossed tomahawks and peace pipes, between them clasped hands and the message: "Peace and Friendship." At the top would be "FORT UNION." At the bottom: "U. M. O."

Striking and distributing medals to Indians happened to be a legal prerogative of the Federal Government, but neither law, tradition nor custom had ever caused McKenzie to hesitate in formulating and carrying forward a scheme he thought might improve his own position and increase trade. He got off an urgent letter to Western Department headquarters, sending along his suggestions and sketches.

Chouteau, who had learned to his own benefit the value of McKenzie's schemes . . . the steamboat, for example . . . passed the idea along to New York, recommending that it be adopted as an aid to improving relations with the upper river tribes, especially at the company's post in the Blackfoot country. "It is at this establishment," Chouteau said, "that we shall have to combat the opposition of the English traders, who have a fort not far distant, and who, as is their custom, will undoubtedly do everything in their power to excite the Indians against us. This difficulty might nevertheless be somewhat diminished if the government could be persuaded to place at our disposal a few presents, which would be delivered to the Indians in the name of the President of the United States. The English government, if I am well informed, allows the Northwest Company an annual sum for this particular purpose.[5] A little indulgence of this nature on the part of the government will secure the confidence and friendship of these savages toward us."

The task of keeping abreast of the affairs of his immense territory was great, but McKenzie found the time to give new attention to his own personal appearance. In maintaining his authority and prestige, he had never neglected the matter of his dress. His uniform had done much to assist him in preserving the high levels of formality and dignity he deemed proper and necessary for a man of his high rank. But it had long been a familiar sight to traders, *voyageurs* and Indians, and he began to fear that it might no longer impress them to the extent that he desired.

In order to prevent this adverse circumstance from developing, he gave thought to devising improvements, or changes, that would without doubt impress upon his subordinates his exalted position in a manner they would not forget.

He designed for himself a glittering coat of chain mail. An accompanying thought was that such splendid and unusual raiment should be complemented with an equally extraordinary gun, and he drew specifications for a weapon that would not only fire six shots but would be decorated with silver platings and ornate engravings.

In view of McKenzie's great achievements, neither Chouteau,

---

[5] The name of the North West Company remained in common usage for some years among traders after its amalgamation with the Hudson's Bay Company.

Crooks nor Astor was willing to chance incurring his displeasure either by criticizing or objecting to his peculiarities. They only shook their heads in disbelief, and approved the requests.

Crooks handled the transactions himself while on one of his many trips to New York, and wrote Chouteau: "For Mr. Mc-Kenzie's *coat of mail* I have sent to England, for nothing of this sort could be found here. His *fusil à six coups* is ordered from Rochester; and the medals for his outfit are in the hands of the die-maker, who, I hope, will give us a good likeness *de notre estimable grand-papa* [Astor]. I wrote to Washington about them, and the War Office made no objections to our having these *ornaments* made. Remember they are *ornaments*, not medals!"

No one objected to McKenzie wearing a knight's coat-of-mail and carrying a fancy and expensive musket, but both the British and the American traders trying to survive under the pressure of the Upper Missouri Outfit looked with disfavor on the medals. Complaints soon came down the river that McKenzie was usurping the functions of the Government by informing the chiefs on whom he bestowed the "ornaments" that they had been sent by the Great White Father in *Washington*. (This was correct.) Indian Agents forwarded the complaints on to headquarters, and official cognizance was taken of them. The wisdom with which Crooks had handled the matter was demonstrated, and at the same time it was revealed that although he had opposed Astor in the fight over the prohibition law, Secretary Cass was still willing to be of some service to his old friend.

Chouteau straightened things out by saying bluntly in reply to an inquiry from Washington that "before the die for the Astor medals was struck the matter was submitted to Governor Cass . . . Secretary of War, who gave his consent to the measure, and a sample of the medals was deposited with the department, accompanied by letters of the President of the American Fur Company."

Strung on a buckskin thong, the likeness of John Jacob Astor was carried into battles along the bloody banks of the Big Horn, the Little Horn and Crazy Woman Creek, the glittering discs rivaling such prizes as scalps and medicine bonnets in value, and held in greater esteem than horses and captive squaws.

10

Hundreds of men, unlimited resources, quality merchandise, a steamboat and a coat of chain mail all brought advantages to the Upper Missouri Outfit and made it an impressive and formidable force that discouraged organized competition. But it did not intimidate all competitors. They continued to appear, and in 1832, the year of McKenzie's great triumphs, he was obliged to reckon with the strongest competition he had ever known. It seemed that some men simply could not be persuaded that the Kingdom of Astor could not be successfully invaded.

One of them was a former American Fur Company trader named Narcisse Leclerc. Two other disbelievers were William L. Sublette of Rocky Mountain fame, and Robert Campbell, who had been a member of Ashley's successful expeditions.

Leclerc had left the American Fur Company filled with bitterness and hatred, convinced he had been cheated out of compensation due him. In 1831 he organized an outfit, and set off up the Missouri from St. Louis to seek revenge for what he believed to be ill-treatment at the hands of Laidlaw and McKenzie. Chouteau quickly apprised them of Leclerc's intentions.

But Leclerc elected to trade that season on the lower river, and in November Laidlaw had written McKenzie from Fort Tecumseh: "I have heard nothing of Leclerc . . . and as the ice is now drifting a little, I am in hopes he will not get up this far. But even if he does, I am well prepared for him and shall have someone at his heels all the time. He told Papin that nothing would do him so much good as to go puffing a cigar alongside of you and put on a dignified look. I expect the gentlemen would take care not to get too close."

Leclerc was next heard of back in St. Louis. He had done well in the lower river trade, and in the spring of 1832 had set out once more with a larger outfit of goods. Orders went out that Leclerc was to be stopped from trading anywhere on the river. J. P. Cabanne, the company agent at Council Bluffs, was also instructed to intercept Leclerc and warn him that he would be inviting serious trouble if he attempted even to enter the domain of McKenzie.

The turn of events provided Cabanne with an opportunity to employ drastic measures. In July the new prohibition law was in effect. Chouteau was aware that Leclerc had a license from Gen. William Clark, the Superintendent of Indian Affairs at St. Louis, to take with him 250 gallons of alcohol up the river. He protested, but Clark refused to revoke Leclerc's license on the ground that it had been issued to him before the law had been signed.

The *Yellowstone* had just returned from its epic trip to Fort Union. Chouteau promptly reloaded it with cargo, among which were 1,400 gallons of liquor, and sent it back upstream to Council Bluffs. At Fort Leavenworth, Federal authorities boarded the boat and confiscated the entire shipment. Leclerc already had managed to slip by the fort and was well on his way to the upper river with his liquor.

When Leclerc hove into sight at Bellevue, it was found that three men who had deserted the company before the expiration of their contracts were working for him. Cabanne promptly clapped them in irons. By what authority Cabanne thought he could commit this act was not stated. However, Cabanne believed that he did have the right to make a "citizen's arrest" of a trader violating the new law forbidding the importation of spirits into the Indian country.

Minus the three deserters, Leclerc and his men pushed on. Cabanne dispatched a force under a trusted trader, Peter Sarpy, to get ahead of Leclerc and capture him and his entire outfit. Sarpy took with him a small cannon, which he mounted on a bluff above the river. When Leclerc came along, he ordered him to surrender or be blown out of the water.

Leclerc had no alternative but to capitulate. The liquor was confiscated and put in a storehouse in Bellevue. Cabanne offered to buy it, but Leclerc refused. He turned about and hastened back down the river to St. Louis, where he reported to General Clark that he had been robbed, brought suit against the American Fur Company and filed criminal charges against Cabanne.

Feeling was already intense against the American Fur Company for its high-handed and brutal methods against both Indians and competitors, and the Indian Service gave support to Leclerc's charges with sympathetic statements. When news of the affair reached Washington, an outcry was raised in various departments against Astor, and it was demanded that he be forced to mend his ways or be driven from the Indian trade.

Chouteau's contention that Cabanne's sole purpose in stopping Leclerc was to prevent a violation of a Federal statute was weakened by Cabanne's offer to buy Leclerc's liquor. The situation looked bad for both the company and its enterprising agent at Bellevue.

Counsel came to the St. Louis office from William Astor, who opined that, "If it were not for the unreasonable excitement that exists against our friend in Missouri [Cabanne], and which no doubt great pains will be taken to keep alive, I should not despair of Mr. Cabanne's escaping with light damages or perhaps acquital. The strong point of defence, in my opinion, should be that at the time Leclerc was stopped and brought back he was violating the law of the land excluding ardent spirits entirely from the Indian Country; that General Clark's permission was no protection after the act of July 9, 1832, was published, and with its provisions Mr. Leclerc was bound to be acquainted. You have, however, I dare say, the best advice your country affords, but it seems to me that in case of defeat I would appeal the case to the Supreme Court of the United States."

Chouteau, quite unfairly, turned on Cabanne for resorting to "such heroic measures." He and Crooks sought a compromise, and found Leclerc a reasonable man. They gave him a check for $9,000, and the suits were withdrawn. Then they fired Cabanne, and Joshua Pilcher was sent to replace him.

Counteracting the new firm of Sublette & Campbell was not as easily or as cheaply accomplished. As soon as McKenzie got wind that it was being organized, he dashed down the river and proposed that he make a fast trip to Washington in another attempt to secure some liberalization of the new prohibition law. True, Crooks and even Astor had failed, but McKenzie had the impression that he might succeed. It was an appalling situation. Sublette and Campbell were shrewd veterans. They would violate the law, and by traveling overland to the mountains they would have greater opportunities to carry liquor than traders importing supplies by way of the river. It would be impossible to cope with them in the upper Missouri country unless permission to take liquor to Fort Union was obtained. Of course, the request would not be made on the ground that it was necessary in order to compete with Sublette and Campbell. The old stock argument would be advanced: British traders were using it freely on United States territory and depriving American traders of business to which they were entitled.

Chouteau, although holding little hope that McKenzie could succeed where so many other prominent men had failed, approved the trip. McKenzie was an impressive person, a forceful talker, who held great confidence in his own powers of persuasion and felt at home among important persons. At least, concluded Chouteau, no harm could be done by letting McKenzie make an appeal in his own way.

If the Washington officials with whom McKenzie talked were impressed by his manner, appearance and personality, they were unmoved by his pleas. Crooks went to Washington from New York to meet him, and wrote Chouteau that McKenzie was "disheartened . . . and he parted with me in desponding anticipations of the future." That was not quite accurate. McKenzie was disappointed when he left Washington for St. Louis, but it was not his way to be despondent.

Organization of the new firm of Sublette & Campbell was completed in December, 1832. General Ashley, from the floor of Congress, gave it his unqualified recommendation and support. This brought forward several bankers with generous offers of credit. By spring, when the firm was ready to begin operations, its resources were extensive enough so that it was generally believed in the trade that competition with the American Fur Company could be successfully conducted.

Campbell led a large expedition to the mountains and met the Rocky Mountain Fur Company partners and the contingents of Drips and Fontenelle at the annual rendezvous on Green River. After that he set out to defy McKenzie at the mouth of the Yellowstone.

Sublette took a brigade on the steamboat *Otto* up the Missouri River. He had an immense amount of equipment and goods, and he put ashore parties to build posts at nearly all sites occupied by American Fur Company establishments. He sent the steamboat back at Fort Clark, and went on with a large company by keelboats. His destination also was the mouth of the Yellowstone. In this way a two-pronged attack was launched toward Fort Union.

Campbell, with Milton Sublette and his men, was already on the Yellowstone when Sublette arrived. The united companies at once set about erecting a post on the north bank of the Missouri only three miles by land (six by water) above Fort Union. It was named Fort William, in honor of the elder Sublette.

The various contingents of the new company soon set out for several destinations, while Campbell remained in command at the post. William Sublette and the partner, Nathaniel Wyeth, left for St. Louis. They would bring out new supplies the following spring, Sublette by way of the Missouri, and Wyeth overland to the Green River. Milton Sublette moved into the mountains; Fitzpatrick, another partner, was already in the Crow country; and several other outfits were dispatched to various trapping areas.

This was a show of force more brazen and well-supported than any with which McKenzie previously had been obliged to contend, but he soon demonstrated that he was equal to the task.

Within a few weeks he wrote to Chouteau that he had received a letter "from Captain Stuart," which had been delivered to him at Fort Union by an Indian messenger. It stated that "Fitzpatrick was robbed of 100 horses, all his merchandise . . ." and "can consequently make no hunt this fall."

This was a most interesting bit of intelligence, disclosing more to Chouteau than was stated in its words. Captain Stuart was not a trapper. He was a titled British Army officer who had gone west with a group of well-to-do sportsmen, had wandered through the mountains with several fur expeditions, during which time he had become a friend of McKenzie's. His full name was Sir William Drummond Stuart, Bart., and his home was in Perthshire, Scotland.

Shortly after sending Stuart's report downriver by express to Chouteau, McKenzie took pen in hand to write a more detailed account to his lieutenant, D. D. Mitchell, up the Missouri at isolated Fort McKenzie. This document revealed more about the methods used by the American Fur Company to maintain its dominant position than any other written during the period.

"Sublette and Campbell arrived here August 29th," he told Mitchell, "and soon fixed on a site for their fort which they have built two miles below me and called Fort William. They came up in great force with a very large outfit and abundance of alcohol and wines highly charged with spirits. They engaged the three young Deschamps as interpreters at salaries of $500 per annum each, and Tom Kipland at $600. They had, moreover, a full complement of clerks and seemed prepared to carry all before them, nothing doubting that they would secure at least one half the trade of the country. They abandoned the idea of sending to the Blackfeet this season. They started a small equipment on horses to the Crow Village on Wind River. They were expected to return early in December but have not yet been heard of. Mr. Winter and J. Beckwith [Upper Missouri Outfit men] passed the fall in the Crow camp and traded [for] all their beaver. While Mr. Winter was with the Crows, Mr. Fitzpatrick . . . my friend Captain Stuart was with him . . . arrived with thirty men, one hundred horses and mules, and merchandise etc. etc. and encamped near the village. He had not been long there before a large party paid him a visit and pillaged everything he had, taking even the watch from his pocket and the capote from his back; also driving off all his horses. This was a severe blow to Sublette and Campbell. And although on their first start they had made a great show and grand promise to the Indians and although among the men nothing was talked about but the new company, they live now at the sign of 'the case is altered.' Their interpreters have quarreled and left them, and are now working hard for me. The Indians find their promise mere empty words and are applying continually to me to engage (fight) them. They have a post near to Rivierre au Tremble in opposition to Chardon [at the mouth of the Poplar River] where they are doing literally nothing. Chardon has it all his own way. They have another post on the Yellowstone in opposition to Pilot and Brazeau and there they get no robes although they offer a blanket of scarlet for a robe.

"You must be aware that I have not been asleep this fall. It has cost me something to secure the Indians to me, but being determined to get the peltries, nothing has been neglected that would carry my point. My opponents cannot by any means get peltries sufficient to pay the wages of their men. At the Gros Ventres and Mandans they have not even robes to sleep on. At the Mandans my last account states that Picotte has eighty packs of robes and five hundred beaver, the opposition two packs of robes and eight beaver, and I hope things are equally promising lower down."

Fitzpatrick filed charges against the American Fur Company, and accused Samuel Tulloch, the company's agent among the Crows, of hiring Indians to rob him. So emboldened were McKenzie and Tulloch, and so unconcerned were they by the possibility of prosecution, that they readily admitted their guilt and made no effort to prevent the Indians who had participated in the plundering from confessing.

Tulloch, however, scoffed at Fitzpatrick's declaration that a large quantity of beaver had been taken, and said he had exchanged goods with the robbers for only forty-three stolen skins. He wrote headquarters that, "The 43 Beaver skins traded, marked 'R.M.F.Co.,' I would in the present instance give up if Mr. Fitzpatrick wishes to have them, on his paying the price the articles . . . were worth on their arrival in the Crow village, and the expense of bringing the beaver in and securing it. My goods are brought into the country to trade and I would as willingly dispose of them to Mr. Fitzpatrick as to any one else for beaver or beaver's worth, if I get my price. I make this proposal as a favor, not as a matter of right, for I consider the Indians entitled to trade any beaver in their possession to me or to any other trader."

After having instigated the robbery, Tulloch offered to sell the skins to the man from whom they had been stolen . . . if he got his price . . . hardly a "favor."

Fitzpatrick did not take advantage of Tulloch's generosity. He placed the matter before his friend and former employer, General Ashley in Congress. More howls of protest came from the enemies of the American Fur Company in Washington, and memories of the Leclerc incident were revived. Hastily Chouteau wrote McKenzie: "In a letter to General Ashley, Fitzpatrick accuses the company of having instigated the savages to commit certain depredations of which he was the victim, and it appears that this letter has been sent to the Department of Indian Affairs. The dragoons will perhaps be ordered to make a tour along the base of the mountains, and in that case it is possible that they will pay you a visit. You will therefore prepare for their reception and especially for any *searches* which they may make if they go."

The troops were coming! McKenzie was warned to hide incriminating evidence.

The desperate straits in which the new firm of Sublette & Campbell found itself after less than a year's operation were indicated by an unexpected visit Campbell paid to McKenzie at Fort Union.

"Campbell called on me," McKenzie wrote Mitchell, "and proposed to sell out to me all their interest on the river. I listened to his terms, but was by no means disposed to buy out an opposition, when all my old experienced and faithful clerks and tradesmen felt so certain of driving them out; especially on my giving them *carte blanche* with respect to trade at their respective posts, of course to be used with discretion but with this condition, that all peltries must be secured for the A. F. Co. and thus far I have no reason to complain. The new company is now in bad odor and must sink."

Charles Larpenteur, who was working for Campbell at Fort William at the very time McKenzie was boasting to Mitchell and Chouteau of his success in combating the opposition, was to substantiate McKenzie's assertions with the statement: "The Indians had no confidence in his [Campbell's] remaining, so that the bulk of the trade went to the big American Fur Company in spite of all we could do . . . This post [Fort William] was not the only one that was out of luck, for all those along the Missouri proved a failure."

The reasons for their failure were not obscure. What McKenzie meant by giving *carte blanche* to his traders and clerks was that they were free to pay any price necessary to get the Indians' furs, and that they could use any amount of alcohol they wished to hold the trade. Profits were not to be considered when it came to preventing Sublette & Campbell from acquiring pelts.

Exorbitant prices were paid, and liquor was dispensed with reckless abandon. At the Mandans, where Sublette & Campbell's men put up a strenuous fight, as much as twelve dollars was paid for a single beaver skin worth no more than two or three dollars.

Sublette and Campbell simply could not stand up under such pressure, and McKenzie had good reason to believe that he soon would be free of them. Consequently he was astonished and infuriated when he received word from St. Louis that William Astor had approved an agreement, proposed by Crooks and Chouteau, under which the investments of Sublette & Campbell on the Missouri would be purchased, and the American Fur Company would withdraw for a year from trading in the mountains.

It was a bitter pill to swallow, and he felt that Crooks and

Chouteau not only had lost their courage but all vestiges of the
business acumen he had believed they possessed. The truth was
that Crooks and Chouteau, fully apprised of the ability of Sublette and Campbell to obtain additional capital through the
good offices of Congressman Ashley, had been more apprehensive
about the future than had McKenzie.

It was with profound disappointment, and not a little chagrin,
that McKenzie perused the letter in which Chouteau told him:
"By the enclosed agreement you will see that we have concluded
an arrangement at New York with Mr. Sublette. We take such of
his equipment in merchandise, utensils, etc., as remains at the
close of the season's trade [for 1834] and we retire from the
mountain trade for the ensuing year . . . In making this arrangement our object was to keep Sublette from purchasing new equipment and from connecting himself with houses that were making
him all sorts of offers. His reputation and that of his patron,
Ashley, whatever may be the cause, are far above their worth.
Nevertheless such is the fact and it is enough to procure them
unlimited credit. It is this which induced us to offer to buy them
out. We hope, therefore, that, taking all things into consideration
you will approve of the transaction."

McKenzie cursed. The last sentence was a gross insult. He had
won the fight, and now he was being asked to approve the defeat
of Chouteau, Crooks and William Astor.

11

Particularly galling to McKenzie were events which transpired in
the mountain trade following the unnecessary agreement to buy
out Sublette & Campbell's Missouri River investments. He had

more than once advised St. Louis not to fear the outcome of the fight to beat the Rocky Mountain Fur Company traders and their allies. His predictions of victory for the American Fur Company had been based on sound reasons. He had confidence in his own ability to smash any competition by legal or illegal means . . . and he cared not which were used . . . and on the intelligence he received from the fearless and competent men he had sent to the far countries beyond the Missouri. This intelligence contained unmistakable indications that Sublette, Fitzpatrick, Wyeth and their associates were themselves creating situations that would contribute to their own destruction.

The accuracy of this analysis soon became apparent. If Fitzpatrick and others had just cause to complain about the violent tactics of the American Fur Company, they were conducting themselves in ways no less deserving of condemnation. Moreover, the great arena of the mountains was no longer the scene of bitter rivalry only between big companies. It had been invaded by numerous small groups, all bent on outdoing each other and picking up the leavings of the large expeditions. These disorganized, poorly financed little bands were not only annoying the strong combines, but were fighting among themselves like a lot of terriers after a bitch.

Robberies and murders were almost daily occurrences. The entire mountain trade was degenerating into a continual running fight between big and little gangs. As a result, the Indians were utterly demoralized by the bitter, brutal and vicious conduct of the whites toward each other, and were rapidly losing confidence in all of them. Taking a leaf from the white man's book, the Indians resorted to all manner of lawlessness, putting the life of every trader in peril at all times.

McKenzie favored a policy of letting the rivals kill each other off, while he operated with expeditions so strong, supplied with merchandise of such good quality and such immense quantities of liquor, that large outfits could not afford to compete, and neither the smaller bands nor the Indians would have the poor sense to attack them.

Also, McKenzie and his agents were fully aware that William Sublette and Robert Campbell were cleverly channeling most of the profits from the mountain trade . . . both those of their own company and the Rocky Mountain Fur Company . . . into their own pockets. This was being accomplished in several ways. They brought out goods from St. Louis to the annual rendezvous for their own partners and those of the Rocky Mountain Fur Company, and by this means they were able to make good money on sales to both organizations. Also, they broke contracts and failed in other commitments if they believed that anticipated returns would not accrue.

Petty quarrels, clashes of personalities, dissension, disloyalty, dishonesty . . . these were the weapons with which McKenzie believed his competitors would destroy themselves. But this conviction was not shared by the executives who occupied the comfortable and safe offices in St. Louis and New York, not to speak of the lovely villas in Europe.

If his superiors had not lost their guts and had listened to him . . . Well, the damn milk was spilt. McKenzie could sense nothing but evil tidings in the wind, and he was deeply disturbed by statements and intimations that continued to come in dispatches from St. Louis. Fontenelle had told Chouteau: "We have always been too late [at rendezvous] and our opponents in the country make a great boast of it." McKenzie cursed Fontenelle. There was no excuse for being late.

Both Chouteau and Crooks intimated, though in different statements, that they were tired of the troubles in the mountains, and would be glad to withdraw the next year. Crooks went so far as to say that it was only because he had feared damage to the company's prestige, especially in the eyes of the Indians, that he had refrained from recalling Drips, Fontenelle and other overland expeditions, and abandoning the mountain trade altogether.

To make things worse, in McKenzie's estimation, Crooks had written Astor: "I am convinced that these expeditions have been an annual loss. But we have hoped for improvement from year to year. Generally the loss falls upon the traders. If the expeditions to the upper Missouri had confined themselves entirely to that trade [at regular posts] its returns would have been greater and its expenses much less. Nevertheless, in spite of the unfavorable prospect, I do not think it politic to abandon this trade for the present . . . it is not for us to leave the mountains exclusively to them."

Yet, Crooks had done that very thing, left the mountains exclusively "to them," by the agreement with Sublette & Campbell to withdraw the next year. What kind of gibberish was Crooks writing? McKenzie resented the implications in the letter. He saw it as a reflection on his own work. Moreover, to tell Astor that a branch of the company was unprofitable was to invite the heavens to fall.

It was a discouraging situation all around, and McKenzie's spirits were not lifted by the information that the $9,000 which the company had paid Leclerc would be deducted from the profits of the Upper Missouri Outfit.

12

McKenzie's futile lobbying trip to Washington had convinced him that no favorable amendments to the prohibition law would be forthcoming in the near future, and he applied himself to the problem of obtaining the liquor he needed to combat the Hudson's Bay Company in the Blackfoot and Sioux countries. He had no intention of giving up his smuggling, but in itself it was an inadequate means, and it was extremely dangerous and undependable as well. If he was not caught by Indian Agents, he might suffer disastrous losses at the hands of rivals. Not only Hudson's Bay men, but the Sublettes, Campbell, Fitzpatrick, and even the righteous New Englander, Wyeth, would hijack a keg of liquor at the first opportunity.

There seemed to be only one course open to him, and that was to make his own whisky. He proposed to Crooks and Chouteau that a still be set up at Fort Union.

They were somewhat stunned by the idea, and labeled it "radical" and an "invitation to the Government to put them in jail." McKenzie argued that, on the contrary, it would not be a violation of the law. He had read the statute with care, and it did no more than forbid the *importation* of alcohol into the Indian country. Distilling spirits at Fort Union, therefore, would not be a strict violation, even though, admittedly, there might be grounds for a charge that an attempt had been made to circumvent the law's intent. It was all a matter of interpretation, and by the time the Government got around to a ruling, which would have to be supported by a court decision, a hell of a fine stock of whisky could be in barrels at Fort Union. If the decision went against them, they would, of course, stop the operation, and find some other means of obtaining the liquid supplies that were necessary if they intended to remain in business.

Convinced that McKenzie's premise was without merit, Chouteau nevertheless agreed to put the question before the company's legal counsel. He was astounded to receive an opinion favoring it. The subterfuge, said the attorneys, might be successful. In any case, considerable time would have to elapse before an adverse ruling could come from the courts, just as McKenzie had stated, and the arguments might well be carried to the United States Supreme Court.

Crooks was back in New York, and despite the opinion of the St. Louis attorneys, he continued to be strongly opposed to the scheme, warning Chouteau that, "The excitement against us is undoubtedly greater than it ought to be, and whether well or ill founded, the effect is not the less injurious, and we are looked upon by many as an association determined to engross the trade of the upper Missouri, by fair means if we can, but by foul proceedings if nothing short will ensure our objects. With such a reputation it becomes us to be more than usually circumspect in all we do. Every eye is upon us, and whoever can will annoy us with all his heart. It will therefore, in my opinion, be madness to attempt your project of the *Alembique*."

Crooks pointed out that the United States was then making overtures to Great Britain to halt traffic in liquor on the Canadian side of the border, and he declared . . . to the surprise of Chouteau and the utter disgust of McKenzie: "If the Government of Britain reject the proposal, their object will evidently be to drive us out of the country, and deprive the United States of a trade which justly belongs to her citizens; and I cannot allow myself to believe that after such unequivocal proof of their real intentions, our own Government will persist in denying us the use of ardent spirits so far as the article is required to place us on an equal footing with our commercial rivals. But still, if in the face of reason and common sense, the Executive will not have the law so modified as to afford us a fair chance with our Hudson Bay opponents, *I would, hard as it is, rather abandon the trade, than violate the statute if that was necessary to sustain ourselves against them.*"

Crooks may have written the letter for the public record, to show the honorable intentions of the American Fur Company. McKenzie thought such a statement, issued for any purpose whatsoever, was a disgrace, and he accused Crooks of disloyalty to the company. Chouteau did not hold such a strong view, but he elected to ignore Crooks's admonitions. He and McKenzie bought the supplies and equipment required for a sizable still.

The *Yellowstone* was scheduled to leave on her spring voyage up the river. Carefully disguised, its parts distributed among other machinery and general cargo, the still went aboard. McKenzie followed in the company of the distinguished Maximilian, Prince of Wied, who was journeying to the Indian country in the interests of sightseeing and doing a bit of shooting.

McKenzie confided to the Prince, who was himself a thorough adventurer, not only about the still but that he had managed to smuggle aboard eleven barrels of liquor under the very eyes of the inspectors. Maximilian greatly enjoyed the game of attempting to outwit the authorities, and he and McKenzie had some good laughs about it as they shared the fine sherry of which the Prince had an ample supply in his personal luggage.

Their smiles vanished suddenly when the boat paused at the Black Snake Hills (St. Joseph, Missouri). McKenzie sent an angry letter to Chouteau complaining about the strictness of the inspection made by Federal officers. "We have been robbed of all our liquors," he wailed, "say seven barrels shrub, one of rum, one of wine and all the fine men and sailors' whisky which was in two barrels. They kicked and knocked about everything they could find and even cut through our bales of blankets which had never been undone since they were put up in England . . . The more I think of it, the clearer I see the injury we are going to sustain by being deprived of that article."

Maximilian also was offended and distressed. He lamented that "they would scarcely permit us to take a small portion to preserve our specimens of natural history."

But there remained one gratifying thought: the inspectors had failed to detect any part of the still.

McKenzie had been thorough in his preparations. At the mouth of the Iowa River he put off a group of laborers to start "a corn plantation." At Council Bluffs he purchased a supply of the same essential ingredient.

No time was wasted in getting the still into operation at Fort Union, and success was immediate and unqualified. McKenzie was elated. There could be no question of liquor supplies now. He was in a position to show the Hudson's Bay Company a thing or two about using firewater in the Indian trade. In no time at all he would have more on hand than he needed, enough to keep every brave and squaw between the Mandans and the Big Horn in a perpetual state of drunkenness. If a Hudson's Bay agent obtained a single beaver skin it would only be because his own traders had drunk too much of the Fort Union "cougar piss," and he would shoot the first Upper Missouri Outfit man who did that.

Joyfully McKenzie wrote Chouteau, "Our manufactory flourishes admirably. We only want corn to keep us going. The Mandan corn yields badly but makes a fine, sweet liquor. Do not load the boat too heavily at St. Louis, that a few hundred bushels of corn may be placed on board at the Bluffs . . . Surely you will contrive some means of passing alcohol to the Bluffs for the Sioux trade."

He took pains to inform Crooks directly of his achievement, writing, "For this post I have established a manufactory of strong water. It succeeds admirably. I have a good corn mill, a respectable distillery, and can produce as fine a liquor as need be drunk. I believe that no law of the United States is thereby broken though perhaps one may be made to break up my distillery. But liquor I must have or quit any pretension to trade in this part."

McKenzie also sent a winter express to Pilcher at Council Bluffs, admonishing him to send up a good supply of corn in the spring, "or my wine vats will be idle."

As he wrote his ecstatic letters and reveled in the pleasant glow of his own handiwork, McKenzie had no way of knowing, or even any reason to suspect, that the days of his venture into moonshining were numbered.

In August, Nathaniel Wyeth, accompanied by the noted trader, M. S. Cerre, had arrived unexpectedly at Fort Union. Although they were competitors, McKenzie did not forget the good manners he had been taught as a youth working for British companies. He entertained his guests with lavish hospitality, placing before them such delicacies as light bread, cheese, milk, fine roast beef and good whisky . . . luxuries they had not tasted for many months. He proudly conducted them on a tour of his splended, efficient post, boasted of the enormous trade he was doing, and in his enthusiasm became so indiscreet as to show them the still.

When Wyeth and Cerre requested that McKenzie sell them some badly needed supplies, McKenzie was only too happy to oblige them. It was the policy of the American Fur Company to sell merchandise to anyone who desired it, providing the price was satisfactory. Wyeth and Cerre were pleased and impressed, and they suggested next that McKenzie also sell them some of his good liquor.

McKenzie, the generous and genial host, was suddenly transformed into McKenzie, the hard, shrewd trader. He had no hesitancy in informing his guests that as competitors he did not propose to arm them with an article that would give them power to oppose him.

Wyeth and Cerre were not a little aggravated, but when they asked the amount of the bill for the goods they had purchased, their aggravation was augmented by profound indignation and bitter resentment. McKenzie had charged them the same exorbitant prices that Indians were obliged to pay for merchandise.

They paid, but not without vicious thoughts, and departed down the river.

The desire for revenge was still burning in them when they reached Fort Leavenworth, and forthwith they appeared at the office of the Indian Agent and swore to an affidavit which stated that Kenneth McKenzie, chief representative of the American Fur Company on the upper Missouri, was "making and vending whiskey in quantity."

Not long afterward the affidavit reached the desk of Gen. William Clark, Superintendent of Indian Affairs in St. Louis. He promptly wrote to Chouteau requesting "what explanation you think proper to give."

For nine days Chouteau wrestled with the problem, but at the end of that time he sent an answer which was nothing if not ingenious. To begin with, he protested that he was totally ignorant of the alleged illicit operation at Fort Union "in the manner and to the extent stated." Next he disclaimed all personal responsibility for such an unauthorized act. The disclaimer was followed with an explanation of the company's position that made General Clark shake his head in wonder.

"The company," declared Chouteau, "believing that wild pears and berries might be converted into wine (which they did not understand to be prohibited), did authorize experiments to be made, and if, under color of this, ardent spirits have been distilled and vended, it was without the knowledge, authority, or direction of the company, and I will take measures, by sending immediately an express to arrest the operation complained of, if found to exist."

General Clark wasted no more time with the Western Department. He prepared a factual report, and sent it off to Washington.

Chouteau's express rider dashed away for Fort Union. Conveniently forgetting his own involvement, Chouteau delivered a stern rebuke to McKenzie for "having placed the company in an unpleasant situation."

This was more than McKenzie would tolerate. He replied that while he was willing to be made the scapegoat, as long as "the company be thereby benefitted," he did not intend to submit to a charge that he had built the still without previously consulting headquarters in St. Louis.

Despite his anger at Chouteau, however, McKenzie concocted a story he thought would be accepted in official circles as a plausible explanation for the presence of the distillery at Fort Union. Actually, his egotism and self-confidence induced the conviction that he himself was untouchable in his far kingdom. He could easily escape from a Federal officer sent to arrest him, and no officer would be foolhardy enough to look for him among the Indians. He wrote to General Clark that a British friend wished to operate a still at Pembina, and had requested him to bring the equipment up the river to Fort Union, after which it would be transported on to Canada. By coincidence, said McKenzie, an American experienced in making liquor happened to be at Fort Union when the still arrived, and he had requested permission to experiment with "the wild fruits of the country." McKenzie had seen no harm in granting the request. A "very palatable article" had been produced, but there had been no intention to manufacture spirits for the purpose of evading the prohibition law. The whole thing had been simply an experiment in which the American had engaged to pass away idle hours.

General Clark was as unimpressed by this defense as he had been by Chouteau's explanation, and after duly noting the discrepancies between the two stories, he sent McKenzie's letter on to Washington. Crooks, advised of the gathering storm, rushed from New York to the capital and closeted himself with Senator Benton.

Officials of the War Department and the Indian Service soon issued a joint opinion that Astor's wanton disregard of the law in the Indian country had become intolerable. They bolstered a demand that the license of the American Fur Company be revoked by citing the illegal arrest of Leclerc and the robbery of Fitzpatrick.

The influence of Astor in Washington and the power of Senator Benton had never been put to a more severe test. The cost to Astor in political contributions and other gratuities without labels was not disclosed, but it was far from being nominal. Despite such persuasive measures, he might well have met defeat had not his old ally, Secretary Cass, seen fit to overrule the actions of subordinates.

Crooks ordered that the still be destroyed, and that McKenzie appear in St. Louis. He wrote a stern letter to Chouteau: "The General [Clark] tells me that you had the address . . ." meaning *brass* or *nerve* ". . . to persuade Judge H—— that your distillery at the Yellowstone was only intended to promote the cause of botony. But *prenez-y-garde.* Don't presume too much on your recent escape from an accusation that might have been attended with serious consequences. The less of this sort of business you do, the better, for the time may, and very probably will, come when you will be exposed by the endless number of spies you have around you."

The summons to McKenzie to appear in St. Louis was reflective of a suggestion, and possibly a demand, of Secretary Cass that he be removed, at least temporarily, from the scene. This maneuver, it was believed, would have a calming effect on the disgruntled officials and Congressmen who had demanded Astor's scalp.

When he reached St. Louis, McKenzie was promptly sent on to New York. There he was given a check for $50,000 . . . profits which had accrued to his credit as King of the Upper Missouri . . . and a ticket to Europe. His violent and dramatic career with the American Fur Company had ended.

When he returned to St. Louis after his journey abroad, he established himself, not without mockery of the misfortunes that had destroyed him, as a wholesale liquor merchant.

13

Robert Stuart could look back to 1830 and remember a letter he had written to the trader John Lawe, of Green Bay. A rumor that Astor would withdraw from the fur trade had been circulating at the time. "Pray," Stuart told Lawe, "give yourself no concern about Mr. Astor's retiring . . . my opinion is that he will never retire *until he is called . . .*"

Lawe was not saddened by such a thought. Astor had ordered that no more credit be given to white men at Green Bay, and was contemplating withdrawing from that area. Lawe's inquiry of Stuart as to the truth of the rumor had been prompted by hope rather than by apprehension. He hated Astor as only an agent from whom virtually every cent of profit had been squeezed for years could be capable of hating.

Stuart's statement to Lawe, however, stemmed from wishful thinking. If he would not admit it to Lawe, he did harbor concern. He could recall that as early as 1825, Astor had remarked, after counseling him to curtail expenditures for merchandise, "I may also wish to sell out." As the decade of the 1820's drew to a close, Astor had begun to dispose of his ships. This meant that furs had to be shipped to Europe and China as freight, with a resultant decrease in profits.

Stuart and Crooks both had access to the American Fur Company letter books, but if they did not keep abreast of the contents of them, they were informed by employees close to Astor of the trend of his thinking. So both of them knew that in the fall of 1831, and in the spring of 1832, Astor had written to his old opponent in Montreal, Joseph McGillivray, and to his friend Benjamin Mooers in Plattsburg, that he was "about to retire from all mercantile or money transactions, my health being feeble."

Soon afterward, in June, 1832, Astor had gone to Paris. He was seriously ill. The world-wide epidemic of cholera seriously damaged the fur trade, and it was practically halted in some countries in the belief that animal pelts were common carriers of the contagion.

Astor escaped infection, although his daughter Eliza and her husband, Viscount Vincent Rumpff, were stricken, and narrowly escaped death. The year 1833 brought distress and sadness in other ways. Henry, Astor's brother who had reached New York on a sutler's wagon in the wake of the British Army, died suddenly, leaving an estate of a million dollars. Starting with a stall in the Fly Market in which he sold meat stolen by British raiders from Yankee farmers, he had become the city's most prosperous butcher. Astor's sister Elizabeth and two grandchildren also died, victims of the terrible plague. On July 17, he was seventy, but his continuing bad health left him no reason to celebrate. The fur market was crippled, and gave no signs of reaching full recovery in the near future. Moreover, a new and menacing factor had come into play. Astor had written Chouteau about it some months before its sinister influence had become fully apparent. "I very much fear," he told Chouteau, "Beaver will not sell well very soon unless very fine, it appears they make *hats of silk* in place of Beaver."

All his adult life Astor's greatest asset was his perspicacity, his God-given talent to look into the future with amazing clarity. He saw the possibilities of reverses before his competitors. He could anticipate with unerring accuracy the trend of the nation's economy. Sickness had not deprived him of these powers, and what he saw ahead of him in Europe, in relation to the fur trade, was unpleasant for him to contemplate. He saw a long hill down which the profits would steadily descend from the great height they had reached, and he did not intend to march down that hill with them.

His reaction to business conditions and his thoughts about retiring were conveyed to New York and St. Louis in various remarks, but no clear-cut decision was stated, and Crooks refused to believe that he was nearing the end of his active days in the fur trade. "The business seems to him," Crooks wrote Chouteau confidently, "like an only child and he cannot muster courage to part with it."

When Astor had gone to Europe in 1832, it had been his hope to return to New York in the fall, and for a time it looked as if he would be able to do that. Then had come the fall from bed that seriously shocked his nerves and forced him to remain confined in his room for some days. This accident was followed by a "painful fistula operation," and he wrote to Chouteau, "I think now to Remain in Europe till Spring in Deed I am not able to go back & in winter I Do not wish to."

Recovery came slowly, but by October, 1832, he felt well enough to hire a carriage and pair. The drives seemed to speed his improvement to such an extent that by December he was able to engage in a recreation he had long loved, riding a good saddlehorse.

Vincent Nolte, a friend, wrote that credit for Astor's progress on the road to restored health was due to the skill of the attending physician, Baron Dupreyten. The Baron, said Nolte, often accompanied his patient on the horseback rides, and "One day when riding, Astor appeared by no means disposed to converse; not a word could be got out of him: and at length Dupreyten declared that he must be suffering from some secret pain or trouble, when he would not speak. He pressed him, and worried him, until finally Astor loosed his tongue—'Look ye, Baron,' Astor said, 'how frightful this is! I have here in the hands of my banker, at Paris, about 2,000,000 francs, and cannot manage, without great effort, to get more than 2½ per cent per annum on it. Now, this very day I have received a letter from my son in New York, informing me that there the best acceptances are at from 1½ to 2 per cent per month. Is it not enough to enrage a man?' "

Setbacks came. His spirits fell, and he was afflicted with extreme nervousness. Instead of taking ship for New York in the spring of 1833, he was obliged to retreat to his villa at Lake Geneva, once more a very sick man and appearing on the verge of a complete collapse.

There he decided that he could postpone no longer the announcement of his pending complete withdrawal from the fur trade. He gave Crooks, Stuart and Chouteau several reasons: Profits were declining and, it was his belief, would continue to decline. Silk was supplanting beaver for hats, and although beaver hats undoubtedly would continue to be made for some years, the quantity would steadily decrease. He reminded them that the original charter of the American Fur Company, granted in 1808 for a period of twenty-five years, had expired. His son William had no desire to carry on in the fur trade, being more interested in managing the family real-estate holdings in Manhattan. Last of all he mentioned that his health would not permit him to carry heavy business burdens, yet it unquestionably was the factor that influenced him the most in reaching an irrevocable decision.

Astor took it upon himself to send a formal notice to Bernard Pratte & Company. "Wishing to retire from the Concern in which I am angaged with your House," he told them, "you will please to take this as notice thereof, & that the agreement entered into on the 7th May 1830—between your House & me on the part of the American Fur Company will expire with the outfit of the present year on the terms expressed in said agreement. I am Gentlemen your humble Servt. . . . ."

Although they were deeply grieved to be separated from the genius who had guided them through so many prosperous years,

Crooks, Chouteau and Stuart determined to carry on. Pratte, Chouteau & Company, as successors to Bernard Pratte & Company, arranged with Astor to purchase his interest in the Western Department. Crooks and a group of traders which included Stuart made a similar agreement by which the Northern Department came into their hands.

Although its name continued in use for many years, the incomparable and impregnable American Fur Company which Astor had conceived, financed and directed for a quarter of a century . . . the greatest force in all the world's fur trade . . . was legally dead.

14

All through the summer and fall of 1833 Astor struggled at Genthod to regain enough strength to let him sail for New York. He was extremely homesick, longing for Sarah, yet he never seemed to think it advisable for her to come to his side. William, deeply concerned, expressed the opinion that his father needed the stimulus of the New York office and its many problems to aid in his recovery, and in January, 1834, he wrote to Count Rumpff, "I was much disappointed by my father's not returning to this Country in October—I hope he will however certainly return in the Spring. Occupation of mind which he will get here only is, I believe, the only cure for his nervous affection." There was no doubt William meant *affliction*.

It was March, 1834, before Astor's physicians grudgingly approved of his departure. Astor at once sought passage on the excellent and fast vessel, *Utica*, and was deeply disappointed when told that all staterooms had been sold.

The captain of the *Utica* was Frederick Augustus De Peyster, the courageous master who, in the China trade years before, had performed numerous invaluable favors for Astor, for which he had never been repaid. When Captain De Peyster was informed that his former employer was in urgent need of accommodations, he did not permit old grudges to influence him. He readily offered to give up his own comfortable stateroom for the voyage to New York.

True to character, Astor thanked De Peyster for his extraordinary kindness, but the Astor purse remained tightly closed. If De Peyster had a desire to repay Astor in kind for this unconscionable niggardliness, it was fulfilled. Upon reaching New York, he gave out for publication a story that branded Astor a coward, a fool, a completely unreasonable rich ass unbalanced by a belief in his own importance, and a tragic figure.

The *Utica* sailed from Le Havre. For several days it fought adverse winds in an attempt to clear the English Channel. Astor became alarmed and asked De Peyster to run into some English port and put him ashore. De Peyster refused, but Astor persisted. "I give you tousand dollars to put me aboard a pilot-boat," he said. In the hope of calming Astor, De Peyster promised that unless they succeeded in getting out of the Channel by morning, he would arrange for him to land.

The winds changed during the day, and the *Utica* reached the open sea. Suddenly a heavy gale arose. The vessel was helpless before it and was driven northward along the Irish coast. For days De Peyster fought the raging storm, only his great skill as a navigator and his thorough knowledge of the waters preventing disaster.

Day by day Astor became more frantic in his demands that he be put ashore, at last becoming so desperate and filled with fear that he raised his offer to $10,000. De Peyster declined it on the premise that to embark on an unscheduled course would result in the forfeiture of his insurance. As long as he continued to fight the storm, no matter where the ship might be driven, its insurance would remain in force.

"Insurance!" cried Astor. "Can't I insure your ship myself!"

De Peyster, his patience on the verge of exhaustion, said he would accept such an agreement, provided the other passengers had no objection and the weather improved. Within a few hours the gale abated, and Astor hurried to the Captain's cabin to write a draft on his son for $10,000 in favor of the ship's owners. Emerging, he handed De Peyster a piece of paper. The captain stared in amazement at it. The paper was covered with writing that was totally illegible.

"What is this?" he demanded.

"A draft for $10,000," Astor replied.

"But no one can read it."

"Oh yes, my son will know what it is. My hand trembles so that I can't write any better."

"But you can at least write your name," De Peyster said. "I am acting for the owners of the ship, and I can't risk their property for a piece of paper that no one can read. Let one of the gentlemen draw up a draft in proper form, you sign it, and I will put you ashore."

Indignantly Astor refused and disappeared into his stateroom.

The winds calmed, the *Utica* recovered its course and beat steadily across the North Atlantic. Astor seldom showed himself on deck. One morning when the *Utica* was off the Banks of Newfoundland, Captain De Peyster mounted the poop to speak a ship bound for Liverpool. Suddenly Astor appeared beside him, yelling: "Tell them I give tousand dollars if they take a passenger."

De Peyster feared that Astor had become deranged. He was asking to be taken back to England! After he had persuaded Astor to go below, he took several stiff drinks to quiet his own nerves.

Understanding and sympathetic friends sought to explain Astor's behavior with the excuse that he was an old man, that his days of voyaging, whether in the North Atlantic or in the equally stormy waters of the commercial world, were ended. It was a reasonable explanation, undoubtedly true, but one close friend . . . Philip Hone, the tireless diarist, was marked as the person . . . expounded a theory that long lingered in the minds of those who knew Astor best. It was that after sailing from Europe, Astor had a premonition of tragedy awaiting him at home, and he could not bring himself to face it.

When Astor came down the gangplank in New York on April 4, 1834, Hone and William were there to tell him that Sarah had died seven days before, when the *Utica* was off the Banks of New-foundland.

Epilogue

They said the feeble old man lived with a regiment of ghosts, and that all of them appeared before him during the sunny hours when he sat, wrapped in a big shawl, in the garden gazing out toward the Hell Gate.

They said he held long talks with some of the ghosts. He talked with his brother Henry, and he cackled a little when he recalled how he had got the best of Henry in a loan. That hadn't been an easy thing to do. Henry was smart and shrewd, and above all else he disliked to loan money.

In those days he was just beginning to buy furs, and at times he found himself committed in transactions that were beyond his available funds, and he would have to borrow a little money. Two or three times he had got loans from Nathaniel Prime, the filthy old usurer in Wall Street, but the rate of interest was outrageous, and more frequently he appealed to Henry for help in moments of financial stress.

Henry had a genuine affection for his young brother, but that did not inspire him to open his sow's ear purse without a blasphemous accompaniment. Henry made the loans, however, and at a reasonable interest rate, but at last Henry decided that Yakob was reckless with money and not very capable of handling it. Henry decided he would relieve himself of an aggravating situation, and at the same time teach Yakob that it was better business to earn money by hard work than to pay a premium on it.

When he asked Henry for a loan of $200 to buy some furs at a bargain price, Henry shrieked and cursed and pounded his butcher's block. Yakob would meet with disaster and end up in a debtor's cell.

"I tell you what I do," Henry said. "No two hundred will I lend you, but I will do this. I will give you the money if you agree never to ask me again for any."

He quickly took the money, agreed to the stipulation, bought the furs and made a hundred dollars profit on them. He didn't think so much of Henry's business ability after that. Of course, as things turned out he never needed to borrow money again.

They said the old man had long and pleasant conversations with Sarah, and he liked to tell his friends who came to sit with him for a time how Sarah, for all her piety, was extremely sharp and clever when it came to business. Philip Hone, always scribbling in a diary, heard about it, and so did Joseph Coggswell, his secretary, and Fitz-Greene Halleck, the poet, and Gerrit Smith, the radical son of his old Utica friend, and Washington Irving, the writer.

Sarah had always been content to remain out of the limelight, however, and even when she was the richest woman in New York she had no wish to be noticed. In the beginning she had beat furs with him, and she had worked long hours in the music shop and later in his offices and display rooms. As soon as he could afford it, he had relieved her of every duty, except those of the home and the family, which really were enough for any woman, but even then she seemed to have no desire to travel. On rare occasions she took the children on a trip up the Hudson to Albany, but she had never wanted to go to Montreal or to Europe. She seemed to dislike the thought of being in a foreign country. She would have gone if he had insisted, of course, but he had not urged her to do it. It wasn't customary for a good German to take his wife on business trips.

The old man swore that he and Sarah had never had a serious disagreement. The nearest they had come to it was one day when Sarah had attempted to correct little . . . What was her name? Oh yes, his little granddaughter, one of the Langdons. She was one of his favorites, and he always spoiled her. Sarah was a great believer in discipline, and she scolded the little girl, and the little girl was angry, and asked him: "Grandfather, why did you marry Grandmother, anyway?"

Oh, he had got the best of Sarah that day. He told the little girl: "Because she was so pretty, my dear." There was nothing Sarah could say to that in front of the child. Sarah just looked frustrated and went out.

Sarah always kept the house open to ministers from any kind of church. She read a little in the Bible every day. That was what he had done when he was a youth boarding in his brother's house in London. He would be awakened by Bow Bells, and he would read a few verses before he got up. Sarah liked books with religious themes. He could remember very well that one of her favorites was *Rise and Progress*. It was written by some fellow named Doddridge.

Sarah always liked to entertain his friends. She liked it best when they brought their families with them. Sarah was a kind, generous, thoughtful hostess, no doubt because she had a genuine liking for people, almost everyone. No man ever had a better wife.

Sarah was even smarter than he was about furs, too, and a better judge of quality.

The old man laughed with watery eyes about the time he badly needed Sarah to go to his warehouse and give him her opinion about some skins.

"I'm very busy," Sarah told him. "If I go it will cost you five hundred dollars an hour."

"Agreed," he had told her, and he had laughed hard about being held up that way. Sarah was a great one.

But mostly the old man talked about things he had never seen with his own eyes. They said that even though he had not seen them in the years gone, he saw them clearly and vividly from his vantage place overlooking the Hell Gate.

He saw the great muddy yellow river reaching out through the western wilderness, and he saw the long file of the Astorians, mites under the immensity of the prairie sky, creeping onward across the sea of grass that washed against the mountains. And he saw the *Tonquin* rising in thunder, torn and splintered, and he heard the screams of the dying savages.

They said the old man had a fine soft sea otter fur, and he fondled it and murmured that there could be nothing more beautiful, and he held it against his shiny wrinkled ivory cheek.

They said Wilson Price Hunt and Ramsay Crooks and Robert Stuart and Pierre Chouteau, dressed in their buckskins, came there to sit with him in the garden, and Kenneth McKenzie strode across the lawn in his glittering coat of chain mail and his waving plume, and old Alexander Henry came, and some days he was surrounded by dark French-Canadians and big gentlemanly Scotsmen and courteous Britishers, and they talked about Michilimackinac and Fort Union, while the war drums sounded in the distance and far out on a ridge a wolf howled. But that traitor McDougal was never allowed to set foot inside the gate, and the old man cried a little when he thought of the North Westers moving into Astoria. Even if he had failed, even if he had never become a king, no one would ever forget what he did on the Columbia. They said the old man's weak voice was filled with deep pride when he spoke of it, and he told them that when everything else he had accomplished was long forgotten, Astoria would stand as an indestructible monument to his memory.

They said that when the wild cold winds blew through the Hell Gate, and the old man could not be carried out to enjoy the fresh air, the strong young men in the white coats went to his room each morning, and they lifted him gently on a blanket, raising him up and down in it, to give him his exercise. Then he was fed from the breast of a wet nurse.

They said he couldn't talk any more, and the regiment of ghosts had passed by for the last time. Then came that evening in 1848 when they looked in on him, and he was asleep.

Bibliographical Note

Many of the major libraries and museums in the United States and Canada possess original material that throws light on the life of John Jacob Astor . . . such things as letters, newspapers, account books, legal documents and commercial records.

Virtually every scrap of this Astoriana is listed in Kenneth Wiggins Porter's, *John Jacob Astor, Business Man,* published by the Harvard University Press in 1931. Porter's two-volume work is by far the most exhaustive and accurate account of Astor's commercial career as a merchant, fur trader, landowner, real estate owner, landlord, ship operator and financier. It is badly organized, often confusing, and completely disregards chronology, but is incomparable as a guide to Astor source material.

The best general work on the western fur trade is Hiram Martin Chittenden's, *History of the American Fur Trade in the Far West,* first published in 1902, a reprint of which was issued in 1954 by Stanford University Press. Chittenden devotes considerable space to Astoria and the operations of the American Fur Company west of the Mississippi.

Regarding Astor's vital Columbia River venture, there is nothing to be compared with Washington Irving's *Astoria,* which has appeared in countless covers in the last century and a quarter. A new paperback edition was published in 1961 by J. B. Lippincott Company. Irving was for many years a close friend of Astor's, and he was given access to Astor's personal papers relating to both the sea and overland expeditions of the Pacific Fur Company.

Irving romanced at times and wandered off on side trails, all to the good of his story, but at the expense of accuracy. The great heavy-handed historian, H. H. Bancroft, accused him of deliberate misrepresentation and distortion in favor of his mentor. However, in time it was shown that Bancroft was guilty of hasty judgment and that his charges were without foundation. Chittenden, indubitably an authority, took the wind out of Bancroft's sails with the rebuttal: "Not in the allurements of style alone, but in the essential respects of accuracy and comprehensive treatment, Irving's work stands immeasurably above all others on the subject."

Gustavus Myers' *History of the Great American Fortunes* is the classic in its field. It was first published in 1910, in Chicago, by Charles H. Kerr. A complete edition is in the Modern Library.

The Fur Trade, by Paul Chrisler Phillips, is a well-documented and studious work covering the trade in all its aspects, from its beginnings in the sixteenth century to the middle of the past century. Needless to say, only the highlights could be treated for such an extensive period in two volumes. It is a new and up-to-date study, published in 1961 by the University of Oklahoma Press.

John Jacob Astor, Landlord of New York, by Arthur D. Howden Smith, and published in 1929 by the J. B. Lippincott Company, is purported to be a biography of its subject. It is fanciful, nonsensical and inaccurate, and of no value to a student, a writer, or for that matter, anybody else.

Robert Stuart wrote a *Travelling Memoranda* of his epic journey of 3,700 miles through unknown country to carry dispatches from the Columbia to Astor. Irving made extensive use of it, working from the manuscript, and sometimes adding dramatic incidents and rather idiotic dialogue that were his own inventions. The Stuart manuscript was "lost" for nearly a hundred years. It was "found" in a cupboard by E. M. Grinnell, a grandnephew of Irving, and is now in the Yale University Library. The University of Oklahoma Press published it in 1953 under the title *On the Oregon Trail, Robert Stuart's Journey of Discovery.*

Alexander Ross, a young Scottish schoolteacher, was one of the original Astorians. He wrote two notable books. The first was, *Adventures of the First Settlers on the Oregon or Columbia River,* and was published in London, in 1849. The second, *Fur Hunters of the Far West,* appeared in 1855, and a reprint was issued by the University of Oklahoma Press, in 1956.

Two other valuable accounts of the Astoria expeditions were written by Gabriel Franchère and Ross Cox. Franchère's *Narrative of a Voyage to the Northwest Coast of America* was first published in French in Montreal, in 1820. An English edition was not issued until 1854. The work of Cox, *Adventures on the Columbia River,* appeared in two volumes in London in 1931.

Ross, Franchère and Cox all began work with the Pacific Fur Company as clerks. Consequently they personally acquired knowledge of the company's affairs and of the partners. Their accounts differ in many instances, even when they were writing about the same events. This undoubtedly was due to different animosities and sympathies. But their books comprise an invaluable record of the time and the place.

I should like to cite a few more authoritative books, magazines, newspapers and public documents—to many of which I was directed by Porter, Myers, Chittenden and Phillips—that supplied valuable source material for this book. They are:

BOOKS, ARTICLES, PAPERS, LETTERS

Armstrong, William, *Aristocracy of New York.* New York, 1848.

Astor Family, *Astor Letters.* New York City.

"The Astor Fortune." *McClure's Magazine* (April, 1905).

Astor Letters. Pennsylvania Historical Society, Philadelphia.

Astor Papers. Baker Library, Boston.

Astor, William Waldorf, "John Jacob Astor." *Pall Mall Magazine* (June, 1899).

Baring Papers. Public Archives of Canada, Ottawa.

Barrett, Walter, *The Old Merchants of New York City,* 5 vols. New York, 1889.

Beach, Moses Yale, *The Wealth and Biography of the Wealthy Citizens of New York City.* New York, 1846.

Brevoort, Henry and Irving, Washington, *Letters of Henry Brevoort to Washington Irving,* George S. Hellman, ed., 2 vols. New York, 1916.

Chouteau, Pierre, *Pierre Chouteau Papers.* Missouri Historical Society, St. Louis.

De Voe, Thomas, F., *The Market Book.* New York, 1862.

"Foreigners in the American Fur Trade." *Mississippi River Valley Historical Review* (1917).

Gallatin, Albert, *The Writings of Albert Gallatin,* Henry Adams, ed. New York, 1879.

Gebhard, Elizabeth Louisa, *Life and Ventures of the Original John Jacob Astor.* Hudson, Bryan, 1915.

Golder, Frank, *Russian Expansion on the Pacific.* Cleveland, 1914.

Greene, Richard Henry, *The Todd Genealogy.* New York, 1867.

Hamm, Margherita Arlina, *Famous Families of New York.* New York, 1902.

Hendrick, Burton J., "The Astor Fortune." *McClure's Magazine* (April, 1905).

Henry, Alexander, *Travels and Adventures in Canada and the Indian Territories, 1760–1776,* James Bain, ed. Montreal, 1901.

Heydenburk, Martin, *Incidents in the Life of Robert Stuart.* Michigan Pioneer and Historical Collections, Detroit.

Hodge, F. W., *Handbook of American Indians North of Mexico.* Washington, D.C., 1907.

Irving, Washington and Brevoort, Henry, *Letters of Washington Irving to Henry Brevoort,* George S. Hellman, ed., 2 vols. New York, 1916.

Jacques, David Ralph, *Lives of American Merchants,* Freeman Hunt, ed. New York, 1856.

Jefferson, Thomas, *The Papers of Thomas Jefferson*, Vols. CLXXV, CLXXVI, CLXXIX. The Library of Congress, Washington, D.C.

"John Jacob Astor." *Pall Mall Magazine* (June, 1899).

Kappler, Charles J., *Indian Affairs, Laws and Treaties*, 3 vols. Washington, 1903.

Larpenteur, Charles, *Forty Years a Fur Trader on the Upper Missouri*. New York, F. P. Harper, 1898.

Leonard, Zenas, *Narrative of Adventures*, W. F. Wagner, ed. Cleveland, 1904.

Lewis, Meriwether, *Lewis & Clark Expedition*. Philadelphia, J. B. Lippincott, 1861.

Longworth's American Almanac, New York Register and City Directory. New York, 1801.

Maximilian, Prince of Weid, *Travels in the Interior of North America*. London, Ackerman, 1843.

Miller, Alfred Jacob, *The West of Alfred Jacob Miller*. Norman, University of Oklahoma Press, 1951.

Monroe, James, *Monroe Papers, Writings of President Monroe*. Library of Congress, Washington, D.C.

New York Directory and Register, 1789–1790. New York City.

Oertel, Philip. *See* Van Horn, W.D.

Parish, John C., "Liquor and the Indians." *Palimpsest Magazine* (July, 1922).

Parton, James, "John Jacob Astor." *Harper's Magazine* (February, 1865).

——— *Life of John Jacob Astor*. New York, 1865.

Robeson, George F. "Fur Trade in Early Iowa." *Palimpsest Magazine* (January, 1925).

——— "Life Among the Fur Trappers." *Ibid.*

——— "Manuel Lisa." *Ibid.*

Schoolcraft, Henry R., *Personal Memoirs*. Philadelphia, 1851.

Scoville, Joseph A. *See* Barrett, Walter.

Smith, Matthew Hale, *Sunshine and Shadow in New York*. New York, 1868.

"Surrender at Astoria." *Oregon Historical Quarterly* (December, 1918).

Van Horn, W. D., *John Jacob Astor*. New York, 1855.

Withington, Lathrop, "Astor Pedigree Upset." *New York Sun* (July 30, 1899).

NEWSPAPERS AND MAGAZINES

Boone's Lick Advertiser, 1830. Columbia, Missouri.
Canadian Magazine, April–May, 1824.
Louisiana Gazette, 1809–1812. St. Louis, Missouri.
Missouri Gazette, 1808, 1809, 1812, 1822. St. Louis, Missouri.
Missouri Intelligencer, 1830. Columbia, Missouri.
Missouri Republican, 1822. St. Louis, Missouri.

U.S. GOVERNMENT DOCUMENTS AND REPORTS

American State Papers, Indian Affairs. United States Department of State, Washington, D.C.

Benton, Thomas H., *Report to the Senate Relative to the Fur Trade*. United States Senate, Exec. Doc. No. 67, 20th Cong., 2nd Sess., 1829.

Message from the President. Sen. Exec. Doc. No. 39, 21st Cong., 1st Sess., 1831.

Sen. Doc. No. 60, 1st Sess., 17th Cong., 1821.

Sen. Doc. No. 60, Vol. 1, 1st Sess., 17th Cong., 1821.

Sen. Doc. No. 58, 1st Sess., 19th Cong., 1825.

Sen. Doc. No. 90, 2nd Sess., 22nd Cong., 1831.

Sen. Doc. No. 90, 1st Sess., 22nd Cong., 1832.

Sen. Doc. No. 1, 2nd Sess., 35th Cong., 1858.

Sen. Exec. Doc. No. 90, 1st Sess., 22nd Cong., 1832.

Sen. Exec. Doc. No. 11, 1st Sess., 35th Cong., 1857.

Reports of Committees, Doc. No. 34, Vol. 1, 2nd Sess., 16th Cong., 1820.

Reports of Committees, Doc. No. 5, 2nd Sess., 22nd Cong., 1832.

Reports of Committees, 1st Sess., 24th Cong., 1836.

Index